The British Prices and Incomes Board

by ALLAN FELS

CAMBRIDGE

AT THE UNIVERSITY PRESS

1972

Published by
the Syndics of the Cambridge University Press
Bentley House, 200 Euston Road, London NW1 2DB
American Branch: 32 East 57th Street, New York, N.Y. 10022

© Crown Copyright 1972

Library of Congress Catalogue Card Number: 78—161285

ISBNS: 0 521 08297 8 clothbound
0 521 09674 X paperback

Set in cold type by E.W.C. Wilkins & Associates Ltd.,
and Printed in Great Britain by Alden & Mowbray Ltd.,
at the Alden Press, Oxford

University of Cambridge Department of Applied Economics

OCCASIONAL PAPER 29

The British Prices and Incomes Board.

University of Cambridge Department of Applied Economics
Occasional Papers

To Maria Isabel

Contents

TABLES

FIGURES

CHART

Preface

This is an independent study of the National Board for Prices and Incomes, commissioned by the NBPI. The study was done from inside the NBPI. I was free to inspect internal files and documents, interview Board Members and staff, and to attend Board and staff meetings, and meetings with parties with a concern in references. The NBPI has no responsibility for the product and, indeed, the final draft was completed well after its demise.

The nature of the study has been partly influenced by the time available, and the uncertainty which surrounded the NBPI's future for the first 6 months or so of the preparation of the study. Initially I decided, with the agreement of the NBPI, to spend 4 months (later extended to 6 months) on what I considered a tractable and useful subject — 'The NBPI as an Investigatory Body'. Following the Government's announcement in November 1970 about the NBPI's future, I was given an extension until March. I then extended my coverage of the original subject and also broadened the scope of the work by covering, in a selective rather than exhaustive fashion, the NBPI's policies, role and relationship to prices and incomes policy. I eventually ended the study after 14 months. I mention all this to explain the emphasis on the NBPI's investigatory methods and work which permeates the book, and the incomplete nature of some parts of the study.

In commissioning the study and allowing me to work from the inside, the NBPI gave me a rare academic opportunity. Members of the Board and staff have been remarkably helpful and co-operative. A considerable number of Board Members and senior staff took pains to comment in detail on several drafts. Three Board Members — Mr. J.E. Mortimer, Mr. Ralph Turvey, and Professor W.B. Reddaway — commented at length on specialised subjects. Mr. Aubrey Jones commented helpfully on factual matters in a draft prepared in March. Although a number of senior staff were especially helpful, I particularly wish to acknowledge comments on specialist matters from Dr. F.J. Bayliss, Mr. R.F. Burch, Mr. H. Christie, Mr. J.N. Harvey, Mr. G. Roberts, Mr M.F. Shutler and Mr. J.N. Stevens. Most of the appendices were prepared by members of the General Branch, the Industrial Relations and Economics Support Unit, the Enquiry Team, the Statistics Branch and the Management Operations Branch. I received extensive help from the members of the typing staff. To all of these persons I express my deepest gratitude.

At various stages in its life part or all of this study was read and commented on very usefully by Dr. A.N.J. Blain, Professor H.A. Clegg, Dr. J. Corina, Mr. D.R. Glynn, Mr. L.A. Gunn, Professor W.J.M. Mackenzie,

Professor D.C. Smith and Dr. G. Whittington. An acknowledgement of help from the late Professor Joan Woodward is made in Chapter 5. The final draft was read and commented on promptly and constructively by Mr. W.A.H. Godley, Director of the Department of Applied Economics, Mr. L.J. Handy, and Mr. D.A.S. Jackson. Finally Professor H.A. Turner, both in his capacity as a Board Member and as Montague Burton Professor of Industrial Relations at the University of Cambridge, helped launch the study and gave constant encouragement and advice. To all of these persons, I am deeply grateful.

I wish to thank the Department of Applied Economics for use of its facilities for the full period of the study. The final draft was typed with great efficiency by members of the D.A.E. typing staff. I am very grateful to them, especially Mrs. Lillian Silk, Miss Audrey Twyman, Miss Christine Hudson and Mrs. Marlene Reardon.

I wish to thank Her Majesty's Stationery Office for granting permission to publish this study independently.

Neither the Prices and Incomes Board nor the Controller of Her Majesty's Stationery Office are in any way responsible for anything that is expressed in this book.

My biggest debt is to my wife for her support, encouragement and understanding, without which this study could never have been written.

Allan Fels

August, 1971

Introduction

The chief object of this study is to provide an historical account of the role, operation and methods of enquiry of the National Board for Prices and Incomes. The study covers economics, industrial relations, management practice and public administration.

The study is not about the productivity, prices and incomes policies of 1965–70 per se, nor is it intended primarily as an analytical study. As it has only been possible to consider the impact of the NBPI in a cursory fashion, the study is not meant to be the last word on the NBPI and I have generally refrained from drawing conclusions which a description alone would not support. To have judged the NBPI adequately would have required an analytical evaluation of the prices and incomes policies of 1965–70 as well as a fuller account and analysis of the NBPI's own policies and practices.

A number of more analytical themes have not been taken up although they arise naturally from the study. Some examples may be given. The NBPI was a very distinctive type of organisation but I have not tried to formulate a precise model of its characteristics. The NBPI sought to influence the industries and firms it investigated and to have a wider impact on those who were not directly reported on, but I have not attempted to trace the mechanism by which it had an effect, if any. The NBPI was mainly concerned with the detailed investigation of particular areas of the economy (and quoted with approval Professor John T. Dunlop's dictum that 'a wage-price policy ... at high levels of utilisation comes down to detailed micro-problems'),[1] but I have not tried to analyse how its microeconomic recommendations linked up with the macroeconomic workings of the policy. Despite their importance there is in fact surprisingly little helpful analysis of these subjects.

In writing some chapters I have had in mind the needs of administrators or potential administrators, in Britain and abroad, of prices and incomes policies, and of those working in public investigatory bodies, but overall I hope the book will be of value and general interest to a wider audience.

Part I outlines the institutional background to the establishment of the NBPI; the economic and policy context in which it operated; and its role.

Chapter 1 describes prices and incomes policy experiments between 1948 and 1962, and includes an account of the work of the Council on Prices,

1 Third General Report, para. 46.

1

Productivity and Incomes. The evolution of the machinery of incomes policy is described and it is noted that by the end of 1962 the foundations of much of the incomes policy of 1965—70 had been laid.

Chapter 2 reviews the work of the National Incomes Commission, identifying some factors which made it a seemingly ineffective instrument of incomes policy administration. Two of these factors were its slowness in reporting, and its inability to determine all the facts relevant to the decisions it was required to make. It is noted in later chapters that the methods of the NBPI were designed to avoid these shortcomings as far as possible.

Chapter 3 describes the productivity, prices and incomes policies of 1965—70, paying attention to matters of greatest relevance to the NBPI. Initially the policies were voluntary and designed to help raise real incomes in the long run. There was a dramatic reversal in 1966 when they became mainly a weapon of short term wage and price restraint. The chapter also discusses the economic environment of 1965—70 and suggests it was unfavourable for the conduct of the NBPI's work.

Chapter 4 is about the general role of the NBPI. The Government had the power of determining which cases of individual incomes and prices increases the NBPI should pronounce upon. It failed to refer to the NBPI a considerable number of important national wage agreements which did not conform with the requirements of the incomes policy, and practically no local agreements were referred. When it did receive references, the NBPI had the task of operating an incomes policy in a vacuum because most incomes were increasing at a rate in excess of the norm. On the prices side the reference policy was similarly weak.

The NBPI always saw its main role as being to help stimulate efficiency and promote change of a longer term kind. In carrying out this role, it sought to use references about particular industries to have a wider impact on those not directly concerned in references. The chapter concludes with a brief account of the relationship of the NBPI to other independent official bodies.

Part II is devoted to a full account of the organisation, procedures and methods of enquiry of the NBPI. The three chapters may be viewed as showing how the NBPI sought to satisfy certain requirements that were necessary to prevent it from being a constraint on the effectiveness of the whole prices and incomes policy. For example, the NBPI believed that if it was to make authoritative judgments of whether wage and price increases were in the national interest, and sound recommendations for longer term change, it needed to make as thorough an independent examination of the issues raised by each reference as possible; and that, if it was to be effective, it needed to produce reports which could withstand critical scrutiny in public and would persuade the Government and the parties to accept its recommendations. Consequently, in seeking to obtain the information necessary to answer the questions posed by each reference, it endeavoured to conduct investigations of a high standard: their main characteristic was a reliance principally upon the NBPI's own enquiries made specially for the reference, and only secondarily upon other sources such as published statistics and submissions of the parties, which were usually inadequate for its purposes. This characteristic explains much of the NBPI's way of conducting a reference.

Another broad theme of Part II is that the NBPI was a new, unusual official body which adopted a number of innovatory procedures and methods of enquiry of considerable interest, and which, as an organisation, was also of considerable interest.

Part III surveys the NBPI's main strategy and policies in the fields of incomes and prices, and also continues with the exposition of its methods of enquiry.

Chapters 8 and 9 outline and comment on the NBPI's attempts to reduce the influence of traditional factors in wage determination, such as comparability, and to inject other factors, most notably the incomes norm and productivity. Chapter 8 deals with the NBPI's policies regarding comparability, the wage and salary structure and low pay. Chapter 9 deals with productivity agreements, payments by results schemes, and the reform of collective bargaining.

Chapter 10 outlines the functions of general study reports and standing references and gives examples of two of the latter – the reports on the pay of the armed forces, and the remuneration of solicitors. These reports are also examples of the NBPI's investigatory expertise.

Chapter 11 is a descriptive account of the NBPI's innovatory methods of assessing managerial efficiency. These were only partly developed by 1971 but it has been thought worthwhile to give them a disproportionate amount of attention because of their novelty and potentialities.

Chapter 12 on Pricing is mainly devoted to analysing how the NBPI assessed profits and how it sought to relate price increases to the investment needs of firms or industries under investigation, but there is also an account of its treatment of costs.

Chapter 13 is about NBPI policy with respect to price structures and gives a description of some pricing studies of nationalised industries.

Chapter 14 is not a summary of the book. Its main conclusions relate to the lessons of the NBPI's methods of enquiry.

Part I The Context of the NBPI and its Role

1. Prices and Incomes Policy 1948–62

1. 1948–50

The first post war attempt to conduct a national wages policy was from 1948–50, under the Labour Government. In 1948 a White Paper *Statement On Personal Incomes, Costs and Prices* [1] stated that in prevailing conditions there was no justification for any general increase of individual money incomes. It conceded that increases might be justifiable from a national point of view in some individual cases citing the need to man up undermanned industries as a possible example. There was, however, no justification for the maintenance of traditional wage differentials for their own sake. The policy was directed at wages, but existing powers were used to check price increases and companies were persuaded not to increase dividends. The achievement of the stabilisation of employment incomes was left by the Government to the individuals and organisations concerned, in order 'to avoid the undesirable necessity for any interference with the existing methods of negotiations ... '.

The Trades Union Congress accepted the White Paper subject to three conditions: it was not prepared to agree to the reduction of established differentials which it considered were required to sustain craftsmanship; nor to refrain from pressing for adjustments in the wages of workers whose incomes were below 'a reasonable standard of subsistence'; and it insisted that increased output must be a ground for increasing wages. Key trade union leaders pledged their acceptance of the White Paper. In practice they did not press for the exceptions to be applied. Indeed,

'... many of them went a good deal further [than their pledge ... to restrict wage claims to those which were compatible with the terms of their declaration] and tried – for a time successfully – to hold back all claims'.[2]

1 Cmnd. 7321.

2 Allan Flanders 'Collective Bargaining' in Allan Flanders and H.A. Clegg (ed.), *The System of Industrial Relations in Great Britain* (Basil Blackwell, 1954), p. 310.

There is wide agreement that the policy restricted the growth of wage rates and earnings: in the two and a half years from February 1948, despite the fact that prices rose at 8 per cent, nationally negotiated wage rates increased by only 5 per cent.[1] Econometric studies are in broad agreement: D.C. Smith found that the annual rate of change of weekly wage rates was lowered by over 2 percentage points with a smaller effect on hourly earnings;[2] Jefferson, Sams and Swann found that wage rates increased in 1948, 1949, and 1950 at the rate of 3.8, 1.8, and 4.4 per cent, in comparison with increases of 8.3, 6.8, and 4.7 per cent which they estimated would otherwise have occurred.[3] These differences were statistically significant. Lipsey and Parkin also found similar results and in a later study Parkin estimated that wage rates grew almost one percentage point less than they would otherwise have done, although prices went up more than was expected.[4]

The trade unions' cooperation seems to have been the result of a widespread sense of crisis in the aftermath of war and the convertibility crisis of 1947, the fact that the population was accustomed to wartime and postwar controls, and the close personal links with, and support for, the Labour Government of key trade union leaders. Nevertheless, trade union restraint crumbled steadily from the second half of 1949 and had ended completely by the end of 1950. The chief factors in the breakdown were the devaluation of September 1949 and the ensuing rise in the cost of living, accelerated further by the rearmament programme and the outbreak of the Korean war in 1950; lack of support at grass roots level from trade union members; and finally because the policy aimed primarily at the restraint of nationally negotiated wage rates rather than earnings. The last of these factors requires elaboration.

Earnings include such elements as extra wage rates negotiated locally over and above nationally agreed wage rates, overtime payments, and bonuses and incentive payments related to individual output. The last element was particularly important, since roughly one—third of the work force was on payments by results wage schemes. The absence of control over earnings did not render the policy entirely ineffective because of the crucial importance in those days of national wage agreements as a determinant of movements of most wages and salaries. Nevertheless the policy apparently gave a stimulus to piecework and perhaps to overtime. In addition the earnings of those receiving piecework or overtime payments seem to have increased

1 J.C.R. Dow, *The Management of the British Economy 1945—60*. (Cambridge University Press, 1964), p. 35.

2 David C. Smith 'Incomes Policy' in Richard E. Caves (ed.) *Britain's Economic Prospects*, (George Allen and Unwin, 1968), p. 141.

3 C.W. Jefferson, K.I. Sams and D. Swann. 'The Control of Incomes and Prices in the United Kingdom, 1964—67: Policy and Experience'. *The Canadian Journal of Economics*, May 1968, p. 283.

4 R.G. Lipsey and J.M. Parkin 'Incomes Policy: A Reappraisal', *Economica*, May 1970, p. 115. J.M. Parkin 'Some Further Results on the Determination of the Rate of Change of Money Wages', *Economica*, November 1970, p. 386.

more rapidly than those receiving time rates or no overtime. This eventually led some unions to seek general increases in time wage rates to maintain their relative positions, and the policy began to disintegrate as one union after another sought increases.

The 1948–50 experiment showed that Government enforcement machinery was not, in those days, an essential requirement for an effective short-term wages policy; indeed it might have been counterproductive by reducing voluntary cooperation. On the other hand, a minority of trade unions and industries did not co-operate in the policy at any stage, and therefore wage rates in some industries went up even in the early stages of the policy. Later, one union after another began to seek and obtain increases. Both of these developments must have weakened the resolve of co-operating unions whose members were falling behind. Official machinery to enforce the policy might have prevented these early sources of anomaly, and then delayed or moderated the sharp increases in wage rates in late 1950 and 1951. Whether official machinery could have dealt at factory level with the growing gap between earnings and nationally negotiated wage rates is a question touched on elsewhere in this book.

2. 1950–7

In 1952 the Conservative Government proposed that a national advisory council with trade union and employer membership be established with a view to finding ways of relating wages to productivity. The Trades Union Congress was opposed to the idea and it lapsed. The Government then repeated its warnings of a dangerous wage-price spiral and it referred back some Wages Councils proposals for wage increases for reconsideration. When the Councils resubmitted their proposals unchanged, the Government let them through.[1]

From 1952 until March 1956 the Government took few steps to influence movements in wages. When industrial action was threatened in 1953 by both railway, and engineering and shipbuilding workers, the Ministry of Labour intervened to set up Courts of Inquiry which gave awards that pacified the unions. The Government 'preferred to support industrial co-operation and its established institutions at almost any cost',[2] and in 1955 accepted the report of a further Court of Inquiry granting significant wage increases to railway workers.

A White Paper *The Economic Implications of Full Employment* published in 1956 stated:

'In order to maintain full employment the Government must ensure that the level of demand for goods and services is high and rises steadily as productive capacity grows. This means a strong demand for labour, and good opportunities to sell goods and services profitably. In these conditions it

---

1 For an account of this, and other wages policy developments in the 1950's, see K. G. J. C. Knowles 'Wages and Productivity' in G. D. N. Worswick and P. H. Ady (ed.), *The British Economy in the 1950's* (Oxford University Press, 1962).

2 Knowles, op.cit., p. 505.

is open to employees to insist on large wage increases, and it is often possible for employers to grant them and pass on the cost to the consumer, so maintaining their profit margin. This is the dilemma which confronts the country. If the prosperous economic conditions necessary to maintain full employment are exploited by trade unions and businessmen, price stability and full employment become incompatible. The solution lies in self-restraint in making wage claims and fixing profit margins and prices, so that total money income rises no faster than total output.' [1]

'... firms should try, wherever possible, to pass on gains from higher productivity in lower prices ... it is essential that there should be a positive reduction in prices in those sections in which productivity tends to rise more rapidly than the average.' [2]

'The counterpart of realism in relation to prices is realism in relation to personal incomes. The Government of this country does not attempt to tell the people what income each one of them ought to be receiving at any given moment ... the satisfactory operation of this whole system depends upon everyone involved being fully aware of the issues at stake, and upon their acceptance of the full duties of citizenship which this realisation places upon them.' [3]

The White Paper thus stated what it saw as the dilemma of a full employment economy — demand management alone could not ensure both full employment and price stability. They were incompatible if self-restraint was not practiced. Otherwise the economic consequences would be dire. It was not said what steps then would be necessary.

There was another theme in the White Paper. Demand management alone could not ensure the attainment of a maximum rate of growth.

'How fast output rises depends on our success in raising productivity. The achievement of a sustained increase in productivity calls for contributions from both management and labour. Management must strive to ensure the maximum expansion of output by progressive investment in the most efficient capital assets, by the introduction of the most modern industrial techniques and by the elimination of all restrictive practices which inhibit the economic growth of production. The contribution of labour lies in co-operating to the full in the adoption of new methods of working and in setting aside all practices which, however much they may have been justified in the past as means of safeguarding status, conditions of work, or the security of employment itself, are not appropriate in conditions of full employment. The healthy functioning of the economy and the progressive growth of its output depend also on cooperation within industry in maintaining an efficient and enlightened system of industrial relations'.

1 Para. 26.
2 Para. 31.
3 Para. 32.

8

The possibility of developing an instrument of policy to ensure the realisation of a maximum rate of growth was not considered. The objective should be met by contributions by labour and management.

The White Paper was soon followed by a Government appeal for a 'price plateau', made after a series of meetings with representatives of employers organisations, the TUC and the nationalised industries. Nationalised industries and private employers were asked to forego price increases for at least a year, and the unions were asked to adopt a policy of wage restraint. The essence of the policy was to secure wage restraint through price restraint. The policy of wage restraint was rejected by the TUC. A number of industries both in the public and private sector appear to have responded to this appeal. The claims of engineering and shipbuilding workers in November and December 1956 and in March 1957 were firmly rejected by employers. A strike followed. Meanwhile the Government permitted or connived in substantial wage increases in the public sector and nationalised industries; and it then proposed a Court of Inquiry whose recommendations for a settlement of the strike were accepted:

'The employers, instead of receiving the support they had anticipated or even being permitted to "go it alone", had been put under pressure. It may be that the Government believed that the economic consequences of continued wage inflation would be bad but that the political as well as the economic consequences of industrial conflict would be worse ...' [1]

The policy is generally thought to have had little effect on the movement of aggregate wages. This conclusion is supported by econometric studies by Smith; Jefferson, Sams and Swann; and Lipsey and Parkin. Studies by the Department of Employment, [2] and the National Board for Prices and Incomes, however, suggest it was of some effect in reducing earnings.

In 1958 the Government, after refusing a Court of Inquiry into a London busmen's pay dispute, enjoyed a success when the busmen settled for a relatively low offer after an unsuccessful strike. Generally, however, in those years it intervened little to prevent wage increases. As in most of the 1950's it generally wished to avoid major strikes or other forms of industrial action.

3. The Council on Prices, Productivity and Incomes

The Government, however, remained concerned about inflation, and in August 1957 the Council on Prices, Productivity and Incomes, a three-man body under the Chairmanship of Lord Cohen, was established with the function of keeping under review changes in prices, productivity and the level of incomes (including wages, salaries, and profits) and of reporting thereon

1 Knowles, op.cit., p. 508.

2 Department of Employment, *Prices and Earnings in 1951—69: an econometric assessment*, (H.M.S.O., 1971).

3 *Third General Report*, Appendix A.

from time to time. The 'Three Wise Men' did not report on specific cases of wage or price increase. The function of the Council was intended to be educational.

The establishment of the Council marked a constitutional innovation: it was independent of the economic policy making machinery of government.

> '... the Government was no doubt moved by the hope that these people would achieve a quasi-judicial standing and that their recommendations on economic policy, even if unpopular, would have a compelling moral force, like those of judges handing down the law. This idea of bringing in a species of economic judiciary, to supplement the efforts of an executive in need of wider support for its policies ... lay behind the establishment of the "Council on Prices Productivity and Incomes" ... which was supposed to provide the country with *ex cathedra* judgements on the permissible increase in wages ... and so on.'[1]

Its first report, heavily influenced by the views of the late Sir Dennis Robertson of Cambridge University, was a largely unqualified endorsement of the view that the main cause of rising prices since the war had been 'an abnormally high level of demand for goods and services in general, maintained for an abnormally long stretch of time'. This was not to deny altogether that 'powerful' trade unions exerted an independent influence on wages. Nevertheless it regarded the stern measures taken by the Government in 1957, which had contributed to an increase in the level of unemployment, as 'justified and indeed overdue', and stated that 'no one should be surprised or shocked if it proves necessary that it should go somewhat further'. The Council was sceptical of the benefits of announcing a permissible percentage increase in wages in view of the risk that the average might come to be treated as the minimum. 'What, it was felt, was being recommended by the Council was a virtual wage standstill ... coupled with an invitation to the Government to allow unemployment to rise with a view to keeping unions in their place'.[2] The TUC which had given evidence to the Council declared that it would have no further truck with it.

The Council issued two more reports before it was reconstituted in 1960 under the Chairmanship of Lord Heyden, with Sir Harold Emmerson and Professor Phelps Brown (who replaced Robertson in 1959). With a change of personnel came a change of view. The 'Three Wiser Men' issued in July 1961 a final study accepting that cost and demand pressures both influenced inflation, emphasising the importance of increased productivity, and discussing possible machinery for a national prices and incomes policy. All in all the Council may have had some educational effects but 'its main achievement was to push the unions into a position of aggressive hostility towards

1 A. Shonfield. *Modern Capitalism* (Oxford University Press, 1965), p. 154.

2 Knowles, p. 512–3.

10

government economic policy, when, if a wages policy was to be evolved, what was wanted was an atmosphere of cooperation'. [1]

As for the experiment in 'independent' as opposed to 'representative' government the sacrosanct character of the views of the economic judiciary may have been somewhat undermined by the change in its views consequent upon the change in personnel, and, more certainly, the experiment 'had not been a success. People kept noticing the unstated political assumptions staring through the cracks in the façade of expert economic argument'.[2]

Perhaps in establishing the Council at a time of increasing wages and prices the Government had hoped the problem would eventually go away. This at any rate proved to be the case for a time because in 1958 and 1959 prices rose little.

4. The 1961–2 Pay Pause

In July 1961 in response to a sterling crisis the Government introduced a package of restrictive measures and announced unexpectedly that there would be a pay pause until productivity had caught up and there was room for further advances. In those areas where Government had direct responsibility, it would act in accordance with this policy. The Government, although taking no new powers, accordingly intervened in wages settlements whenever its existing powers or role as an employer permitted it to do so. Existing commitments and decisions on Civil Service claims already before the Industrial Court would be implemented without any delay, but otherwise Civil Service pay and other public sector pay increases directly under Government control would be delayed without retrospection 'until circumstances permitted'. When in September the Government refused to accept an award in respect of 2,000 Admiralty employees, it was the first time since the establishment of the Industrial Court in 1919 that it had refused to accept one of its awards. Existing powers to hold up Wages Council awards in the private sector were also used.

The July 1961 statement also asked that the same lines should be followed elsewhere both in the private sector and in those parts of the public sector outside the immediate control of the Government. Local authorities and the heads of nationalised industries were asked to observe the policy.

As regards the latter, there were apparently some effects on settlements in the nationalised gas and coalmining industry, but in November there was a serious breach when the Electricity Council, threatened with industrial action, broke the pause. Although quickly chastised by the Prime Minister, he said that the Government had no powers to control the 'precise wage agreements' in the nationalised industries. Except in Wages Council industries, the impact of the pause on the private sector seems to have been limited at most to delaying a few pay increases. In contrast with the 1956

1 G.D.N. Worswick, 'The British Economy 1950–59' in G.D.N. Worswick and P.H. Ady (ed.), op.cit., p. 59.

2 Shonfield, op.cit., p. 154.

policy, the Government had taken the lead in applying pressure for wage reduction, whilst the private sector appeared to follow less vigorously. The TUC opposed the policy.

The pause came to an end in March 1962. Econometric estimates of its effects mostly conclude that the net effect was probably to hold down the rate of wage rate or earnings increases slightly.[1] There were no measures to control wage drift or non-employment incomes; and there were no exceptions to the policy for wages.

There were difficulties in maintaining a policy which was accused of bearing unevenly on employees in the public and private sector; which took no account of exceptional individual cases and which dealt with pay only, and indeed it was made clear when it was introduced that the Government was working out a form for the policy to take in the longer term.

5. 1962

When the longer term policy was introduced in 1962, the political and economic background was very different from in the mid 1950s. A catalogue of problems had emerged: low investment, rising prices, lagging exports, and chronic balance of payments problems culminating in bouts of speculation against sterling. In the 1950's G.N.P. per head grew at about 2 per cent per annum. This was not so slow as to induce a widespread deeply felt sense of crisis, but by the standards of European economies it was low and Britain was christened by some observers as the sick man of Europe.

It was beginning to be more widely believed that demand management, reliance on self-restraint in wage and price determination, and reliance on management and trade unions to bring about higher growth would not ensure simultaneous realisation of the goals of full employment, price stability and maximum possible growth. Associated with this, there was increasing criticism of the Government's failure to attain these goals and particularly of its recourse to 'stop-go' demand management policies; and the publication of the Radcliffe Report in 1959 had led to greater scepticism about the merits of monetary policy. These and other factors led, in the second Conservative period of Government from 1959 to 1964, to attempts to develop new policy instruments and new institutions.

More generally they led to attempts to develop more interventionist styles of managing the economy, and to the emergence of a 'planning mood'. In the public sector in 1961 alone, there was the Plowden Report on the Control of Public Expenditure which recommended more forward planning of, and a more systematic long term approach to the management of, public expenditure; the White Paper on the Financial and Economic Obligations of the Nationalised Industries setting forth a more systematic economic policy for nationalised industries; and the beginning of hospital and National Health Service plans with long term projections of needs and building programmes. There were

[1] e.g. the D.E. study for earnings; Smith for wage rates but not earnings; Jefferson, Sams and Swann found wage rates in 1961 to be lower but the difference was not statistically significant.

also moves toward more manpower planning. There was the Robbins report of 1963 on Higher Education, and from 1956 White Papers regarding Further Education; the 1962 White Paper on Industrial Training; Zuckerman and other reports regarding scientific and technical manpower. In other fields, concerning industrial structure, industrial research and development programmes, there was also more planning.

The most prominent, though not necessarily the most important, result of the change in Conservative Government thinking about economic policy occurred in 1961 when the Government announced its intention to establish what were to become the National Economic Development Council and the supporting National Economic Development Office. The Council was a tripartite independent body consisting of representatives of government, employers and trade unions. There seems to have been some thought initially that it might serve as an incomes policy body. When it was established, however, its function was to examine the future potential economic performance of the nation, and the obstacles to growth, and to seek agreement about means to increase growth. A form of indicative planning on the much admired French model was envisaged. An assumed (rather than a predicted) growth rate of 4.0 per cent per annum of gross domestic product was made the basis for projections of trends in different sectors of the economy. It was clear that a planning exercise of this kind could not be conducted without paying some regard to the future trend of personal incomes, but between 1962—4 such discussions as there were at NEDC about incomes policy were inconclusive.

The Government's longer term incomes policy was the other major new policy instrument. Whilst the incomes policy and machinery of 1962—4 were kept separate from the NEDC venture, a fact which, to some extent, may have contributed to the policy's negative image, the planning mood did, nevertheless, influence the conception of the incomes policy.

The White Paper of February 1962 *Incomes Policy: the Next Step*[1] contained a statement of principles which, during the phase of restraint following the pause, should govern decisions about the scale of increases in incomes. The increase of wages, salaries and all other incomes should be kept within the 'guiding light' figure of 2 to 2½ per cent per year, the past trend rate of increase of national production per head, and the likely rate for 1962. This figure should apply when appropriate to earnings rather than national wage rates and to all forms of personal incomes. Hard and fast rules could not be laid down by which proposals in individual cases for wage and salary increase should be judged, but certain traditional arguments, such as those derived from the increased cost of living, ought not to be given 'the same weight as hitherto'. Comparisons would still have a part to play, but more regard would have to be given in wage and salary negotiations to the general economic considerations set out in the White Paper. It was stated, however, that there might be cases in which an increase could be justified as part of an agreement 'under which those concerned made a direct contribution by accepting more exacting work or more onerous conditions, or by a renunciation of

1 Cmnd. 1626.

restrictive practices, to an increase of productivity and a reduction of costs', or where 'a build up of manpower in one industry relatively to another ... is plainly necessary'. As will be seen, with the exception of the omission of any reference to low paid workers, this approach and phraseology was remarkably similar to the corresponding part of the 1965 White Paper *Prices and Incomes Policy*.

The February 1962 White Paper had stated that it was for employer and employee negotiators in each case to work out the application of these considerations, but the Government asked that all negotiations should reflect them. Shortly after this, in April 1962, several Wages Councils were asked by the Government to reconsider their awards, but after they refused to lower them, the Government reluctantly accepted them. In June 1962 the Civil Service Arbitration Tribunal recommended a 4 per cent increase to civil servants, in contrast to the official offer of 2½ per cent. This was followed by a Government statement denouncing the 'insufficient regard to requirements of national policy' but agreeing to honour the award. It was followed by a series of negotiated and arbitrated awards in excess of the guiding-light figures for nurses, almoners, post office workers and others.

These events suggested that a policy based on exhortation alone could not work effectively. Nor could there simply be a return to the use of pressure on the public sector and elsewhere where the Government had special powers. In July 1962 a further step occurred when the Prime Minister Mr. H. Macmillan made a statement on incomes policy. He said that an incomes policy was necessary as an indispensable permanent feature of economic life, but the problem was to reconcile it with a free society.

> 'In a free society an incomes policy cannot ... be imposed. It can come about only by general acceptance, and if this is to be a permanent feature and not a temporary thing in a difficult crisis ... then it must be regarded both as necessary and as fair ... It must not, as a permanent feature, be rigid. It must be, perhaps, at the beginning but it must take account of all the varying situations. A temporary measure must necessarily be somewhat rigid and sometimes unfair. A permanent policy, however, must be flexible so that it can take account of the different conditions and needs of different services and industries and of the intervals that may have elapsed between the last increase and a new claim.' [1]

The Government would continue to lay down a norm. It would apply to 'incomes' and would cover salaries and earnings as well as wage rates. It would not apply in every case; it might be necessary to provide some special increase to build up manpower in one industry relative to another or to take account of special contributions to productivity or efficiency. On the other hand, the objectives would not be achieved if every case were treated as a special one. It was not enough for the Government to offer guidance in general terms; what was necessary was an impartial and authoritative view on the more important or difficult pay claims given by a body which could see

[1] *Hansard,* July 26, 1962.

these questions both as they affected individual interests and the nation. Accordingly he announced the establishment of the National Incomes Commission (NIC) as a permanent body. Its pronouncements, however, would have no legal effect; the policy would depend upon voluntary cooperation.

Conclusions

Thus the foundations of the criteria and much of the machinery of the incomes side of the prices and incomes policies for the remainder of the 1960's were laid by 1962. They were, in brief, a permanent policy that was to cover all public and private sector incomes, including salaries and earnings as well as wage rates; the establishment of a norm prescribing the generally permissible annual incomes increase, although it was recognised that above norm increases were acceptable in the kinds of exceptional circumstances envisaged in the White Paper *Incomes Policy: The Next Step;* and the establishment of an independent body to judge important pay claims.

There was, however, only a distant connection at best with the economic planning machinery; there was no machinery to detect systematically cases in which incomes at factory level were increased; there was no trade union cooperation; and no powers were taken to enforce the policy or the recommendations of N.I.C.

2. The National Incomes Commission

In this chapter the work of the National Incomes Commission (NIC), the predecessor of the NBPI, is reviewed. Particular attention is given to the difficulties which NIC experienced in determining crucial facts about the subjects on which it was asked to report. The chapter ends with a summary of some general lessons from the NIC experiment. Some of these lessons greatly influenced both the Labour Government and the NBPI in 1965–70.

1. The Commission and its Role

NIC existed from November 1962 until the establishment of the NBPI. As an independent body, its function was 'to provide impartial and authoritative advice'[1] on certain incomes matters. It did not deal with particular cases of increases of prices or profits. It had no substantive powers, nor did the Government take any powers to enforce its findings. Its establishment was opposed by the TUC and it received no co-operation from any trade union at any time.[2]

Three of its five members were full-time. Its full-time Chairman, Sir Geoffrey Laurence,Q.C., was Chairman of the General Council of the Bar. No members were drawn from the ranks of industry or trade unions.[3] There were about 30 staff, but no research or specialist staff. Its terms of reference were: (a) to review certain pay matters where the cost was wholly or partly met from the Exchequer which the Government referred to it;[4]

1 *The National Incomes Commission*, Cmnd 1844 (1962) para 1.

2 University teachers, however, co-operated with its inquiry into their pay.

3 The other members were: Professor H.S. Kirkaldy, Professor of Industrial Relations, University of Cambridge; Sir Harold Banwell, Secretary, Association of Municipal Corporations; Mr. L.C. Hawkins, member of the London Transport Executive; and Professor R.C. Tress, Professor of Economics, University of Bristol.

4 Pay in the nationalised industries and Higher Civil Service and of doctors and dentists was excluded from this category.

(b) to examine retrospectively any particular pay settlement, whether in the public or private sector (other than an award at arbitration), which the Government referred to it.[1] It received one reference under the first head, and three under the second.

NIC was required to have regard to the particular circumstances of cases referred to it and to the national interest. The national interest was not defined, but the White Paper listed some relevant factors e.g. possible repercussions of wage increases on other employments. It was thus left to NIC to define a 'norm'. The figure it arrived at was 3–3½ per cent, 1 per cent above that recommended by the Government in the 1962 White Paper on Incomes Policy on the basis of the then achieved long-term growth rate, but equal to the 3½ per cent growth rate of productivity per head predicted by the National Economic Development Council. 'Purely practical considerations' made it expedient in NIC's view to take a figure which had 'some real chance of general acceptance'.

NIC was instructed to report on the need, if any, for the Government to take action by fiscal or other appropriate means to restrain any undue growth in the aggregate profits in the British economy if it should result from the restraint on earned incomes. It was also empowered to undertake on its own initiative general or particular studies on topics such as the criteria to be taken into account in defining the national interest. NIC undertook no studies on its own initiative, although in each report there was a general discussion of an incomes policy theme (e.g. comparability) relevant to the reference.

2. Findings

Of the wage agreements it examined, NIC unequivocally condemned the following as being against the national interest: the national agreements (of November 1963) in the Engineering and Shipbuilding industry; a Scottish Builders Agreement; and an agreement of the Heating, Ventilation and Domestic Engineering Industry. It acquitted a Scottish Plumbers agreement, and, in its one 'non-retrospective' reference, it recommended salary increases substantially above the norm for academic staff. It found it more difficult to decide about the remainder. It was not prepared to find that an electrical contracting agreement, looked at as a whole, was against the national interest.
'The one circumstance which in our judgement may have the requisite quality [to justify an above-norm wage increase] lies in the past history of time-wasting practices in this industry, which we accept as being of exceptional degree, and in the prospect presented of their renunciations.'[2]

'We do not find it possible to express an opinion whether or not this change will in fact occur. If it does not, the amount of increases in pay will be proved to have been unjustified ... If present hopes and expectations are

1 A further term of reference was to enquire into any pay claim or question referred to it by the parties affected, but no references came to it as a result of this provision.

2 Report 2, para 150.

fulfilled, events may hereafter be said to have proved the wisdom of the Association and the Union in making the agreement. In the face of what we accept is the genuine determination of both sides of the industry to co-operate in producing the fundamental and necessary change, we are not prepared to hold that this agreement, looked at as a whole, is contrary to the national interest. We may be proved to have been wrong; it is for the parties to prove that they have been right.'[1]

In another report, it reached similar verdicts in not condemning above-norm wage agreements of the Vauxhall and Ford companies because Vauxhall had obtained an undertaking of future co-operation from the union, and because of a 'dramatic improvement in industrial relations'[2] in Ford in the twelve months before the settlement. But it did not positively approve the increases either. Its conclusions on a wage agreement of the exhibition contracting industry were:

> '*Prima facie* it is therefore of an inflationary character and could be justified only on the ground of special circumstances. No evidence was placed before us by either of the parties to the agreement of any such circumstances or of any other considerations which might justify the terms of the agreement.' There was, in fact, no evidence from either of the parties concerned because NIC was not afforded any assistance by either the workpeople's or the employer's side of the National Joint Council for the Exhibition Industry. 'The strong *prima facie* case against it was not displaced and we are therefore bound to find, as we do, that this agreement was contrary to the national interest.'[3]

3. Speed of Reporting

NIC's 'retrospective' reports were published well after the wage agreements had occurred. It took about four months to publish its first report, which thus came about five months after the Scottish building agreement it condemned, although seven months before the agreement took effect. The adverse findings of the second 'retrospective' agreement report came about four to five months after the agreements had taken effect. An interim report on the engineering and shipbuilding industry agreement came about five to six months after the agreement had taken effect; the final report came fifteen months later, after a new national agreement – with some important innovations – had been reached. The report was thus mainly of historical interest, rather than likely to have any influence.

The language used and the conclusions reached by NIC suggest that its approach tended to be that of a legal tribunal which waited for what was brought before it and passed judgement in the light of presented evidence.

1 *Ibid.*, para 151

2 Report 4, para 330.

3 Report 2, para 173.

18

That it had the character of a formal inquiry body rather than a probing, investigatory and initiating body is illustrated by its procedures and enquiries.

4. Procedures

NIC relied upon five sources of information: the knowledge of its members, published information of which it was aware, written submissions, oral evidence and enquiries made specially for the reference.

At the start of each reference it invited written submissions from all parties and, by publication of notices in the Press, from any other parties who wished to give evidence. In most cases employers co-operated, but unions never did.[1] In addition, Government departments supplied background information about the industry, and any available wage rates, earnings, profits and productivity data. Several academic experts volunteered written submissions reporting the results of their research. Submissions were circulated amongst the contributors, and released to the press.

Oral hearings were held in public. Written submissions were elaborated and comments made by the different groups on the written and oral submissions of others. Questioning of the witnesses was done by NIC. There were no cross-examinations or legal counsel. After the first round of evidence each party was invited to sum up and to comment on points which had been made during the hearings.

5. Enquiries Made Specially for the Report

NIC made no special enquiries of its own but some bodies which appeared before it did so for its benefit. Thus the University Grants Committee and the Ministry of Education undertook a special survey of 'supplementary earnings' of academics when it emerged that they were relevant.

In the Engineering and Shipbuilding report, NIC persuaded the Purchasing Officers Association to conduct a survey of its members on the effects of the wage agreements under examination on prices. The Engineering Employers' Federation, at NIC's request, also undertook a survey of the effects of the agreement on the unit costs of output to their members. Neither enquiry was entirely satisfactory. The first was qualified in several ways by the Association itself and was generally called into question by the EEF on the grounds that the sample may not have been representative, that an accurate picture of price changes was not given, and that little reliance could be placed on the expressions of opinion for which it asked. The second was an outright failure. Only 240 replies were received from the 1,268 establishments sampled, and NIC concluded the resulting evidence was of no help.

6. Reliance on the Parties for Evidence

The extent to which the NIC was in the hands of the co-operating parties for its information was evident in the second report. Having regard to the

---

[1] In report 3 academic staff did.

terms of reference requiring account to be taken of such matters as pricing, profit margins and dividends, NIC sought to obtain statistics of profits for these industries.

It found published information to be of little use. The two employers associations which co-operated with the inquiry (one did not) kept no data themselves. One informed NIC 'that it was unable to provide a sample of turnover and profits from its members and that there was nothing further it could do to assist the Commission in this respect beyond the written evidence it had already submitted,'[1] which gave very little profits data. The other association, the Association of Heating, Ventilating and Domestic Engineering Employers, advised that it has no figures of profit for its member firms, apart from those of public companies, and had not conducted a survey of profits, nor did it think it could obtain from its members the sample which NIC sought. Finally it considered it had no authority to consent on behalf of members to extraction by the Board of Inland Revenue of relevant information in its possession (which would have been done without revealing the identity of members).

Reliance on such evidence as was submitted by the parties was of limited use at times. In its first report also NIC wished to inquire into profits but published material was unsatisfactory. However, all the responsible heads of the firms in membership of the employers' organisations in the construction industry who appeared before it gave an assurance that, so far as they were aware, the profit margins of their members were not unreasonable or excessive, and that they left no room for the absorption of increased labour costs. Whilst satisfied that the assurances were given in good faith, NIC concluded that no conclusive opinion of the matter could be formed without very much more information than was publicly available:

'All that we can say is that there was no evidence before us that the general level of profits, profit margins and dividends of the construction industry at the present time are excessive or unreasonable.'[2]

NIC's conclusion at the end of these first two references was that there was an urgent case in the national interest for a representative survey of the policies and practices in relation to pricing, profit margins and dividends in the construction industry:

'such a survey in the absence of voluntary agreement, requires an authority and a power of enforcement which we do not possess. Our experience of the two references ... has shown that unless such a survey is conducted ... we shall not have been given the evidence which we require to enable us to observe an important part of our terms of reference ... there is a danger not only that our findings relating to wages will be regarded as

1 Report 2, para 178.

2 Report 1, para 164.

20

one-sided, but that they will again, in terms of an incomes policy, reveal only a part of the picture.'[1]

7. Non-Co-operating Parties

The non-co-operation of trade unions also prevented NIC from receiving information it wanted. A critical issue in the fourth reference concerned the history of attempts in the industry to deal with the matter of the efficient use of manpower. The main evidence came from the two federations of employers. Before reviewing it, NIC said that it had received no evidence on the degree of technical and managerial efficiency in the industry.

A useful purpose would have been served if the unions had given evidence on this. 'As it is we have been able to deal only with questions affecting manpower and even there we have heard only one side of the question. We regret once more that we have been denied the assistance of the trade unions in the examination of vital questions.'[2]

8. Other Investigatory Aspects

NIC preferred some types of evidence to others. In the report on academic remuneration, the least deficient in terms of information available, NIC, in discussing whether university salaries had fallen behind salaries for comparable work, pointed out the inadequacies of the statistical evidence before it. It did:

> 'not think that direct statistical comparisons of this sort are or should be regarded as the determining factors. In our judgment better and more cogent evidence of the true situation was to be found in the frank statement by the University Grants Committee of their own general experience and knowledge of the affairs of the Universities themselves, supported as it was in general by the evidence of the Committee of Vice-Chancellors and Principals and other witnesses from the Universities.'[3]

This was, in the context, a clear statement that in a question of measurement — the measurement of relative change in university salaries — opinions were in principle to be preferred to statistics.

Conclusions

This brief review of NIC may be summed up as follows:

1. NIC did what it was asked to do by the Government. But only wage and salary references came within its province, and very few of them came in 1963—4. Thus only five reports (in four references) were produced in two and a half years. They were mostly published well after the agreements

1 Report 2, para 185.

2 Report 4 (final) para 206.

3 Report 3, para 42.

under investigation had been concluded and were largely or totally irrelevant to the situation when published. NIC did not have trade union support. It operated in an entirely voluntary context. These factors combined to make its impact on the economy minimal.

2. Nearly all reports were weakened in one crucial respect or another by NIC's inability to reach a definite finding, either on a vital issue of fact, or even on the central question of whether or not an agreement was against the national interest. This was largely because it followed the approach of a Court of Inquiry or legal tribunal or Royal Commission[1] of relying for evidence mainly on what co-operating parties submitted and what was already available in a published form or happened to have been the subject of recent academic research. On some questions, such as managerial efficiency in the engineering and shipbuilding industries, independent enquiries would have been necessary for a sound judgment to have been made. The weakness of its investigations lessened the force of its findings, and at times led it to some rather simplistic findings.

3. The rather facile solutions proposed to the wage drift problem in its fourth report (chiefly the elimination of payments by results systems) would probably not have been proposed if it had studied the foreign experience of national incomes policies. This is partly explained by the deliberate choice of NIC not to build up its own research staff.

4. The apparent ineffectiveness of incomes policy between 1962–4 is not primarily attributable to NIC which did what it was asked to do. Moreover, NIC may have had some useful effects on educating the Government and the public. Allowance must also be made for the fact that it was the first body of its kind in Great Britain. There may have been some advantages in its public procedures although their disadvantages are discussed in Chapter 6. But the NIC experiment illustrates an important general point about the administration of incomes policy. An incomes policy can be undermined by a weak instrument of administration. For example, circumstances may require speedy decisions in some cases; or, at other times, well-researched decisions; or both. If the instrument is unable to meet these requirements, it is a serious constraint on the policy.

These points, as will be seen, influenced the NBPI in the development of its methods of enquiry. When additionally the NBPI's greater emphasis on the investigation of cost-saving possibilities and the reform of wage structures and industrial relations is taken into account, the need to establish investigatory methods that went further than those of NIC becomes clear.

1 Of late, Royal Commissions have frequently commissioned or directly controlled research. The approach of NIC resembled that of most Royal Commissions of its time. Royal Commissions are discussed in the final chapter.

3. The Productivity, Prices and Incomes Policies of 1965-70

This study is principally about the NBPI but it is necessary first to outline the main features of the productivity, prices and incomes policies of 1965–70, paying special attention to matters of greatest relevance to the NBPI.

1. The Establishment of the Policy and the Machinery

In December 1964, shortly after the election of the Labour Government, a 'Joint Statement of Intent on Productivity, Prices and Incomes' was signed by the Government, Trades Union Congress, and employers' organisations. The Government declared that their:

'economic objective is to achieve and maintain a rapid increase in output and real incomes combined with full employment. Their social objective is to ensure that the benefits of faster growth are distributed in a way that satisfies the claims of social need and justice.'

Management and trade unions recognised the need to:

'raise productivity throughout industry and commerce, to keep increases in total money incomes in line with increases in real national output and to maintain a stable general price level.'

Various measures were proposed to achieve these aims. One was that the TUC and employers representatives undertook to co-operate in giving effective shape to machinery which the Government intended to set up:

'a. To keep under review the general movement of prices and of money incomes of all kinds.
  b. To examine particular cases in order to advise whether or not the behaviour of prices or of wages, salaries or other money incomes was in the national interest as defined by the Government after consultation with management and unions.'

The first of these tasks was later assigned to the National Economic Development Council which thereafter published annual reviews, and the second to the National Board for Prices and Incomes which was established on 8 April, 1965. The establishment of the NBPI was proposed in the White Paper *Machinery of Prices and Incomes Policy*, February, 1965. The first three references to the NBPI of particular cases for examination were made on May 6, 1965.

'The national interest as defined by the Government after consultation with management and unions', which was inter alia to govern the NBPI's judgement of particular cases, was specified first in the White Paper *Prices and Incomes Policy* of April 1965. The TUC and employers representatives endorsed this formulation. 'The national interest' continued to be spelt out by the Government in a series of White Papers until 1970. Appendix B lists their names and publication dates, along with the legislation which accompanied them in 1966, 1967 and 1968.

'The national interest' required that there should be an incomes 'norm' i.e. a maximum percentage by which the wages and salaries of individuals should increase in any year. This figure, initially of 3–3½ per cent per annum, was derived from the expected annual rate of growth of productivity per head. Exceptional circumstances in which increases above the norm were considered justifiable were also defined. They could be summarised briefly as being that an above-norm increase in pay could be justified only where employees had made a direct contribution towards an increase in productivity; where it was essential in the national interest to secure a redistribution of manpower; where there was general recognition that existing pay was too low to maintain a reasonable standard of living; and where there was widespread recognition that pay had fallen seriously out of line with that found in similar work elsewhere and needed in the national interest to be improved. Two further exceptions were added later, in 1968 for a major reorganisation of a wage or salary structure and, in 1970, for pay increases necessary for bringing about equal pay for women by 1975. The exact definition of criteria are given in Chapter 8.

On the prices side, no 'norm' was laid down for the prices of individual enterprises, but criteria for pricing were prescribed 'with the aim of ensuring that the general level of prices in the economy would remain stable.' Price increases were to be avoided whenever possible, and price reductions to be made whenever circumstances permitted. Enterprises were expected not to raise prices except:

1. a. if output per employee could not be increased sufficiently to allow wages and salaries to increase at a rate consistent with the aforementioned incomes criteria, without some increase in prices, or
b. if there were unavoidable increases in non-labour or capital costs per unit of output,
and if, in these two cases, offsetting reductions could not be made in costs or in the return sought on investment, or

2. if the enterprise was unable to secure the capital required to meet home and overseas demand, after making every effort to reduce costs.

Enterprises were expected to reduce prices in the opposite circumstances or if profits were based on excessive market power. The exact wording of these criteria is given in Chapter 12. There were no significant changes in these criteria in later phases of the policy.

A further important step in establishing the machinery of the administration of the policy was the setting up, at the end of 1965, of an 'early warning' system under which the Government was to be notified in advance of nearly all important wage and price increases. This was to give it adequate time to consider decisions regarding pay and prices before they were put into effect and, in particular, to decide whether or not to refer them to the NBPI. The TUC and CBI co-operated voluntarily although the Government had earlier announced that it would seek statutory powers to enforce the early warning system. Some further comments on this machinery are made in Chapter 4.

2. Some features of the Policy

Several features of the policy as initially formulated should be noted. First, Government statements emphasised the positive nature of the policy and that it bore no comparison with the earlier attempts at 'negative wage restraint' so firmly opposed by the TUC. The Labour Government had returned to power after a campaign directed against the slow growth rate of the economy, 13 years of what were termed 'Conservative misrule' and 'stop-go' demand management policies. It held that the country's problems went deeper than could be handled by deflationary demand management policies or devaluation. A direct 'physical' attack on the weak spots of the economy was necessary to raise efficiency. Fundamental structural reform, conducted on an industry – by – industry, firm – by – firm basis, was the key to growth and the modernisation of the economy which the electorate had been promised. At the same time there was to be a National Plan prepared by a new Ministry, the Department of Economic Affairs (not an independent body like NEDC in 1962–4), with the prime function of raising the growth rate. Planning and intervention was to be by consent, not command, broadly speaking.

The productivity prices and incomes policy was seen as an integral part of the overall programme to raise the long-term growth rate. It was envisaged as helping to secure a planned growth of real incomes at a rate higher than otherwise would be achieved. In the eyes of Mr. George Brown, the First Secretary of State for Economic Affairs, who was the Minister responsible for the administration of the overall strategy, the prices and incomes policy should be designed so as to help bring about higher real incomes, higher productivity, and the efficient utilisation of resources by such means as the elimination of 'restrictive' or 'protective' labour practices, the reform of management and industrial relations and the closer linking of pay and productivity. At the same time prices and incomes rules were necessary to ensure that the Government's total strategy was not frustrated by unjustifiable price increases and by the increase of incomes at a rate that exceeded the growth of productivity. Thus, the emphasis on a productivity-oriented prices and incomes policy was in accord with the Labour Government's general philosophy and, to judge from the election result, the mood of the country.

Second, the policy enjoyed the tripartite support of the Government, employers representatives and the TUC. It was thought that securing the support of the CBI and TUC would help make the policy workable and durable.

Third, the policy applied to 'other money incomes' and prices, as well as to wages and salaries.

Finally, the Government took no powers to deal with those whose behaviour was found to be against the national interest. Observance of the policy, therefore, depended largely upon the voluntary compliance of individual organisations. This was in accord with the philosophy of planning through co-operation, not by force.

3. The Phases of the Policy

There were 5 main phases of the prices and incomes policy between 1965 and 1970.

The first voluntary phase lasted from April 1965 to June 1966. Whilst, in its first twelve or fifteen months, the NBPI had some success in having the recommendations made in its reports accepted by the various parties, the period was marked by a rapid rise in incomes generally, accompanied by a somewhat less rapid rise in prices and a slow growth of output.

The Joint Declaration of Intent had been made against the background of rising demand and a severe balance of payments deficit. The dilemma of reconciling the essentially long term task of accelerating the process of adaptation in the field of prices and incomes with the pressing short term needs of the economy and the balance of payments had on that occasion been resolved by deciding to press on with the long term policies.

In July 1966 following a sterling crisis the priorities were reversed, and there was a dramatic change in the nature of the prices and incomes policy. The Government announced a severe credit squeeze and tax measures aimed to restore equilibrium. The Prices and Incomes Act 1966 was passed giving the Government power to delay pay or price increases taking effect until August 1967. The policy therefore became compulsory. During the first 6 months there were to be no increases in wages, salaries or dividends and there were severe limits on price increases. The exceptional criteria for pay increases were suspended. For the second six months a zero norm was imposed on pay and dividends, but for pay certain exceptions were restored and there were slightly less severe limitations on price increases. The emphasis of this second phase of 'standstill' and 'restraint' was on short-term restraint.

The General Council of the TUC 'reluctantly acquiesced' in the emergency measures of mid 1966 but in 1967 a Congress motion calling for the repeal of the 1966 and 1967 Acts was carried.

The third phase 'the period of moderation' lasted from July 1967 to March 1968. There was a zero norm, but the original criteria were restored. The policy was essentially voluntary, although the Government kept certain powers to delay particular pay or price increases. It had power to impose a 30 day standstill on proposed pay or price rises whilst examining them. It could then order a further delay of up to three months if and only if it referred the proposals to the NBPI. If at the end of three months the NBPI so recommended, the Government could impose a further delay of 3 months on the increase. The maximum period of delay was thus seven months.

This scheme had significant legal implications for the NBPI. Until 1967 an NBPI report had no legal significance in the sense that the Government could ignore it and use its power to delay a wage or price increase, although in practice it never did so. Thereafter anyone whose increase was a candidate for Government delay had the opportunity of persuading the independent NBPI to report favourably upon it, in which case the Government, whose use of its powers was now conditional upon an adverse NBPI report, could take no action. If the NBPI did report adversely, however, the Government was not obliged to act. To this extent the NBPI assumed a quasi-judicial role which continued until 1970.

Moreover, this change meant that the NBPI became an essential part of the machinery of control. Until 1967 it was thought that the Board would only deal with important cases of wage and price increase. Less important cases would be left to the Government to examine and control. Now for the Government to block any increase the only step was to refer it to the NBPI. When an outbreak of above-norm pay increases for busmen occurred in 1968 the Government called in the NBPI to act in effect as a direct instrument of wage restraint. In the view of some major trade unions including the TGWU this established the NBPI as a body whose main purpose was to function as an instrument of wage repression rather than as a body which helped raise wages. [1]

During the third phase the pound sterling was devalued in November 1967 after a further sterling crisis. In response to the wish to make devaluation effective a somewhat belated fourth phase was ushered in in March 1968 and lasted to the end of 1969. The Government's power to delay increases after an adverse NBPI report was extended to eight months and thus the maximum period of delay to twelve months. The 1968 Prices and Incomes Act also conferred on the Government some new powers including powers to order price reductions on an NBPI recommendation.

There was a zero norm, and a ceiling of 3½ per cent on increases in wages and salaries justified on exceptional grounds. However, increases above the ceiling were permitted in three exceptional circumstances — when the effects on productivity of a productivity agreement or of a major wage or salary restructuring were sufficiently great; and for low-paid workers as part of a settlement which, as a whole, was within the ceiling. A voluntary scheme to keep a 3½ per cent ceiling on dividends increases was administered by the Treasury with the co-operation of industry.

In January 1969 the Government published a White Paper *In Place of Strife*. The most controversial proposals sought powers to intervene in certain strike situations.[2] By April opposition to the measures was gaining momentum in the trade unions and in the Labour Party itself. In the Budget speech

1 Andrew W.J. Thomson 'Collective Bargaining under Incomes Legislation: the Case of Britain's Buses', *Industrial and Labour Relations Review*, April 1971, p.389 is an illuminating account of these events.

2 For an account of this and succeeding events see Peter Jenkins *The Battle of 10 Downing Street.* (Charles Knight, 1970).

of April 1969 the Chancellor of the Exchequer announced that a short Bill containing the strike proposals would be introduced without delay. At the same time he announced that the power conferred by the Prices and Incomes Act of 1968 to defer settlements for 12 months would not be renewed at the end of 1969. In June 1969 the Industrial Relations Bill was abandoned in the face of strong opposition from within the Parliamentary Labour Party and from trade unions. In the third quarter of 1969 the Government, without reference to the NBPI, sanctioned a series of much publicised above-norm pay settlements for London firemen, local authority manual workers, nurses and so on and largely abandoned any pretence that the policy was being applied.

The final phase of the Labour Government's policies came into operation at the beginning of 1970. The Government retained only the power to delay proposed wage and salary or prices increases for one month whilst it inspected them, and for three months while the NBPI reported. All the other powers were allowed to lapse. A White Paper stated that pay settlements should fall within the range of 2½ − 4½ per cent. The 3½ per cent ceiling scheme for dividends was dropped. The policy was essentially voluntary.

Following its election in June 1970, the new Conservative Government discontinued these policies, and the NBPI was wound up on March 31st, 1971, after completion of its work on the subjects which the previous Government had referred to it.

4. The Economic Context of 1965–70

The economic context in which the policy and the NBPI operated was unpropitious especially for the conduct of a 'positive' policy.

The poor balance of payments situation until 1969 gave the Government little opportunity to experiment with a long-term positive style of prices and incomes policy. Instead, as has been noted, the policy became a means of restraint in 1966–7. There may have been a degree of public readiness to accept the austere policies of 1966–7, but after the failure of the policies to avert devaluation in 1967, the reservoir of goodwill for any further experiment was depleted, and the atmosphere in which the 1968–9 phase operated was less favourable. As for the effects of the devaluation the NBPI's own comments were apt. After pointing out the difficulty of executing a policy designed to operate on individual incomes when prices were rising, or were thought to be rising, faster than earnings, it noted that devaluation was likely to lead to price increases estimated at about 3 per cent: 'We are ... faced with the paradoxical position that the act of devaluation makes a prices and incomes policy more necessary than before while also making its execution more difficult'. [1]

Table 3.1 shows some indicators of national economic performance for the 5 phases of the policy.

1 *Third General Report*, para. 15.

Table 3.1 *Some Economic Indicators, 1965–70: Gross Domestic Product, Unemployment and Vacancies*

Period of prices and incomes policy	Percent increases at annual rates[a] Gross Domestic Product[b]	As percent of civilian labour force	
		Unemployment[c]	Unfilled Vacancies[d]
April 1965–June 1966	1.2	1.28	1.68
July 1966–June 1967	2.0	1.82	1.26
July 1967–March 1968	4.6	2.30	1.08
April 1968–Dec. 1968[e]	3.4	2.35	1.17
January 1969–Dec. 1969[e]	1.5	2.32	1.24
January 1970–June 1970	1.8	2.44	1.20
April 1965–June 1970	2.1	1.99	1.31

Sources: Blue Book, Monthly Bulletin of Statistics, National Institute Economic Review.

Notes:
  (a) The percentage increases quoted are those from the quarter preceding each period to the final quarter of the period.
  (b) Output based.
  (c) Unemployment registration as percentage of civilian labour force. Seasonally adjusted.
  (d) Unfilled vacancies as percentage of civilian labour force. Seasonally adjusted.
  (e) These are sub-periods of the 1968–9 phase.

They show that economic growth was low throughout the five years, except between July 1967 and December 1968. The failure of growth was contrary to the expectations which accompanied the introduction of the prices and incomes policies and the National Economic Plan. In 1965, for example, a norm of 3½ per cent had been set on the assumption that the national growth rate per head would increase from about 2½ per cent in 1964 to 3½ per cent, whereas in fact it proved to be a little over 1.0 per cent for the first period of the policy. The level of unemployment increased steadily over the whole period. Unfilled vacancies, an indicator of labour market conditions, were low after June 1966.

Turner and Wilkinson[1] have shown that if account is taken of tax and social insurance deductions, the annual change between 1964 and 1968 (the years they quote) in the real income of the median wage earner (married with two children) was only 1 per cent. (For the years 1959–64 the rate was 1.9 per cent and for 1968–70 2.7 per cent (estimated)). A year by year picture is shown in Fig. 3.1.

This must have made it more difficult to secure the acceptability of the incomes policy, and it tended to undermine any underlying concept of the prices and incomes policy as one designed to promote the growth, not the restriction, of incomes.

1 H.A. Turner and Frank Wilkinson. 'Real Net Incomes and the Wage Explosion'. *New Society*, February 25 1971. A lengthier paper on the subject is being prepared. I am grateful to the authors for allowing me to use the graph which is a refined version of the one which appeared in their New Society article.

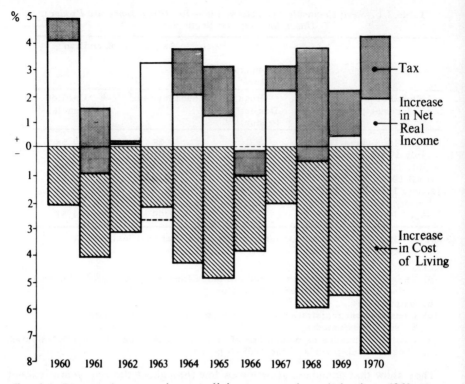

Fig. 3.1 Changes in money income, living costs, and tax deductions 1960-70

The failure of growth along with increasing unemployment, whilst no doubt bringing home an appreciation of the need to raise productivity in the future, and whilst perhaps making management even more cost-conscious than usual, meant that there was a poor climate for the operation of a productivity-oriented prices and incomes policy. In an economy growing below its capacity growth rate attempts to raise productivity per employee may lead to increases in unemployment rather than higher output, and may encounter employee resistance. Thus, Mr. Jack Jones, General Secretary of the Transport and General Workers' Union, speaking on February 10, 1971, said output had been increased through productivity bargaining in recent years, but new jobs had not been created to absorb surplus manpower.

'So the same output has been shared out among fewer men and the dole queues have lengthened. The Government got the productivity and the workers got the sack.' [1]

Table 3.2 shows the course of wage rates, earnings, retail prices and wages and salaries per unit of output during the policy.

1 *The Financial Times*, February 11, 1971, p. 31.

30

Table 3.2 *Hourly Wage Rates, Earnings, Retail Prices, and Wages and Salaries per Unit of Output, 1965–70*

Percentage increases (at annual rates)

Period	Hourly Wage Rates	Earnings (Seasonally adjusted)	Retail Prices	Wages and Salaries per unit of output
April 1965–June 1966	7.4	7.6	5.1	7.0
July 1966–June 1967	2.8	1.7	2.5	0.3
July 1967–March 1968	9.2	8.8	2.8	4.5
April 1968–December 1968	4.5	7.6	5.5	0.7
January 1969–December 1969	5.6	8.3	5.1	7.6
January 1970–June 1970	12.6	13.6	8.8	12.1
April 1965–June 1970	6.5	7.3	4.7	5.0

Notes:
  (a) This table brings up to date a table published in the White Paper '*Productivity, Prices and Incomes Policy after 1969*', p. 6.
  (b) The percentages increases quoted are those from the average for the quarter preceding each period to the average for the final quarter of the period. Quarterly figures have been used which eliminate various fluctuations in the monthly figures.
  (c) Hourly wage rate figures are taken from the Department of Employment's index of basic hourly wages rates and relate to manual workers. Earnings figures are taken from the monthly index of weekly average rates and salary earnings. They relate to all industries and services and are seasonally adjusted.

From the inception of the policy prices and incomes were increasing at high rates. On the incomes side, observance of the norm implied little or negative increase in real incomes. In 1965–66 when the norm was 3.5 per cent, prices increased at the rate of 5.1 per cent annually, and observance of the norm implied a reduction of 1.6 per cent per year in real income, not an increase of 3.5 per cent. In 1966–7 prices increased by 2.5 per cent whilst the norm was zero. A rise in import prices and taxes after devaluation sent the retail price index up sharply. The norm for 1968–9 was zero, although in practice the ceiling of 3.5 per cent was widely regarded as the norm.[1] Even an increase of 3.5 per cent implied a fall in pre-tax real income of about 2 per cent.

Had everyone observed the incomes norm, prices would, no doubt, have increased less and observance of the norm would have been less costly in real terms. But hourly wage rates and earnings rose at rates well above the norm in all periods, and besides giving an element of unreality to the norm, they also prevented there being any prospect that price stability could be achieved.

Whatever the effect of these factors on the success of the prices and incomes policy in general, they made the task of the NBPI much harder in applying the norms and the various criteria to particular cases. During the 1968–9 phase, for example, the NBPI had to decide on the pay increases which should be received by those groups referred to it whilst being aware that average earnings for the rest of the economy were increasing at about 8 per cent per annum. Unless they had made a special contribution to

1 see *Fourth General Report*, para. 57.

productivity or had had a wage and salary reorganisation, they could not receive more than 3½ per cent except in special circumstances for the low-paid.[1] The policy where applied was thus selective and harsh. These factors also made some of the NBPI's long term tasks more difficult. For instance, as is explained in Chapter 8, by reducing the influence of comparability factors in income determination, the Board sought to relate incomes more closely to the norm rather than to what others were receiving. This would clearly have been easier at a time of price stability when incomes were growing at the same rate as national productivity. On the other hand, these factors may have helped in the fulfilment of some of the NBPI's long term goals by adding to the pressure on wage and salary earners to accept ways of relating their pay more closely to productivity, and of reorganising their wage and salary structures on a more rational basis.

The notion, central to the administration of the prices and incomes policy after the middle of 1966 at any rate, that the avoidance of inflation was a primary national economic requirement was undermined at several stages by the conflicting requirements of the Government's economic policy. The most notable example occurred following the stringent tax measures of the 1968 Budget which were estimated at the time as being likely to put up prices by rather more than 1½ per cent.[2] By putting up prices, they made the task of holding down the growth of money incomes to a rate implied by the norm more difficult.

It is outside the mainstream of this study to examine the effects of the productivity, prices and incomes policies of 1965–70. However, the subject is one of some controversy, and the Appendix to this chapter is a brief review of the main econometric contributions to the debate.

Conclusions

This chapter has described the main features and phases of the productivity prices and incomes policies of 1965–70. These policies incorporated several new features compared with the policies of 1961–4. They embraced all incomes and prices, initially enjoyed TUC support and were envisaged as part of an overall programme to raise the long-term growth rate. Machinery was set up for the notification of all important prices and incomes increases.

When the policies were introduced in 1965, their positive long term nature was stressed. It was natural that the NBPI's conception of its role, which is considered in the next chapter, should be influenced by this.

In 1966 there was a dramatic reversal and the policies thereafter became directed at the restraint of incomes and prices, although still retaining a positive note with their emphasis on productivity.

The economic context of 1965–70 was unpropitious for the conduct of policies designed to raise productivity. Moreover, the NBPI was in a difficult situation when examining particular cases of incomes increases

1 see Chapter 8.

2 *NBPI Third General Report*, para. 15.

because it was known that the incomes of others were growing at rates much higher than the norm. It was faced with the problem of applying an incomes policy in a vacuum.

Appendix to Chapter 3   A Note on the Effects of the Policy

The effects of the prices and incomes policies of 1965–70 (which should be regarded as a distinct subject from the effects of the NBPI) on earnings, prices and productivity are a matter of controversy.

Table 3.2 which was discussed earlier is a version (which has been brought up to date) of a table first published in the White Paper of December 1969 on the basis of which the Labour Government claimed success for the policy. The table shows in 1966–67 and in 1968–69, the two periods when the policy was most severely applied, that the growth of wage rates, earnings and wages and salaries per unit of output were all sharply reduced below that of the previous period. The rate of price increase was curtailed in 1966–67, but not in 1968 owing to the effects of devaluation and indirect tax increases rather than to any failure necessarily in the policy. However, it is, or has been, widely believed that in normal times if unemployment is high, wage rates will only increase slowly. If the fiscal and monetary measures that accompanied the two severe phases of the policy increased unemployment — as they seemed to do — there may have been no need for a prices and incomes policy designed to keep down wage rates,[1] and it may even have been counterproductive — incomes norms, guiding lights, ceilings and ranges may have set minimum rather than maximum rates of increases for all wage and salary earners, and significantly lifted a number of wage rates, especially in the nationalised industries and public sector, above the level that they would normally have been, without substantially reducing other increases in wage rates. Table 3.2 then does not constitute proof of the effectiveness of the policy. A more sophisticated study taking account of all the variables which significantly influence changes in wages is necessary.

The NBPI itself made such a study using econometric techniques.[2] Its tentative conclusions were that the policy in 1948–50, 1961–2, 1965 and 1966 had led to a reduction in the rate of increase of earnings by about one percentage point on average. This is a sizeable effect. Prices, however, had increased more quickly than would normally have been expected.

Support for the NBPI's view of the effectiveness of the policy in

---

1 It can be argued that prices and incomes policy is a preferable means of keeping down the growth of wage rates, since it involves less unemployment and lost production.

2 *Third General Report* — Appendix A.

restraining incomes has also come from an econometric study by D. Smith,[1] which found earnings about one percent lower in 1966–7 than expected on the basis of past relationships. J. Corina has also reported calculations covering 1965–69 which show that incomes restraint seems to have had the effect of reducing the rise in incomes by more than one per cent a year, and prices restraint seems to have had a bigger effect[2] (after allowing for the effects of incomes policy on incomes).

Lipsey and Parkin have used a somewhat more refined econometric technique than the others to capture the effects of incomes policy. They sharply distinguished postwar periods when incomes policies were 'on' from periods of 'policy off' to ensure that they correctly isolated the 'policy off' relationship of unemployment and wage rates.[3] The 'policy off' periods were from the third quarter of 1950 to the end of 1955; and from 1957 to until the second quarter of 1961.[4] The advantage of the technique was claimed to be that there was no possibility of the relationship between wage rates and unemployment in 'policy off' periods being distorted by the effects of incomes policy in these years.

They found that changes in wage-rates in 'policy off' periods could be statistically explained by changes in economic variables such as the level of unemployment. In 'policy-on' periods there was practically no observable significant connection between changes in wage rates and changes in unemployment. They attributed this to the effects of incomes policy.

The essence of their findings was that in a 'policy-on' period, the growth rate of wage-rates has always been much the same, and hardly depends at all upon the state of unemployment. In a 'policy-off' period, on the other hand, unemployment is the main determinant of wage-rate increases. The higher it is, the less wage rates increase; above a certain critical point of about 1.8 per cent unemployment, wage-rates will grow less than they do under incomes policy. If, then, one encounters a 'policy-on' period in which unemployment is higher than the critical point, wage rates may grow more than they would at that level of unemployment with 'policy-off'. Since in fact this has happened on several occasions since the war, incomes policy has tended to be counterproductive.

Methodologically their study is interesting and innovatory and several comments may be made about it compared with the orthodox methodology for measuring the effects of incomes policy.

First, however, there is a point about data. The study employs wage rates not earnings as the main variable to be explained. To my mind this is not

1 'Incomes Policy' by D.C. Smith, in *Britain's Economic Prospects*, edited by Richard Caves. (George Allen and Unwin, 1968).

2 The results are reported in an article by Dr. Corina in *The Times*, March 5, 1970.

3 The other studies did this, but somewhat more crudely. Whereas Lipsey and Parkin calculated separate 'policy on' and 'policy off' equations, the other studies used one equation with shift dummy variables to capture the effects of the policies.

4 This conformed with Smith's choice of periods.

entirely unreasonable because incomes policy has largely been directed in practice at wage rates, not earnings. Nevertheless, one would want to explore the effects of incomes policies on hourly earnings, not wage rates, given the choice, since it is the former which tends to be more relevant to unit costs and prices.

In establishing 'policy-on' equations, the different 'policy-on' periods are treated as one, despite their varying intensity, nature, and the differing years, circumstances and governments under which they took place. It is not especially surprising that their study could find no significant relationships between changes in wage-rates and the variables which normally explain such changes. Thus, 1949 was a time of low unemployment, but wage rates grew slowly. In 1963, labelled also as 'policy-on', there was relatively high unemployment and wage rates grew slowly. The Lipsey-Parkin study infers from events of this kind that whether unemployment is high or low has very little effect on increases in wage-rates during 'policy-on'. An alternative hypothesis is that in 1949 the strong policy was effective despite the low level of unemployment and that in 1963 the policy was weak and it was unemployment which kept wage rates down. By failing to take account of this possibility, the Lipsey-Parkin study fails to substantiate its conclusion that incomes policy had greatly weakened any connection between changes in wage rates and other variables. On the prices side it is questionable to regard any period before 1956 as a good guide to the normal behaviour of prices since post war price controls continued to apply up to this point.[1]

A further difficulty arises from their choice of 'policy-on' periods. In Chapter 2 it was made clear that in 1963 and 1964 incomes policy was almost non-existent. Despite this it was included as 'policy-on', as were all of the 1960's. This choice excluded the possibility of testing some alternative hypotheses such as that the relationship between unemployment and wages had altered during the 1960's for reasons unconnected with incomes policy e.g. decentralisation of collective bargaining, increased trade union militancy, a slow down in the rate of growth of real net incomes etc. There is every reason to believe that, as in most industrialised market economies in the 1960's, the relationship between unemployment and wage rates shifted. Pencavel, for example, has found that three of the five best-known econometric wage models of Britain displayed a significant tendency to under-predict wage increases when extended to cover the 1962–7 period.[2] If so, econometric studies may have underestimated the effectiveness of incomes policies.

The latest study published at the time of writing came from the Department of Employment.[3] This rejected the use of unemployment series in explaining

1 Parkin has taken up some other criticisms of the methodology in a recent article 'Incomes Policy: Some Further Results on the Determination of the Rate of Change of Money Wages', *Economica*, November 1970, p. 386.

2 J.H. Pencavel, 'A Note on the Comparative Predictive Performance of Wage Inflation Models of the British Economy', *The Economic Journal*, March 1971.

3 op. cit.

wage movements because of the changed impact of unemployment since 1966 following the increases in unemployment benefits and redundancy, and the introduction of the Selective Employment Tax. Instead vacancies were used. Otherwise this is a test using orthodox variations of the Phillips curve methodology of a number of alternative explanatory models which concludes that the earnings of manual men increased less rapidly than expected in the years 1956, 1957, 1961, 1962, 1965, 1966, 1967, but more rapidly than might have been expected in 1963, 1964, 1968 and 1969. In the three years 1965–7 combined, the total increase in manual earnings amounted to about 4 per cent less than might have been expected from previous relationships; in 1968 and 1969 it was in total about 4 per cent more than might have been expected. On the other hand, over the period 1965–9, the average wages and salaries per employee rose by about 2–4 per cent in total more than past relationships suggested, although this was at least partly the result of measurement factors.

As a result of developments since 1970 the whole question of the validity of the Phillips curve relationship, both at present, and in the 1960's needs reconsidering. Econometric studies of the determinants of wages are subject to a crucial margin of uncertainty depending upon the choice of the original equations with which to test hypotheses. The DE study shows admittedly that a number of alternative equations produce decidedly similar impressions of the effects of incomes policy, but these equations are mostly drawn from conventional variations of the traditional Phillips curve equations, and do not break new ground, for example, by including militancy factors.

The conclusion must be that the question of the effects of the prices and incomes policy of 1965–70 on earnings and prices is unresolved.

4. The National Board for Prices and Incomes and its Role

1. The NBPI

The NBPI was established on April 8, 1965. The first three cases for examination, two concerned with prices, one with wages and prices, arrived on May 6, 1965.

The NBPI was originally established as a Royal Commission but was reconstituted on a statutory basis in 1966. The Prices and Incomes Act gave it, for the first time, powers to call witnesses and require evidence but they were never used. Instead the co-operation of the parties was sought and usually obtained. No doubt co-operation was influenced in some cases by the existence of these powers.

At first the NBPI was under the aegis of the Department of Economic Affairs and later from April 1968 under that of the Department of Employment and Productivity (DEP), now the Department of Employment.

The two most important constitutional facts about the NBPI were:

(I) although an official body, it was constitutionally independent of the Government. It was not obliged to interpret the incomes or prices criteria in the way the Government would. The Members of the Board of the NBPI, drawn from trade unions, business, universities and public life, not from Parliament or the Civil Service, acted in their own capacities.

Compared with direct government conduct of the functions entrusted to the NBPI, this independence had three advantages:

(a) The NBPI was not identified with one or other side of industry and hence had a greater chance of being accepted as impartial.

(b) The application (and the appearance of the application) of the same rules of wage and price fixation to the private and public sector was facilitated. [1]

(c) It was a safeguard on the use of official powers to restrain wage and price increases. After 1967, the Government had no power to delay such increases (except for a 1 month inspection period and for 3 months while the NBPI reported) unless the NBPI reported adversely.

[1] These two points are made in 'Prices and Incomes Policy' by Mr. Aubrey Jones, *The Economic Journal*, December 1968, p. 799.

(II) the NBPI had no substantive powers of its own. Its recommendations never had the force of law but depended on acceptance by the Government and the parties; it had no power to follow up its investigations. The persuasiveness of its reports was its only weapon. Nor could it initiate investigations into particular wage and price increases unless they were referred to it. The critical link in the chain between the prices and incomes policy and the NBPI was the Government, which had the power of reference.

The NBPI was constrained in some further respects. It had no control over the general economic or political environment within which it worked; and its judgements of particular wage and price cases were governed by the criteria outlined in Chapter 3. The criteria thus established a policy framework which both limited its freedom of action and afforded protection from accusations of arbitrariness. When reporting on proposed increases, the Board always endeavoured to show it was merely applying the provisions of the White Paper.

However, the above requires some qualification. The task of interpreting the rather general and occasionally ambiguous provisions of the White Paper left considerable scope for the development of the Board's own policies and emphasis, which in turn fed back into White Papers. It sought to use reports on individual cases to have a wider influence on the development of the policy, and the behaviour of the economy. As will be described in Chapters 9 and 10, the Board was also asked to recommend incomes policy guidelines on productivity agreements, payment by results schemes, job evaluation and so on. It used its five General Reports to comment on and attempt to influence the whole range of Government actions, including monetary and fiscal measures, bearing on the prices and incomes policy. It could also suggest formally and informally subjects for reference; and it could press the Government to follow up reports.

2. Analysis of References

The NBPI published 170 reports. 79 were on pay, 67 on prices, 10 related to both pay and prices, 9 were 'general study' references (which are described in Chapter 10) and 5 were general reports. The pay references were divided almost equally between the public and private sectors. About three quarters of the prices references related to the private sector.

It is possible to make a rough estimate of the numbers employed in those parts of the economy which were covered by NBPI reports (excluding general study reports). The figures obtained are about 18 million, over three quarters of the workforce. This does not mean, of course, that over three-quarters of the economy was subjected to close scrutiny by the NBPI. Its coverage of different sectors necessarily was of various degrees of depth and of differing orientations. Agriculture, for instance, was the subject of two short reports; Armed Forces Pay was investigated exhaustively. Steel prices were examined, but not the wages of steel workers; conversely pay and conditions of service were examined in the clothing manufacturing industry, but not its prices.

Sectors on which the NBPI did not report include: catering, tobacco, footwear, glass, estate agents, accountants, medical and dental professions, school-teachers (excluding Scottish teachers), police and the non-industrial civil service (except for higher civil servants). Dockers were not reviewed except in Bristol. The Engineering Industry was covered in Reports 49 and 104: they excluded shipbuilding entirely. Because of the very large scope of this reference (3,515,000 employees came under the terms of the reference), the separate industries within the term 'Engineering' were not independently reviewed so that for instance nothing was said in detail of the car manufacturing industry, a reference which the Board sought in public unsuccessfully. Price references in the engineering industry were confined entirely to Electrical Engineering products.

Some industries and topics did not come before the NBPI because they were already under investigation by other parts of the Government. The overlap of the Board's work with other bodies is discussed later in this chapter.

There were some 45 references in which a second, third, fourth or, in the case of buses, an eighth look was taken at an industry reported on earlier. A list of such references is given in Appendix D. The NBPI often reported on the same topics in the same industries. Seventeen topics relating to pay were dealt with more than once and twelve relating to prices.

The Government encouraged the NBPI to suggest references and a number of suggestions were accepted. These included suggestions made in NBPI reports for general study references on productivity agreements, payment by results, and overtime; a standing reference on solicitors charges; and coal distribution costs. Unsuccessful published suggestions included those for general study references on merit payments, the contribution made by labour to the more efficient use of all factors of production, negotiated capital savings schemes for workers; and particular firms or industries with inequitable pay structures, enterprises where payment by results wage systems appeared to be out of control, the principles on which prices should respond to new taxes, such as the Selective Employment Tax, or changed tax rates; efficiency studies of local authorities; local authority rates; and newspaper distribution. The Board also pressed with mixed success at various levels of the Government for references on other subjects.

3. Use of the NBPI as a Specialised Investigatory Body

In September 1967 it was announced that before the Cabinet considered proposals for major price increases in the nationalised industries, the NBPI would examine them, and, at the same time, conduct efficiency studies.

Thereafter the NBPI issued some fifteen or so reports on proposals for increases in gas prices, coal prices, London Transport fares, railway fares and charges, the tariff for the bulk supply of electricity by the Central Electricity Generating Board, steel prices and so on. Most of these reports dealt in some depth with the efficiency of selected parts of these industries as well as the immediate price increase proposals. One reason for the

Government's decision was that it seemed anomalous for the NBPI to examine prices in the private sector, without also examining those in the public sector. The decision also illustrates, however, the use made of the NBPI to investigate questions which would have arisen for Government decision, even if no prices and incomes policy had existed. There are numerous other examples, some of which are given in the final Chapter.

They came to the NBPI because as a specialised investigatory body it was often better equipped than Government Departments to make the necessary enquiries. Thus the Chairman in evidence to the Select Committee on Nationalised Industries said that Government Departments supervising nationalised industries had few or no staff with commercial experience. Their staff were mainly of civil service background whose experience consisted mainly of traditional governmental techniques and practices of financial control; these were very different from, and more than, rigid commercial techniques of financial control. Scientific advisers to such departments did not have a background of viewing technology with the same commercial eye as was expected of their counterparts in nationalised industries.[1]

It may be noted at this stage then that the Board's acquisition of a range of professional specialist staff — managers, economists, statisticians, accountants and industrial relations staff, as well as civil service staff — and its development of a variety of enquiry methods, allowed it to fill a gap in the supervision of nationalised industries. An important subsidiary function of the NBPI was in fact to serve as an adjunct to the whole governmental machine as a specialised investigatory body. This point is taken up in the final Chapter.

4. The Role of the NBPI in the Short Term Control of Incomes and Prices, and the Reference Policy of the Government

In this section the use made of the NBPI in the control of incomes and prices increases is described.

The effectiveness of the machinery for enforcing the prices and incomes policy did not depend alone or even primarily on the NBPI. Its centrepiece was the Government which, from the time of the establishment of the voluntary 'early warning' system in November 1965, was notified in advance of a large number of important wage and price increases. For example, over 1,200 incomes increases were notified under the system between August 1968 and January 1969, and 1,130 prices increases between July 1967 and March 1969. Many of these satisfied the requirements of the prices and incomes policy and needed no action; otherwise attempts were usually made to persuade the parties to amend or rescind the increase.[2] If persuasion was unsuccessful

---

1 Memorandum submitted by Rt. Hon. Aubrey Jones in *Select Committee on Nationalised Industries Sub Committee A Minutes of Evidence*, 26th March 1968 (HMSO, 1968), p. 676.

2 The White Paper *Productivity, Prices and Incomes Policy After 1969* stated that 18 per cent of price increases sought in the 1968–69 phase were amended or rescinded in this way.

the Government from July 1966 to June 1967 could delay the increases without reference to the NBPI; after June 1967 if a notified increase did not appear to conform with the policy the choice was to refer it to the NBPI for a recommendation or let it through.

On the incomes side, the NBPI reported on a considerable number of important national agreements but from the start some important above-norm increases were not referred. Three examples were the Doctors Pay Review in 1966, the Liverpool Dock Workers Settlement in 1967, and the Seamen's Settlement of 1966. The Government was criticised for acquiescing in 1968 and early 1969 in a number of settlements seemingly contrary to incomes policy. These included the British Rail Agreement, the Engineering Industry Agreement and settlements for the London Docks Tally Clerks and the Post Office Overseas Telegraphists. In many cases the possibility of industrial action was an important reason for acquiescence.

In its Fifth and Final General Report the Board said that by the beginning of 1969:

'... it had become apparent that the Government was tending to accept wage increases of up to 3½ per cent almost automatically. In many cases where wage increases were referred to the Board, the Government had already agreed to an immediate increase of 3½ per cent and instructed the Board to examine the justification for a larger increase, for example for bus maintenance workers in September 1968, clearing bank employees in November 1968 and workers in the exhibition contracting industries in March 1969. In other words 3½ per cent was becoming a floor rather than a ceiling.

The application of the policy was relaxed still further by the announcement promising a softening of the statutory provisions after the end of 1969. In the public sector an important indication of this trend was provided by the Government's agreement in October 1969 to increases of pay, which were expected to add 8½ per cent to the annual wage bill for its 206,000 industrial workers and subsequently to a similar increase for local authority manual workers. In the private sector an increase of 11 per cent was permitted in November 1969 for 1 million manual workers in the building industry, and larger increases were subsequently allowed for workers in the motor manufacturing industry.' [1]

Even before October, the Government made some much publicised and strategically crucial concessions of above-norm pay increases to London firemen, and nurses and midwives.

The December 1969 White Paper *Productivity, Prices and Incomes Policy After 1969* admitted that 'from the third quarter of 1969, pay settlements have once again begun to break through the restraints of the policy. Settlements reached in September 1969 averaged over 6 per cent; in October they averaged about 8½ per cent, largely due to increases paid to some groups in the public

1 paras. 5 and 6.

sector which matched increases in earning achieved in private industry where local pay arrangements had inflated earnings'. [1]

On 4th March 1970 in reply to a Parliamentary Question, Mr. Harold Walker, then Under Secretary of State for Employment and Productivity, said that the weighted average increase in minimum rates for major wage and salary settlements notified during November and December 1969 and January 1970, taking account only of the first stages of long term agreements, was estimated at 9.7 per cent. On 5 March, when asked how many wage settlements in the public sector during 1970 had fallen inside and outside the current norm Mr. Walker replied: 'Six settlements have been made in the public sector in 1970 within the current range, involving 120,000 workers; 21 settlements were made outside the range, involving 1,028,000 workers'. [2]

Thus, it may be concluded that there were serious omissions in the reference of above-norm nationally negotiated wage rate agreements even before the total breakdown of the policy in July 1969.

A coach and horses was driven through the policy insofar as it purported to control local agreements. Over the period 1965–70 practically no local agreements in excess of the norm were referred. This was partly because under the early warning arrangements firms having fewer than 100 employees were under no obligation to report settlements to the DEP. Small or moderately sized firms with more than 100 employees could escape the net with relative impunity if they wished and it would seem that the DEP received details of about 20 per cent of all cases which would have been notified had the parties to all national company and plant agreements observed the early warning procedures laid down. Most of the multitude of sources of wage and salary drift — in particular the constant re-negotiation of piecework rates under payment by results pay schemes such as are very common in engineering — escaped the net. Of the local settlements which were notified to the DEP, practically none were referred to the Board. Thus some 6 million workers were parties to 3,500 productivity agreements notified to the DEP between 1965 and 1969.[3] Only a handful of such agreements came to the NBPI. This gap in policy is taken up again in Chapter 9 where the NBPI's own recommendations about how to control local agreements are discussed.

On the prices side, the NBPI was openly dissatisfied with the references it received. In its *Third General Report* it commented:

'... we have not been satisfied that the Government have been pursuing a sufficiently purposeful strategy for price references to the Board'. [4]

1 paras. 8 and 9.

2 *Hansard*, Volume 797; Columns 125 and 154. This is quoted in the NBPI's *Final General Report*.

3 *Productivity, Prices and Incomes Policy After 1969*, para. 42.

4 para. 30.

In its *Second General Report* it commented:

'On occasion, however, the Board has been aware of a reluctance on the part of a sponsoring Department to see an industry under its wing referred to the Board; for this reason the Board must attach importance to the concept of an independent Department, not identified with any individual industry or financial institution which is in a position to offset the protectiveness which might be shown to its sponsored industries by the Department more directly involved'. [1]

In its *Third General Report* in July 1968, after the responsibilities for the Prices and Incomes Policy had been transferred from the Department of Economic Affairs to the Department of Employment and Productivity, it observed:

'It remains to be seen, however, whether within the new Department it will be possible to effect the appropriate analyses required in relation to prices policy, and whether the Department can secure the requisite influence with other Departments concerned with pricing, such as the Board of Trade and the Ministry of Technology.' [2]

It suggested that in the post-devaluation context an appropriate reference strategy could involve reference of industries with opportunities for import substitution, exporting or price reduction due to the rapid growth of productivity. [3] In its *Fourth General Report*, it noted in effect that its fears on the prices side had been justified, although in fact after this fourth report the number of price references increased significantly.

Figure 4.1 is based on an analysis of the references received by the NBPI during each quarterly period from April 1965 to June 1970, subdivided into incomes and prices references. [4] Numbers are not of course the main criterion by which the significance of the NBPI's references should be judged. For example although the figure shows the NBPI as receiving three or four incomes references per quarter between mid 1969 and mid 1970, they were of little strategic significance since the NBPI was required to report on 'pay and conditions', not on particular settlements. Thus the diagram exaggerates the significance of NBPI's control role in this period but it gives a reasonable picture of the variability — and uncertainty — of references from one period to another, and from one phase of the policy to the next. It is also interesting to note that the relation between prices and incomes references is almost inverse, especially if one appropriately discounts incomes references after the middle of 1969. Finally, the NBPI was momentarily rescued from near

1 para. 75.

2 para. 5.

3 The last of these three suggestions was also made in the *First General Report* (para.87), *Second General Report* (para.37) and the *Fourth General Report* (para.54).

4 This brings up to date a diagram in the *Fourth General Report*.

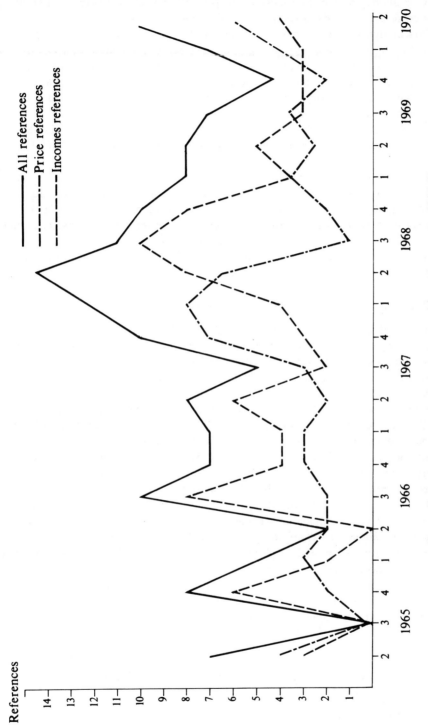

FIG 4.1 References received during each quarterly period, 1965-70

45

oblivion shortly before the elections in June 1970 when it received a series of price references, and a reference on doctors and dentists pay.[1]

This analysis does not mean that the NBPI was always or entirely by-passed as an instrument of short term control before the middle of 1969. It was used in 1968, for example, to control an 'outbreak' of above-norm pay settlements for busmen in different cities[2] and some very important national agreements e.g., construction, electrical contracting, were referred to it for judgement on whether they conformed to the requirements of the norm.

The *Second General Report* of the NBPI stated that it would not wish to contravene the Government's right to determine references. If the NBPI had to determine its own references it would follow, according to the report, that no preliminary screening was necessary, in which case its task would become hopeless. In its *Fourth General Report*, however, the NBPI noted that its functioning differed from the Canadian Prices and Incomes Commission which was not compelled to accept references from the Government if other priorities existed, or if they were not relevant to its primary function, and which was also free to initiate its own enquiries. This is further discussed in the final Chapter.

5. Decisions on Incomes and Prices Increases

Insofar as it had a control role the NBPI operated on a number of occasions to block incomes or prices increases. Of 50 references concerning specific prices increases for example, it recommended rejection in 7 cases, and smaller increases than those sought in 20 cases. In 23 cases it recommended acceptance of the price increases sought. Of 51 incomes references where it had to examine claims, offers or settlements, it recommended against them in 17 cases, and smaller increases than those sought in 24 cases. In 10 other cases it recommended acceptance of the incomes increases sought. In most cases the recommendations were accepted by the Government, and enforced where it had powers to do so. In the voluntary phases of 1965 and 1970 not all recommendations were accepted by the parties.

These classifications are difficult to make, and to some extent arbitrary. They are set out in Appendices E and F so that the reader may know how they have been made. There is not much doubt, however, that the general impression given of a fairly high number of rejections and partial acceptances is correct. Some groups expecting to be referred to the NBPI may have set their prices or incomes increases higher than wanted as a bargaining ploy, but there is no evidence that this was an important phenomenon.

Professor H. A. Clegg has drawn attention to some generous decisions made whilst he was a Member of the Board in 1966–7.[3] These included the

---

1 The doctors and dentists reference was withdrawn by the new Government.

2 These were, however, amongst a very small number of local agreements referred to the NBPI.

3 H. A. Clegg 'The Role of Government Agencies.' *Scottish Journal of Political Economy* June 1970 p. 308, and *How to run an Incomes Policy and Why we made such a mess of the last one.* (Heinemann, 1971), pp. 35–37.

acceptance of a 6.6 per cent pay increase already negotiated for London Busmen (Report 16) when there was likely to be industrial action if the report was adverse. Among other groups for whose pay increases the Board 'devised imaginative justifications were Higher Civil Servants, the fire brigades and employees in electricity supply.' [1]

In *Wages and Conditions in the Electrical Contracting Industry* (24), the Board concluded that the industry's recently negotiated three year agreement was inconsistent with the incomes policy criteria. In the background, however, was the fact that the earnings of contracting electricians were well below the earnings of electricians in many other industries, largely because the tightly controlled national agreement did not permit above-rate payments to be awarded locally. Furthermore, the position of the new leadership of the Electrical Trades Union, who had replaced a Communist leadership group, might have been jeopardised by an adverse verdict.

> '... the political argument was outside their terms of reference, and the restrictive interpretation of the 'out-of-line' argument left them no room to make use of a comparison with electricians elsewhere. So they had recourse to sophistry. The standstill had imposed a delay of six months on increases negotiated but not yet paid. The Board now argued that this meant that the increase had to be paid at the end of the six months, even though the increase was 13 per cent in a period of zero norm. The subsequent stages, said the Board, should be re-negotiated in the light of productivity improvements actually achieved. The government accepted the first of these recommendations, but subsequently allowed the two remaining stages of the agreement to be paid without negotiation'. [2]

> 'However, it would be grossly unfair to the Board to suggest that they have played fast and loose with the successive statements of policy. They have given ground where they thought they must, but generally they have been restrictive in their use of the criteria for exceptional treatment.' [3]

This conclusion is borne out by the analysis above of the number of occasions on which the NBPI operated to block incomes and prices increases.

6. The Long Term Role

In view of its origins in the Joint Declaration of Intent it is perhaps not surprising that the Board, seemingly set up to combat inflation, should regard its primary role as helping to stimulate productivity, raise incomes, and eradicate persistent, underlying sources of inflation and as being, in short, the conduct of a long term, positive prices and incomes policy.

The NBPI in fact enthusiastically seized upon the opportunity provided by the Government and gave a very substantial push of its own to the

1 'The Role of Government Agencies', p. 308.
2 *How to Run an Incomes Policy*, p. 37.
3 'The Role of Government Agencies', p. 308.

establishment and subsequent development of the new style productivity prices and incomes policy. The main reason for the great initial impact of the Board was that it quickly grasped and immediately proceeded to exploit the country's apparent mood after the return to power of the Labour Government. There was at the time a willingness to listen to new ideas about how the growth rate might be accelerated. The Board stepped into something of a vacuum and propounded forcefully and with great apparent authority new answers to the nation's problems.

In particular it stressed that there were factors other than demand at work in generating inflation. This is illustrated in the introduction to its First Report in which the Board explained its role:

'There are two possible causes lying behind the phenomenon of rising prices. First, demand may be too high ... Secondly ... old habits, inherited attitudes and institutional arrangements may all combine to exert an upward pressure on prices ...

It is the treatment of the second cause only i.e. old habits, inherited attitudes and institutional arrangements – which lies with ourselves as a Board. ... we recognise that we have been entrusted with a highly difficult and delicate mission. Experience has shown that attitudes are not changed by a use of the fiscal and monetary weapons at the disposal of Government. Nor are they susceptible to legislation – habits are not changed by law. We see ourselves as promoting change by conducting a continuing dialogue with managements, unions and indeed Government.

The documents establishing the Board have been signed not only by the Government but also by the leaders of the representative organisations of employers and trade unions. We infer from this fact that both employers and trade unions accept the need for change but also recognise the difficulty of effecting change themselves, and the need for the stimulus and help of an independent and impartial agency. We regard ourselves as such an independent agency ... It is with a desire to further change while remaining impartial that we intend to approach all the References that may be made to us.

Since we regard ourselves not just as judges of past events but as intended to influence the shape of things in the future, we also consider it our responsibility to enquire into any methods that can promote a faster rate of increase of productivity in the industry under examination, this being indispensable if the industry is in the future to accomodate desirable increases in wages without however passing these increases on to the consumer.'

In the incomes field, the NBPI's aim was to curtail the influence of traditional factors in wage determination, and inject other considerations most notably productivity and the incomes norm. It regarded traditional factors such as comparability and cost of living movements as making it impossible to relate pay to the norm, as generating inflation, and as an obstacle to the introduction of productivity considerations. Linking pay more closely to performance was thought likely to stimulate efficiency and make it possible to raise incomes without inflation. Every rule laid down by the Government for the incomes behaviour of individuals was interpreted with the emphasis on productivity.

The NBPI's intention was thus to change the subject matter of collective bargaining. This was impossible without change in the system of collective bargaining itself. The existing formal machinery of collective bargaining, established at the national level, was unsuitable for the negotiation of plant productivity agreements. A radical reform of institutions as well as attitudes and habits was required.

The price behaviour criteria required business enterprises to do everything possible to avoid or offset cost increases rather than increase prices. The NBPI believed that no element of a firm or industry's labour or other costs, should be excluded from this effort. In dealing with prices set on an industry-wide basis, it often examined wider matters such as the structure of an industry to determine if costs could be avoided or reduced by mergers, by the abolition of uncompetitive price fixing practices, or by improvements in the functioning of employers associations.

Bank Charges (34) was an example of the wide ranging field of enquiry and radical recommendations which resulted from this approach. The Government asked the Board to review the system and level of charging customers in the light of the banks' profit and dividend record. The Board became the first official body to formulate concrete proposals for widening the area of competition between banks.[1] The main recommendation was that the banks should abolish their collective agreements to pay a common rate of interest on deposits, and on the rates to be charged for advances. There were also recommendations for the disclosure of bank profits and reserves, for the abolition of the collective agreements on commission charges and the publication by each bank of a tariff of main charges. By 1971 the main recommendations were in the process of being implemented. The Board's report, highly controversial at the time, seems to have been one not unimportant factor leading to these changes.

Over the course of time as it became clearer that the NBPI was attempting to operate a prices and incomes policy in a vacuum, the emphasis on its efficiency stimulating role became even greater than at first, and the main part of its work became the detailed investigation of industrial relations, pay structures and managerial efficiency in a host of industries. In assessing the worth of the NBPI, at least in respect of its work done after 1968, the usefulness of these investigations is the major factor to take into account.

The NBPI's approach to the investigation of managerial efficiency stemmed from its analysis of the causes of inefficiency in the economy. Where competition was largely absent as in many nationalised industries but also in some

---

1 There was an implicit criticism of the system in the *Report of the Committee on the Working of the Monetary System* (HMSO, 1959) (para. 132). A Committee of London Clearing Banks (known as the Thomson Committee) unsuccessfully recommended to the Government in 1964 some changes in the cartel system. See B. Griffiths, *Competition in Banking*, Hobart Paper No. 51 (Institute of Economic Affairs, 1971).

private sector industries, and could not be restored by traditional monopoly policy, inefficiency was likely. The role of the NBPI's studies of efficiency in these cases was seen as a substitute for competition or its ineffective working. [1]

Greater efficiency was the key to the reconciliation of the public interest in the avoidance of inflation and the individual interest in higher incomes, as well as the harmonisation of the interests of management and workers. The NBPI's overriding concern in most reports appeared to be the raising, not the restraint, of incomes from wages or profits, by greater efficiency, and a large part of all reports was devoted to specifying acceptable ways by which efficiency and incomes could be improved. This added to the NBPI's acceptability. This is indicated by replies to a questionnaire sent by the TUC in November 1967 to all affiliated unions asking them to comment on their experiences of investigations by the board. No analysis has been published of the replies to this questionnaire but in the TUC General Report for 1968 the following statement appears:

> 'When the General Council considered the replies in March they noted that although unions were not uncritical of the board the general impression given by the replies to the questionnaire was one of general support for what the board was doing. Some unions took the view that the major deficiencies of the board were the fault of Government policy rather than failings of the board itself. Most unions regard the board's reports as providing useful sources of information.' [2]

After referring to some criticisms of the Board's methods of consultation, the TUC noted that another suggestion was:

> 'that contact with the board should continue after the publication of a report, and it was argued that in those industries — particularly in the public sector — where there had been a definite willingness to implement the board's proposals, some difficulties were encountered which the board might help to resolve'. [3]

This statement in fact plays down somewhat the extent of trade union support for the NBPI. The great majority eagerly cooperated with investigations, and many or most were far from critical even publicly of published reports. It is harder to generalise about management which reports often strongly attacked for inefficiency. Its co-operation with enquiries was reasonably good, but in general it did not welcome NBPI investigations.

The NBPI's emphasis on its long term role did not, as has been seen, mean neglect of its role as a short term instrument of control. Rather it aimed to use its short term control function as a lever to stimulate long term change. It tended to take a negative attitude to proposed wage increases unless they

---

1 *Fourth General Report*, para. 52.

2 TUC General Report 1968, p. 316.

3 ibid

were justified by efficiency considerations, and in prices references it put the emphasis on whether the firm or industry was doing enough to raise efficiency. In taking a firm line on short term matters, it always pointed to the one certain way in which it believed individual incomes or profits could be increased without inflation – greater efficiency. More is said in the final chapter about possible conflicts of the NBPI's long term policies with the need between 1965–70 to avoid any immediate increases of inflation.

7. The Educational Role

The NBPI's role was essentially educational in the sense that it had no powers of its own and had always to persuade the Government and the parties to accept its recommendations; and its long term aim of promoting a quicker adaptation of past practices to new needs could only be fulfilled by a 'continuing dialogue' with management, unions and the Government.

There were two main educational tasks which the NBPI saw for itself. The first was to bring home to the parties immediately concerned in references the implications of their actions for others. 'Others' included those who purchased their product and who were affected by wage and price increases through higher prices; other industries which felt the repercussions on themselves of wage and price increases as their effects spread through the economy; and the country at large which suffered from the adverse effects of inefficiency and inflationary practices on the general level of prices, growth and the balance of payments. Thus the Board endeavoured to press for the introduction of public interest criteria into these discussions. As such it acted as a kind of consumer watchdog over price and wage levels, acting 'to intercede on behalf of the consumer when the market may not be operating fully to his advantage'.[1]

In its first two years the NBPI could only handle a few references at a time. Even in later years its capacity was limited to about twenty to twenty-three references at a time. This led it to attempt to identify matters of general significance in particular references and to view each reference from a wider strategic point of view. Its second task thus entailed:

'... Going beyond the parties immediately concerned in a reference to bring home to others the wider implications of their actions. For a reference is scarcely ever unique; the considerations to which it gives rise are more often than not duplicated elsewhere in cases that are not referred to the Board.'[2]

Report 3 *Prices of Bread and Flour* provides an example of this approach in practice.

'We have been told that regular overtime of 14 hours per week is now usual in plant bakeries. In other words, overtime in this industry, as in others,

1 *Prices of Household and Toilet Soaps, Soap Powders and Soap Flakes, and Soapless Detergents*, (4) para. 56.

2 *First General Report*, para. 22.

is an accepted institution, more to maintain earnings than to meet the requirements of production. We consider that not only does it increase wage costs; it also increases other operating costs in that all the other expenses entailed in production tend to be inflated because of the extended working inherent in overtime. That is, the toleration of unnecessary overtime working inculcates slackness into an operation in general. The inefficiencies which go with habitual overtime can be removed by negotiation, provided management uses its initiative'.

At times this appeared to involve a somewhat capricious treatment of the parties directly concerned in a reference. The *Bread and Flour Prices* reference may itself be an example. No evidence was produced to support the assertion that overtime in bakeries was worked to maintain earnings and was unnecessary, but in 1970 in reporting on that industry again in *Bread Prices and Pay in the Baking Industry* (151), the Board found that despite the industry's ready adoption of its proposals for reducing overtime, overtime hours had increased and it also on that occasion conceded that there were 'few apparent signs of overtime being used merely to make up earnings irrespective of production needs'.[1]

Nevertheless the tactic of using individual cases to have a wider effect was a key factor in the Board's considerable initial public impact. This impact was of several kinds. The Board can take credit for getting across quickly several fundamental ideas to the population at large. The best known was that pay and productivity were linked and that it was desirable to relate individual wages and salaries to individual performance more closely than in the past. The Board also can take some credit for securing a more widespread appreciation of the elementary fact that wage increases lead to price increases which in turn can lead to wage increases. Above all the Board seems to have helped get across to a large part of the community the idea that greater efficiency in every sphere of economic activity was of key importance for raising the growth rate of the country.

Another kind of general impact was the deterrence of a significant number of prices, and even some incomes, increases. Management and to some extent trade unions feared exposure of inefficiency and the odium of strong condemnations of wage and price increases as against the public interest. Whether this was good or not, it is known for example, that a significant number of firms significantly reduced proposed price increases when threatened with the possibility of reference to the NBPI. The December 1969 White Paper indicated that some 18 per cent of price increases proposed under the early warning system were withdrawn or substantially amended after discussions with officials whose main weapon, in the last analysis, was threat of reference to the NBPI. There is little evidence that firms proposed high increases initially as a bargaining ploy.

In the longer term, the main way in which the Board regarded itself as

1 Para. 29.

being able to educate industry and to stimulate efficiency was through accelerating the use by industry of the best managerial and industrial relations practices and through eradicating bad practices. It was in an unusually good position to do so for its investigations reached across a large part of the economy and in 'general study references' concerning *Productivity Agreements* (23, 36, 123), *Payment by Results* (65), *Job Evaluation* (83), *Salary Structures* (132), *Hours of Work, Overtime and Shiftwork* (155) and *Low Pay* (169), it undertook studies of best — and worst — practices throughout the economy, and spelt out, on the basis of an up-to-date knowledge of a range of industries and expert opinion, the strengths and weaknesses, the potential areas of application and the best ways of installing and improving on different wage and salary systems.

In this role the NBPI sought results. It eschewed ideal solutions to problems if there was no hope of their implementation. Whilst its recommendations were thus greatly influenced by what it judged would be acceptable to the parties and Government it could not always, however, make recommendations likely to be immediately agreeable.

8. The Relationship to Other Independent Official Bodies

The Board's work overlapped somewhat with that of five other official independent bodies: the Monopolies Commission, the Restrictive Practices Court, the Industrial Reorganisation Corporation, the National Economic Development Council and the Commission on Industrial Relations, as well as, of course, to some extent with Government departments.

It is also overlapped with a plethora of bodies which determined pay in the public sector. An example of the problems which could occur from their use of different methods of pay determination occurred in 1968 when in *Pay of University Teachers* (98), the Board rejected arguments for pay increases based on comparability. Not long after this, the Kindersley Review Body recommended — and the Government accepted — that the pay of doctors and dentists in the National Health Service be increased on grounds of comparability. The Board pointed out that from a wider point of view it was clear that there was a need for a closer co-ordination of pay in the public sector.[1]

There appears to have been a trend at least for a time between 1965 and 1970 to transferring separate pay review bodies to the NBPI. University teachers were denied a separate review body for their pay, but instead the Government made them the subject of a standing reference to the NBPI. The pay of armed forces was determined by application of the Grigg formula, but eventually this was made an NBPI standing reference. The pay of higher civil servants was the subject of recommendation by an independent body, the Standing Advisory Committee on Higher Civil Service Pay. Its recommendations in 1965 were referred to the NBPI.[2] The significance of this

---

1 *Fourth General Report*, para. 69.

2 Although finding them consistent with the criteria of the White Paper *Prices and Incomes Policy*, the NBPI recommended that the Government and the National Staff Side should invite the Standing Advisory Committee in framing future recommendations to take the White Paper into account.

reference was that it was thought to have destroyed the inviolable character of review bodies' recommendations. The Kindersley Review Body, however, remained intact. Of its reports between 1965 and 1970 only the 1970 one went to the NBPI, shortly before the elections, only to be later withdrawn.

A step towards the co-ordination of public service pay determination occurred with the Labour Government's proposals to establish the Commission on Industry and Manpower. Had these proposals come to fruition, the CIM would have recommended to the Government the appropriate pay levels for some of those employed in the public sector. In November 1970 the Conservative Government announced that it proposed to establish three Review Bodies with a degree of interlocking membership which would advise the Government on the remuneration of certain groups in the public sector. They would be serviced by a new Office of Manpower Economics which has subsequently come into operation. This subject is returned to in the final Chapter.

The overlap in the monopolies, mergers and restrictive practices field arose because the White Paper criteria on prices required the NBPI to determine if prices based on excessive market power could be reduced, and if there were any means of avoiding cost increases. The NBPI saw certain practices, such as that of the Road Haulage Association recommending uniform rate increases to its members, as raising costs and tending to perpetuate inflation, and overlap was thus easily possible with other bodies.

In the report on *Portland Cement Prices* (38), the NBPI looked for the first time at an industry with fixed common prices. It was asked to examine the justification for a price increase in cement, and to review the question of the rate of return on capital invested in new works. It interpreted this as leaving it free to judge whether in the circumstances of the present day a regime of free prices would be preferable to the regime of agreed prices.[1] The industry's interpretation was that the latter, having been endorsed by the Restrictive Practices Court in 1961, was a given datum and could not be questioned by the NBPI. Accordingly, the NBPI reached its findings within the framework of the Court's judgement.[2]

There was a near-conflict with the Monopolies Commission after the reference concerning *Bank Charges* (34). The NBPI Report stated that:

'Further amalgamations among the banks, carried through to the appropriate point, could permit some rationalization of existing networks'.[3]

1 *Second General Report*, para. 183.

2 It did, however, recommend that within the framework of a common price agreement, the regional price structure needed to be reviewed. In 1961, the Court had accepted that this structure, basically unchanged since 1935, could not be altered. The NBPI considered that, since then, operational research techniques had been developed which enabled improvements to be made in the structure to ensure it reflected the least cost method of producing and distributing cement. The NBPI also found that the criterion endorsed by the Court, of fixing prices at new works to yield a return of less than 10 per cent on capital, was inadequate and should be abandoned, and replaced by calculations based on the discounted cash flow method of investment appraisal. These recommendations were accepted by the manufacturers.

3 para. 154.

Not long after, a major bank merger occurred, and was referred to the Monopolies Commission which reported against it. The Government accepted this recommendation. It could be said that the conclusions of the two bodies were generally compatible insofar as the Monopolies Commission identified the 'appropriate point' beyond which rationalisation should not occur. The episode did, however, draw attention to the possible conflict of policies which could arise between these bodies. As Beesley points out,[1] the NBPI usually stressed the role of price rises in inducing, directly or indirectly, wage claims, whilst the area of discussion of the Monopolies Commission omitted such considerations. The NBPI also gave more attention to the investigation of managerial efficiency.

There was a considerable number of references in which the NBPI found that the Monopolies Commission was already working or had earlier reported. These included references on *Beer Prices* (136), *Solicitors* (134), *Distributors Margins* (80), *Food Distribution* (165) and *Architects Fees* (71). In general an attempt was made to avoid duplication of work although in more than one reference the report of the Monopolies Commission was considered to be at the heart of the matter concerning the NBPI.[2]

The main distinction drawn between the NBPI's and the Monopolies Commission's work was that the former dealt with the behaviour, whereas the latter dealt with the structure, of an industry. In fact both bodies had to deal in their work with questions both of structure and behaviour. This was one of the reasons why in 1970 the Labour Government eventually proposed a merger of the Monopolies Commission and the NBPI into the Commission for Industry and Manpower, but the legislation lapsed with the dissolution of Parliament before the elections. Apart from the Office of Manpower Economics, the main remnant of the legislation will be an expanded role for the Monopolies Commission in future.

Another important potential area of overlap concerned the relationship of the Commission on Industrial Relations and the NBPI. Both bodies were concerned with achieving the long term reform of collective bargaining, and in some respects the methods of the CIR were inherited from the NBPI. The question of which type of body was a more appropriate one to attempt to play the main part in implementing the reforms in British industrial relations

---

[1] M.E. Beesley 'Economic Effects of National Policies towards Mergers and Acquisitions' in B.S. Denning (ed.) *Corporate Long Range Planning*, (Longmans, 1969).

[2] In references about profit margins in the distribution sector of the economy, an important issue concerned the practice of many manufacturers of recommending retail prices for their products to retailers, including in the price a fixed percentage margin. When manufacturers costs went up after devaluation, the margin expressed in terms of cash thereby automatically increased, even though retailers did not necessarily incur the same percentage cost increases as the manufacturers. However:

'Since the practice of recommending prices is currently under investigation by the Monopolies Commission, we have refrained from considering what we regard as the nub of the question — whether retailers should compete with one another by discounts from a price recommended by the manufacturer or by addition to the manufacturer's ex-factory price.' (*Third General Report*, para. 29).

recommended by the Donovan Commission, and what exact role a body set up as part of a long term incomes policy should have in these reforms, if any, has now been rendered academic by the dissolution of the NBPI, and the somewhat changed role envisaged for the CIR as a result of the 1971 Industrial Relations Act.

Conclusions

Two main conclusions emerge from this Chapter. The first is that in its control role in the prices and incomes policies of 1965–70 the NBPI was largely bypassed. Only some national wage agreements in excess of the norm and hardly any local agreements were referred to the Board. The flow of price references to the NBPI was also small and poorly phased in relation to the different stages of the prices and incomes policy. The breakdown in the short term task of controlling wages and prices came from the reference policy of the Government. It may be noted then that the idea of having an independent impartial agency to control wages and prices did not fail: it was merely that it was not tried.

The second conclusion is that the NBPI saw its main role as helping to stimulate productivity, raise incomes and eradicate persistent underlying sources of inflation. This was seen as the key to the reconciliation of the public interest in the avoidance of inflation and the individual interest in higher incomes. The NBPI's work should be judged largely by its contribution to the efficient utilisation of resources. It attempted to make this contribution both by having an effect on those who were referred to it for examination and by using individual references to have a wider effect.

Part II The Organisation, Procedures and Methods of Enquiry of the NBPI

Introduction to Part II

Certain requirements had to be satisfied if the NBPI was not to be a constraint on the effectiveness of the whole prices and incomes policy in the way that NIC was. One requirement, for instance, was that reports should exercise an influence extending well beyond those directly involved in a reference. Another requirement, obvious but not to be overlooked in the interpretation of reports, was that the NBPI had to reach a definite decision on every short term wage or price proposal submitted to it, no matter how difficult it was to reach a determinate decision that, say, 3 rather than 4 per cent was the 'right' amount.

The NBPI's organisation, procedures and methods of enquiry may be viewed broadly as attempts to meet these and further requirements of an effective policy. Thus the size of the organisation was rapidly increased to enable the investigation in some depth of a significant number of cases and in this way to extend the Board's influence.

The 1965 White Paper *Machinery of Prices and Incomes Policy* stated that the NBPI was free to decide how to conduct its enquiries. The way the NBPI did so was largely dictated by two overriding requirements: the need for speed, and its wish to find out the facts for itself.

The need for speed was recognised by the 1965 White Paper which specified that two to three months should be the maximum for the length of an enquiry. The NBPI, mindful of NIC's experience, accepted the principle underlying the White Paper. In the 1965–6 stage it was felt essential to report speedily, before the matter had slipped away from public attention and the situation had moved on to outdate the report. From 1966, it was frequently necessary to report within 3 months because the Government's powers to freeze proposed wage and price increases only applied for 3 months; even where it was not, the Board chose to report within 3 to 4 months as a rule.

With incomes decisions, particularly under a selective reference policy, the wage earners affected might feel that delay was inequitable[1] and long delays could have led to industrial unrest. With price decisions businessmen feared loss of potential revenue during investigations. Particularly in periods when costs were rising very rapidly, price rises were believed by businesses to be immediately necessary to restore the 'normal' profit of the industry. The situation, moreover, was quite different from that of the Monopolies Commission or the Restrictive Practices Court. Although the decisions of the Commission are sometimes criticised as being unnecessarily slow[2] delay is not necessarily against the interests of the parties, though it may be against the public interest. Furthermore, the habit of quick investigations had useful by-products. It led to great efficiency in the Board's work because of its sense of urgency. There was no question of it engaging in formalised public hearings which would have had certain disadvantages as a method of enquiry, quite apart from being time-consuming. It enabled it to deal with numerous references ranging across most of industry. There was no possibility of reports being produced which were obsolescent in relation to fast changing industrial situations. Some of the disadvantages of quick reporting are noted in the next three chapters, and discussed in Chapter 14.

58 reports were published within 3 months. This is 40 per cent of the 145 reports which had no special characteristics affecting the amount of time taken (such as general reports, general study references, efficiency studies of nationalised industries and standing references). The median time for such reports was 3 months and 28 days. The average was 4 months and 27 days. Average and median figures conceal the somewhat greater speed of reports in the early years.

The NBPI believed that if it was to make authoritative judgments of whether wage and price increases were in the national interest, and sound recommendations for longer term change, it needed to make as thorough an independent examination of the issues raised by each reference as possible; and that, if it was to be effective, it needed to produce reports which could withstand critical scrutiny in public and would persuade the Government and the parties to accept its recommendations on controversial matters. Consequently, in seeking to obtain the information necessary to answer the questions posed by each reference, it endeavoured to conduct investigations of a high standard: their main characteristic was a reliance principally upon the NBPI's own enquiries made specially for the reference, and only secondarily upon other sources such as published statistics and submissions of the parties, which were usually inadequate for its purposes.

1 This can be so even with the guarantees of retrospective awards which are possible in industries with low labour turnover. Even retrospective awards were ruled out in the 1966/7 phase of policy.

2 See C.K. Rowley, *The British Monopolies Commission*, (George Allen and Unwin, 1966) p. 88.

5. Organisation

As an organisation the NBPI is a subject of considerable interest. Its output of 170 reports in six years was immense. They covered the widest diversity of subjects, and were usually based on a substantial amount of investigatory work, often of an innovatory character. The almost continuous uncertainty surrounding the future of the Board was only exceeded by the uncertainty and variability of the day to day workload. As an organisation for getting work done, as an unique, innovatory investigatory body, and as an official body with a number of distinctive characteristics, the NBPI is worthy of study and in this chapter an account of its organisation is given, and in the following two chapters an account is given of its procedures and methods of enquiry. This account, largely in static terms, should be seen against a background of rapid expansion between 1965 and 1968 when expenditure grew from £208,000 in 1965/66 to a peak of £934,000 in 1970 (with the NBPI in all costing some £4 million).[1]

1. Members of the Board

The Prices and Incomes Act provided that membership of the Board should not be less than nine, or more than fifteen.[2] A list of the names and backgrounds of all members is given in Appendix A. The Members of the Board were responsible for policy.

The full-time Chairman, until October 1970, was Mr. Aubrey Jones. His previous career included periods as a Conservative Minister (of Fuel and Power, 1955–57, and of Supply, 1957–59); chairmanship of Staveley Industries (1963–64), a large machine tools concern; an economist; and a journalist; and at the time of his appointment he was a prominent parliamentary

---

1 The NBPI kindly gave me access to the original text of an unpublished organisational review of itself made by the late Professor Joan Woodward in 1968, referred to below, and Miss Woodward was able to comment helpfully on an early draft of this chapter. Her review which could, with a handful of deletions, be usefully published, has been a very helpful source of information for some parts of this chapter, although I have relied primarily upon my own impressions from attendance at meetings of the Board and staff; interviews with some Board Members and staff; and access to answers to an internal NBPI questionnaire sent to about 25 staff seeking their impressions of the working of staff working parties. The report of a NBPI staff committee on staff working parties was also helpful.

2 In the latter part of 1970 and in 1971 the Board's membership dropped below nine, but other provisions in the Act meant that reports were not invalidated.

member of the Conservative Party opposition. To the NBPI he brought this varied experience and an unusual blend of radical-mindedness and political acumen.

The Chairman was the overwhelming influence on the Board's general policies in the early stages of its history, and it is no exaggeration to say that in the early days the organisation was largely shaped around him. He continued to be the principal influence in later years. His control of the Board's output and public impact, again especially in earlier years, was also considerable because his facility as a writer enabled him, after Board discussions of draft reports, often to redraft and at times rearrange them extensively. This practice not infrequently gave him considerable discretion in the final stages of references.

The Chairman can also take much of the credit for seeing clearly at the outset the main lines of the NBPI's approach. As a result there was no initial period of experimentation and delay whilst the organisation tried to find its role in a novel area of Government. This contributed greatly to the NBPI's seizing the opportunity presented to make a strong initial impact on public opinion.

The importance of the Chairman's part should not overshadow the unquestionable importance of the significant contributions which the great majority of full and part-time Members made to general policy as well as in more specialised fields and references. The wide ranging scope of the NBPI's work and the number of problems raised by each reference was such that Members could, if they wished, have a big influence on important matters of policy, and most chose to do so.

There were nearly always three or four full-time Members, including one or two Deputy Chairmen. This relatively large number of full-time Members (compared with bodies such as the Monopolies Commission)[1] was necessary because of the heavy workload, the need for speedy decisions, the need for frequent meetings of Board Members with the parties affected, and the desirability of a measure of Board guidance of the conduct of enquiries by staff.

Part-time members of independent boards such as the NBPI are popularly thought to be in better contact with management and unions and, if practising industrialists or trade unionists, to be more acceptable. Insofar as their function is to bring a range of opinion to bear upon references, full-time

1 Comparisons in this chapter with the Monopolies Commission or the Commission on Industrial Relations are not intended as favourable or unfavourable reflections on their organisation and procedures. Their functions and size are different from the NBPI's.

membership is not necessary, and in some cases this is the only way of obtaining the services of talented people.[1,2]

An approximately even balance was maintained between Members with trade union and business backgrounds, who usually made up over half the Board. Some of these brought specialised knowledge to the Board such as in the fields of personnel management, marketing, and machinery for collective bargaining. Academic Members were from economics, industrial relations and industrial sociology. Two Members were appointed with special responsibilities for the standing references on the Pay of Armed Forces and the Pay of University Teachers, although serving as ordinary Members.

The spread of membership followed from the tripartite character of the prices and incomes policy but was also intended to demonstrate the independent character of the NBPI, to help make its investigations and decisions more acceptable, and the interests of unions and management in specific cases better understood. The Minister responsible for the appointment of the first Board Members, Mr. George Brown, said they had only one characteristic in common — 'They passionately believe in the attempt to achieve a prices and incomes policy as part of the overall planning strategy'.[3]

The Members of the Board displayed a solidarity comparable to, if not better than the Cabinet. At one of the first Board Meetings the Chairman, in the words of the minutes, said:

'that the Board, being a permanent body, was unlike a Royal Commission which, if it failed to reach agreement, produced both majority and minority reports. The Board's authority and influence would be seriously undermined if their recommendations appeared to be other than unanimous. It would be his aim to carry the Board with him but if he failed, he hoped members would accept that they should be bound by the principle of collective responsibility and stand by the majority view'.

In the event no minority reports were issued nor did Members publicly dissent from decisions. There was only one resignation, by Mr. Robert Willis in 1967.

1 The Board could also co-opt members for particular references by drawing upon selected panels of businessmen and trade unionists. This only happened in a few early reports — *Wages, Costs and Prices in the Printing Industry* (2), *Prices of Bread and Flour* (3), *Prices of Household and Toilet Soaps, Soap Powders and Soap Flakes, and Soapless Detergents* (4), *Pay of Industrial Civil Servants* (18), *The Pay and Conditions of Manual Workers in Local Authorities, the National Health Service, Gas and Water Supply* (29). This device was originally thought to be important in ensuring the support of the TUC and CBI.

2 For fuller discussions of these issues, see C.K. Rowley *The British Monopolies Commission*, (London: George Allen and Unwin, 1966) p. 54—55; the Franks Committee Report on Administrative Tribunals and Enquiries, Cmnd. 218, July 1957, passim; Sixth Report from the Select Committee on Estimates, 1952—53, p. 8. As noted below, Board Members, especially full-time ones, had considerable contact with unions and management as a result of the NBPI's refusal to rely on formal hearings alone for its information. It is difficult to sustain the commonly expressed view that there was any danger of full-time Members 'losing touch' with the views of management and unions.

3 TUC Congress 1965, p. 28.

Minority reports would have been possible only until the reconstitution of the NBPI on a statutory basis in 1966. After then the NBPI was a body corporate and as a result their issue was not possible.[1]

This solidarity was surprising considering the diverse origins of Board Members and the controversial nature of their task. The reasons for it seem to have been that the NBPI's scope for action was circumscribed by the criteria laid down in White Papers and there was a large area in which the approach was necessarily pragmatic; there was general agreement on the NBPI's broad line and on the fact that what it was trying to do was good; the need for solidarity itself was appreciated by Members; and the skilful incorporation of differing points of view into reports without compromising their forcefulness and consistency.

There were, nevertheless, disagreements within the Board. The main line of division was not between trade unionists and businessmen as one might expect, though such a division was not altogether absent. Rather there was often a spectrum of opinion ranging from more radically minded Members of the Board wishing to challenge conventional practices to more conservatively minded Members who saw less need for change, though none consistently opposed well-based recommendations for change. It is worth noting some of the arguments for and against the issue of minority or dissenting reports.

For power to make minority reports it can be argued —

(a) individual signatures of minority reports emphasise the Members' personal responsibility for what is said, and by implication, to a more carefully studied report; (b) failing power to publish dissent, the risk of resignations is enhanced; (c) there may well be room for legitimately different conclusions being reached by intelligent men of goodwill after all proper application: the object of a Board, not a single man, is to secure a diversity of view: it should be possible to have it expressed; (d) it is unfair to expect Members to be positively associated with conclusions from which they positively dissent; (e) the weight of a report is strengthened if Members are free to express dissent but have not done so; (f) there are dangers in compromise reports: they may be wishy-washy; and the concealment of serious disagreement and the pressures for compromises may not be helpful to the Government in finding the right solution. Circumstances may be important here. There may be no scope for compromise about a conclusion that a monopoly, or merger, is, or is not, against the public interest; on the other hand, in dealing with wage and price matters there is often no exact 'right' figure for an increase and indeed the broad principles underlying the decision may reflect a compromise between admittedly conflicting considerations: in such cases a compromise is more acceptable.

Arguments for a body corporate, with a single report, are —

(a) a pattern of one or more minority reports, reservations, and dissents, must reduce the board's public standing and give a board's sponsoring department much more trouble in getting and sustaining ministerial decisions on

---

[1] A legal opinion to this effect was obtained in 1969 on the request of a Board Member who disagreed with the recommendations of a report.

follow-up action than would single reports. Two recent examples of the effectiveness of minority reports in undermining the influence of a report are Professor Colin Buchanan's dissent from the Roskill Report on the Siting of the Third London Airport; and Mr. Andrew Shonfield's partial dissent from the Donovan Report on Trade Unions and Employers Associations. Members of the Monopolies Commission can and do issue dissenting reports.

(b) It increases the pressure on individual Members to find compromise conclusions which are generally acceptable.

(c) The practice of unanimity provides to each Board Member both the opportunity to influence his colleagues and some protection against interested parties who feel that it is more important that someone on the Board should act as their advocate than that a common view should emerge as a result of discussion. In particular, independent Members who happen to be appointed from the ranks of one or other side of industry may feel, if there is provision for dissent, under a very real temptation to do so on any report which appears critical of the side of industry from which they come. Under the unanimity rule Members may be prepared to be associated with such criticism coming from the Board as a whole and from which they can say they are not free to dissent.

As observed, much depends on the size of the body, the circumstances of the situation, the objectives of the body, and the influence it wishes to have. For the NBPI influence was of the greatest importance and it was the decisive factor in making it eschew the minority report.

The Board met about once a fortnight. Before 1969 it did not consider a reference until a late stage, when a draft was put before it. From 1969 onwards, it considered a paper reporting the main findings of fact typically about a month before the deadline and frequently reached its main decisions at that stage, and considered a draft report at a later meeting. This change, suggested by Professor Woodward in her organisational review of the Board (see below), to some extent strengthened the participation of Board Members in its decision-making, and gave more leeway for following up their suggestions. More important probably was the catalytic effect on Board Member participation from 1969 onwards of her undertaking the review and interviewing all Board Members.

The Board as a whole took no part in the early stages of the conduct of references. Members did not, for example, discuss new references at Board meetings but sub-committees, appointed by the Chairman, were established for each reference.[1] Their size usually varied from one full-time or part-time

1 Both the Monopolies Commission and the Commission on Industrial Relations operate differently from this. The Monopolies Commission assigns a panel of members to take charge of each reference. The full-time Chairman sits on most panels. The reference is not considered by the Commission as a whole at any stage. The Members of the Commission on Industrial Relations meet at the start of each reference and decide upon the approach which should be taken to a reference. One Member is then appointed to take charge of the handling of the reference. A draft report is sent to a meeting of all Members which has power of final decision. The Commission is much smaller than the NBPI, which makes this procedure easier.

Member at the busiest times to two or three as a rule.[1] They met within two or three weeks of the arrival of a reference to guide the staff working parties in determining the issues for investigation and again before presentation of the findings to the Board. Decisions as to which enquiries should be made and which issues particularly investigated tended to be mainly a staff matter unless Board Members had a good technical grasp of the main issues and a knowledge of how to mount special enquiries. An important function of Board sub-committee Members was to attend formal meetings – and often informal ones – with the parties affected. They also kept in varying degrees of touch with day-to-day developments, depending on whether full-time or part-time, and on working styles and other commitments.

Greater Board control of the conduct of a reference during busy times would only have been possible with a substantially larger membership or an enlarged full-time element. Either such provision might, on the other hand, have reduced the effective or unified functioning of Board Members as a policy making group.

The Board Members did not, as the White Paper establishing the NBPI contemplated, divide into a Prices and an Incomes Division, because it was believed that prices and incomes were closely interrelated and that it would not be sensible to consider them in isolation from one another. [2]

Before turning to an account of staffing, it is worthy of note that the Board itself was assisted by a number of prominent academic figures –
Mr. Allan Flanders, Lord Balogh, Mr. R. Opie, Professor B.R. Williams and Professor J.R. Crossley. Most of these enjoyed good access to the Chairman and exercised a significant amount of influence. The experience of these outsiders in the NBPI seems to have resulted in much less frustation on their part than some outsiders in this period in other areas of British Government. [3]

2. The Staff

The function of the staff was broadly the managerial one of carrying out investigations, maintaining relations with interested parties, including government departments, and of suggesting recommendations.

To the outsider and to the new arrival at the Board, whether coming from the Civil Service, industry, a trade union or the academic world, the most striking feature was the outstanding enthusiasm of staff and rapid pace of work compared with the organisations from which they came.

In the early days the small staff were confronted with a demanding workload requiring the performance at high speed of important tasks of an often

1 The Prices and Incomes Act required that there be 3 Members on each such committee. This was not practicable. For several years it was the practice to appoint, officially, 3 Members, not all of whom were expected to take an active interest in the reference.

2 *First General Report*, para. 25.

3 See T. Balogh, R. Opie, D. Seers and H. Thomas, *Crisis in the Civil Service*, (Anthony Bland, London, 1968), passim.

unfamiliar, pioneering nature. The challenge was willingly accepted, and the nature of the NBPI's work was such that a crusading spirit permeated the atmosphere. Long hours were worked at an intense pace and high morale. The senior civil servants who established the organisation, of whom Mr. A.A. Jarratt the first Secretary of the NBPI may be especially mentioned, made the most, in Professor Woodward's words, 'of the opportunities presented in setting up a completely new organisation to generate a high degree of involvement in the staff of the secretariat, so that people were willing to work long and irregular hours with enthusiasm at far higher than the normal levels.'[1]

The average length of service of staff (at principal level or equivalent or above) was two years and two months. There was little difference in this respect between civil servants on short term loan from Government departments and those from outside the Civil Service who were mostly on two year contracts. Members of the Enquiry Team, whose work is described in Chapter 7, also spent on average two years and one month at the NBPI. Largely because of the almost continuous uncertainty surrounding its future and also because recruitment at each level of the organisational hierarchy was largely from outside, the NBPI was unable to offer good career prospects. This was unfortunate because a maximum of experience was necessary for most work.

An interesting aspect of the NBPI is that staff attitudes varied from those who felt a strong personal commitment to the prices and incomes policy and the need for an independent official agency to stimulate change to those who tended more to see their role as being the provision of technical information and policy advice to Board Members to be disposed of as they wished; this does not mean there was any difference in the relative efficiency of such groups.

3. The Formal Organisation

The Secretary of the Board (of Deputy Secretary level after 1966) was head of the staff. The Board was exceptionally well served in this position by two very able civil servants, Mr. A.A. Jarratt until 1968 and Mr. K.H. Clucas from then until 1971. Although they had somewhat differing conceptions of the way in which the organisation should be run, the former being somewhat less, and the latter rather more disposed to the formalisation of arrangements within the organisation, each style seemed to accord well with the different needs of the organisation in early and late years.

Mr. Clucas came from the Ministry of Labour and has subsequently become First Civil Service Commissioner. Mr. Jarratt had been the Principal Private Secretary to Mr. Jones when he was Minister of Fuel and Power and was appointed Secretary on Mr. Jones' request. In turn some of the senior civil servants in the early days were appointed on the personal request of Mr. Jarratt, who decided that the staff could not be organised along traditional Civil Service lines and took this into account in their selection. As well he looked for senior staff who would engender a sense of enthusiasm

1 'How the P.I.B. Should Work,' *New Society*, 1969.

into the Board's work. In 1968 Mr. Jarratt departed to become a Deputy
Under Secretary of State in charge of the new Prices and Incomes Division
of the Department of Employment and Productivity. Mr. J.M. Woolf left to
take up an appointment as Assistant Under Secretary of State in charge of
the establishment of the new Manpower and Productivity Service division of
the DEP and after completing this task was transferred in 1969 to the Prices
and Incomes Division of the DEP. This illustrates in a small way the feedback of informal influence the NBPI had on the making of policy.

Under the Secretary the staff were organised at first into one, then two,
and finally in 1968 three divisions headed by Under Secretaries. Two
divisions from 1968 consisted of 'generalists' grouped into about ten branches
responsible for executing inquiries into references. Each branch was headed
by an Assistant Secretary, who was usually assigned two or three references.[1]
He thereby became Chairman of the Staff Working Party set up for each reference. One Report Secretary (of Principal or Chief Executive Officer level)
was assigned to each reference, and an Assistant Report Secretary. References were not allocated to divisions or branches in such a way that they
could acquire specialities. Apart from the imbalance at any one time
of prices and incomes references, and the lack of continuity of staff, the
urgency of most references prohibited delay until a particular division or
branch was ready to deal with it; the main reason, however, was that the main
issues in wages and prices references were seen as similar.

The third division consisted of the specialist branches, and several other
branches concerned with general policy, liason with Whitehall, information
including press and public relations[2] and internal administration. An organisational chart of the NBPI in 1970 is shown in Chart 5.1. Further explanation
of the chart is provided in appropriate parts of the text.

4. 'Specialists'

The most novel feature for an official body of the staffing was the large
number and wide interdisciplinary mix of 'specialists'. Of those 99 staff
employed from 1966—70 of rank equivalent to or higher than principal, 57
were generalists and 42 specialists. 47 came from outside the Civil Service.
All of the Management Operations Branch and most of the Industrial Relations

---

1 The limited numbers of references per Assistant Secretary (and their relatively
narrow spans of control) were the result of an early decision in the Board's
history that Assistant Secretaries should participate fairly actively in each reference, and should get out to see the parties frequently. Typically about half of an
Assistant Secretary's time was taken up with meetings, inside and outside the
Board. This is not an abnormal span of control for an Assistant Secretary in
British Government. See *The Civil Service*, Report of the Fulton Committee: Vol. 1,
1968, Cmnd. 3638, June 1968, Page 53, para. 159.

2. One minor task of the information branch was to forward to appropriate government
departments letters of complaint from the public about rising prices. Records of
the numbers of letters received were kept from 1966. The numbers are:
1966 — 2,864; 1967 — 5,398; 1968 — 9,870; 1969 — 5,553; 1970 (first six months) —
1,796.

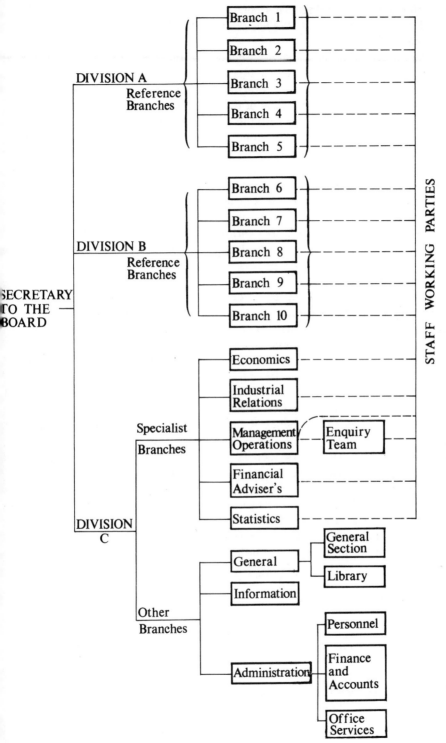

Chart 5.1 N.B.P.I. STAFF: Organisation Chart (July 1969)

Branch came from outside. This points to another distinctive feature of the NBPI as an organisation — the admixture of staff with Civil Service and outside backgrounds.

The specialist branches were: Economics, Industrial Relations, Management Operations, Statistics and Accountancy. Heads of specialist branches were of Assistant Secretary status. After 1968 in accordance with industrial but not Civil Service practice, heads of divisions and branches were responsible for their own personnel work with the assistance of a personnel manager who reported to the secretary. The Economics Branch[1] was relatively small and for fairly long periods of time did not have a senior economist at its head. It worked almost exclusively on price references. The Financial Advisers (originally Accountancy) Branch was established in late 1965. Prior to that the NBPI's accountancy work was done by an outside firm. Because of the difficulty of attracting accountants to Government service, some two-thirds of the NBPI's accountancy work continued after 1965 to be done by outside firms. Accountancy work was done in price references and some pay reference The Industrial Relations Branch was strongly manned from the inception of the NBPI. The experience of its members extended to various specialisms such as industrial relations, labour economics and industrial sociology; personnel and industrial relations management; trade union organisation and operations; work study, industrial consultancy, factory inspection etc.[3] Of the 13 advisers or senior advisers from 1966, 6 came from universities, two from business; two from trade union research departments, and two from the Civil Service. The Statistics Branch was formally established in October 1966 with the arrival of a Chief Statistician although statisticians had worked at the NBPI since its inception. It worked on most references. Its main specialist work was the conduct of some 150 surveys but it also provided published statistics, generally helped in the analysis of all data and took part in other statistical work such as forecasting exercises in price references The Management Operations Branch was set up in mid–1969. At first the NBP relied mainly on commercial management consultancy firms to make efficiency studies for it. The Enquiry Team were at the service of the NBPI to do fact-finding work in a variety of fields. From the second half of 1969 onwards they were attached to the Management Operations Branch. Their work is described further in Chapter 7. Further details of the Management Operations

1 After the decision in September 1967 to refer price increases of nationalised industries to the NBPI the branch was strengthened from three advisers to four plus a senior adviser, a post which, as has been stated, was only filled for a time, for about 18 months.

2 By 1970 the Branch included a Principal Accountant, a Chief Accountant and two Senior Accountants. The Fulton Report discusses the difficulty of attracting accountants to the Civil Service.

3 In October 1966, for example, it had five full-time IR specialists and some part-time members, over half of the NBPI's specialists, and from 1968–1970 there were between about 6–9 advisers including the senior advisers.

4 By 1970 its membership was about 40, including a Chief Statistician and six statisticians.

Branch are given in the chapter on efficiency in view of the novelty of employing businessmen in an official body. Otherwise the principle is adopted of separating the description of specialist branches from the description of specialist work, since much specialist work was the product of interdisciplinary collaboration between specialist branches, the staff working party responsible for references and Board Members.

The Industrial Relations Branch was the most influential specialist branch. From the outset its members aimed to function as a cohesive group rather than as a collection of individuals with different views and consciously sought to ensure that their branch's viewpoint was represented. In the interests of developing a consistent policy and of pooling the varied experience of individuals, its members regularly discussed references as they arose although each was free to take his own line in advising on particular references. This was encouraged by the Secretariat not least because it is not difficult for competent administrators to find specialists to contradict whatever specialist advice they have been given, and there was a wish to get away from such situations.

It would be inaccurate to brand the Branch as a whole as being associated with what is known as the Oxford School view of British industrial relations, but a significant proportion of its members belonged to this school of thought. Perhaps the main reason for the prominence of the Oxford viewpoint in the NBPI's general approach to industrial relations was the presence of Mr. Allan Flanders, the leading exponent of its theories, as an adviser to the NBPI in the crucial early days when doctrine was established, and the appointment from 1966 to 1967 of Professor H.A. Clegg, the other leading exponent of its views, as a Full Time Board Member.

The Management Operations Branch followed a similar approach to the Industrial Relations Branch when it was established as a Branch in the middle of 1969. Unlike the Industrial Relations Branch, however, it was organised along functional lines with different sections being responsible for marketing, operations research etc. The Industrial Relations Branch advisers were, broadly speaking, all purpose general advisers.

The influence of the Industrial Relations Branch was also attributable to defaults in the specialist composition of the organisation in early years. As is explained in the chapter on efficiency, the NBPI lacked staff with senior management experience until 1969. The Economics Branch, rightly or wrongly, was not usually represented on wages references, and the representation of labour economists, whether they should have been in the IRB or Economics Branch, was a little thin, if one considers the economic consequences of such matters as productivity bargaining. The Industrial Relations Branch, rightly or wrongly, was mainly concerned with the 'internal job market' (i.e. labour and wages within a particular firm) rather than primarily with the wider repercussions of wage and labour matters on local, regional or national markets. Some of the I.R. members had personnel management experience which was very useful but this is a rather specialised field of management and no substitute for a management branch.

5. Use of Outside Resources

The NBPI was a heavy consumer of outside expert resources. The role of industrial relations case study workers is dealt with in Chapter 7. Academic experts on specialised subjects or particular industries were sometimes brought in. As noted earlier, more than half of the accountancy work was done by an outside firm.

Management consultants were used heavily even after the establishment of the NBPI's own Management Operations Branch in June 1969. Nearly one-tenth of the NBPI's finance went in the form of payments to consultants.

In assessing what external (or internal) resources should be used for a reference, the likely cost of the alternative methods of obtaining the necessary data were taken into account and from mid–1969 there was a form of ex-post control whereby each staff committee assigned to a reference reviewed and explained the reasons for any departures in actual costs from budgeted figures.

In the *Second General Report*[2], the NBPI gave three reasons for employing consultants or outside independent specialists. First, the range of expert knowledge among the Board's staff could not be made all-embracing without gross waste. Second, a fluctuating workload which involved sharp peaks made outside help intermittently necessary even in fields where the Board's own staff was qualified. Third, there was much to be gained from co-operation between the Board's own staff and outside help. The subject is taken up further in the chapter on efficiency.

Commenting in the *Second General Report* 'about some anxiety expressed about the extent to which consultants contribute to our work', it was pointed out that consultants took no part in policy discussions or drafting which determined the underlying approach to a report, or in determining the shape of the report. They were employed as experts in particular fields and their terms of reference were restricted to their own expertise. It was concluded that 'they are fact-finders, not policy makers, and the Board's recommendations are made on the basis of its own judgements in the light of the evidence.' This hardly meets the not entirely academic point that though the NBPI could designate consultants as 'fact-finders, not policy makers' there are no isolated 'facts' which are not identified and structured in accordance with implicit theories in consultancy practice. The identity and terms of reference of consultants were not disclosed publicly, but only to the party being investigated. They were bound to secrecy by the Official Secrets Act, and by the Prices and Incomes Act.

The NBPI could rightly claim to have been an expert consumer in the use and, later, the control of consultants. Originally there was competitive selection by staff working parties and the secretariat: later there was selection by the Management Operations Branch. A large index was kept with detailed information about which individual consultants in which firms

1 See *Fifth General Report*, para. 87.

2 *Second General Report*, paras. 61–64 has a fairly full discussion of the use of consultants.

specialised in different subjects, and a record was kept of the performance of consultants in references.

Large indexes were also kept of case study workers, research workers and their specialities.

The large and speedy deployment of external resources was one of the keys to the effectiveness of the NBPI as an organisation.

6. 'Specialists', 'Generalists' and Staff Working Parties

The role of specialists in British Government has apparently never been completely satisfactory. Thus the Fulton Committee on the Civil Service expressed the view that many specialists get neither the full responsibilities and corresponding authority, nor the opportunities they ought to have.[1]

The relation of generalists and specialists was a potentially acute problem for the NBPI, but from the outset a method of combining them was found in the system of allocating specialists and generalists to separate hierarchies or divisions whilst bringing them together in Staff Working Parties for particular references. In doing this, the NBPI departed from the practice followed by the Civil Service normally.

The Fulton Report regarded the most common modes of organising administrators and specialists engaged in a common task in British government as obstacles to the effective allocation of responsibility and authority. One mode is that of 'parallel hierarchies' in which responsibility is bisected, with financial and overall policy control being entrusted to administrators organised in one hierarchy, while advice on the technical merits of a case and the execution and development of technical policy is laid to specialists organised in a separate but parallel hierarchy. In 'joint' hierarchies, the other mode, an administrator and a specialist are designated joint heads of a block of work, but at lower levels the separation of functions still occurs, with financial control in the hands of the administrators. Despite certain of their advantages, Fulton viewed these systems unfavourably because they produced delay and inefficiency because of the need for constant reference to and fro between the hierarchies; they prevented specialists from exercising the full range of responsibilities normally associated with their professions and exercised by their counterparts outside the service; and they obscured individual responsibility and accountability as no single person had clear-cut managerial responsibility for the whole task.

The long range solution Fulton saw was for a single integrated structure under a single head, the head being the person most appropriately qualified for the job. For the Board a short term solution was necessary. Its solution, which preceded the Fulton Report, was separate specialists branches; but the combination in staff working parties of specialists engaged in common tasks.

An alternative possibility would have been to abolish the separate hierarchies and develop teams of generalists and specialists concentrating

1 op.cit., chap. 1.

largely on particular types of references. Responsibility for the deployment of specialist staff would not then have been as divided as when they were assigned to more than one reference. The division of control between line managers and a professional head would have been avoided also. There might also have been a better integration of specialists from different and often overlapping branches. Heads of former specialist branches would then also have concentrated more on policy issues and less on the supervision of specialist work. Above all there would have been greater continuity in working relationships, policy making, and investigatory practices. This practice is followed by the Commission on Industrial Relations, though its specialists come primarily from one discipline rather than many which makes it more practicable.

The assignment of specialists to separate branches meant, however, that they could be deployed flexibly and economically, an important consideration when their limited numbers are considered; they could pool and develop their specialist skills better by close contact with fellow specialists and develop a consistent approach to specialised issues; and junior staff could be more easily trained. Generalist branch heads moreover might not have used specialist services to their best advantage. The latter group of considerations were the main factors seen as in practice tipping the balance in favour of separate specialist branches.

A Staff Working Party, comprising an Assistant Secretary, Report Secretary, Assistant Report Secretary, and specialists, as appropriate, worked therefore under the supervision of the Board sub-committee for each references. Generalist members had overall responsibility for the administration and management of the reference, including 'political' aspects of references, meetings with parties with a concern in the reference, co-ordination of specialist enquiries, and report drafting. Treating report drafting as a separate task gave full play to the writing skills of civil servants and allowed more effective use of specialist staff. Civil servants also brought to the NBPI a familiarity with the inner workings of Government departments, and made use of a network of contacts in them. In practice they, especially the Assistant Secretary took a significant part of the responsibility for decisions of the Staff Working Party. In turn, the Under Secretaries, under the Secretary, bore general responsibility to the Board for the references entrusted to their branches.

It might be argued that the assignment of this measure of responsibility to 'generalists' — which of course reflected their large, and by international standards, unique share of responsibility for higher decision making in British government, and the correspondingly 'restricted access to higher management and policy making' of specialists [1] — might have prevented the satisfactory building into the machine of specialist contributions. The traditional arguments for assigning these roles to generalists would be 'that they are trained to tone down specialist enthusiasm with common sense, to make technicalities

1 *Fulton Report,* op.cit., para. 17.

intelligible, and to look at policy proposals from a policy angle';[1] where more than one specialist is involved, administrators are sometimes considered better than specialist heads at holding scales even; many specialists are equipped only to practice their specialism, and anyway are in too short supply to occupy administrative positions. The assignment of the post of Chairman of Staff Working Party to Assistant Secretaries might also be supported on the grounds that it ensured clear line management. The traditional arguments for assigning senior roles to specialists would be that many of them do show administrative ability and that a professional knowledge of a subject is the only proper foundation on which can be built general executive ability. These traditional arguments are, as V. Subramaniam has pointed out, based on convenient but different prototypes and ignore the wide spectrum of individual variations.

It is difficult to go much further than endorse Subramaniam's view. It ought perhaps to be noted that industrial relations (of the kind dealt with by the NBPI), management efficiency, and private sector pricing policy are fields in which the Civil Service has had limited experience, and there was a rather wide variation in the background knowledge which civil servants possessed of these subjects. Some had an excellent knowledge. For example, one Under Secretary, Mr. J.S. Cassels, who came from the Ministry of Labour, had been Secretary of the Donovan Commission and had an expert knowledge of industrial relations institutions. Equally, a small minority of staff with posts as high as Chairman of Staff Working Parties displayed no more apparent previous knowledge of these subjects than might have been acquired from, say, newspaper reading, and their leadership of Staff Working Parties suffered.

Turning to specialists their role was not in fact as restricted as their position in the formal hierarchy might suggest, partly because of their informal access to individual Board members. The main reason, however, why specialists had a satisfactory share in decision making was the effective and flexible working of the Staff Working Party system, a pre-Fulton Report experiment, which facilitated speedy action, effective communication and creative interdisciplinary contact both between specialist branches and between specialists and generalists, reasonably satisfactory co-ordination of different enquiries, and the development of a 'team' feeling. Meetings were conducted in an appropriately informal spirit and a large number of staff commented on the fact that a person's rank or field of specialisation did not guarantee an immediate acceptance of his ideas to the same extent as in other bodies. Any loss as the findings of specialists filtered across and then up the hierarchy during the various drafting stages[2] was presumably offset by the gains from presenting the findings to a variety of questioners.

Any committee system has its shortcomings of course. The main weaknesses of Staff Working Parties seem to have been the lack of continuity in

---

1 V. Subramaniam 'The Relative Status of Generalists and Specialists', *Public Administration* (London) Autumn 1968, Vol. 46, p. 331.

2 Various steps were taken to prevent this happening, e.g. circulation of drafts, and consultation before drafting.

working groups handling references (as when one working party dealing with a price reference found that none of its members had previously worked on a price reference); some inevitable problems of division of control between staff and line management, accentuated by the presence of several different specialists in each team; a tendency to fragmentation of enquiries; and weaknesses in the evaluation of the enquiries of specialist branches because of lack of time; and some inconsistences of approach. Co-ordination, moreover, was not perfect and it may have weakened as the NBPI grew larger. The main theme of the important report in 1970 on *Coal Prices* (153) was the need for management action to raise productivity but the chapter on industrial relations had very little to say on the topic at all and concentrated mainly on those subjects having least to do with productivity. There is no doubt, however, that the Staff Working Party system was fundamentally sound and regarded as such by the staff.

7. Informal Organisation and the Growth of the NBPI

There was a very large and rapid build up in the scale of the organisation between 1965 and 1968, a considerable feat in itself. There was also a change in the nature of the Board's work with a heavier workload and a need for much more enquiry work per reference than in the early days. Although the initial forces making for staff involvement to some extent had slackened by around 1968, there still remained a very high degree of involvement on the part of many of the staff.

The NBPI was a new and unusual organisation, nearly always faced with a heavy workload and the need for quick decision making. Its internal communications and decision making network at Board and staff levels, and between Board members and staff, was more complex than appears from the foregoing account. Thus, a good deal of decision making occurred outside the Staff Working Parties. Often this was because there was no need, and sometimes no time, for all members to be present and also because of the responsibility of Under Secretaries, who were not members of Staff Working Parties, for references. There was no formal machinery to ensure consistency in the policy applied between different references by SWPs, nor to enable heads of specialist branches to make a co-ordinated contribution to the formulation of policies and the development of procedures. In addition, the distinctive nature of each reference and the somewhat varying roles of different Board Members and staff assigned to different references, led to varying procedures in Board sub-committees and Staff Working Parties.

The NBPI was small and personal enough for most of its life to live with this without any obvious loss of efficiency. As it grew larger a trend to greater formalisation occurred. It was always willing to examine its own workings critically and drew upon the services of its specialist branches to do so. In 1968 it commissioned an organisational review by Miss Joan Woodward then a new part-time Board Member and Head of the Industrial Sociology Unit, Imperial College of Science and Technology. The main theme of this report concerned the transition which the NBPI was making from its early phase —

when there was a small staff and Board, and a highly flexible organisation continually relying on improvised and informal methods and continually confronted with unfamiliar problems — to a later phase of being a body with acquired experience and a much heavier workload, whose basic task had become the assembly and analysis of information. Her recommendations were designed to adapt the NBPI's organisation to this task by ensuring not only a fuller participation of Board Members in reference work and decision making but also by recommending a number of internal organisational changes (which are mainly noted elsewhere),[1,2] and accelerating other changes which were likely to come anyway.

It would be interesting to construct an organisation model of the NBPI in the manner of industrial sociologists and others. This has not, however, been attempted in this book, and Miss Woodward of course was not engaged in a study of that kind. Fortunately Burns and Stralker have already constructed a model which they believe characterises many organisations. Most of its elements seem applicable to the NBPI, and indeed it emphasises some of its distinctive features compared with other official organisations.[3]

Burns and Stralker distinguish between two extreme forms of management system, the mechanistic and the organic. The former, which is more suitable for stable conditions, has a proper organisation chart which follows text book rules. The tasks to be performed by the organisation are broken down into specialised sub-tasks and allocated to sub-groups and individuals with precisely defined and delimited responsibilities. The individual's tasks tend to be of an abstract nature pursued with purposes and techniques more or less distinct from the concern as a whole. There is a hierarchical structure of control, authority and communication reinforced by what they term an omniscience imputed to the head of the concern who has final decision making power. The responsibility for co-ordination and reconciliation of sub-tasks at each level of the hierarchy is that of the immediate superior. Communications tend to be vertical between superior and subordinate rather than lateral. In changing conditions which give rise constantly to fresh problems and unforeseen requirements for action, the traditional organisational forms cannot analyse sub-tasks and distribute them automatically to individuals with responsibilities defined within a hierarchic structure. The traditional channels cannot adjust to the situation sufficiently.

The organic form of organisation largely abandons the organisation chart. The tasks of individuals are continually adjusted and redefined through interaction with others; each sub-task is perceived as closely related to the final

---

1 See page 26, *Fourth General Report*, and *New Society* 1969 'How the PIB Should Work' by Miss Woodward, for summaries of the review. The NBPI also had a staff committee examining some of its working procedures at one stage.

2 These included an improved information and storage retrieval system and the appointment of a non-Civil Service personnel manager, along the lines suggested by the Fulton Committee as a new model for the Civil Service.

3 T. Burns and G.M. Stralker, *The Management of Innovation*, 2nd edition. Tavistock Publications, 1961.

ends of the concern; 'responsibility' is not seen as a limited field of rights, obligations and methods and there is less tendency for problems to be posted upwards, downwards or sideways as being someone else's responsibility; the individual is involved not merely in the exercise of a special competence, but is also committed to the success of the concern's undertaking. There is a network structure of control, authority and communication, with lateral rather than vertical communication. The sanctions which apply to the individual's conduct in his working role derive more from a presumed community of interest with the rest of the organisation in the goals of the organisation and less from a contractual relationship between himself and a non-personal corporation, represented for him by an immediate superior; instead of omniscience being imputed to the top of the echelons, the relevant expert knowledge may be located anywhere in the network. The lead is taken by the most informed and capable. The location of expert knowledge becomes the ad hoc centre of control authority and communication. Communication is lateral rather than vertical with communications between people of different ranks resembling consultations rather than command; communication consists of information and advice more than instructions and decisions.

Without sharing all its characteristics the NBPI had more in common with the organic than the mechanic model and in this respect it was unusual for an official organisation. Over the course of time it tended rather more in the direction of the mechanic.

6. Procedures

In this chapter the sequence of events in the NBPI's internal handling of a reference is described. Little is said about the nature of the special enquiries which the NBPI made since this is dealt with in later chapters. Some procedural topics are isolated for discussion — the NBPI's efforts to keep the media informed of its doings; the meetings held with parties affected by the reference; and there is a brief discussion of the advantages and disadvantages of the Board's methods compared with 'judicial' methods of investigation.

1. Sequence of Events in a Reference

Preparations before references were announced: The NBPI was not normally a party to pre-reference negotiations between the Government and the parties affected, nor did it wish to be, although on occasions it was called in to describe the nature of its investigatory procedures. However, before the formal announcement of references in the London Gazette, the staff usually discussed informally their desirability and exact terms with the Government departments involved.

Within the NBPI, to permit staff to get to grips with unfamiliar subjects quickly as soon as references arrived, pre-reference preparations were made by one or two members of staff permanently assigned to the task. They compiled background briefs for references considered likely, drawing on published information and the help of government departments. Enquiries outside the Government were rarely possible before gazettal. The time available for this varied from as little as three or four days to some months. The most extensive of all pre-reference preparations made were those in respect of the motor car industry on which voluminous information was collected over a period of several years, but the reference never came.

Sometimes it was possible for the nucleus of a Staff Working Party to start work before a reference was gazetted.

The planning stage: Once a reference had arrived, it was necessary to identify the key questions likely to arise and to plan special enquiries and a programme of work to ensure the assembly of necessary information. In doing so, a systematic attempt was made, after Professor Woodward's report, to assign broad priorities and to allocate financial and specialist resources to references in the light of budgets estimating likely costs and the demand on staff time of the work programme.

Field enquiries stage: The nature of these enquiries and the co-operation given them is described in Chapter 7.

Evaluation of enquiries and report writing: Even in three months references, it was necessary to allow four or five clear weeks at the end for analysing results, drafting findings papers and reports; and for giving Board Members collectively time to read, consider and discuss them;[1] and re-drafting, securing final approval by the Board, printing and publication had to be done within the last month.[2]

Much of the evaluation of results of enquiries was made outside the Staff Working Party and Board Members Committee by specialists, in some haste at times, often simultaneously with the drafting process. The difficulties of analysis were perhaps greatest in processing reports from case study workers, whether in short or long reports.

Reports and appendices and supplements contain relatively little analysis of data collected, compared with what could have been done had there been more time. The approach was to extract a small amount of essential information from enquiries and to relegate as much technical material to appendices or supplements as possible.

Some indication of the vast amount of enquiry work which went into reports is given in the appendices to this book which summarise most of the special enquiries made by the NBPI. Very often these findings were condensed to a paragraph or less in the interests of brevity.

Report writing was a highly developed art. There was a succession of drafts. The actual evidence for some factual conclusions was not always made clear. Sometimes it was thin and an ex cathedra pronouncement was made. Sometimes it was not possible to give details of such matters as the methodology of case studies and other enquiries without greatly lengthening reports or appendices. In some references it was not possible to disclose the profit position or other financial details of industries or firms because of limitations imposed by the Prices and Incomes Act. Final drafts of reports were disquietingly often completed at the very latest moment possible.

There appear to have been several reasons for the NBPI's preference for short reports. Busy people could read them. Their impact was probably greater. Essentials could be stated without embarrassing errors of detail or 'the less said, the better'. On the other hand, it could be argued that longer reports with a more detailed spelling-out of problems and possible remedies would probably, on some occasions, have brought home more graphically the problems of an industry to its members, and assisted other readers in recognising similar problems in their own firms, industries or trade unions. The NBPI opted almost always for short reports.

Besides issuing reports, the NBPI also prepared after its general study

1 After the Woodward Report, a Findings Paper was sent to the Board Members about five weeks before the publication deadline. In three months references this compressed further the time available for special enquiries.

2 The aim was to *publish* within three months.

reports on wage systems pamphlets for widespread distribution. These explained the nature, advantages, and means of using these systems, and their relation to incomes policy. Something like one million were distributed in all.

A few weeks after publication a post mortem report, written by the Report Secretary and discussed by the Staff Working Party, was circulated to all staff. In practice this dealt mainly with lessons of the reference about procedural matters rather than with the evaluation of the substance of the report's recommendations, or of the enquiries that were made and was not of the value it might have been. After the report by Miss Woodward, which in some respects recommended changes which were coming anyway, the post-mortem reviewed and explained the reasons for any departures in actual costs of enquiries from budgeted figures.

There were a handful of occasions, mainly in 1970 and 1971, when the NBPI was approached after reports by the parties for advice on implementing recommendations or for more information, say from earnings surveys. It generally obliged.

2. Public Relations

Reports, then, were written with a keen eye to their public impact. As is the usual practice for official reports, a 'Confidential Final Revise' — a final, but unofficial, copy of the report — was distributed to the media in advance of publication and there was always a press conference and briefing session. This, however, was only one part of the public relations effort.

From the inception of the NBPI, great pains were taken to inform journalists of its doings and developing philosophy. The Chairman frequently saw reporters informally. So did the Secretary. There was also an Information (or Public Relations) Officer. The Chairman made many television and other appearances and became a nationally known figure. Others at the NBPI also had numerous speaking engagements.

There were several reasons for this active approach to public relations. The NBPI had only one chance of stating its views — at the time it reported. It could not issue a second report to explain further, or rebut critics.[1] It was essential that even if after the briefing the journalists departed disagreeing, the disagreement was real, and not based on a misunderstanding of the facts or the argument. The NBPI's philosophy was relatively novel. For it to be conveyed accurately (especially in the first year or so), quickly and without misunderstanding, considerable efforts extending beyond reliance on minimal dissemination of background information to journalists, were necessary to ensure a full appreciation of its viewpoint. This was not a case of selling conclusions to the public 'as if they were breakfast foods'[2] but of explaining

1 By the same token, the NBPI was fully aware that once its report had been published, it never had to withdraw anything that it said in reports. It could 'get away' with certain types of conclusion that a permanent body with a remit to report on a situation periodically could not.

2 This phrase, and some of the ideas in this paragraph come from Christopher Foster 'On the Rejection of Roskill' *The Listener*, 1 July 1971.

particularly complex processes of reasoning. Nevertheless whilst the NBPI did not seek to mislead with its reports, its aim was more propagandistic than that of a body which simply wanted to present the strongest possible case for each side of the argument to ensure a full, informed public debate. Its reports and the accompanying public relations efforts were designed to achieve public and official understanding and *acceptance* of its views on specific cases; and also to ensure that the general principles applied in specific cases be transmitted to others to whom they were relevant, although not directly involved in a reference.

The NBPI public relations activities partly explain its initial impact and quick establishment as an authorative, important voice. As explained earlier, the NBPI did no more than grasp an opportunity waiting to be exploited. Its public relations made a significant contribution to its doing so, as did the quality of its reports, but their effects should not be exaggerated.

This contrasts with the more passive approach of some other independent bodies. Christopher Foster[1] has suggested that the shallowness of the Commission Roskill's press briefing was probably one telling factor in the poor public reception to, and ultimate political rejection of, its recommendations. Journalists needed every bit of help in understanding and evaluating a dense and complex argument in that instance, but there were signs, he says, that the Commission thought a more ample explanation of their reasons incompatible with their quasi-judicial status. The comparison with the ordinary judicial process is strained, since there is an almost impregnable respect for judicial decisions, and they involve much less in the way of development of new principles than a planning (or a prices and incomes) decision. Where new principles are involved, and need to be debated publicly and politically before they are accepted, it is better to treat the public and the press rather like a jury to whom a judge has a duty to explain the facts and the implications of the facts, and the implications of the principles until he can rely on them to retire to the jury room well-informed.

3. Follow up

The Declaration of Intent and the White Papers leading to the establishment of the NBPI did not contemplate any follow up to reports. After publication of its first report, the NBPI sought to secure implementation of its recommendations by the Road Haulage Association. The Government, in the shape of the Minister responsible for the Board, Mr. George Brown, stepped in and it was at that point settled that it would be the Government which would be responsible for any pressing of the parties to implement reports. Thereafter the NBPI could only press the Government to press for action.

An important question though is whether the NBPI took action to discover the outcome of its recommendations for long term change. Did it for example attempt to learn from the experience of industries which adopted its recommendations?

1 ibid.

Clippings from newspapers were circulated daily to full-time Board Members and a majority of staff. Those with information about industries which had been reported on were then stored in 'follow up' files kept on each reference. An NBPI staff member attended any follow up meetings held by the DEA or DEP staff, and in this way some limited information was obtained about what had happened in the industry. Only a little of this was circulated to staff or Board Members. The information acquired in the above fashion was apparently mainly of interest to staff and Board Members who had worked on the reference. It should be remembered that owing to the high turnover rate of staff and Board Members many new staff would have found this form of follow up somewhat uninstructive.

The main occasions on which the NBPI learnt from experience occurred when it was given a second opportunity to report on industries. With a few exceptions, such as road haulage and buses, this did not occur until 1969. Some of the results of these reports are described briefly in the final chapter.

Despite the fact that it was not responsible for official follow up of reports, the NBPI, in my opinion, would have been more effective in making sound recommendations for change if it had regularly made tactful follow up enquiries of parties affected by its reports. This need not have been done on a formal basis, nor in cases where its intentions were likely to be misunderstood. As noted elsewhere, before 1969 relatively few staff had a background of executive or managerial experience in industry. This made it all the more important to discover why recommendations were not being put into action, or why progress was slow or difficult.

The TUC survey of trade union attitudes noted earlier produced a suggestion that contact with the Board should continue after the publication of a report, and it was argued that in those industries — particularly in the public sector — where there had been a definite willingness to implement the Board's proposals, some difficulties were encountered which the Board might have helped to resolve.

4. Contact and Consultation with the Parties

During the course of a reference there was considerable contact and consultation between the NBPI and parties directly concerned with the report. The objects of the consultations were to inform the parties of the main issues, to ascertain their viewpoints and to acquire knowledge of the industry. The likely acceptability of recommendations could also be sounded out. It was also desirable to be seen to be holding such meetings.

The parties concerned included trade unions, of which several might have an interest in the same reference, and management and/or employers' associations. Employers' associations possessed varying degrees of authority and knowledge depending on the character of the industry, and the number of firms belonging to the association.

There was a genuine problem often in defining exactly who were the parties. Was it the managment of firms named in a reference, the representatives of employers' associations, or the CBI, and so on? The NBPI put a certain amount of emphasis on consulting those whom it regarded as most likely to have something constructive to say, and it was sometimes criticised because of the selectiveness of its informal consultations.

Meetings were also held with other bodies, for example the Consumers' Council. The most important were 'sponsoring' Government departments responsible for the Government's relations with particular industries. Their advice concerning the likely acceptability of recommendations to the Government was sought. Their advice was not always followed, but it was necessary to weigh it heavily, since they were responsible for recommending to Ministers whether to accept reports as well as for follow up.

Contact with the parties occurred at several stages. Immediately after the arrival of the reference, they were contacted and preliminary meetings arranged at which a general idea was given of the likely issues, submissions invited, and co-operation sought in its enquiries. It was necessary to employ diplomacy and sometimes allay unfounded fears about the nature of the investigations. Board Members often played an important part in obtaining co-operation.

The next round of contacts occurred in the course of enquiries when members of staff working parties met members of the industry. The NBPI's specialists, for example, saw much of their opposite numbers in firms, often maintaining contact with them until completing the report. In its investigations, the Enquiry Team interviewed many persons at different levels of management and employment. Many views – often conflicting – were obtained about an industry, even when the primary purpose of the interviews was to obtain technical information.

There was a system of informal consultations. Thus, on the industrial relations side, where the system was most fully developed, there were relatively few references in which staff or Board Members with a trade union background had no previous contacts at the national level of the trade unions involved. They were used fully, often being consulted informally on several occasions during the progress of a reference about their attitude to the main issues.

The NBPI nearly always, however, conducted formal consultations with the parties. Normally one or more Members of the Board sub-committee appointed to deal with the references and the members of the Staff Working Party attended. The meetings were not open to the public. Normally, separate meetings were held with unions and management, and sometimes with different firms. The NBPI usually presented the conflicting views of the parties to each other. It believed that meetings held in private led to freer and less-inhibited discussions than public hearings.

No special procedures were followed. Legal counsel did not attend, but sometimes firms of accountants or management consultants, which had helped parties prepare their case, appeared. At first the main formal consultations took place at an early stage; after 1966 they occurred towards the end when the NBPI felt in a better position to discuss the reference knowledgeably. At this or a later stage and more so in the second than the first half of the NBPI's life, the parties were often shown the factual parts of draft reports, partly as a precaution against error. Alternative possible conclusions were sounded out orally, although this was apparently not always done in early days. As a rule at the formal consultation stage the parties were not told which of the alternative conclusions were likely.

Further informal consultations often occurred as new points and developments arose towards the end of a reference and the Chairman himself would often see some key representatives and other contacts at a late stage. In some cases he showed parties, on the side, at his office, a complete draft report including provisional conclusions. Only occasionally did these consultations at a late stage lead to substantive changes in reports. The NBPI thus normally did not show the full draft of reports to the parties, and sometimes, especially in early days, it showed them nothing in writing.

The NBPI's system of informal contacts with the parties allowed it to see much of representatives and other members of the industry under reference than would have been possible with procedures similar to those of, say, NIC. Discovering the acceptability of recommendations and the likely reactions of parties (which is not exactly the same thing as holding consultations insofar as the latter implies a two way exchange) was regarded as of really great importance and nothing in this account should detract from the great pains normally taken to find out the views of the parties. However, there were certain weaknesses as a result mainly of a wish not to rely much on formal consultations or on showing reports to the parties and the NBPI attracted quite strong criticism concerning its consultations with parties at the report-drafting stage. For example, the otherwise remarkably favourable TUC survey of trade union opinion disclosed that a number of unions regarded the NBPI's consultations with them as falling well short of ideal. Similar criticisms were made by the employers side and the CBI on a number of occasions.

The NBPI was unwilling to show full draft reports to the parties and give them a few days in which to comment. This was partly because there was little time in which to report. Some reports were completed at the very last moment, although this is something that would have been better avoided anyway. The NBPI's fears of the consequences of showing reports to the parties outweighed its wishes to receive the benefits of their considered comments, which it thought could anyway be reasonably well obtained in its formal consultations. The consequences it feared were possible leakages to the stock market, action by the parties to pre-empt recommendations, and, above all, loss of public impact, essential for the success of the Board's wider strategy. To show reports to the parties was to invite carefully selected leakages to the Press in advance of the publication of reports. It also gave parties a chance to prepare rebuttals. Once a draft report criticising an important industry for its failure to save costs was received by it well in advance of publication. On the day of publication it issued a lengthy rebuttal which stole the NBPI's headlines.

This preference left the NBPI open to a number of damaging, even if sometimes unfounded, accusations of unsatisfactory consultations. Moreover, misunderstandings were possible at purely oral proceedings. Even when parties were shown factual parts of reports, their crucial significance for the conclusions were unlikely always to have been made perfectly clear.

Also the NBPI's fallibility, especially when reporting at speed, made it even more important to consult the parties adequately at all stages, especially the last stages. Failure to do so was to the likely detriment of the educational effect on parties.

In the author's view, the NBPI could have been more open in its consultations at the drafting stage. It was perhaps necessary that it should control who saw draft reports, but one has the impression that it was partly a matter of working style, rather than necessity, that led it to keep the parties so much in the dark about its reports.[1]

5. Formal Procedures

A distinctive feature of the NBPI's methods was its eschewal of formal public inquiry procedures. Would it have been prefereable for the Board to have followed more formalised procedures? It is necessary to distinguish between several types of procedures although combinations of the types below are possible.

First, there might have been procedures broadly similar to those of the Restrictive Practices Court or the Roskill Commission. An investigatory body would have presented a case for or against the parties to an independent court presided over by a lawyer or judge, and consisting of lay person including some experts. There would have been written and oral evidence, formal legal proceedings, cross examination and legal counsel. Legal procedures may be unexceptionable in the Restrictive Practices Court when the existence or non-existence of specified, clearly identifiable practices has to be determined; when they are presumed to be against the public interest unless the contrary can be positively established; and where there is no pressing urgency about the decision.[2] Other things being equal, legal procedures seem at present to enjoy greater public support, and thus help to make decisions more acceptable.

However, they would have created problems with the sort of questions investigated by the NBPI. A parade of expert witnesses on both sides might have been played off. NBPI staff could have spent considerable time in court being examined and cross-examined by legal counsel.[3] Even the most streamlined proceedings would have been time-consuming and costly. Enquiries as to whether 2d or 3d was an appropriate price increase would have been arduous

---

1 The Commission on Industrial Relations which has taken over the NBPI's system of extensive informal consultations with the parties said its 'whole approach and working methods are directed' to securing recommendations likely to be acceptable to the parties (*First General Report*, p. 13) and it shows draft reports to parties as a matter of course. Its task is of course different from that of the NBPI. The Monopolies Commission goes to greater pains at the formal consultation stage than the Board, without actually revealing its conclusions.

2 The Restrictive Practices Court has admittedly completed its work at exceptional speed.

3 This admittedly does not happen to staff of the Official Registrar of Restrictive Trade Agreements.

Contentions as to the exact scope for cost-saving, the validity of financial forecasts, the costs and benefits of productivity agreements, the likely effects of wage increases on recruitment to a particular industry, the repercussions of wage restructuring decisions outside the industry, could have occupied an army of counsel, witnesses and judges for months – with little or no gain in the quality of decisions.

Legal procedures on economic matters not requiring yes/no decisions also tend to suffer from the rather indeterminate or imprecise nature of much of the evidence e.g. opinions of economists on consequences of possible courses of action. This at any rate has been the experience of the Australian Commonwealth Arbitration Commission which holds legal hearings on wage matters. Judgements in such matters as those that come before Courts of Inquiry, for example, often are of an intuitive character, not arriving at what is 'right or wrong' but compromising between several views and conflicting desiderata.

Second, even without legal procedures, would it have been preferable to have separated the fact-finding from the decision-making body, to have separated 'prosecution' from 'judge',[1] and at the same time to have held public hearings?

Public hearings would have brought out openly the evidence on which recommendations were based. It would, however, have been difficult to have communicated some findings publicly (commercial secrets, private views of contending parties, statements and facts likely to worsen delicate industrial relations situations) and discussions might often have been less frank than in private. Separation of fact-finding from policy making could have led to research that was misdirected and wasted in anticipation of hypothetical questions of the decision making body; the possibilities for flexible redirection of investigations during the course of a reference would have been reduced. It seems preferable to keep fact-finding and recommending functions together when complex decisions arise as there is inevitably a loss of information in the transmission of findings from one body to another. The case for a more rigorous separation of fact-finding from policy making rests on the fallacy that a Board cannot be trusted to reach fair decisions because of its involvement in the fact-finding. It may be the opposite case in fact. Furthermore, the creative and imaginative approach to problems that characterised the Board and partly arose because of integrated fact-finding and policy making would have disappeared. It would also have been difficult for the decision making body to have urged greater efficiency on the parties and investigators might have thought this outside their brief. The procedures would have been more accusatory, more prolonged and less constructive.

1 It is a misnomer to call the NBPI a prosecutor. Also, acceptance of its recommendations depended on the Government, and some of the blame heaped on its procedures may have been due to poor consultative procedures at this level after the issue of reports. In practice however most short term recommendations were accepted quickly by the Government and this increased the responsibility of the NBPI to act judicially.

7. Investigations

1. Factors Determining the Nature and Depth of Enquiries

The nature and depth of NBPI investigations were mainly determined by the following 9 factors:

1. The White Paper criteria, and the terms of reference of the subject referred for investigation.

2. NBPI Policy. The paramount factor, in the early years at any rate, determining the nature and direction of investigations in the field of management efficiency and industrial relations structures was the NBPI's preconceived policy objectives. It was decided at an early stage that the NBPI was not engaged in research. The policies which it propagated consciously determined the slant of what was looked for. This is not to deny that the NBPI often modified a broad position under the influence of information it collected or that it failed to appreciate that policies had to be adapted to the peculiar character of each industry. Over the course of time the approach became progressively more empirical, both causing and reflecting an increasingly empirical policy on pay references.

The first report on *Pay and Conditions of Service of Engineering Workers* (49) is an example of preconceived policies dominating the enquiries. As this report was an important one, the sources of evidence for the much-publicised main finding of widespread anomalies in pay structures may be considered in detail simultaneously.

Case studies were undertaken in 47 firms. The pre-determined approach, inter alia, was to find examples of anomalies in wage structures, since it was believed that they existed in the industry and should be a major theme of the report. In 38 firms investigators found an overlap in pay for a standard week between skilled time-workers and semi-skilled piece-workers; in 18 firms semi-skilled piece-workers or workers paid by various systems of payment by results were earning more than the highest paid skilled time workers and in three of these 18 firms this applied to more than half of the semi-skilled piece-workers. According to the report 'in two firms we found an even worse anomaly — some semi-skilled workers on payment by results schemes earning even more than any skilled workers on payment by results. Finally in two firms we found that some unskilled payments by results workers were earning more than the highest paid skilled time-workers. These anomalies in the pay of the skilled and the unskilled are once again a source of tension and therefore of inflationary pressure.'[1]

After this evidence was collected and analysed, it was grasped for the first time that this was not necessarily evidence of an anomalous situation (though eventually the report asserted it was). The figures related to weekly earnings. Semi-skilled workers might have received more than skilled workers because they worked longer. Again, the figures did not relate to comparable groups of workers. The highly-paid semi-skilled workers were on incentive pay schemes of one sort or another; the less highly paid skilled workers were paid according to the numbers of hours worked. The 'reverse' differential may have been attributable to no more than the differential payment which those who work on payment by results schemes normally receive over those doing similar work on a payment according to time worked system.

The failure of the case studies to disclose convincing anomalies was not necessarily because they did not exist but may have been because they were not looked for. At an advanced stage of the reference examples were obtained from an unnamed source of actual average hourly earnings in normal working time for semi-skilled and skilled workers in 3 plants, showing the semi-skilled workers to be receiving more than the skilled workers. The three examples were set out in such a way that they were the centrepiece of the analysis. To give these examples their due, they look as if they might be real anomalies. But equally they might have had a good explanation, as is noted in the report rather much in passing. In certain cases, the NBPI notes, technological changes can lead to a position where, because of the nature of the work, semi-skilled production workers should be paid more than skilled men. The changing job content may require that pay be enhanced to compensate for the monotony of certain types of semi-skilled work and that this compensation might be such as properly to exceed that paid for skills. The incentive effects of payment by results might be such that the earnings of semi-skilled grades reflect much greater effort. Nevertheless the reversal of the expected differentials in these three examples 'suggests to us that at least there is a strong *prima facie* case for investigating the situation, and indeed that there are good grounds for arguing that internal wage structures are such that in many cases they need a complete overhaul.'[2] The obvious response to this is to ask why the NBPI did not itself probe deeper to establish whether the 3 examples quoted were genuine anomalies or not. It is clear that wherever the new evidence came from, it was still not conclusive. Nevertheless the NBPI still believed that the industry was rife with anomalous pay structures and gave the evidence full prominence, calculating, no doubt correctly, that it would be persuasive to readers. Whilst reverse differentials might be rationally explicable, 'these decisions should be taken after investigation and due consideration by all the parties concerned.'[3] 'We believe that there is a

1 Para. 32.

2 Para. 34.

3 Para. 34.

strong possibility that all too often the reversed differentials are not the result of considered and agreed policy but of a haphazard development arising from *ad hoc* decisions.'[1] (This, incidentally, is an example of an ex-cathedra statement of the kind referred to in the previous chapter.)

This example is interesting because there is a widely held belief in many different quarters that the pay structure of the engineering industry is, in fact, rife with anomalies. Having to some extent failed in the task of providing supporting evidence for this view, the NBPI was not deterred from pressing on to a conclusion which may well have been true.

This interesting example could give the wrong impression about investigations. It would be an exaggeration to think of preconceived policy objectives taking such a strong hold of enquiries in more than a minority of cases.

This episode may be used to illustrate one further point. Often the problem with investigations is that it does not become clear what evidence is or would be crucial until they are complete. In this instance, of course, it should have been clear in advance what kind of information to seek. In many other instances however, very little information was known in advance about the circumstances of an industry and it was sometimes only towards the end of a reference that the real issues came into sight, and those responsible for the inquiries could only pray that the information already collected would turn out to relate to the real issue.

3. Time and type of reference. The type of reference usually determined the time spent on it. References could very roughly be classified as follows:
(a) Particular pay settlements or price increases. These usually had to be reported on within 3 months. Within this period it was possible to conduct earnings surveys, if essential, and some industrial relations and other case studies. Short studies of managerial efficiency and field studies of one or two selected subjects were usually possible. But the time available for commissioning, briefing, and then analysing reports of outside case workers was short. Analytical work was of course severely hampered in a 3 months reference.
(b) Studies of pay and conditions without regard to a particular settlement; studies of costs and charges; and nationalised industry efficiency audits. These most often took 5–6 months, and required study in some depth.
(c) General Study reports. These required a broader, sometimes more analytical, type of study covering more than one industry. They usually lasted more than 6 months. They are described in Chapter 10.
(d) Standing references. Time was not a very serious problem as these were continuously under review. They are described in Chapter 10. It need only be observed here that the NBPI sought in these references to achieve a very high standard of enquiry e.g. in the references on the remuneration of solicitors and on the pay of the Armed Forces, and as will be explained would have done so in the standing reference on the pay of university teachers had it continued in existence and the reference not been withdrawn.

[1] ibid.

4. Nature and size of industry and complexity of its industrial relations system. The studies of the engineering and construction industries were different from those of the *London Brick Company* (49, 150) for example, because in the latter case it was feasible to study a large proportion of the plants in the firm. In the former there was no hope of examining a statistically significant sample which would permit generalisations about the whole industry.

5. Existing Knowledge. To continue with the bricks, construction and engineering examples, much was known in advance about engineering and construction from published research, official statistics, and previous official enquiries. Little was known of industrial relations in the London Brick Company. A major part of many investigations, especially industry-study references, was to collect basic information about the structure and functioning of the industry's industrial relations system. A few examples of many reports on industrial relations, for example, which provide virtually the first complete picture of an industry include reports on the clothing manufacturing, laundry and dry cleaning, contract cleaning, pottery, brick, and exhibition contracting industries and on the Industrial Civil Service, and the National Health Service. These constitute an invaluable inventory of a large part of the British system of industrial relations.

6. Whether NBPI had previously reported. Typically second reports were done in more detail. Otherwise it was believed that they would have little to contribute that had not already been said.

7. Period of NBPI's Lifetime. The thoroughness and depth of studies progressively increased over the lifetime of the NBPI, reaching a peak in 1970–71, increasing in roughly inverse proportion to the NBPI's apparent influence. The NBPI's seemingly most influential reports were those made at the start, although based on a minimum of special research.

In early days the NBPI did not investigate managerial efficiency, wages structures or industrial relations systems in detail. It tried to identify major problem areas, and suggest broad solutions by collecting enough evidence to support its view. Thus if it believed that an industry had an inequitable wages structure, it might then point out little more than, say, that job evaluation was the answer. It was thought inadvisable to tell an industry in detail how to improve, as the NBPI did not have the detailed knowledge necessary and could make mistakes. There remained however ample scope for pointing out in general terms the kind of new management and industrial techniques which should be applied. Whatever the merits of this, the NBPI's approach had been transformed by 1970. Prescriptions became more detailed. Thus, whereas in an early reference such as *Portland Cement Prices* (38), it was merely recommended that the industry should use operational research to deal with certain specified types of cost and price problems, in later references such as *Bricks* (150) the NBPI actually constructed the basic models which it believed the London Brick Company should use.

8. Early investigations were strongly industrial relations oriented. They did not totally ignore the managerial dimension, but typically they identified

in vacuo what was wrong with, say, the wage structure or the collective bargaining system and then advocated reform without full consideration of its implications for management. The first report on Industrial Civil Servants, described in the next chapter on incomes, is a classical example.

There was a slow period of transition over three to four years towards an appreciation of the need to go beyond this. This transition was perhaps most influenced by the sequence of references concerning busmen. The NBPI's early recommendations on one-man busing were bearing little fruit and it was necessary on each return reference to say more than previously about possible methods of implementation. In these references the NBPI gradually went beyond rather vague textbook style pronouncements on necessary managerial action to a spelling out of action which, in the light of actual investigation of management, seemed appropriate in the circumstances. It was perhaps by early 1969 that this approach had gained ascendancy in reports. It was only with the establishment of a management operations branch in June 1969 that the NBPI really had the tools to do the job. Before then it lacked staff with senior executive experience in industry, and it made relatively poor use of consultants on industrial relations matters. This point is taken up in the chapter on efficiency.

9. The NBPI's view, reflected in its refusal to split into a Prices and an Incomes Division, that there was a need to deal with the whole spectrum of related issues of prices, costs, productivity and incomes, whether in references concerning incomes or prices. This view followed from the NBPI's policy objectives. In practice there were many references where all these issues were visibly interrelated.

There were a number of references in which an attempt was made to reach across the whole spectrum, no matter how thinly, but equally in a large number of cases the NBPI did not, in practice, successfully attain its ideal. Thus there were many wages references in which management efficiency studies could have been done but were not. The efficiency of the clothing manufacturing industry, referred to in the Fourth General Report as an industry in which 'ample scope for using higher efficiency to make higher pay possible' existed, was only investigated by industrial relations case study workers and in general study references only a little use was made of management or economics specialists for enquiries.[1] On the prices side, to take examples from different periods, neither the report on *Brewing* (13) nor on *Steel Prices* (111), although the first was a costs and prices reference and the second a prices reference, made adequate investigations into labour costs and the basis for setting pay, nor produced a comprehensive set of recommendations. The NBPI's second report on *Beer Prices* (136) which took 7 months and included a major study of the financial position of the industry, also gave almost no attention to these matters, and, in addition, was thin on the subject of managerial efficiency. In general, prices references tended to be seen as raising different issues from wages references.

---

1 Some useful general information was obtained from consultants, however, in general study references.

If a full inter-disciplinary view of an industry was not always achieved, the NBPI was rather more successful in striving to consider particular issues in wage and price references against the background of an industry's overall technical, market or financial position. The group of 3 references on low pay reported on in 1971 are a good example. Low pay was found to exist in three not seemingly different industries — laundries and dry cleaning, the NHS, and contract cleaning. But in each case the 'solution' was different. Contract cleaning was an expanding industry in which productivity was reasonably satisfactory. This was a much more appropriate industry in which to attempt to raise pay, on low pay grounds, than in laundries which faced a situation of declining demand, where attempts to improve the plight of the low paid were likely to generate unemployment. In the National Health Service, the low pay problem had to be seen against the background of the enormous possibilities which the NBPI considered to exist for a general increase in the level of productivity.

2. Existing Sources of Information

Before making enquiries of its own the NBPI explored the possibilities of using alternative sources of information.

Official or other Published Statistics:

(a) *Earnings:* The Ministry of Labour's (later DEP's) published earnings statistics were usually inadequate for the NBPI's purposes. They covered relatively broad industrial groups and geographical areas whereas the NBPI usually wanted to know earnings in sub-industries or sub-regions. With certain exceptions, published figures did not show earnings by occupational groups or levels of skill (until the New Earnings Survey of September 1968). Only averages, not ranges, of earnings were published, although ranges are necessary to help determine the incidence of low pay and the nature of wage structures. The published figures also did not show the main components of earnings, such as basic rates of pay, payment by results, shift work bonuses, commissions and other forms of bonus and overtime; nor did they reveal the relationship between earnings and hours worked. As no-one else, e.g. employers' associations or trade unions, normally collected this data, the NBPI very often encountered industries in which practically the only knowledge available was of basic rates of pay; this was usually inadequate to assess the validity of wage and salary claims and it was often considered essential to undertake special earnings surveys.

(b) *Financial:* Published company reports are usually limited to the minimum financial information required by law; and businesses may also be so divided up internally that these accounts give only a part of the picture. Official financial, economic or production statistics alone were rarely sufficiently detailed to be of great use in exploring the kind of issues raised by references.

3. Reliance on the Parties for Information

Trade associations could rarely supply sufficient financial data; and to ask firms to submit financial information was usually impracticable because data was needed on a standardised basis; nor could they judge what was relevant. Reliance was occasionally placed on the parties to make their own financial case usually without problems. However, the Brewers' Society submitted in 1969 as justification for a price increase an elaborate cost index which in essence reflected changes in the price per unit of individual inputs such as labour and materials, between 1964 and 1969; but it took no account of the changed composition of inputs, nor of changes in the volume of production affecting unit costs of output. The NBPI therefore launched, at a late stage, a programme of special investigations, which disclosed amongst other things that inputs whose price had risen most over the period were used relatively less than before, whilst inputs whose price had risen least were used more. Whereas the Brewers Society index showed a rise of 25 per cent between 1964 and 1969, most of which occurred after 1966, the NBPI's investigations showed a rise of less than 5 per cent between 1966 and 1969.[1]

Consultations with leading representatives of industries were rarely a sufficient source of information. National trade union officials, sometimes responsible for several industries besides the one under investigation, were often poorly informed about workplace conditions in different parts and regions of the industry. Representatives of employers' associations were not necessarily closely acquainted with conditions throughout the industry but only in their own firms. Even top management in individual firms was sometimes uninformed about shop floor conditions because of poor management information systems and sometimes apparently because lower level management did not communicate all the information it should have to the top. Nor could management be expected to provide the NBPI with a balanced picture of shop floor conditions if this reflected their own failings or was against the interests of the firm in the reference. It was the least efficient firms which were least able to supply correct information.

There were many cases of the parties — especially industry-wide associations — unintentionally supplying mistaken information to the NBPI. This may be demonstrated by three examples from the Construction Industry references. In their evidence to the Board, Local Authorities attributed their difficulties in recruiting and retaining building maintenance workers to the fact that their earnings compared unfavourably with those of maintenance workers in the private sector. The NBPI's earnings survey showed this to be untrue. The National Federation of Building Trades Employers told the NBPI that the category of 'building craftsmen's mate' did not exist in the industry. The NBPI's survey showed that there were 30,000 craftsmen's mates. The Federation of Civil Engineering Craftsmen described civil engineering as a 'traditional Payment by Results industry'. The NBPI's survey showed that only about half the industry's manual staff were paid by results. There was

1 For more details, see *Beer Prices* (136), paras. 21–36.

a similar occurrence in the clothing manufacturing reference when the parties informed the NBPI that payment by results systems were the main wage systems employed in the industry. The NBPI's survey disclosed that this was not correct and also showed there to be far more part-timers in the industry than was believed. Finally, the National Union of Railwaymen frequently referred to the plight of a large number of their workers whose basic pay was very low, of the order of £10 a week, and whose weekly earnings were little better. Their evident concern was sympathetically endorsed by British Rail. The NBPI conducted a mini-earnings survey which failed to uncover any workers of this type. It asked the NUR to produce a group of men with these low earnings. The NUR was not heard from again.

Most often, however, the parties simply did not know the facts. Few employers' associations — often for their own good reasons — collect information about industry-wide matters — the incidence of low pay, earnings, costs, profits, prices, the effects of industry wage agreements on actual earnings, the best management or industrial relations techniques, the relationship of movements in prices recommended on an industry-wide basis to movements in costs and so on.

Poor information not only impeded the making of decisions about particular cases of wage and price increase, but also clearly impeded sound decision making by management in individual enterprises. This theme is taken up in the chapter on management efficiency.

4. Some Instruments of Enquiry: Case Studies, the Enquiry Team, Statistical Surveys

The NBPI considered it vital for reports to be based on a close knowledge of an industry's industrial relations. Helpful information was usually obtained at informal meetings with employers and trade union officials but was not normally regarded as a substitute for the first hand knowledge of an industry's industrial relations, the foundation on which reports were built. To obtain this it was considered necessary to go to the workplace itself. Some conclusions from the Report of the Royal Commission on Trade Unions and Employers' Associations suggest why it was not enough to confine investigations to examination, at national level, of the working or apparent working of industry-wide collective agreements:

'Britain has two systems of industrial relations. One is the formal system embodied in the official institutions. The other is the informal system created by the actual behaviour of trade unions and employers' associations, of managers, shop stewards and workers.

The keystone of the formal system is the industry-wide collective agreement, in which are supposed to be settled pay, hours of work and other conditions of employment appropriate to regulation by agreement.

The informal system is often at odds with the formal system. Actual earnings have moved far apart from the rates laid down in industry-wide agreements; the ... major elements in the gap ... are all governed by decisions within the factory ... construction site or office ... At the same time, disputes procedures laid down in industry-wide agreements have been subjected to strain by the transfer of authority to the factory and workshop.

The bargaining which takes place within factories is largely outside the control of employers' associations and trade unions. It usually takes place piecemeal and results in competitive sectional wage adjustments and chaotic pay structures. Unwritten understandings and "custom and practice" predominate.'[1]

It is generally accepted that this analysis is true of at least a significant part of the British industrial relations system.

Case Studies: As is apparent from Appendix H, the NBPI conducted numerous case studies and other on-the-spot investigations of industrial relations at the workplace. Case studies, indeed, were of course impossible. Its own advi enquiry methods such as surveys, were of course impossible. Its own advisers undertook some studies themselves. In addition, over 225 specialists in indus trial relations, mainly academics, were commissioned to do others. Their dispersion ensured a wide regional coverage. The absence of tight control was one factor explaining the variation in the quality, technique, depth and approach of studies. The Enquiry Team (see below) also were used for less complex and specialised industrial relations enquiries, and they worked in conjunction with industrial relations advisers in some other references such as *Job Evaluation* (83), *Smithfield Market* (126) and the Low Pay reports on the *National Health Service* (166), *Laundries and Dry Cleaning* (167) and *Contract Cleaning* (168).

Case study workers received a written brief and normally attended a briefing session at the NBPI. The form of the written brief varied, but usually consisted of a list of questions or a check list of topics to be covered. In *Payment by Results* (65), for example, case workers were given a fairly free hand in the sort of information collected because of the wide range of firms and types of scheme. There was, however, a check list of basic information required, and an account of the background to the reference. With *Salary Structures* (132) little previous research had been done on the subject and case study workers had to feel their way. A loosely structured brief was provided initially but supplemented by a meeting held after case study workers had gained their first impressions. An example of a brief is given in Appendix

Case study workers often spent up to ten to fourteen days or more studying industrial relations in depth at one or a few plants. They normally approached several levels of the organisation, especially the shop floor, and if possible more than one person at the same level of the hierarchy. On the shop floor, the persons interviewed typically were the production managers, supervisors or personnel officers, shop stewards, convenors, local union officials and some workers. Usually co-operation was good. In some cases management refused to allow such interviews. Where this happened but the union co-operated, the NBPI sometimes went out of its way to interview workers in their homes. At other times unions did not co-operate.

1 Rogal Commission on Trade Unions and Employers Associations 1965—68 : *Report* (HMSO, 1968), paras. 1007—1010.

Case study investigations tended to cover the following areas:

(a) The industrial relations system, especially at establishment level. This included trade union organisation, inter-union problems, arrangements for collective bargaining and dispute settlement at plant level, and other aspects of management-worker relations, including personnel management policies.

(b) The efficiency of labour utilisation and the degree of managerial control of overtime and labour costs; the use of management techniques.

(c) Wages. The role of local labour market factors, how payment by results and other wage systems worked, what inequities were perceived by workers, the effects of previous wage settlements, especially productivity agreements, the relationship of local and national wages.

(d) The nature and extent of labour 'restrictive' or 'protective' practices. Some typical enquiries concerned whether workers of one type or grade performed work normally done by others of a different type or grade; whether jobs were overmanned; whether there were occupation bars to some activities. This was a difficult area to investigate.

Further details of the subjects covered in investigations are given in Appendices G and H.

In selecting establishments for study, some assistance was obtained from trade unions and employers. In this way, it was often possible to locate highly efficient plants with techniques worth publicising, and highly inefficient ones for examples of what not to do. The NBPI always attempted to avoid over-reliance on these sources, however, and to study a selection of plants of its own choice.

A basic methodological issue about all case studies is whether the choice is consciously or subconsciously biased to establishments most likely to demonstrate the truth of the chooser's hypothesis. Certain precautions were taken against this, for example, a wide dispersion of studies and a selection of large and small plants, but methods of random choice were not used to select what it would study. To this extent, case studies did not form a basis from which it was possible to make scientifically established generalisations.

The exact number of case studies varied. Sometimes if an industry with few firms was under investigation, all could be studied. At the other extreme, the general study reference related to all sectors of the economy. When there was sufficient time, the studies could be monitored as they progressed; if they all pointed in the same direction, it was unnecessary to do more. Another factor was homogeneity. Although there are thousands of bank branches, it seemed safe to generalise from studies of a few (*Hours of Work and Overtime in London Clearing Banks* (143).

The problem of making case studies of representative sites in large heterogeneous industries was more serious. Three reports dealt with the construction industries, which employ 1,800,000 workers in 81,000 firms.[1] In the civil engineering part, industrial relations case studies were made on 12 sites.

1 *Pay and Conditions in the Civil Engineering Industry* (91); *Pay and Conditions in the Building Industry* (92); *Pay and Conditions in the Construction Industry other than Building and Civil Engineering* (93).

Management consultants did efficiency studies of 5 of the same 12 sites.
In the building industry management consultants made efficiency studies of
20 of the 26 sites covered by IR case workers. The sites covered a variety
of conditions and there was no evidence that there was anything unrepresentative about the sites studied, or that they were biased towards the inefficient
The consultants produced a study – set out in detail in the report – showing
apparently wide variation in labour efficiency on the 20 building sites, mainly
indicated by their estimates of the amount of productive working time as a pro
portion of total working time (and also by the rate of working, which showed
less variation). If the performance of the average site could have been brough
up to that of the best site, itself capable of great improvement, the gain in
labour efficiency would have been of the order of 20 per cent. The NBPI
concluded that even on a conservative view it should have been practicable
to raise labour efficiency by 10 per cent and more on many sites. This became
a major conclusion. The consultants had previous experience of the industry
and said their conclusions were consistent with their previous experience.
A further 5 cases done by other consultants produced similar results. A third
firm using the same method undertook 5 studies in civil engineering – these
suggested that an average increase of between an eighth and a fifth in
efficiency could be achieved. This sample was extremely small for such swee
ing conclusions. On the other hand, its evidence was difficult to ignore.

The function of case studies was not (or should not have been) to prove
conclusively the existence of a particular state of affairs throughout an industry. The NBPI used their results, however, to draw such conclusions. The
Engineering and Construction Industry references are examples. They were
also used to illustrate generalisations, presumably based on other evidence.

In defence of the habit of generalising, it can be said that the NBPI conducted over 600 case studies over its lifetime. These were done, as mentioned
by over 225 different outsiders, whose findings were remarkably consistent
despite variations in other respects. As a result, an appreciation of the industrial relations problems in other industries was in the background of each
reference. If a certain problem was observed in a study of a number of plants
in an industry then the Board, having encountered the same situation in a
number of industries earlier, felt more easily able to draw conclusions about
the industry under reference. An example concerned payment by results system
Once the NBPI had investigated their working in a general study report, it
believed it was able to spot their shortcomings speedily in specific industries,
such as clothing manufacturing.

Use of the Enquiry Team: At first the Board drew mainly upon outside resource
to conduct special enquiries, but an innovation occurred in October 1966, when
it established its own Enquiry Team. This was used for obtaining information
at first hand and for making detailed study of operations at source, at first
mainly in industrial relations, and later more on the management side.

The team totalled about 30 members by 1970. It was headed by a Principal
or equivalent. In Civil Service terms the rank of other members was Senior
or Higher Executive Officer, (i.e. they were not of a level equivalent to

management consultants, or industrial relations advisers). There was also some recruitment at a junior level of graduates direct from University studies.

A minority of its members had a background as specialists with expertise in organisation and methods, work study and other areas of management services. The background of the majority, however, was 'generalist', but with experience of fact-finding and sifting in central or local government or business. Thus almost one-half of the team had previously worked in the Board of Customs and Excise interviewing in industry and commerce and inspecting production or accounting records. The majority of members could be regarded as 'specialists in interviewing and fact-finding'.

An important element in the work of the Enquiry Team was its accumulation of experience derived from working on about two-thirds of the Board's references and the planned development of the ability of various of its generalist members to handle on their own more specialised investigations. The team, however, mainly had a support role in specialist enquiries. Guidance from NBPI specialists also contributed to its development of an enquiry methodology, and to its ability to formulate guidelines for the examination of management problems. From the middle of 1969 it was attached to the Management Operations Branch.

Team members worked at a rapid tempo and with a high sense of team spirit. They had to be prepared to be mobile at short notice or to work inconvenient hours. During the course of the duties, team members went underground in coal mines and visited rock stationed lighthouses and in studying the jobs of members of the Armed Forces they lived and worked aboard submarines and naval ships while they were on passage and they travelled in tanks on Army exercises.

Use was made of the Enquiry Team for conducting interviews, case studies, collecting data and obtaining general information from business establishments. Other tasks included obtaining answers to questionnaires where postal methods were unsuitable, and desk-work fact-finding of a miscellaneous nature, but it was adaptable for the widest variety of tasks.

Tasks ranged from attitude survey interviews of a sample of wives of members of the Armed Forces to visits to twenty-three potteries to find out about payment systems and agreements, labour turnover and absenteeism, training, industrial relations and efficiency. In the reference on *Pay and Conditions of Smithfield Market Workers* (126), the team undertook a series of enquiries in and around the market. Information on earnings, hours of work and conditions of drivers and porters was sought from firms of carriers; more circumspect enquiries were needed to ascertain the probable earnings of self-employed porters which they were themselves reluctant to divulge. Six case studies of wholesalers operating in the market were undertaken lasting 2 to 5 days. Enquiries were conducted at irregular hours including a twelve hour session started on Sunday evening.

There was a wide variation in the numbers of visits made and cases chosen for study depending on the circumstances of the reference. 350 visits were made in the Beer Prices reference; in Report 87 on *Taxi Fares*, 280 or so cab drivers were interviewed; in *Solicitors* (54) 123 firms were visited and interviews were held lasting from between two hours to all day. In the job evaluation reference, about one hundred firms with job evaluation schemes were interviewed. The length and depth of studies in that reference varied widely, e.g. interviews generally lasted from 2–6 hours but there were other cases studied in greater depth which involved visits to a factory or establishment lasting up to three weeks. At the other extreme, sometimes only a handful of short visits were made. In the reference on Manufacturers' Prices of Toilet Preparations, six visits to manufacturers lasting up to half a day each were made. In the Bristol Docks Staff Pay reference, where one employer was involved, only one member of the team conducted the enquiry which required five days' fieldwork. Further details are given in Appendix I which attests to the range, volume, and usefulness of the Enquiry Team's work.

Whilst nothing here is intended to detract from the Team's efforts and contribution to the work of the NBPI, one issue ought not to be passed over. There seems to be a general tendency in the British Government to overextend the use of Executive Officer ranks in assessing efficiency. E.L. Normanton in his comparative analysis of efficiency auditing in government in several countries noted that the British Exchequer and Audit Department relied almost exclusively upon Executive Class civil servants recruited directly from school and, after comparing their qualifications with the much higher ones required for similar work in the USA, France and Germany, concluded that while they did excellent work in detecting irregularities and extravagance they appeared to have neither the skills nor sufficient status within the Civil Service to attempt efficiency auditing.[1] A fortiori, one would expect that in moving outside the public sector, as the NBPI did, a higher level of personnel would be involved. One of the Enquiry Team's main tasks was the collection of factual information and answers to set questions, but in practice it often became fairly heavily involved in the assessment of management and industrial relations. Although receiving specialist guidance, it seemed in fact at times to be used for tasks beyond its competence, usually in default of the availability of other investigatory resources. The youth of some of its members also counted against it in confronting experienced management. What was really required for the higher level tasks was a team consisting of junior management consultants with some industrial experience, supported by the Enquiry Team.

Statistical Surveys: In the four and a half years from October 1966 the NBPI conducted some 150 statistical surveys for about half the 145 reports issued in that time, an average of two per report for which such surveys were considered necessary. Best known are the NBPI's ad hoc earnings surveys which obtained information about the pay of nearly 300,000 workers drawn from samples of nearly six million workers. Typically the NBPI surveys sought details of hours of work and earnings for a sample week for a sample of workers classified by skill and occupation. The detailed composition of earnings such as according to whether overtime, payment by results, shift pay,

1 E.L. Normanton, *The Accountability and Audit of Governments* (Manchester University Press, 1966).

bonuses etc. was sought. Ranges as well as averages of earnings were calculated. The size and type of undertakings and region was often taken into account. These surveys of earnings were generally coupled with questionnaires to firms asking about the manpower structure, conditions of service, recruitment and labour market problems, seasonality of earnings, timing of wage increases or other related factors. Much cross-tabular analysis was possible, only some of which could be shown in appendices or supplements e.g. analyses of hours and details of earnings could be produced by sector, agreement, grade, occupation, age, region, full and part-time, etc. with some degree of cross analysis. Other statistical surveys analysed prices, costs, margins, charges for services, professional fees and costs, the characteristics and attitudes of workers and the views of management as well as various aspects of the subject covered by the general study references. Appendix K summarises the NBPI's surveys.

An outstanding feature was the speed at which all surveys were completed. Many of the smaller surveys were completed for three-month references in about six weeks from the first drafting of the questionnaire to the production of tabulations and most were completed in under four months though a few took much longer.

To speed up enquiries the pilot stage of postal surveys was eliminated. Instead there was informal testing by interview coupled with continuous revision. Successive drafts were discussed with a series of trade associations, large and small firms and each would be asked to comment question by question on the latest draft available without providing answers to them. The whole process was often completed in under 2 weeks.

Non-piloting actually had advantages. Numerous amendments could be tested. Close questioning at an interview produces better comments and suggestions than written requests. Informal testing makes it easier to adapt the questionnaire for ease of completion. It was less wasteful than a pilot survey.

Surveys were based on scientifically reliable samples and were generally representative of the firms and industries covered. The high scientific standards were accompanied by average survey response rates of around 70 per cent, a high figure for surveys.[1]

The NBPI pioneered the regular conduct of detailed earnings surveys on an industry-wide basis in Great Britain. The New Earnings Survey, an important step forward in the collection of earnings data in Great Britain introduced in September 1968, was in fact suggested by the NBPI and uses the same methods as the NBPI used in its surveys for a small sample of employees throughout industry.

In general the Board's many pioneering surveys, besides being a powerful, wide-ranging instrument of enquiry, uncovered a vast amount of information,

1 For further technical information about the conduct of these surveys, see an article by Mr. R.F. Burch, the Chief Statistician of the NBPI, entitled 'Statistical surveys conducted by the National Board for Prices and Incomes', *Statistical News*, May 1971. (HMSO, 1971).

e.g. about earnings structures, which will continue to be of value for some ye
to come. Moreover, many of the Board's surveys, particularly on the general
study references (e.g. on job evaluation, salary structures and overtime and
shiftwork) and other reports of general interest such as on London weighting
in the non-industrial civil service, local authority rents, top salaries in
private and nationalised industries, solicitors' remuneration, architects' fees
and low pay, have a long-term interest and application that is not greatly
affected by changing attitudes to incomes policy.

Other Enquiry Methods: Financial enquiries are described in chapter 12; and
management efficiency studies in chapter 11.

5. Some Miscellaneous Issues

Burdensome Enquiries: The NBPI's enquiries at times imposed a good deal
of work on some firms, who were expected to reply quickly, and there was
occasional overlapping of enquiries made by different members of the Staff
Working Parties. Some steps were taken to avoid overwhelming firms with
requests for information. Thus in earnings surveys, normally all the largest
firms down to small samples of small firms were sent questionnaires, but
large firms usually were asked to select small samples of workers while processing up to large samples for small firms. This was to avoid asking any
one firm to undertake excessive form filling. Simple instructions about a
correct, scientific manner of doing this were given to the firms selecting
their own samples. Sometimes in price references companies were given a
choice either of answering the NBPI's questions bit by bit as the need for
new information emerged, or else of submitting everything of conceivable
relevance at the start. Most chose the latter. The Board believed that the
accounting information it sought was almost always of the kind that well-
managed businesses firmly in control of their materials, overheads and wages
costs could expect to have at their disposal for day-to-day purposes, and that
therefore where managements were fully effective, its requests usually produced little difficulty; in other cases, the Board's pressure for this information was likely to work in the interests of prices and incomes policy by
encouraging a sharper awareness of the need for close cost-consciousness.[1]

There were numerous complaints about burdensome enquiries, sometimes
from firms which were under investigation by more than one official body.
Because of the possibility, indeed the likelihood, of an adverse report, firms
usually assigned a top executive to spend a good deal of time watching
investigations. There were complaints that this prevented them from completing other tasks. This should not be exaggerated but it was a small part
of the cost of the NBPI's work; there would be very few at all who would
say, however, that the burdensome enquiries in themselves amounted to a
weighty reason for not having them; and there was often an inconsistency
between denunciations of reports for their over-burdensome enquiries and
their allegedly superficial character.

[1] *Third General Report*, para. 65.

Co-operation in Enquiries: The high degree of co-operation which the NBPI received in its inquiries was impressive. An objective measure of this was the response rate to all surveys, including financial ones, of about 70 per cent. There were some disappointments, as can be seen from the details of Statistical Surveys in Appendix K, but only in a few cases. The NBPI's case study workers and Enquiry Team also received a similarly high degree of co-operation. There were some references, however, in which trade unions refused any co-operation at all in any part of the enquiry and there was a steady increase in their numbers over the course of time.

Were Earnings Surveys Inflationary? There is no real evidence to test the claims which have been sometimes made about the inflationary repercussions of information collecting, but it is worth discussing some aspects of the issue.

Certainly some of the NBPI's findings removed pressure for wage increases. Some earnings surveys conclusively disproved the existence of low pay thought to be widespread in an industry, (e.g. in the clothing manufacturing, pottery, and several other references). In other cases there may have been an opposite effect. A case can be made, however, for the proposition that it is best that reliable results rather than rumour determine the situation.

The Board's preoccupation was with the internal labour market within firms or industries. It did not collect regional or local labour market information which, it can be argued, is more likely to stimulate inflation, particularly as very large differences are known to exist at this level.

Nevertheless, the repercussive effects of internal job markets earnings surveys are not known with any certainty. The Board's final report on *Productivity Agreements* (123) contains a discussion based on surveys of local labour markets suggesting the repercussive effects of productivity agreements were slight. As it never published the surveys, this evidence is of little weight. It is known that one of the most important pay claims to break the back of the incomes policy in 1969, that of London Firemen, based part of its case on comparisons with the pay of firemen at airports, revealed in an obscure part of an NBPI earnings survey to be unusually high.

On the whole, the writer's view is that earnings surveys had at most a marginally inflationary effect. This is not to deny that other actions of the NBPI may have raised pay expectations e.g. the emphasis on increased productivity as a source of pay increase, and the pointing up of differentials in the engineering industry. These were not the result of earnings surveys.. They are discussed later.

Part III The Policies and Work of the NBPI

8. Comparability, Wage and Salary Structures, and Low Pay

The main strategy of the NBPI in the incomes field was to break the accepted conventions for claiming and conceding pay increases such as comparability and to substitute other considerations such as the incomes norm and productivity. This chapter gives a history and analysis of the NBPI's treatment of comparability. A further related element in the strategy was to bring about changes in the wage structure: this is also examined in this chapter. Consideration of the NBPI's policies on wage structures leads naturally to a consideration of its treatment of low pay, the third main topic of the chapter.

1. White Papers

The 1965 White Paper *Prices and Incomes Policy* stated the principles which should govern increases in money incomes if they were to conform to the national interest. Although it was recognised that wages and salaries were determined by many factors, 'including changes in the supply and demand for different kinds of labour, trends in productivity and profits, comparisons with levels or trends of incomes in other employments and changes in the cost of living,' it was also noted that if wages and salaries per head were to keep in step with the long-term rate of increase in national productivity, 'less weight than hitherto will have to be given to the factors' mentioned and 'more weight will have to be given to the incomes norm'. Only in exceptional cases should individuals receive pay increases greater than the norm.

The original criteria justifying exceptional pay increases above the norm were:

(i) where employees made a direct contribution towards increasing productivity in a particular firm or industry, for example by accepting more exacting work or a major change in working practices. Some of this benefit should accrue to the community, however, in the form of lower prices.

Following the two NBPI reports on productivity agreements, more detailed guidelines were drawn up for this criterion;

(ii) where it was essential in the national interest to secure (or prevent) a change in the distribution of manpower and a pay increase would be both necessary and effective for this purpose;

(iii) where there was general recognition that existing wage or salary levels were too low to maintain a reasonable standard of living;

(iv) where there was a widespread recognition that the pay of a group of workers had fallen out of line with the level of remuneration for similar work and needed in the national interest to be improved.

To these was added in 1968:

(v) re-organisations of wage and salary structures which could be justified on grounds of economic efficiency and increased productivity,

and in 1970:

(vi) increases necessary for the implementation of equal pay legislation.

Apart from the additional criteria, subsequent White Papers followed substantially the same pattern. Two variations concerning low pay in the April 1968 White Paper and comparability in the December 1969 White Paper are discussed later in this chapter.

The NBPI's application of these criteria in particular references spanned the entire field of incomes from top salaries in big business to low pay in agriculture, from the remuneration of solicitors to the earnings of lightkeepers.

2. The General Strategy in Incomes References

The NBPI quickly decided that *much* 'less weight than hitherto' should be given to traditional factors in wage determination. Before the end of 1965 it had formulated a radical strategy which it then pursued in incomes references for most of the remainder of its existence. Very crudely this was to break the accepted conventions for claiming and conceding pay increases, and substitute other considerations, most notably the incomes norm, and productivity. The intention was to change the subject matter of collective bargaining. This strategy was spelt out in the *Second General Report:*

> 'The Board's general approach to the whole problem has been to try and loosen the relationship between pay within a factory or an industry and the pay thought to be paid elsewhere ... the Board has instead tried to substitute ... a close relationship between internal pay and internal performance.' [1]

The NBPI wished to reduce the hold of three traditional factors referred to in the White Paper: changes in the cost of living; recruitment needs; and, especially, comparability.

1 para. 47.

3. The Cost of Living

The White Paper left no room for cost of living considerations to enter into individual wage determination. 'Less weight than hitherto' was to be attached to them, and the rules for pay increases — the norm, and the criteria for exceptional pay increases — implied that changes in the cost of living were irrelevant in particular cases of pay increase. In addition, the NBPI believed that the linking of wage increases to price increases was likely to give rise to an endless inflationary spiral as wages and prices chased each other. In individual cases linking would conflict with the goal of relating wage increases to the national norm, especially as at all stages between 1965 and 1970 the retail price index was rising sharply.

The most obvious cases in which pay increases were linked with increases in the cost of living arose in industries which automatically adjusted wages in accordance with movements in the Index of Retail Prices. In its first wages reference, *Wages, Costs and Prices in the Printing Industry* (2), the NPBI recommended that use of such a formula be discontinued in the printing industry. Soon afterwards the Midland Bank based its case for a 5 per cent (and upwards) pay increase partly on the fact that in the twelve months preceding the wage settlement (in April 1965) prices had risen by 5½ per cent. The NBPI rejected this argument in its Report, *Midland Bank Salaries* (6). After this, there were very few cases in which rises in the cost of living were advanced as justification for a wage increase.

4. Recruitment Needs and Essential Manpower Redistribution

The Government White Paper conceded that pay increases for the purposes of attracting or retaining labour were justifiable but only in very limited circumstances:

> 'Where it is essential in the national interest to secure a change in the distribution of manpower (or to prevent a change which would otherwise take place) and a pay increase would be both necessary and effective for this purpose'.

The Board's policy with regard to this problem was laid down in its report on *Pay and Conditions of Busmen* (16):

> 'How is a labour shortage best met? The White Paper on Prices and Incomes Policy states that labour shortage can justify an exceptional pay increase only if such an increase would be both "necessary and effective" for the purpose of redistributing manpower. In an area of general labour shortage a pay increase has to be very large if it is to be effective. And a very large increase in pay in a labour intensive industry such as the bus industry, without an equivalent increase in productivity, would hasten its contraction. The pay increases to London busmen following the Phelps Brown report were intended to increase the labour force "up to the present establishment". The resulting advantage to the London busmen has not yet been eroded to any great extent by subsequent pay increases to other Londoners, but no

permanent addition has been secured to London Transport's labour force. Had other London employers followed the L.T.B. with comparable increases in pay there would have been an inflationary effect all round, but without any change in the distribution of labour.

The most effective remedy for an undertaking suffering from a shortage of labour in an area of general manpower shortage is to make use of the labour which it already has; just as this is the only effective remedy for a shortage of labour for the country as a whole. From the point of view of an individual undertaking an exceptional pay increase which is justified by a better use of the existing labour force offers it also the secondary advantage of protecting it against a loss of manpower.' [1]

The doctrine was firmly applied in reference after reference, with few exceptions, and investigations in particular cases were designed to show the futility of overcoming labour shortages by means of pay increases. The Midland Bank, besides granting a general pay increase to all staff, had made a special increase to attract younger staff. The NBPI found that this was speedily followed by the other clearing banks and by some insurance companies, and to that extent the effectiveness of the increase was largely reduced.[2]

Investigations primarily sought to uncover practical possibilities for increasing labour productivity. The eight references concerning busmen were good examples: in the NBPI's view the answer to the industry's staffing shortages consisted in better use of the existing labour force principally by means of one-man busing, the elimination of 'restrictive' or 'protective' labour practices, the application of operations research techniques to bus scheduling, and finally a policy of recruitment in a wider field, including women and part-time labour.

Even if a pay increase were necessary to attract recruits, when the shortage related only to a particular group of workers there was the obvious question whether an across-the-board increase for all classes of worker in the industry was necessary. Thus in *Pay of Nurses and Midwives in the National Health Service* (60), the NBPI's investigations confirmed that there was no general shortage of nurses affecting every grade and every type of hospital, but there were serious shortages in particular grades e.g. the staff nursing grade, in staffing at nights and weekends, and in psychiatric hospitals, and in hospitals for the chronic sick including geriatric hospitals. The same pay increase for all nurses was not therefore regarded as an appropriate solution. Apart from special measures that management might take such as a reorganisation of the shift system, the remedy consisted in special above average pay increases to deal specifically with these problems, linked with a general reorganisation of the salary structure.

In passing it is worth noting that in a sense it was fairly widely known all along that nursing shortages were not general. What was new politically

---

1 paras. 64, 65.

2 *Pay of Midland Bank Staff* (6).

was to place the problem of particular shortages in the context of an argument about differentials — which had hardly been mentioned before. Indeed it was a general theme in the Board's reports that each industry should move towards the construction of a wage structure tailored to its own needs even if this meant a deliberate change of wage structures.

The Board did not get the opportunity of examining the salary structure of teachers, despite its yearning to do so, but obiter dicta in the report on *Scottish Teachers Salaries* (15) provide clues to the approach it might have taken:

'Each system of education (the English, Welsh, and the Scottish) has a recruitment problem but the nature of the problem is not necessarily the same for each system. In each case a solution requires an examination of the use made of existing manpower resources. Such an examination would also call for a thorough review of the most desirable method of determining the composition of teachers' salaries and of the relative emphasis to be placed on academic qualifications as opposed to teaching ability and responsibilities undertaken.' [1]

However the NBPI did not always reject pay increases based on recruitment needs. Recruitment needs were, for example, the grounds for pay increases to members of the armed forces[2] and higher civil servants.[3]

5. Comparability

It was implicit in the 1965 White Paper that comparability should have some role to play in wage determination. It was relevant to the criterion concerning the pay of groups of workers which had fallen seriously out of line with that for those doing similar work; in judging whether an exceptional pay increase was necessary to help secure an essential change in the distribution of manpower, comparability was also a factor to be taken into account. Comparisons were also relevant to the low pay criterion. The White Paper had not defined low pay, and in judging whether pay was low it was necessary to consider the relative level of pay elsewhere. Finally, comparisons enter into major wage and salary reorganisations, since these are usually made on the basis of detailed comparisons with pay for similar work in other industries. However, any role implied for comparability was severely qualified in the White Paper. For example there had to be 'widespread recognition' that pay was 'seriously' out of line, and it needed to be 'in the national interest' to correct it. Moreover, the White Paper implied that arguments based on comparisons in themselves were not acceptable; they were clearly subordinated to the criteria. Finally 'comparisons with levels or trends of incomes in other employments' was one of the traditional factors to which less weight

1 para. 46, loc.cit.

2 *Pay of the Armed Forces* (116), para. 34. This was an interim increase, though.

3 *Pay of the Higher Civil Service* (11), para. 14.

than hitherto should be given. Later White Papers discouraged the use of comparisons even more strongly: the 1968 White Paper for instance stated that the 'seriously out of line' criterion should be applied selectively; the 1969 White Paper reversed some important aspects of these policies. It is returned to below.

There were several reasons why the NBPI sought to reduce the role of comparability. A long term voluntary incomes policy would not work unless individual pay increases were related to the norm, rather than the increases other people were receiving; and initially it would be impossible to bring down the level of wage settlements to that required by the norm. Even if there were general observance of the norm, this could be undermined if exceptional pay increases for higher productivity or low pay spread to groups with no special claim for exceptional treatment. In practice the prices and incomes policy acted mainly on nationally negotiated wages rates: but it was also necessary to contain the effects of wage drift as much as possible by preventing the automatic linking of earnings among sectors. Second, the widespread use of comparability tended to set off a process of leap frogging or a 'wage-wage' spiral. Increases in wage rates granted to one section of the work force, sometimes for special reasons, tended to be quickly imitated by other sections; in return the original group then applied pressure to restore its differential; and so on. The well known 1961 OECD Report by a Group of Experts 'The Problem of Rising Prices' had regarded this as a major cause of excessive wage increases.[1] Third, the NBPI's aim of relating pay more to individual performance could be frustrated by the use of comparability arguments. If the increases given for special effort by some workers were followed on the grounds of comparability by similar increases for groups of workers who had made no such effort, the earnings-productivity link would be weakened. Fourth, the use of comparisons often tended to distract attention from individual circumstances within groups, and from the need to take specific measures to deal with the problems of each sub-group, e.g. by altering the wage structure rather than granting uniform increases. Finally, the NBPI was concerned at the manner in which comparisons were used in pay negotiations. Some examples of this are given below. These reasons did not amount to a total rejection of comparability. Rather, as was made clear in early reports, the aim was to reduce its importance, and to prevent it from being the sole factor in pay negotiations.

The comparability issue arose in numerous references especially those concerning wages and salaries in the public sector. The nature and evolution of the NBPI's policies may be illustrated from some landmark references, mainly those in which the greatest difficulties were encountered. The issue arose in several early references, in 1965 and 1966 in such cases as *Midland Bank Salaries* (6), *Armed Forces Pay* (10), *Pay of the Higher Civil Service* (11) and *Pay of the London Busmen* (16). Thus *Pay of Busmen* (16) was an important reference because the NBPI strongly criticised the use of

---

[1] W. Fellner and others, *The Problem of Rising Prices*, (O.E.C.D., Paris, 1964) ch.5 esp. p.54.

automatic comparability formula linking the pay increases of London busmen with earnings in other industries. In addition the NBPI did not accept the claims of provincial busmen which were mainly based on comparisons with the claim of the London busmen. But the main attempts, perhaps, to dethrone comparability were made in *Railways Pay* (8) and *Pay of the Industrial Civil Service* (18) in January and June 1966.

In 1960, the Report of an Inquiry into Railway Pay (The Guillebaud Report) had recommended increases in the wage rates of railways staff in 1960, largely on the basis of comparisons of the levels of basic rates with those in other selected industries. Following the acceptance of these recommendations by unions and management, wage settlements in subsequent years had been based largely upon an updating of the Guillebaud comparisons. In 1965 the British Railways Board offered manual workers increases in basic rates of 3½ per cent in October 1965 and October 1966, a 40 hour week (in place of 42 hours) and improved holidays and pensions. The likely effect on earnings (in the first part of 1966) was calculated by the Railways Board as being a 6½ to 7½ per cent increase. This offer was rejected by the trade unions, with a threat of industrial action.

The NBPI refused to countenance an increase in the offer.[1] It attacked the comparisons in question as incomplete. The Guillebaud Report had not disclosed all the comparisons it had made and it was wrong to claim some of the comparisons in that report as the sole determinant of wage increases. They were also made between wage rates and wage rates, not between earnings and earnings. The NBPI's calculations showed that the earnings of railways manual staff had kept pace with the average for industrial workers even if wage rates had not. The comparisons led to the application of a uniform formula for pay increases to all railways manual staff. This perpetuated the 1960 relationships in wage rates:

> 'at a time of rapid technical advance and altering responsibilities for the railways, regardless of the changing demand by the railways for different kinds of labour, the changing contributions that are required from different groups of workers, and even the fact that the earnings of different groups of workers (as distinct from their rates) may be moving differently'.[2]

The formula also fed upon itself. Increases in the pay of industrial civil servants were derived in part from an increase in the basic rate of the railways workers pay. Such increases were in turn used by the railways unions as part of their claim. Finally comparisons excluded all the other considerations set out in White Paper on Prices and Incomes Policy, such as the need to relate pay increase to the norm and exceptional criteria. However, the NBPI disclaimed any absolute opposition to the use of comparisons in wage determination. It merely wished that, in line with the White Paper, they be given 'less weight than hitherto', that they should not be the sole

1 It did support an increase for clerical workers.

2 para. 19.

consideration in wage bargaining; and that if comparisons were relevant they should not be misused. It did object to the way in which comparability was being used in the case of the railways and it was made especially clear that it would attack the application of automatic or semi-automatic formulas linking pay increases in one sector with those in others. But in recommending a a special pay increase for railway clerical workers, one of the main grounds was that their pay was below that of their counterparts in other industries. This illustrated that it was not altogether attempting to banish comparability from the wage scene.

The NBPI then indicated various ways in which it would be legitimate for the pay of railway workers to be increased. This required the full co-operation of management and unions in making the railways operate more efficiently. The two sets of negotiating machinery which dealt separately with pay and productivity should be merged. Management preparation and initiative was necessary to achieve greater productivity. Above all, unions needed to co-operate in the more economical use of manpower by reducing the number of men employed on particular tasks and by allowing greater versatility in their employment, and by cutting back on overtime. Specific examples of how this could be done were given. These included more single manning of locomotives at night; less use of guards on modern freight trains and the assignment of a wider range of duties to them; the employment of suitably trained permanent way staff as guards on ballast trains; and the abolition of traditional demarcation lines between the work of station and parcels porters at one London main line station.

There was stiff resistance to these recommendations by the trade unions who threatened a national rail strike. Following the Prime Minister's intervention, there was a slight improvement in the management's offer and the question of pay and productivity was referred to the Ministry of Labour, not the NBPI, and the threat was then withdrawn.

'... but the main concession was a promise of a further review of the whole question of railway pay under the aegis of the Prime Minister, and outside the scope of the Board. Disaster had been avoided, but the Board's value as an instrument for securing the acceptance of the policy had diminished, at least for the time being.'[1]

The difficulties that arose as a result of the Board's recommendations and the subsequent concessions to the railway workers showed how politically difficult its task was.

The next major attack on comparability was launched in *Pay of Industrial Civil Servants* (18) in June 1966. As this reference is important in other respects, a full account is given. The NBPI was asked to report on the pay system of industrial civil servants (which was derived from the 1946 version of the Fair Wages Resolution of the House of Commons).

The Industrial Civil Service comprised over 200,000 manual employees in

1 H.A. Clegg, *The System of Industrial Relations in Great Britain* (Basil Blackwell, Oxford, 1970), p.422.

many different occupations, in a wide range of Central Government industrial activities including armament factories, naval dockyards, storage depots and in a variety of establishments engaged in engineering, shipbuilding, building and in vehicle maintenance and repair; there were others who did ancillary work in research establishments, H.M. Forces camps and elsewhere. The majority worked in establishments employing a thousand people or more, but there were many who worked in small groups as cooks, domestics, stokers, gardeners, and general labourers in non-industrial establishments. Industrial civil servants were employed in the main by eleven Government departments.

A uniform percentage increase in wage rates was granted every six months to all employees. The increase was derived from the automatic application of a formula — the average increase of minimum wage rates paid in a wide spectrum of outside industries. This reference was significant because the Government itself was the employer; and the NBPI was asked not to pass judgement on a specific settlement but on the system of fixing pay.

The NBPI argued first that the existing system caused the Government to follow everybody else when its own White Paper urged the need to attach less weight than hitherto to comparisons. Second, the comparisons were made between wage rates and wage rates, not earnings and earnings. The effect of this was the opposite to that of railway workers. The pay of industrial civil servants lagged behind that of their counterparts in private industry; and there were some serious labour shortages and recruitment problems. Taking into account that attempts to improve recruitment by giving all round pay increases in 1959 and 1963 had failed to overcome the problem, and that attempts to improve pay without changing the basis on which it was determined were unlikely to achieve their objective, the Board recommended 'a radical reform of the whole of its pay system'.[1]

Third, the system ignored the variety of conditions obtaining both inside the industrial civil service and outside it.

The Fair Wages Resolution had required wage rates to be no less favourable than in the appropriate trade or industry in the district. Only from 1940 were nationally bargained rates developed for different industries, and then the different national rates were compressed into an average. In view of the numerous occupations, industries and regions involved it might be expected that the application of this crude average would lead to relative under payment in some cases and relative over payment in others.

Fourth, the prices and incomes policy was concerned with the relationship between incomes and the more effective use of national manpower. It was therefore concerned with methods and systems of remuneration as facilitating or impeding the more effective use of national manpower. The larger role now played by the Government in economic affairs seemed to require that the Government should for its own part pioneer in this respect. The present system allowed little scope for this.

1 para. 31.

'We consider that a new payment system should rest on the recognition that Government industrial civil servants are employed in a great diversity of undertakings, that there is no single formula which can conceivably meet the needs of this highly heterogeneous group of workers, and that the application of such a formula ignores the existence up and down the country of different labour markets and the desirability of accepting this fact. This is not one industry but a number of industries with one employer. It follows that for pay purposes the 210,000 workers in the Government industrial civil service should be subdivided into smaller groupings. Equally, however, the groupings should not be so small as to render impossible a desirable degree of central control.'[1]

Separate pay structures should be speedily introduced for each of the nine main industrial groups. Since the pay structure would bear little relationship to previous practice, regard would need to be paid initially to the level of pay of those engaged in similar activities in outside employment. Following this, pay increases should be negotiated in a Trade Joint Council for each industrial group. The negotiations should not be concerned with outside movements in basic pay rates (which may or may not have been determined in accordance with the White Paper) but with the needs of each industrial group. These should be assessed in the light of any national standard for pay increases laid down by the Government and of criteria for exceptions from the standard on the ground, for example, that a major change in working practices had taken place.

Pay was so seriously out of line for some jobs that the new system proposed would bring increases in pay to many workers. It was important, therefore, to realise the considerable potential that existed for savings to be made by the better utilisation of labour. There was scope for improvements in efficiency and productivity, coupled with reductions in numbers employed, greater cost consciousness and more effective management. The initiative in improving the utilisation of manpower could be more effectively taken locally than nationally and there was, in particular, an important need to give much greater discretion to unit managers in deciding numbers and grades of workers employed; and at the same time for local management to be complemented by strengthened arrangements for central management services. A recently established inter-departmental committee to promote efficiency in the Industrial Civil Service should also consider what arrangements should be made for co-ordination since the proposed industrial groupings would not necessarily coincide with Departmental responsibilities. A possible solution would be the establishment of a central 'efficiency' inspectorate which would complement but not take over the managerial functions of the responsible Departments and their local managers. The recommendations were accepted by the official and trade union side of the Industrial Civil Service. The fate of the attempts to implement them is described later in this chapter.

The use of automatic or semi-automatic formulas has its strongest force

1 para. 33.

in the public service. After dealing with industrial civil servants, the NBPI appears to have wished to consider the pay of local government officers, teachers[1] and finally the non-industrial civil service which was seen as the citadel protecting comparability. Only the first of these three references came. The pay of teachers might well have come to the NBPI in 1968 had they not settled for what was offered. Although the pay of local government officers did come to the Board, its recommendations for the introduction of more refined methods into the determination of their pay were largely ignored; and

> 'In 1968 a general agreement provided for pay increases [for civil servants] based on Civil Service Pay Research Unit investigations. Each grade was to receive up to 7 per cent from the beginning of that year (representing a 3.5 per cent ceiling over two years since the previous increases) and the balance, if any and whatever it might be, was to be paid a year later. Thus fair comparisons continued to apply, but only after a delay.'[2]

It was only with the publication of the report in December 1968 on the less economically significant reference *Pay of University Teachers* (98) that the battle against comparability could be continued in the public sector.

The Association of University Teachers sought a 15 per cent pay increase on the grounds that there was a need to restore competitive equivalence with other salaries. The NBPI pointed out that in recent years the movement in salaries in general had been faster than the movement in national productivity and had therefore been inflationary. An all round percentage increase based on this movement would add to the inflation. The resulting rise in the index of salaries could cause groups which earlier obtained increases to seek to maintain their differential, and so on ad infinitum. Whilst comparisons of pay were not the sole cause of cost inflation, they played a contributory part. It was recognised that to cut the chain was hard on those waiting at the point where it was broken. 'Not to seek to cut it, however, would help to perpetuate the national situation of recurring financial crises arising in large part from a growth in money incomes relative to productivity greater than elsewhere.'[3] The NBPI thus rejected the claim. It also considered that the salary and career structure was biased towards research and that steps were necessary to encourage and reward excellence in teaching. It recommended that each university authority should have freedom within 4 per cent of the relevant salary bill to grant teachers (except professors) discretionary payments based on the extent and quality of teaching and in exceptional cases their administrative load. The quality of teaching was to be partly measured by a carefully drafted questionnaire to students. These recommendations were challenged

---

1 The comments quoted earlier in this chapter from *Scottish Teachers Salaries* (15) indicate the kind of line the NBPI would have taken. They also foreshadow the approach taken in the reference *Pay of University Teachers* (98).

2 H.A. Clegg *The System of Industrial Relations in Great Britain*, pp. 432—33.

3 para. 97.

by an articulate opposition. One argument was that productivity considerations of this kind could not be applied to university teachers. It was difficult in practice to measure their productivity and thus to link future movements in their pay to their performance. They also complained of being singled out. The report, moreover, was soon followed by Government acceptance of the report of the Kindersley Review Body which reported in favour of an increase for doctors and dentists based on general grounds of comparability fully up to the ceiling permitted by the White Paper. Kindersley had allowed comparability because the Government had earlier allowed it for its own employees. The acceptance of Kindersley indicated the Government's unwillingness to apply comparability criteria up to the hilt. The fairly widespread criticism of the report on University teachers, about which there had been controversy between Board Members, influenced the subsequent thinking of the Board on comparability.

Around this time there happened to be several other references in which the NBPI found it difficult to measure productivity: e.g. banking staff, journalists, lightkeepers. The best example was *The Pay of Armed Forces* (116), published in June 1969, which did involve considerations of comparability, and in fact showed some change in the NBPI's philosophy.

In an earlier reference on the subject,[1] in which comparability was not the central issue, the NBPI had expressed doubts about the crude comparability formula used to determine the Services' pay, especially because of the wholly automatic nature of its application, and the fact that it was the sole determinant of movements in Service pay. Other factors, such as the manning situation, and the extent to which the pay structure continued to contribute to the efficient use of manpower within the Services, tended to be overlooked. But the earlier report conceded, that comparability considerations were of some relevance to the determination of Service pay. In the later report the NBPI was asked to recommend a reorganisation of the structure of pay throughout the armed forces. One object was to ensure that given recruitment targets were met. It recognised that the efficiency of a military force was 'hard to measure', and other standards must therefore be used for the determination of pay. This was one of the first references in which the NBPI conceded that productivity considerations were inapplicable. The reference seems to have marked the beginning of a more cautious approach to linking pay and productivity and a recognition of the difficulties of determining or measuring productivity.

In its Fourth General Report published shortly afterwards in July 1969 the NBPI commented on this:

'There are fields from which the concept of "comparability" cannot be excluded. One clear case is that of the armed forces. We have suggested here the use of job evaluation with a dual purpose. Internally its use should help a structure to be devised in which pay is related more logically to the job servicemen are required to do, with the result that differences

1 *Pay of the Armed Forces*, 10.

114

in pay should be more acceptable. This is the normal use of job evaluation. But we also went further and suggested an external use. The skills and qualities required of certain military jobs might be matched against those of certain civilian jobs, the ranges of pay obtaining for the latter would be identified, and in this way pay levels and changes in those levels could be settled for servicemen in the light of directly relevant information rather than of averages based on general movements in pay throughout the economy. "Comparability" would thus be used with greater precision and selectivity than has hitherto been the case.'

'Since the concept of comparability has its dangers, but is at the same time so deeply rooted and cannot entirely be discarded, we consider that our work needs to be complemented by a fuller reference on the subject, particularly where it relates to activities which cannot be priced, and where benefits cannot easily be measured against costs.'[1]

In December 1969, the Government published its White Paper *Productivity, Prices and Incomes Policy after 1969.* This contained an extended discussion of the role of 'comparability' considerations in wage determination, stressing the limited role they should have in private sector negotiations. As regards the public sector, several special circumstances applied — often output was not measurable in a way that enabled a direct link between efficiency and pay e.g. the output of teachers, doctors or nurses; nor could a market price be assigned to the value of output because it was not sold in a competitive market. The special nature of some public service jobs, and the career nature of such employment, meant that if an unduly low level of pay were allowed to develop in the public service, it would take a relatively long time to show itself in labour supply difficulties. Finally, since the Government was directly or indirectly involved in all pay settlements in most of the public services, there were strong pressures for uniformity of treatment, in spite of the large numbers and varied occupations involved. Hence in determining the pay of many public servants, more reliance had to be placed on the closest comparisons possible with the pay of workers doing similar jobs in the private sector. In some cases, there were no or too few counterparts in private employment for such comparisons; in such cases, regard would have to be paid to more generalised comparisons with pay elsewhere as well as to other relevant comparisons. This did not mean that every measure should not be taken to ensure efficient labour utilisation in the public sector.

It was hardly to be expected after this White Paper that the Board would pursue its policies on comparability in the public sector as vigorously as before. Also, by 1970 earnings were moving quickly upwards at a rate well in excess of the 2½–4½ per cent range suggested by the Government for 1970 and there were virtually no wage controls. In such circumstances it was difficult to deny salary increases when a second report on pay of university teachers was made in April 1970. The NBPI reported that an interim pay increase was necessary pending the results of a study of the university

1 para. 67, 68.

115

labour market commissioned from the University of London's Higher Education Research Unit, when a full review of their position could be made. In the meantime, in the light of comparisons with pay movements of those similarly placed, an increase of 9 per cent was granted. Although this could be rationalised as an interim decision, it suggested some second thoughts on the part of the NBPI about the applicability of productivity considerations to pay determination in other parts of the economy, besides the armed forces.

The second report on the *Industrial Civil Service* (146), published in April 1970, could be described as the formal occasion on which the NBPI recanted and reversed its previous decisions on comparability. The report also showed a keen appreciation of the real difficulties of applying productivity considerations to pay, and a recognition of the importance of the collective bargaining structure in doing this. On examining the consequences of its recommendations in Report 18 on Industrial Civil Servants, the NBPI noted that the system 'was unable to withstand the strong tendency for the method of pay determination to revert to its previous form.'[1] New pay arrangements based on the recommendations of the Board's first report had been brought into force in 1967. The Industrial Civil Service was divided into ten groups. Each group had pay related to earnings outside on the lines recommended. An average rise in wage rates of 7½ per cent was entailed. In 1968 there was an across-the-board increase of 3½ per cent. This was the maximum increase within the incomes policy ceiling then current, and in justification it was argued that many industrial civil servants had low pay and that earnings were seriously out of line with those outside. The pay arrangements of industrial civil servants were again revised in a further central agreement which was implemented as from 1st July 1969. Under this agreement the number of industrial groups was reduced to four. The opportunity was also taken to reduce by approximately a half the number of 'bands' into which semi-skilled workers were grouped for pay purposes. This settlement, a crucial test case for the incomes policy as a whole, resulted in pay increases averaging 8½ per cent and was justified by the Government on the grounds that it was necessary to prevent pay falling seriously out of line with that outside and that it constituted a major re-organisation of the wage structure aimed at increasing efficiency by reducing anomalies and permitting greater flexibility in the use of manpower. This settlement was described as an interim one pending a general review of pay and conditions by the NBPI.

It will be seen that pay arrangements did not develop on the lines suggested by the NBPI following the settlement of 1967. Instead of each industrial group negotiating separately, there were central settlements. Arguments based on the relationship with pay outside continued to exercise a very strong influence. Moreover, because negotiations were centralised it was not possible to have regard to the needs of each industrial group in settling pay. The number of industrial groups was reduced from ten to four. The reversion to the previous arrangements was not costless; each reorganisation had been used to justify above-norm increases.

1 para. 16.

There were a number of reasons why events took this turn. The grouping on industrial lines adopted in 1967 had the result of creating differences in pay between workers doing similar jobs (sometimes within the same perimeter) according to the industrial group to which the employing unit was allocated. Industrial civil servants had long regarded themselves as being employed essentially by a single employer — the Government — rather than by the particular enterprises or units in which they happened to work. The pay differences created by the new system of groups were therefore regarded as anomalous and indefensible both by workers themselves and by their unions; and managements often found the outcome in particular cases difficult to defend in equity. Secondly, the industrial pay groups largely cut across other Departmental boundaries and did not constitute natural entities for management purposes. They therefore did not readily lend themselves to negotiations in Trade Joint Councils whose aim was to relate pay increases more closely to management needs and in particular to improvements in the use of manpower. Thirdly, the civil service faced problems of its own in attempting to move from reliance on comparisons with pay outside towards relating pay more closely with productivity. In particular, the structure and organisation of management could not in practice be rapidly adapted to permit this.

The publication of Report No. 18 did help nevertheless to stimulate efforts to relate higher productivity to higher pay in various parts of the civil service by means of work studied incentive payment schemes and productivity agreements. The agreement concluded in 1967 recorded the intention of both union and official representatives to promote greater efficiency and productivity by the use of recognised techniques of work study and work measurement, by co-operation in such matters as increasing versatility and interchangeability between jobs and by jointly devising new or improved systems of payment based on the more efficient use of manpower and productive resources and some progress did in fact occur in this direction.

Nevertheless, it was apparent that attempts to replace comparability with other considerations could encounter serious difficulties in the necessary accompanying reorganisation of collective bargaining. In its second report on the Industrial Civil Service, therefore, the NBPI first had to determine the appropriate structure for collective bargaining and whether central or local bargaining was to be encouraged. There were advantages in delegating to line management units, but if pay decisions were referred to them they did not have the means by which to monitor performance or keep costs under control and if they did, some central co-ordination would still remain necessary to prevent pay inequities developing between different units. On the other hand it was not practicable in the Industrial Civil Service to negotiate centrally general pay increases based on productivity, owing to problems in measuring output and labour productivity, and the diversity of conditions of the Industrial Civil Service. It was recognised, therefore, that it was necessary for the collective bargaining structure to accommodate both central and local negotiations. Central negotiations would thus be concerned to establish a framework of pay and conditions of employment; within this, line management should be encouraged to relate pay to performance. Detailed suggestions were made about how to do this at local level. As for the central negotiations, they would determine the initial pay structure with the aid of comparisons with pay outside. It was spelt out in some detail exactly how these comparisons should be made for each main class of job. It was clearly difficult for them to be made on a very refined basis, however. Once these levels were established, future central adjustments should depend partly on movements in the economy in general. In the absence of a clear government policy at the time little else could be said.

There are other conclusions which may be drawn from the Industrial Civil Service reports. Recommendations which originally appeared to be sound in terms of rationalisation of the wage structure were not necessarily practicable from a management point of view. The first report had failed to take adequate account of the managerial dimension. The account given earlier in this chapter of the first report indicates that there was some recognition that pay anomalies would occur and that there would be problems because the industrial groups cut across departmental boundaries. But the Board's proposals did not really meet these problems. An 'efficiency' inspectorate and Joint Trade Councils were not enough and the devolution of responsibility to unit managers was not always desirable.

To some extent the first report on the Industrial Civil Service reflected the NBPI's heavy orientation to industrial relations in the early days and weaknesses in its ability to follow through the implications of changes in industrial relations for the managerial system. One might be tempted to conclude that the preponderance of the Industrial Relations Branch and the absence of a Management Branch was the cause of the trouble. It was in fact more complicated than this. The main proposals for change were the brainchild of a relatively senior civil servant working on the reference. Management-oriented Board Members knew what was involved in the recommendations. Consultants reported at length on management aspects of the Industrial Civil Service though their reports were uneven in quality and of limited value. But the report nevertheless typified the NBPI's concern in early years with the industrial relations and wage aspects of a problem.

This completes a sketch of the NBPI's treatment on comparability, at least in the public sector, where the issue was most important and arose most often. In private sector references, the NBPI generally pursued a similar line. There were less complications here, because output was much easier to measure, and in one way or the other, productivity or performance considerations could enter into the process of wage determination. Where comparability had a role, it could be recommended that 'refined' comparisons, based on job evaluation, should be made.

The NBPI's position on comparisons was not rigid, however. It supported pay increases on comparability grounds in a number of references, for example, railway clerks in *Railway Pay* (8); for the *Industrial Civil Service* (146); *Insurance Staff* (41); the *Armed Forces* (116)(as well as in Reports 10 and 70 for very special reasons); and *Pay of University Teachers* (145). In some other references it recommended pay increases for some groups of workers

118

when others lower in the pay structure[1] or working in the same industry[2] had received them.

However, the NBPI's policies look more consistent it the distinction is made between 'crude' and 'refined' comparability, and if account is taken of the following factors:

a. The distinction between comparisons of movements of pay and comparisons of levels of pay.

The NBPI nearly always refused to recommend pay increases for one group because other groups had received *increases*. It especially opposed the use of automatic or near automatic formulas which linked movements in pay in one group with movements in pay in another group e.g. *Railway Pay* (8); *London Transport Busmen* (16); *Industrial Civil Servants* (18); *Lightkeepers* (114). The main exceptions to this rule were nearly all special cases, such as in *Report 10* where the Government was committed to the Grigg Formula (although even then the Board disliked the nature and automaticity of the formula) and an increase was given to university teachers on the basis of movements in pay of comparable occupations as an interim measure.

On the other hand, the NBPI was in certain circumstances prepared to take account of comparisons of *levels* of pay. This was in accord with the White Paper criterion permitting exceptional increases in certain circumstances where pay was seriously out of line with that for similar work and in line with the NBPI's emphasis on the usefulness of job evaluation techniques, which essentially are based on refined comparisons of levels of pay; and in recommending the establishment of new pay structures, the NBPI often had to allow the starting point for each job to be related to the level of pay elsewhere for similar work.[3]

This distinction between levels of pay and movements of pay is meaningful. Comparison of movements in pay carry the implication that the implied base is acceptable. What is needed, however, is to get the base right. One way of doing so is by comparisons of pay levels. It is true that if the pay of one group increases less than another's it may open up a gap in the level of pay, *if* the group receiving the smaller increase had a lower level to begin with. But from the Board's point of view, differences in levels of pay had to be 'serious' before it recommended a restoration of levels and even then 'only when it was in the national interest'. Failure to keep pace in the short term with changes in pay would rarely open up such differences.

A close study of the NBPI's reports concerning private and public sector

1 *Pay and Conditions of Merchant Navy Officers* (35).

2 *Remuneration of Administrative and Clerical Staff in the Electricity Supply Industry* (5).

3 It may be observed that the White Paper wording was 'where pay has fallen out of line'. This was a little unfortunate, since it failed to distinguish between the movement and the being out of line. An alternative wording would have been 'when it *is* out of line'. The White Paper also stated that 'comparisons with levels or trends of incomes in other employments' should receive less weight than hitherto.

pay shows that this distinction played a large part in determining its attitude to pay increases on comparability grounds. However, the distinction was rarely spelt out in the reports. If it had been, it might have removed some misunderstanding and the Board's development of a policy on comparability could have been taken further. It is to be noted, however, that the NBPI in *Top Salaries in the Private and Nationalised Industries* (107) expressed reservations about even this distinction. It conceded that the use of comparisons of salary levels in this way is 'clearly not quite the same' as using comparisons of changes in salary, but, 'unless great care is exercised, could have very much the same drawbacks'. If each company followed this method, others would follow suit, and a self-perpetuating and self-defeating round of increases would follow. It would have little effect on the retention of manpower, as the Board's studies suggested executive mobility was low, and little influenced by salary factors.

(b) The preciseness and appropriateness of comparisons.

In some references the standard of comparison used in fixing pay was found to be the pay of others doing the same work in other industries or localities; in some the standard was of those doing different work in the same industry or locality. Basically the NBPI considered the standard of comparison if any, should be of similar work. Other comparisons could be largely irrelevant or inappropriate – in the *Pay of the University Teachers* the NBPI pointed out that whilst it was true that higher managers in industry, university teachers and higher civil servants all came from the same ranks, it did not follow that the pull to one or other of the three different careers depended mainly upon salary differences. The rewards of university life were not solely to be measured in terms of salary. The individual who adopts a career in university teaching has, for example, a freedom in organising his life which is probably found in few other professions. He would not, therefore, necessarily seek the same salary in university life as might be obtained outside it. Occasionally as an exception the NBPI recognised that within a plant or enterprise or industry it was necessary to adjust the pay of all workers, once the pay of some had been altered for special reasons. When productivity agreements were negotiated, some adjustments were recognised as necessary to avoid serious repercussions. Thus the pay of white collar workers in electricity supply might need adjustment in the light of increases of pay for manual workers in the industry due to productivity agreements.[1] Such adjustments needed to be taken into account in costing the original agreement. But the NBPI argued that such repercussions should be contained as much as possible.

Generally where comparisons were to be made, as for example in establishing a new pay structure, they should be as precise as possible and should involve the use of job evaluation techniques. *The Pay of Armed Forces* references were perhaps the ultimate example of the NBPI's wish to introduce refinement into comparisons. The detailed investigations made are described in Chapter 10 on standing references but it may be noted here that it was

1 Report 5. *Pay of Electricity clerical and administrative staff.*

found that military jobs could not be compared exactly with civilian jobs. After making comparisons that were as precise as possible, the NBPI had to add an 'X' factor to take account of the special conditions of military life. A list of disadvantages — and also the substantial advantages — of the military career was drawn up. No scientifically based attempt was made to assign weights to these or to determine if advantages outweighed disadvantages but an essentially arbitrary substantial positive amount 'the X factor' was added to each pay level.

In the second reference on *Pay of Industrial Civil Servants* there were considerable difficulties in arriving at very refined comparisons. There were also some references in which 'crude' comparisons were judged to furnish sufficiently compelling evidence of pay being seriously out of line for the NBPI to go ahead and recommend pay increases.[1]

(c) The distinction between wage rates, and earnings. The NBPI's preference, already noted, for comparisons to be based on earnings, rather than wage rates, was partly derived from the White Paper's emphasis on earnings as the relevant factor in any decisions on incomes policy.

(d) The fact that no other means of pay determination were available. The interim award to University Teachers was an example of this, and the use of comparisons to determine Armed Forces pay also. Also, lightkeepers was an example.

(e) The change of Government policy in December 1969, when the White Paper spelled out some of the special wage problems facing the public sector.

Thus taking account of the above factors there was a reasonable consistency in the NBPI treatment of comparability. It sought to break the force of crude comparability and if any comparability factor was to enter thereafter, it should be 'refined'. The rationale for 'refined' as opposed to 'crude' comparisons was presumably that they were fairer; and that they were a means of reducing the influence of comparability considerations. The risks of repercussions from the pay increases given to some groups would possibly be reduced (though hardly eliminated) if the comparisons were 'precise'. Even so there was a risk that a 'catching up' increase justified by 'fair comparisons' with outside employments, could in turn stimulate new increases in those employments. The risk of circularity was therefore inherent in any system of comparisons, however carefully defined.

It is perhaps to be added, however, that whilst a careful reading of reports shows a degree of consistency and sophistication in the Board's comparability policies, the general idea conveyed to the world at large was, as the Board well knew, that it was totally against comparability. Not only could subtle distinctions between levels and movements not be easily conveyed to the general public (which might have ridiculed them) but the 'political' ingredient in the Board's approach was important insofar as it regarded the first requirement of reports as being to make an impact.

---

[1] Pay of clerical workers in *Pay of British Railways Staff* (8); and in *Staff salaries of General Accident Group* (41).

6. Conclusions on Comparability

During the period 1965–70 there was apparently some success in reducing the role of traditional factors in wage determination, particularly the use of cost of living adjustments and of arguments based on the need for manpower redistribution.

The reduction of the role of comparability in incomes negotiations was more difficult to accomplish. The notion of comparability as a fair method of fixing pay is deeply embedded in the thinking of wage and salary earners, and is seen as a means of protecting their position in the wage structure, and it is a factor which enters into their expectations concerning annual increases. Comparability is fundamental to trade unionism. It can be argued against this that the influence of comparisons on pay negotiations only reflects the workings of the labour market and the bargaining strength of the parties, and therefore that its influence as an independent factor is slight, and unworthy of attention. But it can equally be argued that comparability considerations exert an independent influence on the bargaining behaviour of both employers and trade unionists, and hence directly affect the outcome of negotiations. There is evidence from this survey of the NBPI's experience of the tenacity of comparability and of the difficulties of replacing it with other acceptable considerations, and of making the necessary appropriate reforms in the collective bargaining structure. Also it is of course easier, though perhaps less necessary, to suppress comparability when the price level is stable, and incomes are only rising slowly. One reason why the NBPI was forced back to comparability more and more was the policy's failure to prevent rapid wage increases in most parts of the economy.

Nevertheless the NBPI appears to have enjoyed some success during the period of the policy in helping to reduce the role of comparability in the private sector and nationalised industries both in respect of industries referred to it for report and in others which feared reference. Whether these effects will be enduring is hard to foretell. The NBPI may prove to have had more success in injecting the consideration of productivity than in tempering the influence of comparability.

As for the public sector, the NBPI's influence appears to have been negligible because it could not attract sufficient references concerning the pay of civil servants, teachers, doctors and dentists, and many parts of local government. The public service, both local and central government, was exempt from the Government's incomes policy because it was guaranteed whatever others got and productivity was never a factor in negotiations. It is an important sidelight of incomes policy between 1965 and 1970 that the public sector was so successful in evading the full rigours of the policy.

Of course, civil service employees did not benefit from wage and salary drift attributable to local bargaining and similar factors as did a substantial part of the private sector (though they may have benefited from 'grade' drift). Consequently they would have felt it unfair if they had been singled out whilst in their view a great part of the workforce was de facto escaping the rigours of the policy through local bargaining.

It must also be recognised that there is a strong case for the use of comparisons to determine pay in the public service and that the use of comparability in fixing civil service pay is refined. Thus the Priestley Report of 1955 said:

'If the Government, which represents him, pays what other responsible employers pay for comparable work the citizen cannot reasonably complain that he is being exploited. Equally we consider that he would agree that he could not, in the long run, obtain an efficient service by paying less'.

The whole incomes policy and procedures represented a challenge to Civil Service expectations about pay-settlement which had grown up from the Government's acceptance of the Priestley Report and the existence of a variety of devices — internal relativities, fair comparisons, independent fact-finding (via the Pay Research Unit), and arbitration (via the Civil Service Arbitration Tribunal). These could scarcely be reconciled with the NBPI's approach and staff associations, notably the Society of Civil Servants and Institution of Professional Civil Servants, were upset that the 'ethical bargain' between the government and its employees was in danger of being unilaterally breached. The NBPI, however, did not have the opportunity of re-examining these matters in the context of a productivity prices and incomes policy, and it would have been valuable for it to have explored the scope for a closer relation of pay to productivity or individual performance in the public sector — and whether there is more scope than is commonly thought for the measurement of performance changes from year to year in this sector. Whatever the merits of this argument, the failure to break the force of comparability in the public sector to some extent undermined the NBPI's broad strategy of linking pay to performance in other sectors.

7. Wage and Salary Structures and Overtime

In a paper given to a symposium in Geneva in 1966, the Chairman of the NBPI stated:

'The objectives of incomes policy in Britain have required a weakening of the force of comparability and a deliberate change of wage structures ... the Board has directed attention towards the need for the construction of wage structures which are tailored to the needs of each industry. Pursuing the example of the industrial civil service, the Board recommended the grouping of establishments on the basis of homogeneity of processes and products and the negotiation of a wage structure for each group.'[1]

The NBPI's *First General Report* stated:

'Our observations have led us to the conclusion that the nature of the British earnings structure is itself an impediment to the more effective use of men and capital assets'.[2]

1 Mr. Aubrey Jones 'Wage Relativities' in A.D. Smith (ed.) *The Labour Market and Inflation*, (Macmillan, 1968), pp.115–6.

2 para. 48.

There were, in fact, three main subjects of concern for the NBPI in the wage and salary structure field. The first was its wish for changes in wage structures aimed at securing greater efficiency. The Board found, for example, that the complicated wage structures of manual workers in local authorities, the National Health Service, Gas and Water Supply called for a detailed examination using techniques of job evaluation with a view to abolishing unnecessary demarcations between levels of skill, ensuring that genuinely higher levels of skill and responsibility were properly rewarded, and securing greater flexibility of movement between the existing occupational groupings.

The NBPI's numerous recommendations for productivity agreements implied changes in earnings structures both within and between industries. It recognised the need for care to be taken not to create pressures from those who felt their relative position had worsened. Two of the guidelines for productivity agreements related to this: 'An agreement covering part of an undertaking should bear the cost of consequential increases if any have to be granted' and 'In all cases negotiators should beware of setting extravagant levels of pay which would provoke resentment outside'.

Second, the NBPI drew attention to the existence of inequitable wage structures in various industries in which employees doing similar work received widely differing wage rates and earnings. One source of these inequitie seemed to be the extension of fragmented shop floor bargaining as against national wage determination; this bargaining by establishing a standard for one group gave rise to resentment and pressures by other groups, first within the plant or enterprise, and then outside it, the net result conceivably being inflationary. Another source was the existence of payments by results scheme some largely out of managerial control, which generated anomalies and dispute Finally many wage structures had arisen as a result of historical evolution rather than from a conscious effort to relate pay to the job.

Apart from the reform of industrial relations collective bargaining institutions and the reform of payment by results wage schemes, the NBPI's most favoured remedy was the use of job evaluation techniques which were recommended in a large number of industries.

The NBPI's main views on job evaluation were set out in an impressive general study report on *Job Evaluation* (83). Job evaluation broadly means the comparison of jobs by the use of formal and systematic procedures in order to determine the relative position of one job to another in a wage or salary hierarchy. The report stressed that job evaluation was concerned with the reform of pay structures, whether associated with managerial, technical, clerical or manual workers. Since it considered that pay structure reform was an important means of achieving greater economic efficiency and that inadequate payment systems often lay at the root of industrial disputes, the Board favoured the use of job evaluation as an instrument of reform. The Report suggested that the need for reform was likely to continue because of the pressures generated by the rate of technical change, the growth in size of organisations due to mergers and take-overs, and the decline in the regulative force of industry-wide collective agreements.

It concluded that job evaluation could yield valuable advantages for both sides of industry. Management had the advantage of greater order and accept-ability in its pay arrangements, and of being able to control their development. It also benefited from having to look at its pay problems in a more disciplined way. Unions and employees benefited from a greater sense of fairness and rationality in pay matters, from being involved in the determination of pay relationships, and from having a payment system wherein additional responsi-bility could be recognised and rewarded. In so far as the introduction and implementation of job evaluation was concerned the Board recommended that wherever possible trade unions should be actively involved.

The Board attached a great deal of importance to job evaluation. But it warned management that the introduction of job evaluation would almost certainly lead to increased costs, particularly in the short term. There was the danger that a major reorganisation of pay structure might in the short term conflict with the requirements of the incomes policy. In the long term, however, were the job evaluation properly carried out and full use made of the data emerging from it, it could result in greater economic efficiency. Thus in the long term the objectives of incomes policy and those of major pay structure reorganisations could still co-incide. To overcome the cost problem, it recommended that the introduction of job evaluation should be accompanied by arrangements to increase productivity. Additionally, where the introduction of a job evaluation scheme required an increase in a firm's annual earnings bill in excess of the 3½ per cent ceiling established in the White Paper for 1968–69, and which could not be offset by other savings, it should be scrutinised with exceptional thoroughness by the Department of Employment and Productivity.

The NBPI never advocated the introduction of a national system of job evaluation:

'The Dutch and Soviet experiences suggest that, even on the technical plane, the application of a national job evaluation system is far from easy. It appears extremely difficult to devise an evaluation scheme which will embrace the great variety of skill requirements, responsibilities, and working conditions to be found over the whole range of employment. At present, we are concerned in this country with the urgent need to reduce confusion, obvious inequity, and economic inefficiency in pay structures. For the time being, the fulfilment of this need will best be furthered by the appli-cation of job evaluation at the enterprise or plant level, aided and promoted by action at the level of the industry such as we have proposed. It is possible, of course, that over time anomalies might develop between industry and industry, but this is a problem for the future.'[1]

The NBPI's main interest was in pressing for repairs to the existing struc-ture, where it was impeding efficiency, generating inflation or creating gross anomalies. In its investigations of specific industries it usually attempted no more than to put its finger on a few important examples of the deficiencies of the structure, and to suggest a general method of reform — normally job

1 para. 121.

evaluation. This was the case especially in the early days, but recommendations for the adoption of job evaluation can be found in numerous reports at all stages of the life of the Board. There is, in fact, an inconsistency between the restraint of the NBPI's advocacy of job evaluation in its general study report and its wholehearted recommendations, sometimes after fairly superficial investigations, of job evaluation in references about specific industries. This, of course, does not mean that the recommendations for job evaluation in the reports on specific industries were unsound, but the tenor of the general reports certainly suggested that it may not always have been wise to press job evaluation as a virtually standard solution to all wage structure problems encountered. More generally it may be noted that this contrast between a general study report and specific industry report seemed to be a characteristic of much of the NBPI's work in the wages field.

The third main field of concern for the NBPI about the wage structure was the wide gap which it often found to exist between basic rates and earnings. It believed this impeded the more effective use of men and capital assets. Large overtime earnings components in the earnings packet were looked upon with reservations. They were thought to make for the retention of undesirable work practices which spun out work into overtime hours. Dependence on a large number of supplements to the basic rate which are uncertain in their nature were thought likely to make workers resistant to change. The NBPI recommended in some cases that a minimum weekly earnings guarantee should replace low basic rates and overtime pay supplements in the hope that the greater security thereby attained by workers would lead to less resistance to change.

The Board's view on overtime has been quoted in Chapter 4. The Board in fact put the reduction of overtime at the forefront of many reports. It was, for example, a major objective of productivity agreements. Its recommendations in this field were, however, outstandingly unsuccessful, as far as is known at present. Proposals for reducing overtime in the road haulage industry and in the bakery industry for example met with no success.

It was only with the publication in October 1970 of a massive general study report *Hours of Work, Overtime and Shiftworking* (161) that the NBPI's discussions of overtime took on a more balanced character reflecting a compromise between different views among Board Members. It found that overtime in Great Britain was high compared with other countries though only for male manual workers. It recognised that many employers and manual workers found that overtime served various needs but reiterated the view that it was often associated with inefficiency and emphasised that wherever it was high, management and workers should jointly study whether it was necessary or desirable. The Board also considered the economic justification and social effects of shiftwork as well as other hours of work problems.

The Board conducted several major surveys for this reference. Three surveys elicited the views of trade associations, large companies and trade unions on hours of work questions. Another important survey covered a sample of establishments throughout the production industries to obtain the views of management on the reasons for overtime and shiftwork and many other questions. Another survey was based on interviews of samples of shift and overtime workers and their wives as well as a control group to study the reasons for and acceptability of shiftwork and overtime and the effects on social life. This survey showed surprisingly little disturbance to social life or health of shiftworkers and that most accepted it for the sake of higher earnings but that there was more discontent among shiftworkers' wives. Finally the Board arranged for the Department of Employment to carry out a special study from the New Earnings Survey of September 1968 of overtime and shiftwork in relation to age, absenteeism and sickness, and levels of pay. This also showed relatively little difference in health between day and shiftworkers and provided evidence, contrary to the general belief, that high overtime workers had exceptionally good sickness and absenteeism records. This survey also concluded that, at least above a certain level of pay, overtime was inversely related to hourly earnings.

Consideration of the NBPI's views on the wage structure leads naturally onto an account of its treatment of low pay.

8. Low Pay

White Papers: Successive White Papers permitted exceptional pay increases 'where there is general recognition that existing wage and salary levels are too low to maintain a reasonable standard of living'.

At first 'above-norm' wage increases were permitted for low-paid workers, but in the 1968–69 phase, there was a 3½ per cent ceiling for such increases although an above-ceiling increase was permitted for low-paid workers as part of a settlement which, taken as a whole, was within the ceiling.

Report 101 on Agricultural Workers drew attention to the difficulties of the ceiling. The Board recommended that a 7 per cent increase granted to agricultural workers should go through, despite the ceiling, as a very special case. This was accepted by the Government. Indeed it became clear during the 1968–9 phase that the low paid worker was a more central figure in the strategy of an incomes policy than was previously thought. Thus, in 1969, above-ceiling settlements for low-paid workers, such as dustmen, were not referred to the NBPI. If they had been, the NBPI would not have been able to recommend increases of more than 3½ per cent. These low pay settlements were widely acknowledged as crucial to the premature breakdown of the policy, paving the way for above-ceiling settlements in a number of other sectors.

Defining Low Pay: The question of whether an incomes policy should accord special treatment to the low-paid was considered foreclosed:

> 'In implying that exceptional treatment may be accorded to a wage increase on the ground that it improves the standard of living of the worst off, we understand the White Paper to be pointing out that when the social services have done what they can, need will still be greatest where wages and salaries are lowest and that the recipients of these should have a prior claim on the use of resources available for pay increase.'[1]

1 *Pay of Agricultural Workers* (25), para. 49.

At first the Board decided not to define a figure which separated the lowest-paid from the rest. It considered that to lay down an absolute 'standard of need' for the purpose of settling pay required assumptions about needs that were arbitrary, and did not take account of varying family size. Any comparison in terms of needs was at best a method of drawing very broad distinctions. 'Clearly anyone whose pay is scarcely above the level of national assistance is low paid. By and large, however, the concept of low pay is a relative rather than an absolute one; the most that can be said in most cases — and even this is difficult — is that pay is too low, or alternatively too high, in relation to somebody else's'. [1]

The identification of the lowest-paid required an examination of the distribution of earnings in the industry and a comparison with earnings in other industries. Moreover, if the wages of the lowest-paid were to be improved relatively, a distinction should be drawn between differentials which should be maintained to avoid anomalies and which it would be 'economically unwise and socially unjust' to narrow, and those differentials which it would not be anomalous to narrow.

In 1971 in a general study report *General Problems of Low Pay* (169), the NBPI reiterated that it would not define low pay in absolute terms. Nevertheless 'a consistent approach makes it necessary to adopt some conventional criterion by which to identify areas of low pay'. [2] Regarding low pay as essentially a relative problem, it treated full-time workers with average weekly earnings lower than 90 per cent of manual workers as low-paid. Men were compared separately with men, women with women, and for part-time workers, hourly earnings were compared. Its main use was to focus attention explicitly on the lowest-paid tenth of the work force, to consider what if anything could be done to secure an improvement. It was stressed that this one-dimensional approach could not be used on its own. To determine if an industry was low-paid, its median earnings should be compared with the national median; the earnings of a predominantly unskilled workforce should be compared with the earnings of unskilled workers nationally; and, if possible such factors as the age distribution, hours of work, hourly earnings, fringe benefits and so on should be taken into account.

Moreover, the NBPI said, it could not be suggested that to belong to the low-paid group gave an automatic right to have one's pay level lifted to that of the lowest national decile. There was always a lowest ten per cent in any group. Many factors which determined the position of a low-paid worker were within his control — the effort he contributed under incentive payment schemes and whether he worked overtime or shifts. Other factors, even if not under the worker's control, made it difficult to improve their pay — if they were seriously handicapped or would have difficulty in raising their level of pay. If a target was required, it should be set in terms of lifting the bottom earning decile closer to the median from its level of under 70 per cent. Finally, low pay and poverty were not the same thing.

1 *Second General Report*, para. 51.

2 para. 9.

NBPI Policies: Two central themes emerge from the NBPI's reports on industries with low pay. The first was stated in the *Fifth General Report:*

> '... our studies emphasised that there was no single set of factors which was responsible for low pay and hence that there was no single set of measures which was appropriate to improve low pay in all circumstances. The need was to study individual situations and to take whatever measures might be appropriate to deal with them.'[1]

The second was stated in the *Fourth General Report:*

> 'In so far as improving the position of the low paid is one of the purposes of a productivity, prices and incomes policy — which in our view it should be — the main remedy is to be found in the improvement of efficiency. Except in a minority of instances, therefore, we consider that the improvement of the position of the low paid can be subsumed in the general problem of improving efficiency'.[2]

The first main attempt by the NBPI to arrive at a low pay policy came when it reported at the beginning of 1967 on *Pay of Agricultural Workers* (25), *Pay of Retail Drapery, Outfitting and Footwear Trade Workers* (27) and *Pay of Manual Workers in Local Authorities, the National Health Service, Gas and Water Supply* (29): these cases illustrate the two themes of higher productivity as a solution, and of the need to take account of the differing circumstances of each industry.

Pay of Agricultural Workers (25) was about an industry in which the great majority of workers were low-paid. Differentials were already very narrow, and in most cases could not have been compressed without anomalies. The NBPI accepted that the decision of the Agricultural Wages Board in the period of Severe Restraint to increase the minimum rate of pay which would have resulted in most workers in the industry receiving an above-norm increase was in full accord with the provisions of the White Paper.

Pay of Workers in the Retail Drapery, Outfitting and Footwear Trades (27) posed a different kind of problem. Although it was claimed that this was a low pay industry the NBPI's earnings surveys demonstrated that only a minority of workers could be so regarded. There was a wide spread of differentials. The Board therefore was willing to support a Wages Council decision to recommend some increase in the statutory minimum for all workers, but urged that representative organisations in the trade should make arrangements to confine the increases to the lowest paid by providing for 'tapering' increases so that they disappeared when earnings were more than £3 (for men) or £1 (for women) above the minimum.

The *Pay and Conditions of Manual Workers in Local Authorities, the National Health Service, Gas and Water Supply* (29) concerned 1,100,000 workers whose pay was closely related. Although the four industries had certain things in common — origins in local government, complicated

1 para. 53.

2 para. 59.

129

structures of time rates, broadly comparable levels of basic pay, and scope for significant improvements in productivity — they also had important differences such as the level and distribution of earnings, the numbers of women employed, and the scope for technological change. The tendency was for the links between the industries to become looser and the NBPI's recommendation were designed to meet the individual needs of each group of workers.

Local government and the National Health Service were the two fields which contained large concentrations of workers who were among the lowest paid in the country. While the national rates of pay compared favourably with those negotiated for similar occupations in other industries, the low level of earnings reflected the limited opportunities of adding to basic rates. The close relationship between earnings for a normal working week and the standard wage rate prevented the Board from repeating its recommendations of the retail drapery report of relating pay increases to different earnings levels. Nor was it possible to confine increases to particular wage rates. The wage rate structures of the two services were so compressed that to increase the wage rates of the bottom grades, to an extent which would provide meaningful assistance to the lowest paid, would swamp many differentials in the structure and diminish others to the point at which they would lose significance. Such a course, the Board considered, would inevitably result in pressures to restore the differentials. A general increase in wage rates was also ruled out. There was no immediate solution to the problem.

The main finding of the NBPI's studies of the efficiency of the two industries was that poor use was made of manual labour. The root cause of the problem of low pay was low productivity. In the long term the solution must lie in the effective use of labour through the introduction of properly constructed and controlled schemes of payment relating earnings to performance. The systems of payment to be considered should include not only incentive bonus schemes in which payment varied directly with performance but also measured day work and productivity agreements in which increased pay was related to an acceptance of different working methods. Since such schemes took a long time to plan, an interim scheme was proposed, which proved to be totally without effect.

Generally, the NBPI's approach to low pay was empirical not only in that it believed different situations required different solutions but also in that it sought always first to find the facts. By pinpointing the exact incidence of low pay, it was often able to narrow greatly the area of contention. Thus, in references concerning buses, retail drapery, clothing manufacturing and pottery, the NBPI's earnings surveys showed that low pay was not widespread in those industries, as had been claimed, but at most confined to specific groups. This information suggested that general pay increases throughout these industries were inappropriate and that measures to help the low-paid worker directly were necessary.

In the second reference on buses, the Board was able to carry its investigations further. The earnings survey identified the existence of low pay in a small number of establishments only. It also showed that most of the difference between low-paid and high-paid workers was accounted for by the different number of hours they worked each week. Members of the Enquiry Team visited eleven of these establishments and interviewed some of the low-paid individuals, and management and unions. It was confirmed that low pay went with low hours per week, which were in turn largely governed by personal preferences or by the health or domestic circumstances of individuals e.g. a number of those who worked relatively short hours were from families with more than one wage earner. In some other references it was found that low pay hardly existed, but there were low basic rates of pay and long hours of work. The NBPI diagnosed the essence of these problems as being the need to reduce hours of work, not to raise pay. Surveys did, of course, sometimes confirm that low pay was a serious, relatively general problem in some industries such as local authorities and the National Health Service.

Productivity as the solution to low pay in many circumstances was the other most frequent theme of the Board's low pay reports as is evident from the above. In a number of instances the low pay problem was seen as being closely related to the Wages Council system of determining pay which was considered an obstacle to raising productivity. This is discussed in the next chapter.

Tapering Formulae: The NBPI's recommendation in the report on retail drapery for the adoption of a tapering formula providing relatively larger increases for the lowest-paid has already been noted. Until 1967 this was in fact an important element in the NBPI's low pay policy and was recommended whenever feasible, for example in *Wages in the Bakery Industry* (17) and *Road Haulage* (48). In none of the three cases was the trade union involved prepared to support the tapering proposal, although the Road Haulage Wages Council, at the insistence of its independent member, did adopt it. The TUC, in its Economic Review for 1968, said about pro tanto increases:

'Unions have, often after considerable efforts to establish a viable basis on which this can be done, either tacitly decided that it was not practicable — at least in the short run — or have explicitly said that it would not be possible because of the marked effect on differentials'.

After this, the NBPI abandoned this aspect of its low pay policy, and after 1967 no tapering formulas were recommended.

The Wage Structure: The NBPI's attempt to support tapering formulas reflected a concern that by transmitting themselves throughout the wage structure increases granted specially to low paid workers would be self-defeating and inflationary. This had been a factor in the early decision not to define low pay, and although not always stated in reports, influenced its rather cautious recommendations for the improvement of those with low pay.

The report *General Problems of Low Pay* contained analysis relevant to the problem. The Board's historical, statistical analysis of movements in the distribution of earnings in Great Britain over the period 1884 to 1970 was directed to substantiating the thesis that there has been remarkably little change in the spread of earnings. Money earnings over that period increased more than twentyfold, but the bottom earnings decile for men was never less than 66.5 per cent and never more than 70.6 per cent of median earnings. During the 1960's there had again been little change. It concluded:

'It can be concluded from the evidence that pay differentials have a great capacity to reassert themselves. There appears to have been remarkable stability in the overall distribution of earnings and considerable, if lesser, stability in inter-industry, sex, occupational and regional earnings differentials'.[1]

This suggested the great difficulty of using a wage policy to change the relative position of the low-paid.

Some Conclusions

The NBPI, and the prices and incomes policies, both accorded a lower priority to low pay than to other wage problems, and up to a point tried to subsume the problem into that of raising productivity.

The NBPI's early reports contain little recognition of the possibility that low wage low productivity sectors may be exactly the ones in which it is hardest, not easiest, to raise productivity. On the other hand, the approach of the Board was constructive in that improved performance by low paid workers would eventually certainly help raise their real pay and might in fact prove to be the only way of ensuring that their real level of pay rises in the long run.

The NBPI's generally empirical approach to low pay problems was highlighted by its recognition that the nature of, and possible solutions to, the low pay problem depended on the circumstances of each industry.

The analysis of the general study report on low pay showing the distribution of earnings in Britain since 1884 suggested the difficulty of changing the relative position of the low paid, a difficulty of which the NBPI had always been aware. The analysis, however, was relevant to all of the NBPI's wage policies discussed in this and the next chapter. Attempts to alter the relative structure of wages should not be lightly embarked upon. The evidence suggest that pay differentials reassert themselves and so the attempts may be unsuccessful and inflationary. This cannot be proved but it is a definite possibility. If the NBPI's wage policies tended to add to inflation, which in my opinion is likely but cannot be proved, they would need to be weighed up against possible productivity gains from the policy. In the following chapter then the NBPI's policies regarding pay and productivity are examined.

This is an appropriate place to note one other point: the NBPI was less vociferous about low pay as a social and economic problem than about other wage problems. This illustrates a general theme which applies to nearly all of the NBPI's work. It did not regard the alteration of the existing distribution of income as one of the main purposes of incomes policy, unless greater efficiency or wage stability was likely to result.

1 para. 44.

9. Pay and Productivity

1. Productivity

One part of the NBPI's strategy was to break the hold of traditional factors in income determination: the other was to introduce different factors, such as the incomes norm, and, most notably, productivity.[1] This was attempted in one form or another across nearly the whole field of incomes, from low pay to top salaries, and the aim was never abandoned.

The reasons for this were stated earlier — higher productivity permitted some combination of higher pay, higher profits, lower costs and lower prices; the policy could be based on an appeal to the interests of the parties; and the closer linking of pay to individual performance would stimulate performance itself. The NBPI also believed that genuine productivity agreements, for example, could have very useful side-effects, such as improving management, by increasing cost-consciousness, by providing new information about performance and new methods of assessing it, and by directing attention to the possibility of changing methods of work. Management negotiators were brought into closer touch with unions, and more managers became aware of the implications for industrial relations of technical and financial decisions. The experience of applying the agreements with their provisions on overtime, flexibility, manning and so on often brought a revolution in managerial control over working hours and practices. There were changes in organisation, personnel and the provision of training, and senior and other managers were better informed and organised than before the agreements.[2]

1 The policy did not mean that pay increases were to be strictly tied to the rate of productivity increases in each plant or industry. The national 'norm' was initially based on the projected average rate of productivity increase for the economy as a whole, but tying wage increases to productivity increases at a micro-economic level would have led to large disparities in pay increases between low and high productivity growth sectors, even for those in the same occupations. Furthermore, much of the productivity increase in particular sectors of the economy resulted from added contributions by capital, not labour, inputs, so that there was no particular reason for awarding higher pay to labour in these sectors. Finally, the demand for labour in labour-intensive industries with a low rate of productivity increase may increase more rapidly than in capital-intensive industries with a higher elasticity of capital-labour substitution, and this would require a higher rate of wage increase to attract labour. See H.A. Turner and D. Jackson, 'On the Stability of Wage Differences and Productivity — based Wage Policies: An International Analysis,' *British Journal of Industrial Relations*, Vol. VII, No. 1, March 1969.

2 *Productivity Agreements* (36), Chapter 5.

The aim was not limited to achieving some once-for-all productivity increases by buying out some restrictive labour practices but to achieve as far as possible a continuous linking of pay and productivity or individual performance. There was no one way of relating pay to productivity or performance; nor of raising productivity. It was necessary to investigate the facts in each reference, to determine the possibilities for improved labour performance, and to point out in broad terms the action necessary to raise productivity.

2. Productivity Agreements

The NBPI's approach received its fullest expression in its treatment of productivity agreements though they were only one of several ways in which it pressed for the introduction of productivity considerations in the pay field. Other methods were recommended in appropriate circumstances such as forms of Payment by Results and relating salary scales to individual performance more closely.

A productivity agreement, as defined by the NBPI in Report 36, is an agreement 'in which workers make a change, or a number of changes, in workin practices that will lead in itself — leaving out any compensating pay increase to more economical working; and in return the employer agrees to a higher level of pay or other benefits'.[1]

Report 36 indicated that some of the main objectives of productivity agreements should be: reductions of unnecessary overtime; freer interchange of tasks between different groups (e.g. craft groups) of workers; the removal of restrictions on output (e.g. limitations on speed of vehicles in oil distribution) improved manpower practices (e.g. reduction of number of craftsmen's mates); and changes in patterns of work (e.g. shiftwork).

The NBPI issued three general study reports on productivity agreements.[2] These references were used to fulfil the NBPI's strategy of injecting productivity considerations into wage and salary negotiations throughout the economy as well as into individual industries it dealt with. This was carried out as a mixture of accident and deliberate policy decision.

The main accident was the timing of the first reference to the NBPI on productivity agreements. Before July 1966, the NBPI had suggested to the Government that it should be allowed to examine a number of selected productivity agreements in order to have an opportunity of clarifying their benefits as well as their dangers. By the time this reference had arrived in August 1966 the Government had introduced the six months 'Standstill' on wages. Looking to the future, it had to determine how the standstill was to give way to a period of 'Severe Restraint'. It asked the NBPI to produce a special interim report in order to suggest guidelines for judging circumstances in which higher pay in return for increased productivity might be justified in the first half of 1967.

1 Para. 3.

2 *Productivity Agreements* (23), (36), (123).

The Board's guidelines[1] were enshrined in appendices to White Papers[2] and they became the basis of the administration of the inspection system of wage claims and settlements purporting to be productivity agreements. Accordingly, the general study references came to be closely connected with the development and operation of the whole Prices and Incomes policy and were regarded by the Board as a unique opportunity to influence the whole economy.

The NBPI's first report was strong endorsement of the virtues and potentialities of genuine productivity agreements, and concluded that there was a strong case for encouraging their spread. This was qualified in three ways. Firstly, it was pointed out that preparation, negotiation and implementation of a sound agreement would be a lengthy process. Productivity agreements were likely to remain exceptional in the near future, since most managements were far from ready to consider undertaking the tasks of preparation, negotiation and control required for their success. Secondly the NBPI laid down stringent guidelines showing the requirements which productivity agreements would need to meet in order to qualify for exceptional pay increases. These were:

'(1) It should be shown that the workers are making a direct contribution towards increasing productivity by accepting more exacting work or a major change in working practices.

(2) Forecasts of increased productivity should be derived by the application of proper work-standards.

(3) An accurate calculation of the gains and the costs should normally show that the total capital cost per unit of output, taking into account the effect on capital, will be reduced.

(4) The scheme should contain effective controls to ensure that the projected increase in productivity is achieved, and that payment is made only as productivity increases or as changes in working practice take place.

(5) The undertaking should be ready to show clear benefits to the consumer through a contribution to stable prices.

(6) An agreement covering part of an undertaking should bear the cost of consequential increases elsewhere in the same undertaking, if any have to be granted.

(7) In all cases negotiators should beware of setting extravagant levels of pay which would provoke resentment outside.'

These were criticised at the time by Mr. Hugh Scanlon as an impediment to the development of productivity bargaining. Thirdly, an apparently minor change of wording was intended to restrict the scope for productivity agreements. The original White Paper had stated that exceptional pay increases were justified 'where employees, *for example* by accepting more exacting

1 As set out in the Report 23, and later amended in Report 36, para. 215.

2 In 1968 and at the end of 1969.

work or a major change in working practices, made a direct contribution towards increasing productivity.' The words 'for example' were omitted from the guidelines.

The above were the guidelines suggested in Report 36. The only important difference from Report 23 was in the fifth guideline which in the earlier report had been: 'there should be a clear benefit to the consumer, in lower prices or in improved quality ...'. The Ministry of Labour had found this guideline the hardest to apply because firms' pricing decisions were often difficult to relate directly to the outcome of productivity agreements. The NBPI's 7 case studies for Report 36 showed that several agreements would not have satisfied this guideline, and that those which did so affected prices only to a minor extent, sometimes because the savings were only fractional in relation to the price of a product and sometimes because substantial savings were offset by increases in costs arising for other reasons.

In Report 123 issued in 1969, the NBPI reported that there was wide scope for the application of productivity agreements in areas such as clerical and other non-manual work, where their use had been rare. Work measurement techniques and other methods of improving efficiency could be applied to a wide variety of clerical and other non-manual jobs, with the likelihood of substantial increases in efficiency and reductions in labour costs. In view of the generally co-operative attitude of non-manual workers, productivity agreements of the traditional kind which spelt out specific changes in working practices were often not desirable or necessary. The main requirement was a willingness to adapt working patterns continuously to changing techniques.

A broader view of productivity agreements also emerged as a result of the requirement of the terms of references that the NBPI investigate 'the renewal and later development of existing agreements' or 'second generation' productivity agreements, that is productivity agreements which succeeded previous productivity agreements, covering the same workers. It traced the development in companies whose earlier productivity agreements were dealt with in Report 36. This showed

'that the earlier agreements later gave rise to further agreements, partly from intent since the earlier agreements could not attempt too much at once, partly because the execution of the earlier agreements revealed a scope and an opportunity for further agreements, partly because changing technology dictated a need for further agreements, the entire history culminating in a recognition that what was required was the continuous adaptation of working patterns to changing technology, with periodic pay or salary reviews. This history does not confirm the commonly expressed definition of a productivity agreement as "a sale of restrictive practices"... It suggests rather that the negotiation of productivity agreements may help companies to move towards the goal of continuous adaptation to changing technology'.[1]

It was thus necessary to revise and broaden the guidelines, to emphasise

1 para. 31.

136

the underlying aim of constantly raising efficiency on the basis of close and continuous co-operation between management and workers, and to express them in terms clearly applicable to workers of all kinds, including non-manual workers for whom it was not appropriate to specify changes in working practices, and manual workers who might have previously concluded agreements specifying changes in working practices but for whom such agreements were no longer appropriate. The term 'efficiency agreement' was adopted to cover both productivity agreements and the new classes of agreement not spelling out changes. The only major[1] change in the wording of the guidelines was the first which now read:

> 'Guidelines for Efficiency Agreements including Productivity Agreements. 1st Guideline: It should be shown that the workers are contributing towards the achievment of constantly rising levels of efficiency. Where appropriate, major changes in working practice or working methods should be specified in the agreement'.[2]

The NBPI said the word 'direct' was dropped not because of any abandonment of the principle that a differentiation between contributions to productivity increases by labour and capital was necessary (no matter how hard it might be to make such a differentiation), but because it could give a misleadingly narrow impression and might be thought to exclude, for example, co-operation which took the form of acceptance of changes in working practices and methods which did not have to be spelt out. The effect of this change of wording, then, was to broaden substantially the criteria, to encompass all possible cases of a labour contribution to higher productivity.

This broader conception whilst showing the possibilities also showed the difficulties of efficiency agreements. It was difficult enough under the old guidelines to measure the contribution of labour to higher productivity in order to reward it appropriately. But to think of rewarding labour for continuing co-operation in the implementation of higher productivity raised seemingly insuperable measurement problems. The guidelines seemed to embrace a wide range of situations where workers benefited by accepting normal changes in working practices resulting from investment's contribution to increased efficiency. The report was not very convincing on this point – it reflected differences of views within the NBPI – and contained a suggestion that the Government should consider the possibility of a further reference regarding methods of measuring the labour contribution to productivity. The broader conception was influenced by the NBPI's awareness that the incomes policy was starting to collapse.

The third report on productivity agreements showed that 25 per cent of all workers had been involved in productivity agreements mainly in 1968 and 1969. The case studies for this reference undoubtedly demonstrated that a proportion of the 3,000 or so agreements were genuine. The NBPI went further than this.

1 A number of less significant amendments were made to guidelines in the light of the broader conception of efficiency agreements and of experience.

2 para. 133.

In three quarters of the 46 cases studied it concluded that the net effect of the agreement was the achievement of lower costs per unit of output or, where it was not possible to tell the effect on unit costs, worthwhile reductions in wage or salary bills:

'Our studies do not suggest that productivity bargaining has so far inflated earnings in relation to increases in productivity and has therefore been on balance disadvantageous from a national point of view; rather the reverse.'[1]

In an earlier part of the report, however, it was stated that the selection of case studies was not intended to provide a representative sample of industry. Rather

'We deliberately selected examples of the types of agreement which we considered best calculated to answer the questions specified in the reference',[2]

i.e. the effects of partial agreements, non-manual work agreements, second generation agreements and industry and company-wide agreements.

It is difficult to see how such a confident generalisation could be made from such a sample. It is also difficult to reconcile it with their apparently negligible effect on the national rate of productivity growth, and the assertion of the NBPI's Report 36 that productivity agreements would be an exception in the future because of the difficulty of establishing them.

Although little direct evidence exists, it is likely that the majority of productivity agreements during this period were simply devices to raise wages in the only way permitted by the incomes policy. Professor H.A. Turner has suggested that the avalanche of agreements can be explained as follows:

'First, a very large proportion of these agreements mainly involved revisions of obsolete or troublesome pay systems and structures, the cost of which revisions the companies concerned could argue to be mostly met by normal productivity growth. Second, another large proportion of agreements in the main merely set out in formal terms changes in working methods or practices which would have had to occur anyway, as a result of technical change, and put a price on them. That is, the productivity increase was mostly that which would have happened in any case; so that what many so-called "productivity bargains" really did was to use this to justify an exceptional wage increase'.[3]

Much of the trouble stemmed from the leniency of the inspection machinery. Only 130 cases covering some 48,000 workers were rejected. This did not reflect the difficulties of applying the NBPI's guidelines, but what must have

1 para. 136.

2 para. 6.

3 H.A. Turner. 'Collective Bargaining and the Eclipse of Incomes Policy: Retrospect, Prospect and Possibilities,' *British Journal of Industrial Relations*, Vol. VIII, No. 2. July 1970. p. 203.

been a conscious political choice. Moreover, inspection became increasingly lenient with the sharp rise in productivity agreements.

The apparently bogus nature of many productivity agreements in this period does not mean that they could not have a legitimate role in a properly administered policy in the future. In 1968—9 they (with wage and salary reorganisations) provided the only means of escaping the rigours of the policy. They were strongly encouraged by the Government and their inspection was fairly lax. In the circumstances they were bound to be abused.

The Board must take some of the blame for the over-rapid spread of productivity agreements, and probably for their encouragement in the Government's policy. Although the Board laid down strict guidelines for the application of productivity agreements, it must have known that in practice the net effect of its reports would be greatly to accelerate their spread. However it is well worth assessing the reports at their face value, ignoring the question of the wider effects of the way in which the report was presented. The three general reports remain the most valuable source of information there is on productivity agreements, and represent an authoritative attempt to work out in detail how they fit into an incomes policy. As such they will, or should be, the main source of guidance for any future experiments with productivity agreements in incomes policy. Nevertheless the reports taken at face value seem to have some weaknesses, and indeed some of the questions left unanswered suggest that it would have been wise for the Board to have exhibited less enthusiasm for them.

The NBPI never really satisfactorily answered the objection that an incomes policy which favours productivity agreements tends to favour the higher-paid worker more than the lower-paid since the former usually works in a better managed, rapidly changing industry with more opportunities for productivity agreements. On the other hand the NBPI's final report on productivity agreements appears to have gone a good deal of the way to meeting the objection that such agreements favour the inefficient or those who have restrictive practices to sell, but it only did so by broadening the conception of productivity agreements to a point dangerously close to the acceptance of any co-operation in technical change as being grounds for a pay rise. The NBPI might thus have found it fruitful to draw a sharper distinction between the acceptance of more exacting work and the acceptance of a major change in working practices. The former seems a more justifiable reason for a wage increase than the latter.

In some cases, the negotiation of productivity agreements particularly regarding overtime may not have been the right priority for management. The NBPI's reports show very clearly the extensive preparation necessary for the conclusion of a satisfactory agreement. The Board saw productivity agreements, indeed, as a means of bringing about improved managerial performance, but a more direct approach would have been to assess what was wrong with management without going by the indirect route of pressing for productivity agreements. This comment probably applies more generally to some of the NBPI's suggestions for the adoption of technique — oriented solutions such as work study, job evaluation and so on to problems of inefficiency in the managerial field. This does not mean that its work was wasted. Broadly it aimed in the right direction for change but may have been a little off target.

The emphasis accorded to productivity agreements as a means of raising efficiency may also be questioned. In the first place the NBPI, for all its qualifications, seems to have had an exaggerated view of their potential for raising efficiency. Their effects on productivity were not shown to be dramatic enough to justify the hope that the increased wages associated with them would not result in cost increases. And, to judge from some of the NBPI's reports on managerial efficiency, it was not clear that there would be much scope for any large cost-saving to occur in the immediate future. The most that could be hoped for was the taking of the first steps to ensure that eventually management would be of sufficiently good quality to include the negotiation of productivity agreements as one part of its programme for securing efficiency within enterprises.

Another problem was the difficulty the Board encountered in trying to relate pay to productivity meaningfully in certain sectors of the economy. When one looks through the list of references, there are many for whom it was hard even in principle to suggest satisfactory measures of productivity – nurses and midwives, Scottish schoolteachers, university teachers, armed forces, lightkeepers, top management, middle management, firemen, local chief officers, merchant navy officers, bank staff, higher civil service, agricultural workers, journalists, pilots. There were other sectors in which no measures of productivity existed, even though there were no difficulties in principle about doing so.

What were the repercussive effects of productivity agreements outside the plant or industry?

The NBPI made studies of possible repercussive effects of productivity agreements on local labour markets. Although little detail is given about the basis of these studies, they suggested that productivity agreements had little effect on pay rates in these markets. No attempt was made to examine the charge sometimes made that the encouragement of and publicity given to productivity agreements, sometimes involving very large pay increases, was a factor lifting the whole level of wage increase expectations throughout the economy, even if their effects on nearby markets were slight. More generally, very little is known about the different ways in which wage increases granted in one plant, firm or industry may influence wage increases in other parts of the economy. Their effects on neighbouring plants is not the only possible way in which their influence may spread. They may spread to other firms in the industry. They might not directly affect rates of pay in neighbouring plants but trade unionists in them might be led to press their national conferences to seek higher increases than would otherwise have been sought in national negotiations: they could affect claims based on comparability. Where as is sometimes the case, employers' clubs in the same areas exchange information about their rates of pay so that each firm can maintain its competitive, relative position in the local labour market, they may set off an upward spiral.[1] The NBPI's analysis in Report 169 of the stability of the British earnings structure, referred to in the previous chapter, suggests that it did not investigate these possibilities adequately. However, one may then conclude on a positive note by quoting the verdict of H.A. Turner:

> 'Perhaps the most important achievement of productivity bargaining is that it is helping to undermine the iron curtain which for nearly half-a-century has restricted negotiations between managements and employees over a large area of industry, setting off "managerial functions" on the one hand and "craft regulations" on the other as areas which are not subject to bargaining. This advantage alone will certainly lead to a continued spread of productivity agreements ...'[2]

3. Payments by Results

In this section an account of NBPI policy with respect to payment by results is given, concentrating especially on the general study report *Payment By Results* (65). The main theme concerns the NBPI's attempt to use the report to draw up guidelines, as it had done in respect of productivity agreements, which could be used by the vetting machinery to get a grip on payment systems which were generating 'drift'. However, a full account of the report is given also to illustrate the nature of a general study report.

In Part I of this book it was noted that the failure to control adequately the working of payments by results wage systems was seemingly one of the factors in the downfall of the 1948—50 wage freeze experiment. The NBPI recognised that an important gap had always existed in incomes policy in Great Britain because in practice it only dealt with claims and settlements for changes in rates of pay and never sought to deal with those causes of increases in earnings which lay outside this process. P.B.R. systems were the most important example. It estimated that about 33 per cent of the work force — and 42 per cent of manufacturing workers — are paid by results in Great Britain.

The NBPI's report 23 on Productivity Agreements referred to the fact that 'direct contributions towards increasing productivity may be made through systems of payment by results'.

The NBPI argued that there was often an element of looseness inherent in managerial control of these systems, and that where this was so, there was a tendency for a general loosening of the relationship between pay and effort, and an upward drift in earnings. Often then there was no justification for exceptional pay increases to such workers. In view of the serious nature of the problem, the Board asked for a general reference concerning it.

The NBPI's intention was to draw up guidelines, as it had done in respect of productivity agreements, which could be used by the vetting machinery to

1 see 'Practical Conclusion' by Derek Robinson in *Local Labour Markets and Wage Structures*, edited by Derek Robinson, (Gower Press, 1970.) pp. 283—285.

2 H.A. Turner, op.cit., p. 207.

get a grip on payment systems which were generating 'drift'. Thus, besides having an educational purpose, this report was connected with the overall operation of the prices and incomes policy.

Wide-ranging investigations were undertaken for the reference. Case studies lasting on average 15 days were made by outside case workers in some 40 different factories, and covered a variety of industries, regions and types of payment systems, as well as examples of P.B.R. systems recently abandoned or introduced. Among the chief topics examined were the effects of P.B.R. on productivity, the pay packet of workers, the wage and salary structure, and workplace bargaining; also studied were such matters as the local effects of national bargaining, trade union organisation, the use of work measurement practices and management control of costs. Selected case studies were summarised in moderate detail in a supplement to the report – they give, incidentally, an indication of the quality of an above-average NBPI case study. Academic, management and union literature of the previous seven years on P.B.R. was exhaustively reviewed. Discussions were held with trade unions; and with employers and professional bodies such as the Institute of Personnel Management, the Institution of Production Engineers and the Institution of Works Managers, some of whom made extensive enquiries on the NBPI's behalf and finally with the Industrial Society and some leading firms of management consultants.

Relying mainly on official data from 1961 it was estimated that about 33 per cent of all workers, and 42 per cent in manufacturing industry, were paid by results. It was recommended that a new and more detailed official statistical enquiry into the incidence of P.B.R. systems be made as a matter of urgency.

There was found to be a diversity of P.B.R. systems, varying according to many factors including the relationship of the individual worker's earnings to his own or his group's performance; the proportion of bonus elements in his pay packet; the period of performance to which the bonus related; the quantity of output, time or effort, or the quality of output, or the nature of the task according to which the bonus varied. The old clear-cut distinction between payment by output and payment by time had become blurred, and many intermediate systems incorporating elements of both had sprung up. The NBPI distinguished two main categories of P.B.R.: 'conventional P.B.R.' i.e. piece work and incentive schemes related to individuals or small groups, and 'alternative systems' such as measured daywork or plant-wide incentive schemes which are explained below.

The NBPI was required to give special attention to the connection between P.B.R. and 'wage drift', the persistent tendency for wages actually paid at the workshop to rise, on average, faster than would result from the increases arranged from time to time under national agreements. The source of drift is the 'workplace margin' between actual wages paid by employers and rates laid down as minimum or standard rates by agreements at national level. (The gap between actual earnings and wage rates due to overtime is not part of the concept of drift).

142

Drift is quantitatively significant in the British economy, and poses a crucial problem of incomes policy. Official estimates showed it to have been about 2 per cent higher than the average for the preceding decade. Taking account of certain deficiencies in the official measures,[1] the NBPI calculated that 4 per cent would be a reasonable approximation of its true extent — in other words drift alone exceeded the national annual rate of productivity increase. If wage inflation was to be avoided, drift left no room, for instance, for selective wage increases to workers not benefiting from it. The NBPI believed therefore that there were good reasons for attempting to bring drift under some effective supervision.

The 'primary process' of drift was strongly associated with conventional P.B.R. Four factors were responsible. First, the effect of many piece-rate or incentive systems linking earnings with output was inevitably to raise hourly earnings as productivity rose with technical progress, independently of the degree of effort involved. Second, there was the 'learning curve' phenomenon. It had been empirically observed by industrial engineers that the output per hour of workers tended to rise, without any apparant change in the process or increase in effort on the workers' part, the more of any given product was produced, even over a lengthy period such as several years. Under most P.B.R. systems, the effect of this was for earnings to increase over the period of the production run. Third, frequent bargaining necessary about the fixing of new piece-rates or work standards against a background of strong union organisation in the workplace and of high employment, inevitably tended to induce a steady increase in the actual hourly wages paid. Fourth, there was the common practice of fixing new piece-rates, times or prices so that P.B.R. workers would earn at least as much as in the concluding sequence of their previous task. This also implied that only those errors in workload fixing which favoured the worker were acceptable, and tended to produce an upward 'ratchet' effect on earnings.

The primary process set off a serious secondary process of drift. Increases in earnings from P.B.R. were unevenly distributed, even among P.B.R. workers themselves, according to their different circumstances. 'Indirect' workers (i.e. those in ancillary services feeding the 'direct' workers on the production line) and other time-workers working alongside P.B.R. workers, often performing unmeasurable, non-repetitive skilled work, often found that unskilled workers on P.B.R. were overtaking their earnings. Evidence for this was to be found in the fact that earnings of semi-skilled P.B.R. workers in the motor industry exceeded those of time-working craftsmen, (and rivalled those of skilled pieceworkers)[2]. Rightly or wrongly, this generated resentment amongst time workers. Devices such as 'lieu bonuses' which adjusted the pay of time workers in accordance with the average bonus of direct workers, went some way to meet the problem of relativities, but in themselves were unrelated to the recipients' own performance, and it was hardly satisfactory to have an element of one individual's pay packet fluctuating according to the effort of

1 See paras. 35 to 39 for the derivation of the NBPI's own approximation.

2 See Chapter 7 for discussion of similar evidence in the engineering report.

others and anomalies in relative pay were, in the NBPI's view, a frequent and recurring consequence of P.B.R. systems, and led to pressure for other wage adjustments to bring workers who had fallen behind the leading groups back into line.

The above mentioned secondary processes apparently were mainly believed to be confined to the 'internal labour market' i.e. within a plant or firm, but it was also asserted that a high rate of drift associated with P.B.R. often had effects outside the firms or sectors directly concerned, leading to matching increases elsewhere in the industry or district concerned, which in turn could spread through other industries or services including the public sector. This easy and probably correct affirmation contrasts with the NBPI's denials in its other reports that productivity agreements had repercussive effects outside the internal labour market. It seems valid to distinguish between the effects of productivity agreements and P.B.R. on the internal labour market, for the former should have had less serious effects since one of its aims usua was to make an agreement covering all workers at the same time in the interna market, but there is little reason to suppose that their repercussive effects of local and outside labour markets should differ markedly.

To sum up, in the Board's view it was not simply tight labour markets and excessive demand pressures in general which alone caused wage drift and, consequently, inflation (though their contributory role was acknowledged): the actual mechanism of wage drift itself made an important independent contribution to inflation; evidence that firms with similar product and labour market situations had experienced different rates of wage drift was considered to bear this out.

Against these apparently inflationary effects were to be set the benefits (and certain other disadvantages) of P.B.R. systems, which the NBPI then turned to analysing. In so doing, however, it had to be taken into account that payments systems were often affected by the general social and economic environment and by factors peculiar to a firm or industry, so that it was impossible to assess any system in isolation from its setting. Indeed in the NBPI's view the intrinsic character of a payment system was of less importance in detail than the context in which it was expected to operate. In particular the following factors were important:

(a) the nature of the particular product market and the general state of the labour market. Since the Second World War, bouyant demand and labour shortages had promoted favourable conditions for the introduction and continued use of P.B.R. systems, but they also gave rise to attitudes and behaviour which could weaken their effectiveness — a feeling that it was more important to meet the order book than to keep down production costs, which tended to lead to a slackening of management control over the payment system a tendency to relax control over the payment system to let wages drift up so as to ensure retention of the labour force and recruitment of new labour in competitive labour market conditions (instead of raising basic rates of pay);

(b) the climate of industrial relations which both influenced, and was influenced by, P.B.R. With full employment conditions, management control tended to be undermined by a tendency for extensive, fragmented bargaining on the shop floor over individual jobs.

(c) social attitudes. The NBPI's case studies disclosed acute differences between the attitudes of predominantly female and male labour forces, the former being more co-operative, and acquiescent in management control.

(d) regional differences.

Against this background, the main advantage claimed for P.B.R. systems was that they usually raised output. The NBPI accepted this mainly in view of the great weight of opinion it received to this effect, in its case studies and consultations with experts. But it did note the difficulty of isolating the productivity gains resulting from the introduction of P.B.R., from the other changes that occurred with its introduction e.g. method study, work measurement, improved managerial organisation; also over the course of time, systems often decayed, or else shopfloor manipulation often removed any clear relationship between effort and output. Furthermore, group incentive schemes, necessary because of the nature of the production process, often diminished the relationship between pay and effort. Bonus elements were sometimes too small to stimulate effort and the period for which they were calculated was sometimes too long, ironing out fluctuations in performance. The incentive also had to be simple and intelligible to workers. Thus: 'whilst we would not entirely accept the claims on behalf of P.B.R. as advanced by managements and consultants ... we concede that conventional P.B.R. systems can be a useful tool for raising effort in situations of low performance with time-rate systems'.[1] This somewhat unenthusiastic tone contrasts with the more receptive attitude to productivity agreements in other reports.

Higher labour productivity, furthermore, did not guarantee lower wage cost per unit. In the longer run, with weak management control, there was a tendency for earnings to rise continually year by year, irrespective or output; a great deal of time was lost on the administration of schemes; often management possessed inadequate data for the accurate measurement of performance. Thus, despite the claims of consultants that P.B.R. schemes generally resulted in net savings in costs, the NBPI concluded: 'there is some suggestion therefore that even with more sophisticated managements increases in effort following on P.B.R. systems may over time be at least matched, if not outweighted, by increases in costs'.[2]

As for other effects, the NBPI concluded that whilst they might partially compensate for the inadequacy of supervision, the real problems probably stemmed from weaknesses in management rather than the payment system itself; and there was little evidence that on balance P.B.R. impeded job flexibility, the quality of output or the acceptance of technical progress.

The advantages of P.B.R. for workers were that they could earn more than on daywork or by bargaining; they could work largely at the pace they chose

1 para. 78.

2 para. 83.

to and with freedom from supervision; variations in individual capacity and earnings ambitions could be accommodated, especially in the case of low performers who might otherwise find pressures of supervision under daywork intolerable; and it could be argued that to some extent there was more security of employment when demand was low because earnings fell and lessened the prospect of redundancy. But the NBPI's case studies showed that to a large extent workers were also disenchanted with the lack of stability in weekly earnings, the constant time-consuming process of shop floor haggling over piece-rates for new tasks, inequity, inversion of customary skill differentials, and the falsification of work records to even out earnings; workers were as concerned with the equity and stability of earnings as with their level. They were prepared to make concessions (in exchange for alternative advantages). There were therefore some grounds for optimism as to the willingness of workers to accept a reform of payment systems.

The final assessment was inconclusive: 'In view of the varying conditions of different industries we are unable to make a simple blanket commendation or condemnation of such systems'.[1] It was recognised instead that sometimes P.B.R. raised productivity and lessened costs; at other times, it had few advantages, and many disadvantages. It was a feature of the report that its tone was non-dogmatic. The absence of an overall verdict did not mean the NBPI could not produce a report which had little of value to say to management and trade unions, for, as in most general study reports, a large part consisted of a detailed guide, almost an instructional handbook, on the installation, reform or replacement of P.B.R. systems of various kinds, together with examples of some practical difficulties encountered in case studies. This was an important part of the educational function of general study reports.

To start with, the type of work systems in which it was thought a conventional P.B.R. system was likely to be appropriate were defined. They were those where work was measurable and directly attributable to those being paid for it; the pace to a significant degree controlled by the worker; the management capable of maintaining a steady flow of work; and the work not subject to frequent changes in methods, materials and equipment.

It seemed futile to attempt to reform or modify a system if the main conditions were not met, for in such situations an entirely new payment system was necessary. On the other hand, if the conditions were appropriate, management faced a choice, either of negotiating a change to an alternative payment system or of reforming the existing one.

Much of the remainder of the report was devoted broadly to exploring the means of following these alternative paths. But whichever was followed, there was an overriding need first to create the right climate for change, and to recognise the responsibility upon managements to secure reform. This theme is taken up in Chapter 11.

Where management chose to reform rather than replace existing systems, the NBPI placed special stress on the following factors which it regarded as

1 para. 250.

146

fundamental to the failure of many systems:

First, a well regulated P.B.R. system needed first to measure all work paid under it so that as far as possible the same earnings were always received for identical effort expended in work of a given skill category. Under 'Rate fixing', the predominant method of measurement, a time or price was set by foremen, or specialist 'rate fixers' with reference only to their own knowledge and experience. The NBPI's evidence was that this was usually unsatisfactory and inequitable, because of its subjective nature, and its vulnerability to bargaining pressures. Instead there was a need for the use of formal 'work study' which combined 'method study' and 'work measurement'. Although involving a degree of subjective judgement, systematic work study techniques on the whole appeared to produce standards of acceptable consistency; and work-studied incentive bonus schemes had the great advantage over piecework that money values were not negotiated with each task: a money rate was agreed on for a standard effort, expended in a given time, and this remained constant while tasks changed. Second, work measurement should be scrupulously separated from bargaining pressures to avoid the problems which arose with simple rate fixing. Third, notwithstanding the dangers of bonuses that were too small, a larger stable element in total earnings was necessary in many P.B.R. systems. It would be dangerous to allow the variable bonus element to comprise more than one-third of the pay packet. Otherwise workplace bargaining was likely to lead to attempts to force up the bonus element to increase earnings, rather than negotiate increases in the wage's fixed elements. Fourth, work standards should be expressed in terms of 'allowed' or 'standard' times rather than as piecework prices, to ensure that comparable efforts yielded equal earnings, to keep bargaining concepts out of measurement as far as possible, and to facilitate comparison of short and long jobs. Fifth, greater priority should be given to the problems of P.B.R. by management, and they should better integrate it into the overall objectives and activities of the company; and steps should be taken to involve first-line supervisors more in the working of the system. Specific proposals were made on this subject. Sixth, comprehensive formal arrangements for joint control should be negotiated between management and men. The great diversity of practice at workplace level on numerous matters such as the extent to which workers' earnings were guaranteed on a change in jobs, methods or equipment, was often the result of unrecorded sometimes obscure or uncertain understandings, varying between and within establishments. It was therefore essential that unambiguous 'ground rules' should be negotiated for a unit larger than the individual workshop or workplace, specifying the provisions for standard setting, pay-performance relationships, and disputes, and also a formal structure of occupational rates or 'standard earnings'.

Where existing industry-level machinery was inadequate for the negotiation of such ground rates, they were the proper subject for plant or enterprise bargaining. The intention was not to weaken collective bargaining but to replace the present fragmented workplace bargaining by negotiation through representative bodies at a level where the full effects of P.B.R. on earnings could be taken into account.

These recommendations led inevitably to a full discussion of the role of national, local and company bargaining in relation to P.B.R. The NBPI's views on this are explained later.

The final part of the report dealt with the relationship between P.B.R. and incomes policy. Two difficulties in controlling inflation generated by P.B.R. were underlined. First, for reasons explained earlier, earnings could increase without any increase in effort or changes in rates. This difficulty existed no matter whether the attempt to control inflation was made by inducing a higher level of unemployment, or through an incomes policy, or through a combination of both. Second, the incomes policy required the notification to the Government of pay claims and settlements involving more than 100 workers, but a large part of the increases in earnings under P.B.R. systems did not, on this definition, require notification because the setting each day of thousands of new piecework prices and so forth nearly always involved fewer than 100 workers, though the aggregate and indirect effects of these bargains were very great.

The NBPI had found little apparent recognition of the problem, at least so far as national policy was concerned, among those operating P.B.R., and it came across only one instance where a firm was attempting to apply the policy to P.B.R. earnings in any way. To help management and unions determine how far existing P.B.R. systems were working in accordance with the aims of the policy, and also to provide indicators of good practice to assist in the operation of P.B.R. systems, the NBPI compiled two sets of generally applicable guidelines which could be used to indicate when a P.B.R. system was working well, and when it needed urgent overhaul. The latter set was as follows:

'(a) the rate of increase of average hourly earnings (excluding overtime and increases paid under industry-wide agreements or their equivalent in non-federated firms, and excluding also increases demonstrably attributable to increased worker effort) exceeds 2½ per cent a year;

(b) the proportion of average earnings (excluding overtime) which takes the form of variable output bonus is over one third;

(c) the use of work study or measured work standards is not attempted by management, or is prevented or limited by workers;

(d) all or most prices and times are fixed by bargaining between individuals or small groups of workers and management representatives, and there is no clear separation of the processes of standard setting and pay negotiation;

(e) no account is taken of the "learning curve" or "improvement effect" when establishing work standards for new jobs and new workers, or in revising them for old jobs;

(f) there are obvious anomalies in the pay of different occupational groups, and between workers in different departments;

(g) the suitability and administration of the system has not been fully investigated within the past 5 years;

148

(h) where the information necessary to establish (a) to (f) is lacking.'[1]

The NBPI referred to the implication of the current White Paper that the Government should concern itself more closely than in the past with the operation of payment systems at the local or plant level, and in selected cases make references to itself. In the same way as in the Netherlands, the Government should have, or consider having, a small number of regional officers to collect information on the operation of plant and company P.B.R. systems, and advise firms on their improvement in line with the needs of the incomes policy. This would be one useful step in an education campaign that was necessary to influence the development of payment systems in line with incomes policy requirements.

The Department of Employment and Productivity did not attempt to apply seriously the vetting system suggested.

In its *Fourth General Report*, the NBPI pointed out that drift, even if not the result of decisions notifiable under the early warning system, could be detected through movements in the official statistics, supplemented by the detailed knowledge of the Department of Employment and Productivity (to which information supplied in connection with decisions which did have to be notified under the early warning system could have contributed). It recommended that in view of the prevalence and magnitude of movements in earnings resulting from 'drift', they should be made the subject of reference to the NBPI as occasion demanded. This implied examination by the NBPI of individual pay systems, for example, payments by results schemes and the earnings or salary bills of firms or groups of firms. Very few or no references were received as a result. This was perhaps the most serious failure of all in the vetting machinery between 1965 and 1970.

The NBPI also tried to use some other general study references in the same way to influence the development of the whole policy and to provide guidelines for the vetting machinery. More is said about general study reports in the following chapter.

This was one of the NBPI's most successful and useful reports as is attested by its sales figures of over 20,000. Something like a hundred thousand popular guides were distributed throughout industry. The report (and the more detailed supplement) was a mine of up-to-date new information and advice for management, unions, management consultants and professional bodies, research workers and government officials.

To my mind, one of the features of this report, and some of the NBPI's other general study reports, was the absence of either a one-sided enthusiasm for, or condemnation of, P.B.R. Rather there was an attempt to advance an appropriately balanced statement of its strengths and weaknesses, and a fairly successful attempt to specify how they could be identified in individual cases. The crucial importance of the economic and social context in which a system was applied was also stressed.

1 para. 257.

4. The Machinery of Wage Determination

The NBPI's recommendations on pay policy often required changes in the machinery of wage determination; in addition, the incomes policy was often used as a Trojan horse to bring about reforms in collective bargaining institutions.

This was because first, the British system of industrial relations traditionally had separated management-trade union negotiations about pay from negotiations if any about efficiency. Second, the traditional pattern of wage bargaining had been one of negotiations covering all firms and workers in an industry simultaneously. With some exceptions such industry-wide structures did not permit productivity agreements to be introduced easily, since they were most easily negotiated locally; in any event, plant or company bargaining of some kind is practically always a sine qua non for a productivity agreement.

Alongside this existing system there had, however, been a good deal of bargaining about pay in individual plants. Much of this had been of a fragmented nature, with the result that bargains struck with one group of workers often gave rise to resentment on the part of others and therefore ultimately to similar concessions to them. It had therefore exacerbated 'leapfrogging'.

A central concern of the NBPI was thus to define the relationship and roles of national, company and plant bargaining. An important example was Report No. 49, the first of its two reports on the engineering industry:

'The purposes of national agreements should be threefold:

(i) to lay down criteria for and establish, when appropriate, minima for pay and conditions;

(ii) to lay down *criteria* for determining the pay structures that arise as a result of plant or company bargaining — i.e. to lay down criteria governing the relationship between the pay of one grade and another.

(iii) to establish machinery to maintain, and if necessary correct, the relationship in pay and conditions between grade and grade or the relationship between actual levels of earnings and actual conditions and the minima stipulated in national agreements, should this relationship develop different from the manner envisaged in national agreements.'[1]

The NBPI 'tentatively sketched' the outlines of new negotiating machinery. In place of the machinery for national negotiations and conciliation, which was only ad hoc, the NBPI suggested there should be more formal machinery, in the shape of a Joint National Council. Appropriate joint negotiating machinery should also be established in every plant or company. The Joint National Council would collect information and disseminate advice and other services. There should be an independent Chairman. One of his functions would be as final conciliator for disputes in the industry. His main function would be to help secure the co-ordination of pay both between grade and grade and between actual earnings and nationally agreed minima, and he would also

1 para. 128.

150

have regard to the prices and incomes policy.

These radical recommendations were ignored by the industry and informed opinion picked holes in the prescriptions mainly on the grounds that an independent Chairman, even if he was wanted, was unlikely to be able to eliminate anomalies and control wage structures in the industry. This was one of the Board's less successful reports. In its second report the NBPI did not mention the recommendations again but generally followed the line of the Donovan Commission in recommending comprehensive plant or company agreements.

Nevertheless the Board pressed on with the task of reforming collective bargaining. In the building industry it recommended the NJCBI should establish joint machinery at industry level to which company agreements would be referred for scrutiny before finally being put into effect.

'The ideal condition would be that in which the national and company agreements dovetail in such a way that between them they cover the whole field of industrial relations. The spheres of operation should be clearly defined so that both parties know which of them applies to any particular issue.'[1]

There is a series of reports aimed at working out the relationship. There is a very noticeable concern on the NBPI's part to preserve and encourage a full role for national wage bargaining institutions and to enable them to exercise a measure of control or surveillance over the development of local bargaining. This was worked out for example in references concerning *The Industrial Civil Service* (146) and the *Milk* (140), *Pottery* (149) and *Water Supply* (152) industries.

The NBPI also dealt with Wages Councils in a number of references. Statute does not allow bargaining about pay and productivity in them. The Board believed that Wages Councils were often an obstacle to the development of voluntary collective bargaining, to trade union membership and to the development of machinery which would link pay changes to productivity. Nor were they usually found to be serving their original primary purpose of protecting the lowest paid workers in the industry. The NBPI's statistical investigations established that they tended to lead to uniform pay increases for all employees, whether well-paid or not. Accordingly in a number of references the Board called for their abolition, and replacement by new machinery, for example in the case of clothing manufacturing and road haulage.

The wisdom of this may be questioned. Whilst the existence of Wages Councils may have made it more difficult for trade unions to build up their membership the underlying reasons for their weak organisation were often to be found in the nature of the industry. In its report on clothing manufacturing the Board ascribed the weakness of the trade unions to several factors, only one of which was Wages Councils. The influence of each factor was not separated, but the Board believed that the removal of the Wages Councils in

1 *Pay and Conditions in the Building Industry* (92), para. 167.

the industry would strengthen trade union organisation.

Even if this was right, it would still not necessarily follow that their abolition was desirable. An alternative possibility would have been to press for modification of the Act governing Wages Councils and to have sought to modify existing structures along the right lines. Instead the Board recommende radical reforms, where a more moderate approach might have won wider support.

It would take a separate volume to review adequately the NBPI's numerous and valuable studies of industrial relations institutions and its countless suggestions for their reform and modernisation. But one central dilemma which it sought to resolve in numerous cases may be referred to in conclusion. The NBPI wished to see local bargaining developed in order to permit the negotiation of productivity agreements; and, to some extent, it recognised that, anyway, a shift to local bargaining was occurring and it sought to steer it in useful directions. On the other hand it recognised that to develop local bargaining might be to stimulate leapfrogging and it would reduce the possibilit of the exercise of some measure of control over local wage fixing by national negotiating bodies which themselves might be more easily controlled by an incomes policy. Against this background its detailed proposals for reform should be considered.

Conclusion

It is difficult to draw definite conclusions about the NBPI's work on relating pay to productivity. The overall impression is that some useful changes may have been brought about in the field of reforming industrial relations institution and in bringing productivity into the wage bargaining process. Against this has to be weighed the possibility that in bringing about some changes its attempts to disturb the wage structure may have been inflationary. The evidenc is not at hand to weigh these factors.

10. General Study and Standing References

In Chapters 8 and 9 several of the NBPI's general study reports were referred to and described. Against that background the first part of this Chapter outlines the origins of such studies, reviews briefly the methods of enquiry used, and some of the difficulties encountered, and goes on to discuss briefly the function of general study reports.

The second part of this Chapter describes the NBPI's work on standing references on the Pay of Armed Forces and the Remuneration of Solicitors. The latter also serves as an example of an NBPI price structure study.

There is a link between the two parts of this chapter. The NBPI's work in both general study and standing references illustrates its investigatory skills and the range of problem solving tasks it was assigned.

A second less important link is that the investigations made in connection with the reference Pay of the Armed Forces represented a further development of the NBPI's work in the field of job evaluation, the subject of a general study report.

1. General Study References

'General study' reports dealt with general subjects such as wage and salary systems or the criteria for exceptional wage increases, and were not confined to any one firm or industry.

The NBPI issued eight such reports, covering a wide field — *Productivity Agreements* (23, 36, 123), *Payment by Results* (65 with supplement), *Job Evaluation* (83 with supplement), *Salary Structures* (132), *Hours of Work, Overtime and Shiftwork* (160 with supplement) and *General Problems of Low Pay* (169). The report on *Top Salaries in Private and Nationalised Industries* (107) was a hybrid, recommending salaries for certain posts in the nationalised industries, but also dealing with general matters relating to top salaries in private and nationalised industries.

General study reports are worthy of attention because they comprise what are widely recognised as some of the NBPI's best reports, and contain the results of useful enquiry work. They also provide an insight into the NBPI's general views, for they helped to establish a framework within which the rest of its work could be conducted.

Most of the general studies were interlinked. *Productivity Agreements* (23) drew attention to P.B.R. systems as a way of linking pay to productivity that required examination, and, as has been seen, led to a general study reference on the subject. The NBPI's next general study report *Job Evaluation* (83) followed naturally from *Payment By Results* (65) in that it could be viewed as a continuation of the series of general studies of the underlying problems of payment systems and pay structures. Furthermore, as the report on P.B.R. (and Engineering) had highlighted the anomalies and inflationary consequences of P.B.R., a question for the report was the extent to which job evaluation could contribute to a solution of the problem. Another major preoccupation of the two early reports on productivity agreements was with overtime working, later reported on as a subject in its own right in 1970. This reference was sought in the NBPI's *Third General Report* in 1968. The NBPI commented in its *Third General Report* after receiving the reference on top salaries, that a reference on middle management salaries would be a logical sequence. Soon afterwards it did receive such a reference.

The origins of the low pay general study report were slightly different. By the end of 1969 when the Government published the White Paper *Productivity, Prices and Incomes Policy after 1969* low pay had emerged as a prominent problem of incomes policy, as the White Paper admitted:

'Recent wage claims by dustmen and firemen aroused a good deal of public sympathy in the belief that the pay of these groups of essential workers had fallen behind those of workers in manufacturing industry. Yet once substantial increases had been granted, others — many of whom are on higher levels of pay — promptly began to argue that these settlements entitled them to similar increases.'[1]

Accordingly the Government stated that it would ask the NBPI to initiate investigations in depth into those cases where low pay was a major problem and to suggest the means by which progress could be made case by case, industry by industry. When the NBPI was then asked to investigate the question of low pay in the contract cleaning trade, among laundry and dry cleaning workers and among ancillary workers in the National Health Service, it decided in addition to present a report on the general aspects of low pay.

Most general study reports followed a common pattern, similar to that of Payment By Results which was described in the previous chapter. The extensive case studies in the P.B.R. report were referred to in the previous chapter and the extensive consultations with all sources of expert opinion. This was in fact a typical feature of all general study reports. Large scale surveys seeking basic information were also a feature. In *Job Evaluation* there was a large scale postal survey (8,000 qustionnaires were sent out) to ascertain how far and in what areas of industry job evaluation was used, at what rate its use was growing, what methods were in most common use and to what extent it was the sole determinant of relationships in pay in particular enterprises, and there were questions about its effectiveness from the user's standpoint. In *Salary Structures*, a survey was conducted covering many of the managerial, executive, professional and technical staff in the economy, about the main incidence, methods and characteristics of salary

1 Para. 68.

structuring and the impact of incomes policy on the structuring. For *Top Salaries in the Private Sector and Nationalised Industries* the Board conducted an interesting survey of pay and other remuneration of top executives in the main nationalised industries and a stratified sample of the 300 largest industrial, commercial and financial companies securing a response rate of 88 per cent and a coverage of 99 organisations. This asked for detailed information about the company or corporation, the composition of pay, fringe benefits, conditions of service and various measures of responsibility for some 2.000 full-time main Board Members and other senior managers reporting direct to a member of the main Board. In the analysis various broad measures of responsibility were employed not only for comparing pay between nationalised and private sectors but also between different sizes of organisation and parts of the private sectors. The extent of bonuses, pensions and other benefits, age, length of service, main function, qualifications and retirement age were analysed. There was also an analysis of movements in pay over the past six years which showed that there had been restraint and that there was no evidence that excessive increases had taken place at these levels on any general scale. Other interesting surveys were made in *General Problems of Low Pay* and *Hours of Work, Overtime and Shiftwork*, and some of these were noted earlier.

In *Payment by Results* overseas experience was considered unlikely to be relevant, and was not studied at first hand. In other references, such as *Low Pay* and *Hours of Work, Overtime and Shiftworking*, studies of overseas practices were made, and in *Job Evaluation* limited studies were made of industry and nation-wide job evaluation in the Federal German Republic and the Netherlands, and studies were commissioned on the operation of job evaluation in Sweden, the U.S.A. and the U.S.S.R.

The NBPI's earlier reports, especially the one on Payment by Results, appeared to be a good deal more successful than some later reports. P.B.R was a subject about which a good deal was known at the start of the reference. It was possible to achieve a good combination of generality and concreteness in recommendations partly because it was possible to measure the costs of a P.B.R. scheme and compare them with output. The last three general study reports *Salary Structures, Hours of Work, Overtime and Shiftwork* and *General Problems of Low Pay* were more difficult subjects from an investigatory viewpoint, since much more difficult conceptual problems arose, less prior knowledge of the subject existed and many key factors were not measurable. It was difficult to get away from generalities. Thus the reference on *Salary Structures* seems to have presented substantial problems. The reference might usefully have been about the more tractable subject of salary *systems* than salary *structures*. Whilst much of the report as published concerns salary systems anyway, it is evident that most of the enquiries concerned salary structures. In addition, relatively little previous knowledge of the subject was available compared with the reports on Job Evaluation and P.B.R. For several reasons, it was difficult to produce concrete guidelines. Optimum salary systems and structures depend upon the objectives and the type of company. Very little was discovered about what type of system went best with what type of company. The resulting guidelines represented not much more than canons which management might apply to any subject e.g. stock control. This reflected the fact that salaries were a more complex subject than, say, P.B.R. where output and labour costs were measurable, goals well-defined, and relatively fewer factors had to be taken into account. There were some similar difficulties about the report on top salaries. This does not mean that the two salaries reports were of no value. Rather they should be seen as pioneering explorations transversing new territory. If the NBPI had remained in existence for several more years, it would have been useful if, having initiated thinking on the relationship of salaries to incomes policy, it could have returned to the subject after an interval of, say, three years in order to take it further.

There has already been some discussion in an earlier part of this book of *Hours of Work, Overtime and Shiftwork* and *General Problems of Low Pay*. Both of these reports were of considerable use in furthering knowledge, and in establishing a framework within which future discussions of the relationship of these subjects to incomes policy could occur. In the conduct of these references, nevertheless, difficulties were encountered in devising a conceptual framework within which enquiries should take place, and again within which the report was written. The *Hours of Work, Overtime and Shiftwork* report clearly represented a compromise between two conflicting points of view about overtime, points of view which were both represented at Board, staff and expert outside advisers level. If the NBPI had adopted its simpler stance of earlier days and regarded most overtime as a generally bad thing, the report could have contained clearer, more specific guidelines for negotiators and others than it did, but they might have been misleading. Overtime working is according to the NBPI's view in this report a complex subject to which there are no easy answers uniformly applicable to the myriad of circumstances in which it exists. The best that could be done was to state in very general terms what action should be taken to identify and get rid of inefficient working. The resulting guidelines were clearly of little assistance for management. This may be illustrated by quoting them:

'... in many companies and plants the means of telling whether a serious problem exists are lacking, and we suggest that all managements which make use of overtime would do well to ask themselves the following questions:

(1) Does management collect regular data about how much overtime is worked, by what sections, occupational groups or departments, and for what purposes?

(2) Is substantial overtime regularly worked by any section, occupational group or department and if so why?

(3) Does management have relevant indices of performance or work standards which enable it to tell whether manpower and other resources are being used effectively?

(4) How much scope is there for raising productivity by means of impro-ved methods, changes in working practices, better manpower planning, the provision of better incentives and so on?

(5) Do the answers to the previous questions reveal that there is sub-stantial regular overtime combined with considerable scope for improving efficiency?

(6) If so, what should be done? In particular:

(a) to what extent is it possible to secure higher efficiency simply by exercising greater care in the use of overtime?

(b) can hourly productivity be raised to satisfactory levels by negotia-ting the introduction (or revision) of work-studied incentive payment schemes?

(c) is an appraisal of the possibility of shiftwork desirable ... ?

(d) is it desirable to negotiate a comprehensive agreement embracing hours, pay and improved methods and working practices?

(7) What new controls, including arrangements for joint scrutiny of hours of work, will be desirable to ensure that satisfactory levels of efficiency once achieved are maintained?'[1]

The Functions of General Study Reports

This brief overview may be concluded by summarising the main purposes of general study references.

A principal function of general study references was educational. There is no doubt that there was a demand from industry for authoritative studies of these subjects. The survey of job evaluation revealed for example that some 7½ per cent of establishments surveyed were actively considering its introduction, and, of course, something like one quarter of the workforce had been covered by productivity agreements by 1969. Rightly or wrongly, no Government department or official body had met the demand until the NBPI stepped in.

The NBPI had certain advantages in comparison with text book writers, official ad hoc commissions and so forth who *might* otherwise have filled the gap. As an official body it received better access to and co-operation from industry and unions than would academics or consultants mounting such research. It had resources of staff and finance sufficient to conduct investigations on a large enough scale to be capable of generalisation beyond the immediate workplace situations studied and to analyse them on an inter-disciplinary basis. It could draw upon experience from earlier references. It conducted these investigations in fourteen months on average. Normally, for an academic team, investigations of comparable breadth would take several years. Consequently the reports far from being out of date by the time they were published, served as a useful guide to some of the latest techniques and developments in more advanced firms, and in this way helped to accelerate change.

1 Para. 157.

Another function of general study references was to develop thinking and policies about particular subjects on the basis of more general, fundamental and analytical research than was possible in reports dealing with particular industries or pay claims.

These general studies were helpful in establishing a general framework of policy within which the work of the NBPI in particular reference could be carried on, in providing guidelines for the use of the vetting machinery in scrutinising proposals for wage increases, and in laying the groundwork for an elaboration of the rather simple criteria of incomes policy given in the White Papers.

Although it is over 35 years since Keynes pointed the way to full employment and nearly the same time since some writers have pointed out that the solution of the full employment problem would give rise to problems of inflation, relatively little systematic research into basic policy issues of incomes and prices policies has been conducted. Thus very little policy development has occurred in the low pay field, partly because of a lack of knowledge of the subject and partly because possible policy solutions to the problem by means of incomes policy have not received attention. If there are to be any future attempts to conduct prices and incomes policies it seems urgently necessary to investigate a host of similar problems and to develop appropriately sophisticated policy criteria to reconcile incomes policies as far as possible with the attainment of such economic goals as efficiency, growth, and equitable income distribution as well as price stability. The potential of general study reports for making a start to the solution of such problems was demonstrated by the NBPI's studies. The NBPI's general study references however, constituted only a beginning to more detailed research needed in the prices and incomes policy field.

There were no general references about prices — a reference about the problem of the rate of return on capital might have come partly in preparation for the replacement of the NBPI with the CIM, had the Labour Government remained in office longer. No references directly concerned managerial efficiency in fields other than industrial relations — with the development of the NBPI reviews of managerial efficiency, in 1970 and 1971, references concerning corporate planning, marketing and similar subjects might eventually have come. Finally, the NBPI's reports only covered a part of the industrial relations field: this is shown by the fact both that the new Office of Manpower Economics has received references concerning measured day work, wage drift, and equal pay and the NBPI unsuccessfully sought references about merit payments, the contribution of labour to higher productivity, and negotiated capital savings schemes for workers.

Besides serving a useful function for prices and incomes policy, the NBPI's general studies must have been an eye opener for other investigatory bodies in Great Britain which have rarely conducted such studies.[1] In my opinion they are the NBPI reports which will prove to be of most enduring value.

1 See M. Peston 'A New Look at Monopoly Policy', *Political Quarterly* (1970), vol. 41, no. 3, p.328.

2. Standing References

There were three standing references on Pay of the Armed Forces, Pay of University Teachers, and the Remuneration of Solicitors. The NBPI was required to keep these subjects under continuous review. Instead of passing judgment on decisions made by other bodies, it was required to initiate recommendations on the pay or fee increases, if any, which should be given and on other action which the Government should take. The reports included some of the NBPI's most interesting and innovatory enquiries.

Pay of the Armed Forces: The standing reference on pay and allowances of the Armed Forces was one of the NBPI's largest studies. The NBPI was assigned the responsibility of investigating and recommending changes in the level and structure of armed forces pay and allowances at a time when recruitment had fallen below requirements. There was one simplifying element as regards the level of pay. The Board was to take as given the numbers of men required: its task was to see that sufficient numbers were obtained to meet the target, but without granting excessive pay increases.

The NBPI, for the first main report (116), conducted three surveys of attitudes and opinion to supplement the evidence presented by the Ministry of Defence on the needs and views of servicemen. The first, of a sample of serving officers and men, sought information about their backgrounds, attitudes and intentions with regard to the Services and their views on a number of specific issues. The second, of officers and men leaving the Service, aimed at finding their reasons for leaving, and the problems they encountered in settling themselves in civilian life. The third was a series of interviews with the wives of officers and men in the United Kingdom and Germany, designed to discover their attitudes to Service life and to find what were the pressures on family life in a Service environment.

The NBPI considered that there were a number of objections to the existing pay structure. First, it remunerated married men more highly than single men for the same work and thus offered the lowest emoluments to those whom the services were most anxious to attract. Secondly, the combination of pay, allowances and benefits in kind was so complicated that it was difficult to convey to potential recruits what their earnings in the Services would be. And thirdly, it was difficult even for servicemen themselves to calculate their true earnings. It concluded that a new pay structure was needed which would:

(a) remunerate married and single men equally for similar work; (b) be based on one comprehensive basic rate of pay for each rank and trade; (c) be so devised that earnings could be known; (d) be capable of adjustment, when necessary, by a system which could be seen to be fair; and (e) help to promote efficiency.

It recommended, as the most satisfactory and the simplest way of achieving these objectives, that all servicemen should be paid a comprehensive salary which would be subject to tax in the normal way and out of which they would be required to pay for food, lodging and clothing (excluding uniform) in the same way as a civilian. It referred to this concept of service pay as the 'military salary'.

Second, a study was undertaken in order to examine and alter relationships in pay between different ranks and employments within the Armed Forces.

Consideration was given to adopting the method employed in Civil Service pay negotiations. This is based on the selection of certain civilian jobs as 'broadly comparable' with the Service jobs being studied. There were, however, very few jobs in the armed forces and in the civilian world which were exact counterparts, since the Services required all their members to have certain basic military skills and frequently required greater versatility, different mixes of skill or different supervisory content from industry.

It was thought that job evaluation methods instead might work satisfactorily. This was confirmed by making initial studies into the feasibility of assessing the content of jobs inside the Services as compared with outside. These prepared the way for the second main report (142) which was based on the results of job evaluation enquiries. These were made by a joint services job evaluation team set up by the Ministry of Defence, working under the supervision of the NBPI's staff and of consultants retained by the NBPI. Its membership totalled 55, including 4 controlling staff from the NBPI and consultants, and supporting staff. Members worked closely together at all stages and seem to have been successful in their aim of comparing particular military and civilian jobs as carefully as possible, with full regard for the somewhat different elements which entered into civilian and military jobs.

The main comparisons related to officers and to other ranks. In addition, some comparisons were made relating to the similarities and differences of the work of certain groups — lawyers, doctors, chaplains, etc. — inside and outside the Armed Forces.

Rigorous descriptions were produced of jobs carried out by about 80 per cent of the other ranks. The components of each job were broken down into seven common factors, such as mental, physical or skill requirements, responsibility and working conditions. A scale was prepared for each factor showing a range of points which could be alloted to any job in respect of that factor. For example, it was possible to receive anything from zero to 340 points for the factor 'previous training and experience', 0—160 for 'responsibility for supervision' etc. In this way the internal relationships of jobs were assessed.

The next step was to convert the points into monetary values. 728 civilian jobs in 321 different civilian organisations from the same broad occupational fields as Service trades were then analysed and evaluated in the same way and by the same teams as in the job evaluation study of Armed Forces. In this way the relative content of Service and civilian jobs was compared and measured.

A serious difficulty arose, however, because there was a wide range of earnings for different civilian jobs receiving the same points score, as a scatter diagram in the appendix to Report 142 vividly illustrates. Nevertheless, an earnings figure appropriate for each job receiving the same points score was somehow devised, and the pay for each Armed Forces job was thereby derived. This difficulty does not seem to have been the result of using a bad method, but of the remarkable spread of earnings for jobs involving similar features in the British labour market.

This method was not able and was not intended to take account of the fact that there were special conditions of employment which were common to all servicemen and which made Service life more uncertain and on occasion more hazardous than the normal run of employment in civilian life. It had always been held that the basic pay of the Armed Forces included an increment to take care of these conditions, although it had never been quantified, nor the conditions defined.

The elements which constituted what the NBPI termed the X factor were defined as follows:

(i) The serviceman was wholly committed to the Service and was subject to a code of discipline which reached far beyond that obtaining in any form of civilian employment.

(ii) He was liable to be exposed to danger on active service.

(iii) He was required as part of his normal peace time service to endure bad or uncomfortable conditions while in the field or on board ship.

(iv) He was subject to the constant upheaval and uncertainty — or what has been called the 'turbulence' — imposed by the need for high mobility in a military force.

In short, therefore, the NBPI regarded the X factor as comprising the combination of exposure to danger, discipline, total commitment to the Service and the frequent uprooting that was inseparable from Service life. This combination of factors had to be set against advantages which the serviceman had over most civilians. Some of these were the counterpart of the disadvantages mentioned above: adventure, variety, and chance to travel, although this was diminishing. Moreover, servicemen had greater security in many ways than most civilians and those who committed themselves to longer engagements received extra pay, which was preserved in the NBPI's recommendations. There were opportunities to be trained in a trade and to earn promotion and carry responsibility while still very young. These opportunities were, the NBPI believed, a powerful attraction to the type of men the Services need to recruit and retain.

Since there was no civilian counterpart to the combination of adverse factors in military life, there could be no direct measurement in civilian terms of the net balance of advantage and disadvantage. A measure might be the serviceman's own assessment of the attractions of his job compared with that of an equivalent job in civilian life. An indication of this assessment over time was not then possible since recruiting and retention rates varied for reasons which were not fully understood.

In the end, therefore, no scientifically based attempt was made to assign weights to these conflicting factors or to determine if the advantages of of service life outweighed the disadvantages. It was simply assumed that the disadvantages predominated and an essentially arbitrary positive amount (of £500) was added to each pay level.

This factor certainly looks odd compared with the rather refined comparison used to determine the level of pay for each job. In addition, the refined comparisons themselves, although no doubt the best possible, had subjective elements on an even greater scale than ordinary job evaluation methods.

But the NBPI's whole approach could probably be defended as an attempt to be as precise as possible. A less elaborate study would have been even more arbitrary. Moreover, the job evaluation study did result in a substantial alteration of internal pay relationships in the Armed Forces, which indicates the weaknesses and possible inefficiencies of the previous structure. Also, in this reference the main requirement was really to eliminate the old system for determining forces pay and up to a certain point what was put in its place was a secondary consideration.

These studies broke new ground, for job evaluation of this kind has rarely been used in the United Kingdom, except at managerial level, and the method were experimental.

The Remuneration of Solicitors: The Remuneration of Solicitors was the subject of three reports. Solicitors' charges for non-contentious business are controlled by rules made up by a Committee under the Chairmanship of the Lord Chancellor, who also has a veto over its decisions.

The relationship between the earnings for a given class of work and the expense involved had never featured in the previous reviews of that large portion of solicitors' earnings arising from these charges. The NBPI stated in Report No. 54 that whatever other factors might influence the final judgment on the level of a particular charge, this relationship must serve as the starting point. It therefore sent a detailed questionnaire to a random sample of nearly 700 firms of solicitors, about 10 per cent of the total. The response rate was about 70 per cent. The results were an analysis of relative cost and profitability of different types of solicitors work which established that there was substantial – and in the Board's view unwarranted – cross-subsidisation of uneconomic activities (e.g. contentious work) by profitable activities (such as conveyancing); and of the structure of practices, all earnings and capital investment (in their own businesses) by solicitors, and the pay of their own staff.

One outcome of this report was that the subject became one of the NBPI's standing references. Its first task under the standing references was to 'investigate and report on all changes in the revenue, expenses and profits of solicitors' since the last report, assessing their effect on its previous recommendations. The new survey of solicitors' earnings showed that the median income of principals had risen by 8 per cent between 1966 and 1968, from £4,180 to £4,514. Practice expenses in the period rose on average by 29 per cent while the average revenue increase was 24 per cent. Average profits per practice rose by 16 per cent. The NBPI looked particularly at the impact of S.E.T. which was an important element in cost increases (averaging £590 per practice in the 1968 accounting year). It found that the profession had offset the effect of S.E.T. by increased revenue from 2 main sources – an increase in some types of work (particularly conveyancing and schedule II work) and what amounted to a rise in prices (stemming in conveyancing from rises in house prices and in contentious work from increased 'solicitor and own client' charges). It took the broad view that the trend of incomes in the profession over recent years had not been out of keeping with the incomes policy. From its studies of manpower in the profession, it also found no reason to suppose that the trend and level of remuneration constituted any obstacle to recruitment plans.

As in the previous report, however, the NBPI was concerned about the uneven distribution of manpower, and the disparity between income and expense, in the different classes of legal business. Thus it found that fewer firms than in 1966 were prepared to take on unremunerative work like county court cases and legal aid and advice. Recognising the urgent need for remedial action, it recommended that the profession's income from county court work should be increased by £3.5 million by the introduction of a new scale of costs, though it hoped that there would be an offsetting decrease in 'solicitor and own client' charges of about £1 million. To assist solicitors in rural areas and in some less prosperous urban areas who met important social needs and had inevitably to incur above average expense per case, it advocated greater flexibility in the application of the scale of costs by Registrars. It recommended that there should be an explicit arrangement enabling county court Registrars to exceed the scale fee for 'preparation for trial' at their discretion. It also recommended that legal advice fees should be increased from £2 to £4 an hour.

On conveyancing fees, it set out in detail its reasons for concluding, as in the first Report, that this class of work was highly profitable. It demonstrated that in 1966 revenue derived from conveyancing amounted to £91 million, whereas the expense involved, including the cost of staff time and principals' remuneration, amounted to £67 million. The new information on conveyancing in 1968 did not affect these conclusions in any major respect. It therefore repeated earlier recommendations that conveyancing fees should be reduced by 6 per cent in total on properties between £4,000 and £20,000 though they should be increased on properties below £2,000.

As regards the future, it emphasised that a standing reference enabled the Board to undertake regular reviews on the revenue and expense involved in different classes of solicitor's work and to conduct detailed investigations of a longer-term nature.

Following the second report the Board undertook a detailed time cost survey of conveyancing and other related studies. Although the coverage of the survey was not as wide as the Board hoped, it received 910 records from 97 practices of broadly similar sizes. Together these provided a unique source of information about the costs and charges attributed to different kinds of conveyancing work, though some adjustment had to be made in the figures of times and costs produced in the survey when considering overall conveyancing costs and profits in the profession as a whole and for considering possible changes in the scale charges.

The survey evidence showed that in all kinds of conveyances the time spent increased consistently with the value of the property, ranging from 4¼ hours (after adjustment) for properties below £1,000 to over 16 hours on properties above £20,000. There was in consequence also a fairly consistent relationship between the cost of the work and the price of the property. The cost of conveying registered property was on average about 85 per cent of the cost of conveying unregistered property in the price ranges covering the great majority of conveyances. This comparison was based on comparable values the totals. The average saving in cost to solicitors acting for a vender was about 20 percent as compared with acting for a purchaser, excluding mortgage and ancillary work.

Over the survey as a whole, work for purchasers was generally less profitable than for vendors. On properties below about £1,000, a registered purchase was likely to be handled at a loss on the fees prevailing in April 1970. Profitability increased substantially with increases in property value. Registered work was not quite as profitable as unregistered work throughout the range of property up to £20,000. Nevertheless, the average cost a conveyance, after adjustment by one-third, was £31.7, compared with a bill of £57.2: in other words, the average cost, which included the principal's average profit, was only 55 per cent of the total charge. The costs to solicitors of purchasers' mortgages, even when adjusted, were on average only 32 percent of the amount charged and thus even more profitable than other conveyancing work; profitability also rose in general with the amount of the mortgage advance. By contrast, mortgage work for vendors at most levels appeared to be unremunerative; but it formed only about 4 per cent of the total cost figure.

The Board did not think that the level of profitability shown in the survey for the period April to May 1970 was greater than the high level shown in 1966 (Report No. 54) mainly because of other relevant factors relating to conveyancing not covered by the survey. The evidence from the survey showed that conveyancing continued to be very profitable work in relation to the total costs (including an average profit) incurred in undertaking it. On the other hand the Board had no evidence that levels of remuneration in the profession as a whole were too high. Conveyancing profits were used to subsidise other less remunerative forms of work. The nature of a solicitor's work was such that it was neither desirable nor practicable to attempt to eliminate cross subsidisation entirely, though the Board pointed out — and the profession itself recognised — that there were serious disadvantages in the extent of the existing imbalance. If conveyancing were looked at in isolation, there would be justification for a larger net cut in conveyancing income than the £2.5 million recommended in its last report.[1] However, the Board did not recommend this because, although it was clear that the revenue of the profession had risen considerably in the previous two years, so also had costs and the overall effect on the profession's income was not known with certainty.

[1] The Board's previous recommendations for increases in the lower value conveyancing scales had been implemented, at a considerably higher level than it suggested. Its recommendations for decreases in the higher value conveyancing scales were to be reconsidered in the light of this report.

The Board recommended reductions in some conveyancing and mortgage charges amounting to about £6 million a year. It estimated that the effect of these changes on conveyancing income, when coupled with the increases of £5 million flowing from the increased charges granted in February 1971 would be a net reduction of £1 million a year or less than 1 per cent. In considering the implications of this for the total incomes of solicitors, it said it was pertinent to bear in mind the increases in charges for other types of work which were implemented following the second report.

The alteration of the scale charges in the way proposed by the Board would also have a continuing effect, in that revenue from conveyancing and mortgage charges would no longer rise to the same extent in response to rising property values.

The specific recommendations were that the Remuneration Orders for conveyancing should be amended immediately to make it clear that the scale charges for conveyancing and mortgages were not fixed charges but maxima (subject to the solicitor's right to elect at the outset for Schedule II charging). The Law Society should also make it clear, amending the Practice Rules as appropriate, that solicitors were at liberty to reduce their charges in cases where the work involved did not justify charging according to the scale. For the future, the conveyancing scales should bear a closer relationship to the cost of the work, though it will not be possible for the relationship to be a precise one.

The NBPI recommended that the existing two-thirds relationship between the statutory conveyancing scales for registered and unregistered land should be changed. A relationship more closely based on the relative costs and responsibilities of the work would be one of 75 per cent. It made concrete proposals as to how this might be achieved. It estimated that the effect of these changes would be to reduce gross conveyancing revenue by some £2.5 million a year.

Further consideration should be given to the means of achieving 'more simple, cheap and reliable' registered conveyancing. In the longer term it was also desirable that the Land Registry fees should be related more closely to the costs of the work involved and, in future, that changes in the fees should have regard to the need to establish a proper relationship between the registered and unregistered conveyancing scales. It recommended that the existing mixture of statutory and voluntary scales for mortgage work should be replaced by a new statutory scale (applying to mortgages of both registered and unregistered land) with charges set at 40 per cent of those proposed for the conveyancing of registered land. The charges would apply equally for solicitors acting for mortgagor only, or for mortgagor and mortgagee, in all transactions where mortgage was contemporaneous with purchase. The Board suggested that they should also provide the normal basis of remuneration for mortgagees' solicitors. In those cases where mortgages were not contemporaneous with purchase, further study should be undertaken with the aim of reducing the level of charges and of establishing a single statutory basis of charging. The statutory scale for negotiating loans should be abolished and charges for this work should be regulated according to Schedule II. These changes would reduce gross mortgage income by some £1.5 million a year.

It expressed no view on the desirability of solicitors acting for both vendor and purchaser, but so long as the practice continued the charges should be no more than 1½ times the scale charges, to be apportioned equally between vendor and purchaser. This would reduce gross income by up to £2 million a year.

The profession should continue to develop the use of simple methods of costing legal work in individual practices.

Finally, it considered that the way in which the statutory machinery for regulating solicitors' remuneration had operated had contributed to the development of the present imbalance in solicitor's remuneration. It recommended that, so long as a major part of solicitors' income was regulated by statute, there should be an independent review body to advise on solicitor's remuneration. It suggested some of the considerations by which this body might be guided. To work effectively, it would require systematic and expert evaluation of financial and other data about the profession, and it would seem appropriate for the Office of Manpower Economics to be charged with this.

For the *Pay of University Teachers* reference, the Board commissioned the Higher Education Research Unit of London University to undertake a major study of all the main aspects of the academic labour market. When the study comes to fruition it is likely to provide information of value in the future determination of University pay. As there are few labour markets about which such detailed information can be obtained, the study should also add to the knowledge of the workings of labour markets in general.

11. Managerial Efficiency

Where inefficiency existed, the NBPI believed that management had a key role in its elimination. 'Our general experience is that the crucial factor in raising productivity is almost always the quality of management and management control'.[1] This applied to nearly all facets of business activity and to management at all levels of organisations. Thus improvements which the NBPI suggested concerning reformed negotiating machinery and the laying down of guidelines for incentive payment schemes 'will be of no avail if the managers and foremen on the spot do not have the ability or the training to put improved methods into effect and are not supported by an adequate control system'.[1] The theme of managerial control was pursued in numerous reports whether the main concern was with labour management or with other aspects of the management function. Whilst it was from management that the main initiative for change and innovation must come, this did not mean, the NBPI said, that trade unions had no role to play or that they were always ready to respond as positively as they might, and investigations were designed to ascertain union and worker attitudes to efficiency and change.

This chapter contains an outline of the nature, procedures, techniques and some findings of the NBPI's studies of managerial efficiency, especially those made after 1968. The subject of efficiency in pricing is dealt with in Chapters 12 and 13. Industrial relations and wage matters have to some extent been dealt with in Chapters 7, 8 and 9.

It should be understood that this chapter very much picks out the NBPI's own 'best practices', rather than surveys all the methods used to assess and help improve efficiency. It is not then a survey of all NBPI studies of efficiency. Rather by concentrating on the NBPI's better studies, the aim has been to record some of the best ways of going about assessing efficiency, and to suggest the potentiality of efficiency studies.

1. The Development of NBPI Efficiency Studies

In the early days the NBPI's reports touched on many aspects of managerial efficiency, but the main emphases were on the problem of managing labour — matters relating to industrial relations, wage and salary systems, and labour utilisation — and on the problem of forecasting output, investment appraisal and pricing. There were also a considerable number of recommendations

---

1 4th General Report.

concerning the structure of industry, most often in the direction of mergers, as in *Bank Charges* (34), *Coal Distribution* (21) and *Laundries and Dry Cleaning* (20), but also in other respects, such as *Motor Repairs and Servicing* (37) where the main recommendations were directed towards securing more purposeful external pressure on the industry from its chief groups of 'organised' customers, such as insurance companies and motor manufacturers.

In studying managerial efficiency, the NBPI at first relied mainly on commercial management consultancy groups and to some extent on its own generalist, industrial relations and enquiry team staff and the help of Board Members with industrial experience. Consultants took no part in policy discussions or drafting which determined the underlying approach to a report, or in determining the shape of the report. The identity and terms of reference of consultants were not disclosed publicly, but only to the party being investigated. They were, of course, bound to secrecy by the Official Secrets Act, and by the Prices and Incomes Act.

The NBPI's early work in these fields was probably quite successful and it is apparent that no high level of management expertise was necessary to uncover and suggest broad solutions to the many fundamental shortcomings exposed in early reports. Nevertheless, early investigations fell short of the ideal. Consultants were generally given wide-ranging briefs and were not in general closely supervised by the NBPI. They were sometimes asked to perform, at short notice, unfamiliar tasks, for example assessing the efficiency of an entire industry. They were not members of staff working parties and so were not able to keep in touch with daily developments in the conduct of references; nor were they in a position to influence the report as much as were NBPI staff. Some consultants produced excellent studies, but equally they sometimes produced reports of an extremely general character of little value. This is no general indictment of consultants but it does suggest that there was a need for closer direction of their activities.

There were several other failings in early investigations. In some references, such as that concerning the printing industry, the condemnation of inefficiency focussed mainly on shortcomings on the industrial relations side, with the trade unions as the proximate cause (though management was also condemned for its role). A full systematic survey of the efficiency of the whole industry, treating labour efficiency as only part of the story, might have been more useful and less one-sided. There was a lack of refined diagnostic and investigatory techniques for correctly identifying likely weaknesses at an early stage; a failure to cover some key areas of business such as purchasing and marketing, together with a bias to pursuing hobby horses; the lack of industrial experience at senior levels had given the NBPI staff relatively little feel for industrial management and, combined with the frequent use of junior or inexperienced staff to check efficiency, which exposed their inexperience to not uncritical executives, led to only a moderately satisfactory 'interface' with industrial management.

In retrospect, it is difficult to understand why the NBPI did not seek to acquire its own management experts at an early date. The reasons were perhaps that it thought its main staffing weaknesses would be on the industrial relations side, a novel field of official reformist activity in those days, and so it concentrated on acquiring this type of expertise, thinking that Board Members and consultants could fill the gap on the management side; and the main attention in early days was given to labour costs and to the reform of industrial relations.

The Government's decision of September 1967 to refer nationalised industry prices increases to the NBPI was a landmark for there was an accompanying decision to strengthen the NBPI to enable it to carry out efficiency enquiries.

During 1968, four management consultants were recruited, one a general management consultant, the other three specialists in operational research, production engineering and management accountancy. They did not form a branch and largely worked independently of each other. Not all were especially satisfactorily integrated into the organisation. In the meantime there was a lack of references about nationalised industries and so it was decided to use the consultants on private sector references. There was also a delay until June 1969 in recruiting a Director of Management Operations Branch, who then headed and directed the team which then started to function as a unified branch, the Management Operations Branch. At the same time the Enquiry Team was transferred to the Management Operations Branch's charge to play a support role (although it also continued to play a part in industrial relations and other studies). Attempts were then made to broaden the range of experience to cover the whole management field from purchasing to marketing. By the end of 1970, after taking into account changes of staff, the Management Operations Branch consisted of its Director, three Managers (in Operational Research, Marketing Activities and Industrial Operations), two assistant Managers, and five management assistants.

Most of the senior members had had line management experience at a senior level and had held down more than one industrial post and thus had a background of broad executive experience in industry. The Director was a former Ford executive, and the three managers were a leading operational research consultant, a Marketing Manager from British Domestic Appliances and a Director of Planning from United Glass. The assistant managers were an ex-OR manager of IPC, and an ex-marketing manager of Morgan Crucible. This industrial experience, rather than consultancy necessarily, experience sought in recruiting was considered an advantage in dealing with managers in industries under reference and as necessary to provide a basis for practical recommendations. Another emphasis in recruitment was on businessmen who could marshall their evidence and communicate their findings effectively in writing and at meetings. The NBPI was selective in its choice of members for this work, and although paying market rates for jobs, there were problems in building up a team of industrial advisers. Thus, it never had assistant managers in production engineering, work study nor purchasing, nor managers in management accountancy, and it never achieved its target membership of 12 managers or assistant managers. This was partly because of the NBPI's uncertain future and the offering of a 'specialist' role instead of a line career.

It is worth dwelling on the reasons why the NBPI built up its team of industrial advisers, or at least why in retrospect this seemed to have advantages. The nature of the NBPI's work was novel, and different from that of the great majority of consultants who normally deal with relatively specific, well-defined problems. Accordingly it was necessary to develop and refine techniques of designing, conducting and analysing appropriate studies. This was best done by continuous, not ad hoc, involvement in such studies. It was also possible to capitalise on the ability to study a particular group of activities in a variety of industries, an opportunity which consultants might not always have. As an example, the NBPI in some half dozen references made some 35 case studies into clerical work measurement obtaining in this way much information on the subject. There were similar types of exercises conducted in some other fields such as corporate planning and sales efficiency. In these two instances, a number of non-reference firms in various industries co-operated in the studies.

The aim was nevertheless to get the best of both worlds and even after the establishment of its own Management Operations Branch the NBPI made use of commercial management consultancy firms in something like one-third of all references. It was felt it would be wasteful to attempt to build up a staff with a full range of expert knowledge extending across all subjects and industries. The main difference after the establishment of the Branch was that the Branch assumed the effective responsibility for the choice of consultants and exerted a closer control over their investigations, usually by means of briefs specifying the main questions for investigation.

Other advantages from developing the NBPI's team were that it was easier to redirect studies during the course of a reference when done internally; outside consultants were not always immediately available to start work when needed due to other commitments; and use of the NBPI's own staff and resources was cheaper. The NBPI had full independence of the industry it reported on. Finally the presence of a management team led to a much greater consciousness throughout the NBPI organisation of the managerial dimension in references. There was a greater attempt, for example, to look at wage problems from a management viewpoint and to see wages as a tool of management. There was also a more systematic attempt to examine the totality of the managerial function rather than to isolate selected aspects

2. The Nature of Efficiency Studies

Efficiency studies compromise essentially two lines of enquiry, the first dealing with the technical competence of an industry, the second its managerial competence. The NBPI was concerned with the latter. It did not, for example, consider the merits of investment in one type of machinery rather than another – it did, however, assess the methods used by management to make such decisions, and it examined their outcome by comparing results and forecasts. It was believed that if correct managerial methods were used, then technical efficiency was likely to result.

The function of an efficiency study was not to review individual decisions by managements so much as to examine the processes by which decisions were reached and in this way to help undertakings to improve the quality of their decisions and hence their performance. The Board thus had to satisfy itself that the objectives of the undertaking were well defined, and properly communicated to the sub-divisions so as to ensure that objectives were met. This did not preclude it from examining the performance of undertakings in the field, but this was done principally to assess the adequacy of the managerial system.

Efficiency audits were concerned mainly with the efficient utilisation of all resources in a firm or industry, including not only finance, plant, materials and labour but also sales and distribution networks and to some extent with the realisation of market potential. The demonstration by firms of a continuing record of improvement in relevant areas together with evidence of a realistic programme of future objectives and action to achieve them and the use of relevant good management practices and techniques was also sought.

The NBPI did not wish to overlap with, or duplicate the work of, departments supervising nationalised industries. Sometimes, as it found in its first investigation of the London Transport Board, the Government or the industry itself had already undertaken an extensive investigation through the use of consultants. Its aim was to choose areas with significant implications for prices but which, because of the relative absence of external constraints, seemed to merit deeper investigations.

The term 'efficiency audit' was not regarded as an appropriate description of studies of efficiency because of its implication that the main concern was with the past, rather than the present and future. The Chairman in his evidence to the Select Parliamentary Committee on Nationalised Industries said:

'I would describe the exercise, not as an inquest into what has happened in the past but as a giving of counsel and of help for the future'. [1]

There is another reason as well. The term audit conveys an impression of completeness of coverage. Whilst the NBPI endeavoured at the outset of a reference to examine the totality of the managerial function, this was only in order to pick a few significant subjects which were then examined in depth. Often there were conscious decisions to sacrifice breadth in order to achieve greater depth. It was thought, however, that good studies of selected subjects might well have a catalytic effect in areas not studied.

Efficiency studies were only partly analogous with the work of commercial management consultants. Broadly speaking, the NBPI was involved only in diagnosis and prescription and was not concerned, as consultants usually are, with the implementation of cures (though care was taken to spell out feasible solutions); it often stopped where a consultant began by

1 p. 684, Minutes of Evidence, op. cit.

171

pointing to areas where an industry needed outside assistance. The NBPI was not invited by the client nor were its terms of reference determined by him. It was probably less welcome, even if cheaper, than an invited consultant; it had less time in which to work; and management was under a greater temptation to steer it away from problem areas. The NBPI was not obliged to satisfy the client: it did not, as a consultant might, run the risk of losing business because of unpopular or revolutionary suggestions. This freedom did not remove the incentive for producing sound acceptable reports since otherwise they would be exposed publicly and to Government departments responsible for followup, and since it wished its recommendations to gain the acceptance of parties.

Nevertheless, the NBPI's position freed it to work in a wider area in a firm or industry than most consultants, and often it investigated areas of the economy such as in many parts of nationalised industries, in which the engagement of consultants had never previously occurred and was not in prospect. A final difference was that its function was to bring the public interest to bear on firms rather than necessarily help them maximise profits.

There was relatively little difference in principle or technique of enquiry between studies of efficiency in the private and the public sectors. The main differences reflected the larger scale of nationalised industries such as coal or gas, the fact that the main nationalised industries are subject to less competition, and that there was a specific government charter to study their efficiency in some depth. The major efficiency studies were thus about nationalised industries and the three largest concerned *Gas* (102, 155) and *Coal* (153).

Not all studies of nationalised industries were on a major scale. Consultants were not engaged in *Bulk Supply Tariff of the Central Electricity Generating Board* (59) principally because there were no counterparts with which to compare the industry. Instead it was decided to concentrate on a few areas in which even marginal improvements involved millions of pounds. This strategy seems to have paid off because the NBPI was successful in obtaining an admission from the CEGB that cost-savings of the order of £60 million would have resulted if delays had not occurred in the construction of new plant. The cost of late commissioning had not been measured previously (and certainly not published), and the disclosure of this information seems to have startled the Government into taking some useful follow-up action including the setting up of a NEDO working party on the management of large construction sites.

A further factor which occasionally limited the scope of a nationalised industry efficiency study was the government's occasional use, in making references, of a distinction between an efficiency and a cost-saving study. A covering letter from the Minister of Power requested the NBPI to treat *Steel Prices* (111) 'as a matter of special urgency' in the light of the then poor revenue position of the British Steel Corporation and the need to determine at an early date the Corporation's likely borrowing requirement. It was recognised that a judgment on the price proposals would require some assessment of the cost-saving opportunities open to the industry, through the timetable set (as well as the organisational changes which the industry was undergoing) precluded a full efficiency study. When the NBPI sought to hold a small scale field study of the efficiency (or cost-saving opportunities or whatever) of the Corporation, there was a clash with the Corporation over the meaning of the letter, and the Corporation resisted rather strongly the attempt to study it in depth, and certainly succeeded in impeding considerably the NBPI's proposed studies. Commenting on the reference in the Fourth General Report, the NBPI said:

> 'The distinction between an efficiency study and an examination of cost-saving opportunities is one not of kind but of time. An examination of the scope for cost reductions is in fact an examination of efficiency but a full efficiency study takes longer'. [1]

Studies of efficiency could be roughly classified under three main headings:

(a) short studies of managerial efficiency in three month private sector price references. These could be termed 'vetting' exercises.

(b) at the other extreme, 'depth' studies of large nationalised industries, which often took more than 6 months. The three most important examples were the reports *Gas Prices (Second Report)* (102), published in February 1969; *Coal Prices (Second Report)* (153), published in August 1970; and *Costs and Efficiency in the Gas Industry*, (155) published in August 1970.

(c) an intermediate group in terms of scale and, to some extent, scope, of studies of the private and public sector. Some examples of these in 1970-1 were the reports on *Pay and Conditions of Workers in the Milk Industry* (140), *Costs and Revenue of National Newspapers* (141), *Bread Prices and Pay in the Baking Industry* (151), *Costs and Revenues of Independent Television Companies* (156) and *Pay and Conditions of Service of Ancillary Workers in National Health Service Hospitals* (166). In these cases there was no requirement to report on a particular settlement within three months, and there was enough time and staff resources to explore managerial efficiency in greater depth.

Underlying these three types of study was a similar approach to the principles of good management, but the procedures were somewhat different in each case.

3. Diagnosis

At the outset it was necessary to select particular areas of a firm or industry for examination. From 1969 onwards the Management Operations Branch and Staff Working Parties systematically attempted in major references to choose what seemed likely to be the most rewarding subjects for study. This was done by using submissions from the parties, any preliminary accounting data showing exceptional cost increases in some areas, the main sources of

1 Para. 49

costs and revenues, prior or published knowledge of the industry, and any preliminary assessment possible of its strengths and weaknesses. An attempt was made to consider all dimensions, not simply more conventional fields such as production. Thus in *Bread* (151) 40 per cent of costs were accounted for by retail distribution. As this is an area that is often neglected by management in industry generally, it was decided to single it out for special study. On the other hand 40 per cent of costs were accounted for by purchase of raw materials, but bakers have little influence on these prices, so relatively little attention was given to the subject. Again in the study of *Newspapers* (141), the temptation to concentrate as in the first report on the sensitive areas of labour and printing was avoided, and neglected but important areas such as the selling of advertising, materials utilisation, distribution and the level of overheads were examined.

The sales area in both gas and coal received considerable attention because it was judged likely that there would be considerable potential for savings and improvements, a judgment which in the event seemed to prove sound.

A further feature of the selection process, especially in later days, was an attempt, not entirely successful, to get away from studying subjects in which NBPI's own interests and expertise was greatest to subjects which appeared to be of the greatest importance. Thus the first major efficiency study of *Gas Prices* (102) dealt mainly with forecasting and planning techniques, pricing policies, and some aspects of labour utilisation; these were not necessarily studies likely to yield the greatest benefit (though they were important); the second study of *Cost and Efficiency of Gas* (155) by contrast, covered important areas, previously untouched by the NBPI, such as purchasing and stock control, the effectiveness of the sales force, the location and number of showrooms, as well as staff efficiency and labour utilisation.

Parallels between apparently different industries often reduced the need for diagnosis and enquiry. For example, the problems of getting products from the factory to the consumer were often similar in different industries.

The areas identified in the preliminary stage were discussed with management or the industry representatives and occasionally with the trade unions, and their agreement was sought and usually obtained for the NBPI's proposals. In a few cases the NBPI over-rode objections and did the studies anyway.

4. Short Studies

In short 'vetting' references concerned with medium or large sized monopolistic or oligopolistic firms the top management of firms under reference was visited. In the interests of constructive discussion it was made clear that the managers themselves had industrial experience, and understood business problems. Discussions were then held, typically for several hours about the way the business was run.

To take marketing as an example, the marketing management were questioned about the broad marketing background of the industry and firm; whether the objectives, strategy and policies of the firm's marketing were precisely defined; whether marketing considerations contributed to product planning and design and packaging and whether product decisions were based on adequate market research; about their use of advertising, sales promotion and market research techniques; the structure and organisation of its marketing department and its activities, and whether its place in the overall organisational structure was satisfactory; what attention was given to training, recruitment of salesmen, and other matters where relevant, e.g. use of R. and D.; and finally whether there was a positive approach aimed at realising the potential of markets and maximising revenue.

Particular attention was paid to those aspects of marketing in which a numerate approach can be taken such as whether there was adequate planning and control of sales forces. The firms would be asked to demonstrate that they kept detailed data on the objectives and performance of the different parts and area of the sales force and for data showing if performance had improved. Particular emphasis was placed on whether action programmes to improve performance existed, and on whether a positive approach existed and on attempts to use experiments to develop important areas, e.g. the efficiency of retailing.

Information was taken from the financial questionnaire on the interrelationships of the cost of various elements in the marketing and distribution mix and some attempts were also made to judge the activities of the firm in the light of comparative data from other firms in the industry and even in broad terms by drawing upon the small 'library' of comparative performance data from other industries which was starting to be built up during 1970-71.

Whilst recognising that every aspect of the marketing field was not susceptible to scientific judgment, it was felt possible on the basis of the experience of the NBPI's managers and by taking the most numerate approach possible to form a judgment as to whether or not marketing activities were well conducted; operated at least possible cost; and under adequate control.

If weaknesses in specific areas were suspected, it was possible to probe somewhat deeper in the time available and to produce some general conclusions.

More generally these short types of studies were of a 'vetting' kind insofar as they simply tested whether some of the essentials of good management in big firms were present. If a firm produced detailed cost and performance data, showed a record of improvement, and concrete plans for improvement in weak areas (of which there are always some), possessed a set of plans and well-defined future objectives for the organisation and its various parts, and used good management techniques, then this was regarded as constituting a necessary, though not sufficient, requirement for optimum efficiency. If it could not meet this requirement, and there were no exonerating circumstances, such as its small size, then there was a strong presumption that it was operating at less than optimum efficiency: whether a big firm achieved maximum efficiency without meeting these requirements was at best a matter of hit-and-miss. This at any rate was the theory of short-run vetting studies, and it is not surprising that in the few references in which such studies were conducted in 1970-71 relatively little emerged from them by way of specific recommendations for improvements, perhaps because a good proportion of those investigated in this way — margarine, ice-cream, tea companies — were from among the better managed British companies.

This method of enquiry, however, represented a considerable advance on the mere interviewing of top management without calling for data, plans, and so on. To the extent that it investigates management efficiency, this is the method normally used by the Monopolies Commission. And the Industrial Reorganisation Corporation, which said it regarded a high quality of management as a prerequisite to its investment of funds in a firm, likewise called for little information which would give an indication of its quality. The NBPI was always sceptical of using interviews with top management as its only instrument of enquiry. In some cases such interviews were enough to disclose whether or not a firm had an adequate and well organised data flow by which its management could control its performance; and whether it had planned its future strategy and activities carefully. In dealing with well-organised monopolistic or oligopolistic firms it was possible to find out much in this way; and it was often all that was possible in three months. It was generally desirable, if there was time, to go deeper than this, and to investigate performance and industrial relations at plant level. In the following section some techniques for conducting field studies of efficiency are described.

5. Some Techniques of Study

In this section, an account is given of some techniques of study employed in more probing efficiency studies, together with examples of their application in practice. This account, which is not comprehensive, partly merges into the next section of this chapter about the findings of some efficiency studies.

The section is broadly organised around an outline of a number of different techniques which the NBPI used to assess and help improve efficiency. These techniques were all closely interrelated and overlapping, and it is principally for expository reasons that a rough distinction is made between them.

The different techniques, then, were:

(a) comparisons, either quantified or non-quantified, of costs, performance, management practices or techniques in different firms in the same industry;

(b) NBPI collection of information about performance in an industry to assess and help improve efficiency;

(c) inter-industry and international comparisons;

(d) case studies designed to identify best and worst managerial practices and to help accelerate the spread of best practices;

(e) studies to determine if industries were using appropriate management decision making tools and techniques, such as operational research; and the construction of operational research and other models which would launch the use of such models in the industry.

Intra-industry comparisons: Perhaps the most powerful method of enquiry was comparisons of costs, performance or management practices or techniques of firms conducting similar operations within an industry. With monopolies or nationalised industries, comparisons of different plants or areas were possible.

Quantified intra-industry comparisons: In some studies, quantified comparisons were made to show the exact scope for possible savings. On most references rough comparisons of the pattern of costs in different firms were made where possible, but they rarely were precise or detailed enough to lead to definite conclusions. The other main quantifiable indicators of comparative efficiency were 'performance indicators' which are partly or fully physical, rather than financial, measures e.g. the quantity of output per man hour is a simple example.

Intra-industry variations in performance do not prove conclusively the existence of inefficiency, because differences in circumstances or methods of production may explain the variations. Nevertheless striking variations of performance in similar situations suggest that inefficiency exists, and that there may be a reasonable prospect of bringing low performers up to the average level of others. Performance indicators also show whether and how much improvement has been occurring from year to year in the same firm or plant.

An example of the NBPI's use of performance indicators was in the second *Newspapers* reference (141). It collected figures of newsprint wastage by ten newspapers. The percentage of waste had increased from 6.1 per cent in 1967 to 6.8 per cent in 1969. There was a wide range of wastage levels — from 4.4 per cent to 12.2 per cent. Only two newspapers showed a downward trend; one, with the lowest wastage, had established an effective control system and had a target figure of less than 3 per cent. The majority showed an upward trend. Three had wastage figures above 9 per cent. For all papers to attain 3 per cent would entail a net benefit of £1.2 million, varying from £38,000 to £364,000 for different papers. In the USA, some newspapers had wastage figures as low as 1.5 to 2.0 per cent, so that this target was not unreasonable. If a less ambitious target of 5 per cent were chosen, approximately £0.6 million could be saved.

In a similar study on *Bread Prices and Pay* (151), wastage in production and distribution was reported to vary from 3 per cent to 8 per cent of retail sales value and it was calculated that if losses could be reduced to 3 per cent in all cases then savings averaging about ½d per loaf could be achieved. [1]

---

[1] The NBPI made a slip here. It should have calculated percentage savings in relation to ex-factory value, not retail sales value. Its calculation of losses should have been correspondingly reduced, to about ¼d per loaf.

In *Costs and Efficiency of the Gas Industry* (155) a basically similar method – quantified inter-area comparisons of performance – was adopted. This was possible because the gas industry was largely confined to urban areas and had relatively uniform characteristics and problems. A number of fields in which cost-savings were considered possible were initially identified and data collected. Thus the Enquiry Team collected data about the numbers of manual employees to whom Work-Studied Incentive Payment schemes had been applied in each area, the savings which had been obtained, and the speed at which the schemes had been and would be introduced. In this way it was possible to calculate the future savings which would result from a more rapid adoption, especially in lagging areas, of Work-Studied Incentive Payment schemes than planned by the industry.

A similar method was employed for the showrooms of the 12 Area Gas Boards. Showrooms were classified into groups according to the size of their turnover. The average numbers of staff per showroom for different Boards varied widely in a way that could not be attributed to differences in their locations and functions. As they had a turnover of some £40 million and a staff of over 3,000, large savings would have occurred – 852 staff, and, by 1972-3, an annual saving of £1.3 million per year – if they were brought up to the level achieved in the upper quartile of Area Boards. [1]

The above was only one of several proposals which resulted from the exercise. The same information revealed that about one-half of showrooms had an annual turnover of less then £20,000, which suggested that they sold less than 8 appliances per week. They employed some 20 per cent of staff, but accounted for only 12 per cent of total turnover, 15 per cent of total bill payments and 16 per cent of total services enquiries. [2] About one-third of all showrooms, and nearly all of the 200 or so with turnover of less than £5,000, were unprofitable. The NBPI estimated, after consideration of the consequences, that some 200 showrooms could, with comfort, be closed down.

Intra-industry comparisons in this reference for a number of fields showed that in toto cost reductions of the order of £100 million were possible over the following quinquennium. Over and above the industry's own plans to effect savings of about one-third of this amount, the NBPI recommended savings of a further two-thirds or so of this amount.

Having identified and perhaps quantified a potential source of savings, it was then necessary to show how it could be achieved. In the Newspapers reference, for example, a little information was published about how the better companies controlled newsprint utilisation. The NBPI regarded the key to an effective control system as the availability of detailed information on the sources and quantities of newsprint utilisation to enable management to take corrective action. It recommended the introduction of systems for the control of newsprint usage for all newspapers, and suggested that experience of such systems might with advantage be shared on an industry-wide

1 Appendix D, page 58 of the report shows exact comparisons.

2 Para. 82.

basis, possibly through the Newspapers Proprietors' Association. In *Gas* (155) a detailed scheme was specified showing the Gas Council and Area Boards exactly how to go about achieving savings. At a later stage of this chapter more is said about how the NBPI investigated best practices in industry and attempted to accelerate their spread.

Non-quantified intra-industry comparisons: The coal industry's complex technology, diversified conditions, and an immense work force of 400,000 made *Coal Prices* (153) one of the most challenging studies the NBPI faced. Quantified inter-area comparisons were however not possible. Within the coal industry, for instance, mines differ greatly in terms of product, geological conditions, equipment and labour attitudes, and even within a mine face, conditions change rapidly. Thus it was not practicable to compare one part of the industry with another. Even data published within the industry, such as output per manshift, could not be used as a meaningful industry-wide measure in view of variations in the 'blend' i.e. the proportion of rock and dirt extracted to coal mined, an unknown factor.

A further problem for the NBPI was that the NCB was well accustomed to handling official enquiries and had developed a high level of debating skills and its managers were very knowledgeable of the intricate technicalities of the industry; the NBPI therefore undertook a different kind of study from that made of the gas industry.

Despite the impossibility of a quantified comparative study of the industry, it was still possible to compare management practices and techniques in different regions on a non-quantified basis and this formed one major part of the study. At the same time, in contrast to the more or less unrelated separate studies of different fields in the Gas industry, an interlocking, overlapping series of studies were planned.

A number of elements in the industry were initially selected for study — forecasting and planning, because it had been off the mark; marketing and pricing, because little attention had been paid to this area and because of its importance in relation to the Coal Board's long term strategy; industrial relations, manpower and pay, because of recent changes created by the 1966 National Power Loading Agreement.

For the mining side of operations, the Enquiry Team visited 30 selected pits for periods of one or two days and obtained general background information about the mine, production data and discussed with the local management such topics as forecasting; management and supervisory structure; labour costs, overtime and management information related thereto; machine utilisation; mine organisation and planning; the relationships with marketing and other departments; and so on.

Industrial relations case study workers visited 30 pits mainly for periods of one to two weeks, looking more deeply or more generally at similar or related subjects, discussing them in detail with managers, supervisors, Area officials and union officials. The case studies were compared with one another and also, insofar as they overlapped, with the Enquiry Team's studies so as to compare and check statements and views throughout the organisation. Thus when Coal Board officials challenged the Enquiry Team's conclusions about overtime supporting evidence from the industrial relations case studies was produced.

The subject of forecasting was tackled by teams operating at three levels — the NCB Head Office in both the marketing and production departments; at the Area and Sales Regions levels; and at pit level. At a later stage, there was a special study of differences in practice between certain areas. There were also studies of such topics as management services, purchasing, and organisation, and marketing by different teams or individual specialists.

Thus the initial findings were based on enquiries by staff of different disciplines, some from the NBPI, some independent. Their unanimity was high.

In order to check the initial findings, additional independent studies were carried out. A marketing study was made by consultants specialising in market research who asked industrial clients to compare Coal Board sales effectiveness with that of other industrial selling activities. A consultant studied the key role of first line supervision in face operations. In the management field, consultants held confidential detailed interviews with a sample of middle management from finance, marketing and production at various levels, seeking their views on such matters as the strengths and weaknesses of current management practices in their areas, their views on what change was necessary, and so on. This study largely tended to confirm and reinforce other findings of field studies.

The NBPI diagnosed the central problem of the industry as its recent, unforecast, falling rate of increase of productivity, after a period of rapid productivity increase. This was occurring against the background of an industry running at a loss and for whose product demand was falling.

Top management, however, was poorly organised to take action. The Coal Board only loosely super vised the 17 Area Directors, stressing their autonomy: this was in contrast with Area Directors' tight control of colliery managers. There was, even after allowing fully for local differences, very little attempt to achieve greater standardisation of approach and procedures between Areas based on best practices in the industry. The Coal Board went to some lenghts to disseminate knowledge of progress in various fields, but there was room for more vigorous follow up. There were also wide differences in practices and procedures in different areas. The NBPI's examination of the Coal Board's organisation and methods branch, mainly deployed in the areas, disclosed different approaches in applying work measurement to staff. There was also scope for standardising the flow of management information. There were differences between the areas in the use made of, and benefit gained from, method study, a key source of productivity gain in such a labour-intensive industry as coal. The discretion left to Area Directors as to the numbers of method study staff had led to their hardly being used in some areas. At colliery level, more specialists, such as accountants, had been recently introduced, but there was widely differing use of them.

In the absence of firm guidance from the centre, a variety of forecasting and planning methods were found to exist in differnt areas, probably one of the main reasons for the serious discrepancies between financial forecasts and results. There was also a need to make sales regions and areas more closely accountable for their respective marketing functions, based on a more standardised information flow which specified profitability as well as revenue objectives.

The reasons for these variations were partly ascribed to varying local situations and traditions, but mainly to the Coal Board's somewhat loose super vision and control of the performance of area directors, with stress on occasional intervention rather than continuous supervision. Whilst it was necessary to achieve a balance between central direction and local auton- omy, the NBPI believed that its examination of the effects of widespread local variations showed that the Coal Board had gone too far towards local autonomy. Although the Coal Board went to some lengths to disseminate knowledge of progress in various fields, there was need for more vigorous follow-up.

Initially it was not intended to study the Coal Board's top management organisation but the evidence from the detailed studies was such that fol- lowing further supporting work, management structure became the main fea- ture of the report. The report was not aimed to produce detailed cost savings, as in the case of gas, for reasons given earlier, but partly also be- cause the key problems seemed to lie in top management organisation and it was believed that action at lower levels would follow improvements at this level.

The NBPI's main recommendations were for organisational changes at the top management level. Once these were accomplished, it believed that other changes would follow; and it indicated the main changes which a newly organ- ised Board should make. This is taken up later.

The *Coal Prices* study, although one of the largest and most ambitious of the NBPI's studies, was not without shortcomings. The lack of co-ordination between industrial relations and management studies has already been men- tioned (despite the useful or fortuitous overlapping of management and indus- trial relations studies of overtime). The members of the Enquiry Team lacked the managerial exper ience necessary to hold their own with NCB managers in the field. The studies of face management were moderately suc- cessful at best. The important subject of machine utilisation was inad- equately covered and in the event a good part of the report's comments on face management was based upon the report of a lone consultant who was brought in at a late stage. Little that was produced by the NBPI's staff on the subject of face management went into the report (despite a considerable expenditure of effort on their part). However, it is fair to add that nearly all the NBPI staff involved in this refe rence believed that a major cause of the difficulties they encountered was the obstructive and unhelpful attitude of some NCB managers and officials.[1]

1 In this reference, the NCB was invited to participate directly in some of the NBPI studies. Mixed teams were appointed to conduct some key studies. Most NBPI staff subsequently felt that this was a tactical mistake. The NCB was too strongly placed to influence the direction of the studies and to stifle criticism.

NBPI Collection of Information to Assess and Help Improve Efficiency:
Where information was not available to enable quantified comparisons of
efficiency, the NBPI on some occasions used its Enquiry Team or consultants to collect the basic data from firms and constructed appropriate performance indicators. This not only allowed it to assess efficiency, but also
to show the industry how to do so for itself in future, and how to employ it
to improve their efficiency. For example, in studying the efficiency of various parts of Independent Television programme production, the NBPI found
that there were no readily available indicators of the utilisation of resources
by individual companies, nor relative figures across the industry. Thus,
there were no useful performance indicators.

Data was therefore obtained on the major component activities of production: studio rehearsal, camera rehearsal, setting and lighting, transmission or recording, set striking, sound dubbing and editing. To obtain
comparable indices, data collection was confined to programme types which
were broadly similar across the industry, namely the one-hour drama, the
half hour comedy and the regional news programme. Wide variations of
studio time and manpower allocation were found between contractors within
each category of production activity.

To make a regional news programme, the average time in 12 studios
varied from 5.5 hours to 2.0 hours with an average of 3.8. The number of
electricians used varied from six to one and so on. In most, but not all,
cases, setting and lighting crews stayed with a production during camera rehearsal and programme production, although there appeared to be no need for
more than one or two at most, and there were adjacent studios in which work
could have been performed at these times by a pool of labour.

The NBPI concluded that there was a strong case for individual contractors to establish indicators with which to monitor performance; with some
standardisation, inter-company comparison could be made, if desired. It
appreciated that variations in performance indicators to some extent reflected the creative latitude required by individual directors, which it would
not suggest be curtailed. Nevertheless, as well as measuring efficiency, the
proper use of established indices would enable companies to be aware of
the detailed implications of differing creative approaches and to evaluate
their relative merits more easily.

The above could not be regarded as in itself a perfect example of this
genre of study. Variations between companies were shown by the use of
ranges, instead of using a measure of dispersion which took account of the
variations of all companies around the average; and there was little attempt
to examine whether or not variations in programme performance indicators
were due to differences in the circumstances of individual companies; and
whether or not different, but not necessarily uneconomic, patterns of input
usage explained the variations. The study was, however, supported by
findings from visits to studios, and the results were checked with some
companies.

The study was more than sufficient to suggest the likelihood of inefficiency, to demonstrate the need for a full scale study to be undertaken,

and to show the nature of the methods which ought to be followed. Finally it may be remarked that relative to most commercial studies of industrial efficiency, this was highly sophisticated.

A few months later, in 1971, a somewhat similar, but more refined, study was published in *Pay and Conditions of Service of Ancillary Workers in National Health Service Hospitals* (166). The NBPI collected information about the numbers of ancillary staff working in catering, domestic services and portering in a sample of hospitals. Different hospitals used different numbers of staff, but in itself this did not suggest inefficiency. Statistical regression analysis showed that 88 per cent of the differences between the numbers of porters employed in different hospitals could be explained by the number of beds, and the floor space of hospitals. On the other hand certain other factors which might have explained these differences proved not to be statistically significant. A (regression) line was then drawn (with appropriate confidence limits) showing the average number of porters for each hospital with different numbers of beds, and different floor spaces. It was suggested that each hospital with more than this average number of porters should reduce their number to the average. In this way some 13 per cent of the labour force could be saved. Further technical details of the study were given in the Appendix D to the report.

There will always be deviations from an average, so that to suggest that below-average performers reach the average level does not prove that it is possible to do so. But it can equally be atgued that this method may understate the possible savings. The average is not the most efficient — perhaps all could emulate the performance of the top 10 per cent; moreover, there is nothing to say that the performance of the top 10 per cent represents optimum efficiency; if, in this report, one looks at the NBPI's overall assessment of the efficiency of hospitals, there is every reason to believe that a far greater saving could be achieved.

Perhaps the most important point to stress about this study was the development in technique and refinement which occurred in a fairly short interval of time after the ITV study. This suggests a general point about the NBPI's management efficiency studies: most were of a pioneering nature. By the time the NBPI closed down, its full potentialities in the management studies field had only been partly realised.

Inter-industry and International Comparisons: Thus far, intra-industry comparative methods have been outlined. In many cases, however, there were strong parallels between similar parts of different industries. The NBPI used comparative research both in other countries and industries where this could be of use. In *BOAC Pilots*, the proposed recommendations were found to be in use in the Scandinavian Airlines which was visited, and in *Gas*, targets for salesmen were checked against confidential data from other similar industries.

As part of a continuous review of developments in management, various studies were made using material collected in reference enquiries and by means of special studies mounted as time permitted in efficient and co-operative non-reference organisations. A number of organisations were in fact willing to co-operate in this way. Areas covered by such studies included white collar efficiency schemes, the use and organisation of management services, the use of data banks, purchasing and stock control, packaging, materials handling and distribution planning. In some confidential areas various non-reference companies co-operated with the research undertaken into corporate planning and their approach to handling important organisation and strategic changes (Plessey, Rio Tinto, Texas Instruments, The Electricity Council and various Unilever companies etc.). Thus recommendations were based so far as possible upon what was known to be feasible and had been achieved in actual management situations.

Case Studies: Of course, it was never enough merely to establish that some parts of an industry were performing worse than others. It was necessary to examine why the differences existed, and the means by which the better outperformed others. This was done by use of a number of methods, but especially by case studies of superior performers and by attempting to identify the techniques used and other factors responsible for their better performance. Case studies were described in Chapter 7.

Recommendations for the use of new management tools: Another method of study was to identify areas of industries under reference to which new management tools could usefully be applied, but in fact were not being used.

The leading examples of the NBPI's recommendations for the adoption of sophisticated techniques in industry were in the operations research (OR) field. OR involves the use of mathematics to solve complex problems, and by no means all businesses which could use it have done so. The main applications by the NBPI were in the fields of the distribution of products, pricing, nationalised industries and drawing up public transport routes in large cities and scheduling particular vehicles and crews. The NBPI recommended the introduction of OR techniques in reports concerning buses, brewing, cement, bricks, milk, car delivery, post office parcels charges and extension of its use in many others such as Gas and the National Freight Corporation. The Coal cost optimisation study which is described in Chapter 13, and other studies of pricing or nationalised industries, involved the use of operational research techniques, as did some of the intra-industry studies referred to earlier.

In large industries such as in the nationalised sector, the introduction of such techniques can lead to substantial savings. Even in a study of a relatively small scale, the Board was able to show how 59 of 475 buses in 4 towns could have been saved by interchanging buses between routes, applying OR techniques to determine the programme of interchanging, instead of running them backwards and forwards over the same route, thus saving significant proportions of time when buses remained stationary at terminals. [1]

In some cases there was time to construct very detailed models of the operation of a single company. This was particularly true in the case of the

1 *Pay of Municipal Busmen* (63)

London Brick Company (150) in which the company had to determine how to deliver bricks to all parts of the country at least cost. The production and distribution systems were so interdependent that it was impossible to take an optimal decision with respect to one part without assuming a decision had been taken on the other. For example, given the demand pattern, it had to choose first between combinations of delivery by its own vehicles, either in one stage or in two stages via the use of sub-depots, by two-stage delivery and by commercial road hauliers' vehicles when demand peaked; second, it had to determine what number of sub-depots it could have and where; third, what number and size of trucks; fourth, how daily trips should be planned so that drivers did not arrive back too early or too late, and how they should combine with vehicles of differing sizes.

But if prices were related to costs, demand itself would vary as a function of the decisions described. Rule of thumb methods would be unlikely to lead to a least cost solution in such a complex situation. The NBPI however set out a detailed model for the company (in Appendix IV) which identified the bulk of the decision rules that the company would need and established recommended prices which, as we have noted later, would increase the competitiveness of the company. LBC was recommended to construct a total systems model, work on which has in fact begun.

6. Some Principles and Findings

In this section some of the principles which the NBPI believed good management should follow are described; and so are some of its substantive findings in particular references.

Management Information: The NBPI stressed that a fundamental requirement for good management was a flow of information to top management about performance in all parts of the business. Despite this, there is an almost endless list of references in which information even of an elementary kind was found to be lacking. 91 out of 100 firms did not know what the introduction of job evaluation schemes had cost them. The optimum number of pages per newspaper from day to day for maximising profitability depends largely on the relationship between variable costs and additional advertising revenue, but few newspapers could provide information on the marginal costs of collecting and producing advertising matter. (More generally, few related their paging decisions positively and systematically to the financial implications, although one paper which did, had made annual savings of the order of £100,000).

Budgetary control using standard costs is an established technique, but in the British Steel Corporation (111) only some 30 per cent of plants were using them. There were many areas in the Industrial Civil Service (146) in which standard industrial costing practices could have been used but were not, with the result that inadequate management information, particularly on the cost of resources required to carry out individual activities, was tending to confine attention to limited aspects of productivity such as getting rid of obvious impediments to efficiency rather than to improving the total management of resources. Two monopolies (in terms of the Monopolies Act) also did not have standard costs information. In the Plasterboard reference, BPB could not make meaningful comparisons of the relative efficiency of its different works, in spite of collecting much financial and statistical information – the NBPI recommended that standards based on universal work study would be the best foundation on which to construct such information. The London Brick Company could not provide discounted cash flow appraisals of two new large works, one already completed, one under contemplation. Nor could it specify what costs would be saved if output were reduced, as it had no standard costs. It could not, for example, distinguish between the effect of input cost increases and the effect of changes in the volume of through-put. Similar deficiencies and inappropriate management accounting were revealed in laundries and dry cleaning, motor garages, and a host of others.

Nationalised industries were no exception. In *Gas Prices* (155), the NBPI, whilst conceding that a mass of information was available to the managements of Area Boards, pointed out that it was difficult to isolate significant items and some important information was missing. Thus, the gas industry used a high proportion of contractors' labour, but it was not possible to get a clear statement from all individual Area Boards of the number of contractors' men currently employed, the proportion of particular kinds of work or jobs done by them, and the relative costs of using contractors' labour or the Boards' own labour. It was difficult to establish what proportion of Area Boards' own labour forces were doing particular jobs and to get any physical measure over time of how many jobs were done. Nor was it at the time possible to get precise figures for the cost of particular services. It was also noted in some Area Boards that management control information existed but was not used as a basis for control. (For example, in one Area Board the basic work sheets showed evidence of delays incurred in waiting for transport, equipment and other facilities, but this information was not collated for submission to senior management for action.)

Management accounts are necessary not only to enable management to make informed decisions, but also to maintain control of its labour and all other resources. They allow assessment after the event of change, but equally importantly they allow budgeting and setting targets. Management accounts also provide a source from which measures or indicators of performance can be established. These are essential for the control of incentive pay schemes, schemes which the NBPI often encouraged.

Performance indicators can vary between industries and sometimes between firms in the same industry according to their method of operating and hence they must be selected discriminatingly, and their use constantly reviewed. They provide a flow of information from which top management can monitor the level and especially the trend of efficiency in different areas and plants. Thus in the Gas Industry they were recommended as of value to the autonomous Area Gas Boards in comparing themselves with others and as indicating the scope for improvements and cost savings, after taking due account of special factors in their area. Indices could also have a useful effect in concentrating effort on specific short term objectives. They also lead naturally to development of management by objectives. The indices for top management could be supported by detailed objectives for managers at each level, which both clarify the action required to support programmes' and provide a simple basis of assessing management performance and ability. (Their chief significance was perhaps as indicators of changes over the course of time rather than as cross-sectional indicators of performance.)

Some examples may be used to illustrate further a point noted earlier that the NBPI besides collecting information necessary to answer the questions posed by a reference, also often sought to demonstrate to management how it should go about obtaining information, in short to install the elements of a management control information system.

In the Gas references (102) and (155) the subject of recall visits by gas fitters and gas fitter improvers employed in the consumer services divisions the Gas Board was dealt with. In its first major efficiency study of the Gas Industry (102) the NBPI had pointed out that despite the industry's concern to provide a high level of service to customers, there was practically no formal information on the levels actually attained. Consultants engaged by the NBPI advocated the establishment of quantitative measures of the various elements of customer service and cost, partly to ensure effective managerial control and partly to help evaluate alternative policies. The opportunity to introduce these measurements could be taken by the industry as part of the review of existing systems then being undertaken in various Boards. It would also provide a basis for reviewing the effectiveness of consumer services in the industry as a whole. Elements of consumer service which were suggested as being amenable to measurement included the range of appliances stocked, the availability of appliances, installation delays, customer convenience with regard to installation, adherence to quality standards for work done, the ease of communication when seeking service, the promptness of service provided, the standard of performance on first call and the total delay and the number of calls required to complete the job.

Reporting some eighteen months later in the next efficiency study of gas, the NBPI found that most Area Boards still had no detailed information on most of these points, including recall visits, a subject which several of the User Consultative Councils had raised with it. The need for recall visits commonly arises from incomplete equipment — usually spares — on the first visit, the fact that the appropriate part is not available, unsatisfactory workmanship, or sending the wrong type of employee for the job. In order to obtain some indication of the extent to which multiple visits took place for any one job the NBPI therefore commissioned a market research firm to conduct a survey among 1,000 customers in each of two Area Boards. In one Board 11 per cent of customers interviewed had had *three* or more visits; in the other 14 per cent. (It appeared that the latter had a higher proportion because it frequently carried out a survey before work was done, a practice which had some advantages). If the pattern were general throughout the industry, this represented some 12 per cent of fitters workload. The elimination of 1 in 12 of repeat visits would have resulted in a decrease of 1 per cent in the number of fitters required giving a saving of £¼ million. More importantly, the NBPI had shown the industry an area in which there was savings potential and about which it needed more information; a method of obtaining it and of making possible savings; and a method which could more generally be applied or transferred to other areas so as to lead to significant savings.

There were other examples of the NBPI installing the elements of an information system. It conducted an earnings survey of Industrial Civil Servants which was intended to set the pattern for future earnings surveys by the Civil Service Department. Another was in the Plasterboard reference in which the NBPI helped to refine discounted cash flow calculations of the forecast return from new investment projects, partly to help determine whether an immediate price increase in plasterboard products could be justified, but also to show how in future, to go about making such calculations.

One of the most important examples of information gathering has already been referred to in Chapter 7. The NBPI's pioneering of regular detailed earnings surveys in particular references stimulated the DEP to expand greatly the scope of its own, economy-wide earnings survey and to follow the NBPI's methods.

When industries lacked data about their own performance, this greatly impeded the NBPI not only in assessing the scope for savings but also in helping to improve performance in weak areas . Paradoxically when business is least efficient it is most difficult for outsiders — whether consultants or government agencies — to help it improve performance in the short term. The groundwork can only be laid for later improvement. This point is suggested, though not demonstrated, by the report on the *Bulk Supply Tariff of the Central Electricity Generating Board* (59) in which it has already been mentioned that the CEGB on request produced a quantified estimate of the cost of late commissioning of plant. This would not have been possible for the NBPI to do itself, nor for the CEGB had it not possessed a sophisticated operational research model of electricity generation and distribution system. Admittedly this is one of a few cases where in effect the NBPI turned clients' analytical strength against themselves, though even here it can be argued that this was the industry's good, as well as the public's.

Management Control: Adequate information was a necessary but not sufficient condition to ensure good management.

A related and vital theme stressed throughout the NBPI's lifetime was the need for adequately tight managerial control. This was stressed especially on the side of industrial relations and wage systems. The report on PBR discussed in Chapter 9 was an example. Management had a key role in control but especially at lower levels where they had a crucial part in the day-to-day deployment of resources.

'... the crucial factor in exercising control is the quality and experience of management at all levels. We have often found that the roles of middle and particularly lower management levels are not fully recognised and given the emphasis which they require. First and second line supervisors and shop stewards are often not given the opportunity and the necessary training for the initiation, supervision and understanding of schemes for improving efficiency on the shop floor. This failure leads to disillusionment and resistance to change. We draw attention to this matter in many reports, particularly those on industries in the public sector, for example the gas industry.' [1]

The crucial role of first line supervision in controlling and deploying resources was stressed in reports on the National Health Service, Industrial Civil Servants, Water, Gas, Local Authorities and Coal.

Supervision is often the forgotten level in management.

In the gas industry, the NBPI found wide variations in the duties and span of control of the supervisors of some 60,000 manual workers. On the customer service side, in some cases they planned the timetable of gas fitters: in others they checked disputed accounts, subcontracted work and quality and quantity control: in many cases they were heavily involved in paper work. Surveys in two Area Gas Boards had shown that some spent as little as 10 to 20 per cent of the time in supervision. As was common in a number of other industries investigated, such as the N.H.S. and in some ways coal, many supervisors were more concerned with technical aspects than with supervisory or management problems. Most supervisors were promoted from within the industry and were self taught: management was reluctant to release them for training in the early days when they could most benefit from it.

Partly because the marketing section of the MOB was well-manned, and partly because marketing is a neglected area of management in some important industries, the NBPI found weaknesses in marketing and sales in several references in 1970-71. Thus it recommended greater use of sales planning throughout the gas industry's Area Boards, making specific recommendations designed to improve the effectiveness of the work done by sales forces and showrooms such as the establishment of realistic targets for salesmen and the application of rigorous levels of staffing. In the private sector both newspapers and independent television companies were found to have serious shortcomings in their marketing strategy and the effectiveness of sales forces.

In its *Fifth General Report* the NBPI expressed the view that marketing was as important as cost minimisation in the contribution which it could make to increased efficiency, whether in the private or public sector. Its marketing studies were designed to increase the revenues of the organisations under reference, provided always that increases in revenue were not obtained by the exercise of monopoly power.

Demand Forecasting and Investment Appraisal: The interlinked subjects of demand forecasting and investment appraisal are another important element in corporate planning. Throughout its six years the NBPI stressed the importance of their contribution to the more effective investment of capital

1 *Fifth General Report*, para. 73.

resources and therefore to stimulating the growth of output per head. In capital-intensive industries especially, under-utilisation of plant capacity can give rise to high costs.

As early as in its *First General Report* the NBPI observed that some current cost increases in the gas industry had occurred because of unnecessary investment resulting from faulty demand forecasts, using inappropriate methods; and in coal forecasting errors had led to overinvestment. In 'these cases, investment would have been better directed, assets would have been better used, and costs would have been better contained, had more critical methods of control been used.'[1]

The NBPI thus often recommended the use of more critical techniques in determining new investment or in determining the use of existing assets.

Correct investment decisions could not be taken, even with discounted cash flow methods, if demand had been wrongly forecast. Few undertakings were found to use econometric techniques in forecasting demand. The NBPI believed that there was a need in many fields for experiments with econometric models to compare outturns with forecasts in order to identify sources of error. Whilst not underestimating the difficulties, it was only through a logical process such as this that improvements in forecasting techniques were likely to be achieved. Thus it recommended for example the adoption of econometric forecasting procedures by the British Plaster Board Ltd., the monopoly plasterboard supplier in the country.

In nationalised industries millions of pounds were involved in many investments and it was to them that the NBPI devoted the most attention in the forecasting and investment appraisal field. The NBPI's studies of forecasting at all levels of the coal industry have already been referred to. The gas industry was the subject of an even more exhaustive study. It was undertaking a very large investments programme as part of the changeover to North Sea gas. The NBPI recommended that a more scientific and explicit approach be followed in providing for uncertainty (breakdown of equipment, temperature variations etc.) by making this factor the subject of numerical assessments of probability, and by a more systematic exploration of the results of alternative assumptions. Investment appraisal methods were also found to differ widely among Area Boards. The adoption of criteria laid down by the Government in the White Paper on the Economic and Financial Objectives of the Nationalised Industries needed to be speeded up and present appraisal methods should be overhauled and standardised.

As will be seen in the following Chapter on prices, these topics were also relevant to the evaluation of price increase proposals. In connection with references where the case for a price increase depended on the rate of return on new investment compared with the cost of capital, the NBPI made some general study of methods of appraising rates of return on new investment which included such factors as the forecasting of cash flows, the allowance for risk and uncertainty, and technological progress as well as the

---

1 *First General Report,* para. 45.

different approaches to the costing of capital from different sources.

Organisational Structure: Top management could hardly exercise the necessary control and influence over an organisation if the organisation structure was basically defective.

The NBPI concluded that the way in which the hospital service had been organised was the most important factor causing slow progress in improving the pay and efficiency of *Ancillary Workers in National Health Service Hospitals* (166). Regional hospital boards and hospital authorities, the second and third tiers of the service, enjoyed considerable freedom of action. They had no common strategy for improving the pay and efficiency of ancillary workers. In many regions it had been left to individual hospital authorities to decide whether and how quickly they should implement the recommendations for improving the pay and performance of ancillary workers endorsed by the Ancillary Staff Council and the Health Departments.

The financial control exercised by the Health Department, in the NBPI's view, placed insufficient pressures upon Regional Hospital Boards and hospital authorities to respond to opportunities for reducing costs. The system, which had to meet the requirements of Parliamentary accounting, worked primarily through pressure to keep expenditure down to the amount in the estimate. However, there was little pressure to reduce costs in areas where expenditure for one reason or another was stable. If anything, the system encouraged excessive expenditure in these areas for three reasons. First, money could not be transferred between expenditure heads except with the approval of the Regional Hospital Board. Secondly, money could not be carried over to the next financial year. Finally, any shortfall in expenditure was liable to be matched by a cutback in the budget for that item in the following year. The budget thus tended to become self-fulfilling as the authorities strove towards the end of the year to keep expenditure up.

On the other hand they were not provided with specific funds to encourage performance-related schemes. They were required to finance the cost of introducing schemes from the savings which they generated but for several reasons given in the report this was likely to hold up progress. It was recommended that they be given financial resources and incentives to stimulate faster progress.

Coal Prices (153) was the most prominent report in which many of an industry's problems were diagnosed as flowing from a faulty organisation structure. In the NBPI's view it was essential in the first place to strengthen the amount of control exercised from the centre over operations in the field. Central action was also required to improve standards of supervision and colliery face management; to put forecasting and planning on a uniform and reliable basis; and to develop further the means of involving workers in the achievement of the industry's objectives. Changes in the top management structure in the industry were necessary to achieve this. In particular, it considered that there should be an individual Board member, preferably a Deputy Chairman, to whom the Areas were directly responsible. There should also be a central management services department, which might be responsible to the same member.

Management Services: In a number of references, both public and private sector, the NBPI found that management services were fragmented and lacked a cohesive approach to the problems of the industry or company. Small technique based sections such as work study, O and M and operational research, worked independently and even on occasion in opposition to one another with the result that maximum benefit could not be realised, certainly not within a short time scale. *Coal* (153) and *Gas* (155) are examples.

In those enterprises where an central management service department had been created under the control of a senior Board member the NBPI found various improvement programmes were dovetailed together and greater savings achieved much more rapidly.

In *Coal* (153) it was believed that there was a need for strengthening some important management services at the centre. Even after allowing for the industry's contraction, the numbers of staff employed on method study had in recent years been allowed to run down overmuch, despite the great importance of their work for the improvement of productivity. Business planning staff needed strengthening. In examining the organisation and methods branch, deployed mainly in the Areas, the NBPI found evidence of different approaches in applying work measurement to staff, and also scope for standardising the flow of management information. The operational research executive, and the computer services section, needed stronger central direction to ensure that they were used within the organisation to best advantage, e.g. by guiding departments in choosing between the use of computers and other means of tackling a given problem. Hence, there was a strong case for locating the Coal Board's various management services in a single department at Headquarters, and possibly making it responsible to the Coal Board member exercising supervision over Area Directors. It was felt that this would help to ensure the spread of best practices throughout industry.

Corporate Planning: Under the influence of the corporate planning approach to management, which has started to be applied to a number of leading large firms in Britain and is more widely practised in the United States, the NBPI gave considerable attention in 1970-71 to the role and performance of top management in larger businesses.

The NBPI sought to determine whether companies and industries adopted a planned logical approach to the overall conduct of their business. Ideally, a number of elements were considered necessary for this:

(a) A clearly defined, quantified set of long term, medium term and short term objectives for the business as a whole. Flowing from this, measured goals for the different parts of the business, and related programmes of action designed to achieve these goals. Regular systematic analysis of the strengths and weaknesses of the organisation, and relevant programmes of action to eliminate weaknesses.

(b) Adequate forecasting, research and forward planning procedures to ensure the formulation and attainment of feasible objectives.

(c) Integration of planning of all elements of the business, production, marketing, distribution etc. by means of an overall strategy relating and co-ordinating the individual objectives to overall objectives. For example production strategy should be related to marketing needs and marketing to production. The organisational structure should conform to the requirements of the objectives, and in particular the same importance in the organisational structure should be given to the main sections of the business needing to be co-ordinated so that no part was likely to dominate decision making at the expense of others.

(d) A management services department can be a key factor in introducing change. Top management in big business at times needed a management services department to report directly on the appropriate techniques for use in the business. In turn, it was well placed to ensure their speedy adoption.

(e) There should a flow of quantitative information to top management about performance at each level in every part of the business to enable weak points to be detected and action taken. The flow of information was thus a mechanism of control over the performance of the organisation.

(f) Efficiency was likely to be highest when the way of doing each job in the organisation had been subjected to systematic study. At the same time, targets of performance could be established, e.g. retail sales value per man hour of production and in this way control maintained. Work study and measurement was not, however, universally applicable. Incentive schemes were often desirable.

(g) Management in the field or at lower levels was important. Particular attention should thus be paid to recruiting and training of first and second level supervisors. Training for all staff was important.

In the course of its studies on several references the NBPI came across many good and efficient operations. It also looked at some efficient organisations as part of special non-reference studies. These organisations operated in a wide variety of fields, had very different internal organisations and quite different approaches to management, but all were identified as having one thing in common; the willingness of management to experiment in a controlled way with new ideas — be it a product or a technique. The NBPI's belief was that this willingness to try out new approaches under controlled conditions, then to modify and progress, was a key factor in success. To take but one example, commercially and financially the most successful of the 12 Area Boards in the Gas Industry was believed to be one where all levels of management from the top down were actively seeking new and improved methods of operating. Nothing was taken for granted, all procedures and methods were constantly questioned and a continual process of change and improvement followed. In contrast some of the less successful Area Boards showed a greater reluctance to change anything; methods used for years continued without question and were only modified in the face of external pressure.

This attitude of 'its always worked well in the past so it is alright now' was found to be common in many of the less efficient organisations examined, not necessarily throughout management but certainly in the upper levels where policy decisions rest. It applied to structure and organisation, methods, marketing and even products. In such situations operating costs tended to rise to unnecessarily high levels, market opportunities were missed and products sometimes superseded by more advanced items produced by other companies.

Some examples of organisations which failed to meet these desiderata may now be considered.

The *National Freight Corporation* (162) was a prime example of an organisation without a strategy for dealing with change. The NBPI regarded it as needing as a matter of urgency to put an intensive effort into planning and to prepare plans based on studies covering all its plans for some years ahead. About £75 million of the Corporation's turnover came from the carriage of parcels by its subsidiaries, including National Carriers Ltd (NCL) and BRS Parcels Ltd. Their market had been contracting on average by around 4 per cent per year between 1965 and 1969, and competition from the private sector was likely to intensify. Productivity was rising each year and in the NBPI's view, the numbers of employees might well need to be reduced from 35,000 to 17,500.

Despite this NCL (whose current losses were £15 million per annum) had been planning on the assumption that over the next few years its traffic would increase sufficiently to absorb its current surplus capacity of 20 per cent. There had only been very limited market research into the potential parcels market of the NFC; it was not known whether the decline had been due to a falling share of the public sector, or an overall decline in demand, and whether the trend was likely to continue. It was not possible for the NBPI or the NFC to forecast accurately the future trend. All that could be said with certainty was that failure to adapt would lead to far more drastic and painful adjustment later.

The whole future organisation of the Corporation's parcels subsidiaries needed to be called into question. Should NCL and BRS Parcels Ltd. merge, or specialise in different kinds of parcel carriage, or should the BRS whose efficiency was only about half of the NCL's, bear the brunt of the rundown? These and other possibilities needed to be evaluated in the light of market research, O.R., and other studies suggested by the NBPI. Once the Corporation's marketing objectives were clear, the most appropriate form of organisation could be chosen, and objectives laid down for the constituent companies. There could be many manpower problems. By planning carefully much of the reduction could be effected through normal wastage, and careful transference of workers between depots.

The National Coal Board was also found to be in need of a corporate plan:

'Under such a system we envisage that the Board would define the operating policies and objectives for all major aspects of its activities and compare these objectives with an analysis of the strengths and weaknesses of each sector of the organisation. From this analysis would ensue detailed and systematically formulated programmes of management action and responsibility which would bring together as necessary the separate organisational functions required for their execution. Such a plan would reinforce the system of management by objectives which the Board has been operating in its Area organisation over the last few years by imposing a comparable discipline on the whole organisation. In doing so it would create stronger relations of accountability between top management and the decentralised sectors of the organisation, and would show more clearly where special management attention was most needed at any time. The case for a formalised system of corporate planning on these lines is particularly strong in the coalmining industry because of its size and complexity, the need to regain a higher rate of productivity improvement and the present lack of clarity about its long-term prospects and objectives.'[1]

A related question concerned the degree of control exercised by the Government over the activities of the nationalised industries. The NBPI recommended in the report on the *National Freight Corporation* (162) that, provided the Government has discussed and agreed the forward plans of a nationalised industry, it should not intervene in their detailed execution. However, in the examination of the nationalised industries the NBPI noted in some instances a lack of overall co-ordination at Government level as between the plans of different but connected industries, for example coal and electricity supply, and British Rail and the National Freight Corporation, which detracted from promoting efficiency. The former case is dealt with in Chapter 13.

Marketing: Marketing was a particular aspect of corporate planning which the NBPI often found to be neglected. In a relatively short space of time the National Coal Board had undergone a major change from being almost the sole primary energy supplier in an expanding market to facing sharp competition from other fuel supplies and a declining demand for coal. The NBPI conceded that there was no strong case for the NCB trying to keep the contracting general industrial and domestic markets at their present size, but believed it should try to identify profitable parts of the market which could be retained, such as in smokeless fuel. The NCB's annual expenditure on advertising and sales promotion was low in relation to its total expenditure. Expenditure on market research, less than £20,000, was confined to the minimum essential. More needed to be done both on attitudes and on the effect of advertising and the information thus obtained, together with internal data, needed to be used in planning models for both industrial and domestic markets and for monitoring marketing activities. There was also scope for a greater effort in such critical fields as research and development, liason with the coal distribution trade, and a closer integration of the NBPI's marketing and production activities. After its very searching

1 Coal Prices (153), para. 30.

analysis of NCB's marketing activities, the NBPI's general verdict was that in the face of change the NCB had remained too production oriented and was 'unduly defensive'.[1]

Labour Utilisation: The NBPI identified a surprisingly large number of industries in which the standard of labour utilisation was poor and in which the most elementary techniques for remedying it were absent. A selection would include *Local Authorities, the National Health Service, Gas and Water Supply manual workers* (29), *Pay of Maintenance Workers in Bus Industry* (99), *Gas* (155), *Electrical contracting* (120).

It has not been possible to survey the NBPI's views on labour management and utilisation in all references, which could be the subject of a separate volume, but a typical example comes from the PBR reference already described in Chapter 9. In deciding either to negotiate a change to an alternative payment system or to reform an existing system, when a PBR scheme was out of control, the NBPI stressed the importance of creating the right climate and above all of recognising the responsibility upon managements to secure reform. Despite this, it found considerable managerial inertia. Only rarely was change instituted because of a desire by management to operate as efficiently as possible. The idea of regular audits and reviews of payment systems appeared to be very little known despite a rapidly changing environment.

This inertia persisted in some cases even where the payment system was in danger of ruining the firm, and the NBPI, giving three examples of firms where payment systems seemed to be dangerously out of control, wondered aloud 'whether the traditional sanctions against management inefficiency (of lost trade and profits or bankruptcy) are at all effective.'

The NBPI concluded that it was necessary for managements at the highest level to take a much greater interest in payment systems than many did at that moment; to question the functioning of their payment systems; and to commit their organisations to negotiating changes where the situation seemed to call for them. Later in the report, it recommended steps that might usefully be taken in this direction.

A development in sophistication and in the detail of studies may be illustrated from several references.

In the *Local Authorities, National Health Service, Gas and Water Supply Workers* (29) reference concerning over 1,000,000 workers in four differing, decentralised industries, the NBPI outlined the elements of a solution to the widespread problems of low pay and low productivity in the local authorities and National Health Service. Its main source of information was a firm of management consultants with experience in the local authority field, which visited 37 local authorities for the reference and hospitals, water undertakings and Gas Area Boards. NBPI staff also visited some establishments.

The NBPI's solution was that properly worked out and controlled schemes

1 Para. 107.

196

directly relating pay and productivity should be introduced. A table indicating substantial labour productivity increases achieved in 29 local authorities following introduction of work studied-incentive payments schemes was published in support of the conclusions. Three prerequisites were specified for securing a closer relationship between pay and effective labour utilisation: higher standards of labour management, and more extensive training in management; better supervision, probably by better pay; and an increase in work study staff and possibly consultants.

Report 29 seems to have exaggerated the potential for improvements in productivity in local authorities and the National Health Service and also to have taken an unrealistic view of the potentialities of work study, overlooking the fact that a formidable team of work study specialists would need to be built up; union and worker acceptance would take time; and great time and effort in general would have been required to implement such schemes which might have diverted management from other tasks. Once established such schemes must be tightly controlled and the problems of maintaining them after installation and preventing wage drift were largely ignored. Work study can hardly be always decried since, as both the early Report 29 and the later *Gas* (155) showed, there are cases where it has led to, or been associated with, very substantial productivity improvements, especially where large groups of men were engaged in repetitive work. On the other hand there have been circumstances when the cost and effort of installing these schemes has outweighed the gains in productivity. Such problems have occurred, for example, with irregular work (such as hospital work and small dispersed groups of staff.

This is not to say that the NBPI's recommendations failed to be of value since they may have at least stimulated some kind of managerial action in the right direction but there could possibly have been a more discriminating approach to the whole subject of work study, a greater emphasis on ascertaining the real priorities of management, and an attempt to tailor it to the situation.

In *Gas* (155) the Board's sixth reference concerning the gas industry, a very detailed report was made indicating how work-studied incentive payment schemes, already underway, could be accelerated, and other improvements in labour utilisation made, with special emphasis on how management should proceed and on its need for information on performance.

Rather slow progress had been made in the spread of work-studied incentive payments schemes. The Board undertook 13 case studies of particular work-studied incentive payment schemes, had extensive consultations with officials and unions and evaluated the working of the schemes in the light of experience in other industries. It made many specific suggestions as to how the introduction and spread of the schemes might be greatly accelerated — for example by using less skilled personnel to carry out tasks such as routine maintenance of work-studied incentive payments schemes — which were preventing highly trained work study personnel from being effectively used; use of standards from other Area Boards; establishment of a central data bank, establishment of a Management Service Department etc. It also proposed more ambitious targets for the introduction of such schemes which would have lead to savings of over £30 million by 1974 if adopted.

Two somewhat conflicting tendencies are noticeable in the development of the NBPI's studies of labour utilisation. The first is a tendency to formula or standard prescriptions — work study, and productivity agreements are examples. The second, contrary tendency was for the NBPI to move away somewhat during 1970-71 from emphasising the importance of work study techniques for raising productivity. In a number of references it was indicated that savings could be realised more rapidly by the establishment of simple yardsticks and more effective management and supervisory control in the areas of workload, material and plant utilisation as well as labour utilisation. For example, it was stated that savings would have been achieved more quickly in NHS laundries by standardising the frequency of linen changing in similar hospitals and the establishment of linen pools than from introducing incentives. These conflicting tendencies — one rather oriented to the tailoring of recommendations to individual circumstances, the other in the opposite direction — were partly attributable to differing approaches to these subjects in the Industrial Relations Branch and Management Operations Branch. Recommendations could be explained partly in terms of which specialists from which branches were responsible for them.

Conclusion.

This chapter has reviewed selected aspects of the procedures, techniques and findings of NBPI studies of managerial efficiency, concentrating on those made after 1968. These studies were of a pioneering kind and were not fully developed by 1971. Their conduct was also hampered by a lack of staff. Nevertheless this review has indicated their potentialities for stimulating improvements in managerial practice in a wide range of situations, as well as in assessing efficiency. It is difficult to say more than this at present because it seems unlikely that these kinds of studies will be undertaken by official bodies in Great Britain in the immediate future.

12. Pricing

Section 1 of this Chapter records the White Paper criteria concerning the pricing behaviour of business enterprises and draws attention to the lack of guidance the White Papers gave the NBPI in assessing profits when examining individual cases of price increase. Section 2 is a brief account of the NBPI's financial investigations.

Section 3 describes the NBPI's treatment of cases in which cost increases were proposed as the justification for price increases. The NBPI put great emphasis on the requirement that firms should do everything possible to avoid or offset cost increases before raising prices. This was an unusual and interesting feature for a pricing policy and an assessment is made of it at the conclusion of the Chapter.

Sections 4 to 12 gives a full treatment of how the NBPI attempted to assess private sector profits. Here, unlike in Incomes references, the NBPI mostly lacked an explicit strategy. However, towards the end of 1969 it started to compare discounted cash flow forecasts from new investment projects with the cost of capital required to finance them in order to reach a judgement about firms' needs for price rises. A full account is given of how this was done in sections 8, 9 and 10.

This Chapter then is mainly about costs and profits. It is important to remember, however, that the NBPI was not called upon to fix either profits or costs but to make a single recommendation in each reference about the sum, i.e. prices. Very often the NBPI had dubious data about costs, inconclusive principles (and dubious data) on profits, and it had to come to an agreed decision on prices, but without necessarily agreeing on the propriety of the components. It did not usually matter too much if different Board Members had different reasons for accepting the same answer.

It would be possible to approach the subject of the NBPI's pricing recommendations by treating it as a problem in decision making, showing how internal differences of view between Board Members about costs and profits were finally reconciled at the stage when specific recommendations on prices were made. Such a study would also consider how wider factors — such as the desire to use individual cases to have a wider effect on the development of the overall prices and incomes policy — entered into decisions in individual cases. However, mainly by treating NBPI reports at face value, it is possible to give an account of the main objective elements which influenced decisions. This chapter then mainly abstracts from the internal decision making process.

The following chapter, entitled 'Price Structure and Pricing Studies', should be read in conjunction with this one.

1. The White Paper Prices Criteria

The 1965 White Paper 'Prices and Incomes Policy' stated that:

'Enterprises will not be expected to raise their prices except in the following circumstances:

i. if output per employee cannot be increased sufficiently to allow wages and salaries to increase at a rate consistent with the criteria for incomes ... without some increase in prices, and no offsetting reductions can be made in non-labour costs per unit of output or in the return sought on investment;

ii. if there are unavoidable increases in non-labour costs such as materials, fuel, services or marketing costs per unit of output which cannot be offset by reductions in labour or capital costs per unit of output or in the return sought on investment;

iii. if there are unavoidable increases in capital costs per unit of output, which cannot be offset by reductions in non-capital costs per unit of output or in the return sought on investment;

iv. if, after every effort has been made to reduce costs, the enterprise is unable to secure the capital required to meet home and overseas demand.'[1]

Enterprises were expected to reduce their prices in the opposite circumstances, and if profits were 'based on excessive market power'.

Successive White Papers stressed the importance of efficiency: 'All enterprises will be expected to make every effort to absorb increases in costs by means of increased efficiency'[2] and stated that it should be a normal part of an enterprising business's behaviour to increase efficiency, keep down costs and hold prices at a level compatible with its long-term growth. This would speed up the replacement of old techniques and out-of-date equipment by new techniques and modern equipment. The criteria were not intended to inhibit the structural changes necessary in the interests of economic growth. The considerations, it said, recognised that a vigorous and efficient enterprise could reasonably expect a higher level of profit than one that was not. Nationalised industries were under the same obligations, while taking account of the White Paper 'A Review of the Economic and Financial Objectives of Nationalised Industries'.[3]

---

1 Para. 9.

2 Para. 3, Cmnd. 3073 (1966). This point is repeated in para. 7, Cmnd 3150; para. 10, Cmnd. 3235; and para. 16, Cmnd. 3590.

3 Cmnd 3437. 1967. This followed the 1961 White Paper 'The Financial and Economic Obligations of the Nationalised Industries', Cmnd. 1337.

Private sector profit rates [1] were not to be increased by raising prices, except where necessary to secure capital to meet demand.

If the White Paper had been silent about reductions in profit rates the NBPI could justifiably have regarded its principal task as simply the policing of price increase proposals to ensure that through them no firm enjoyed an increase (nor suffered a decline) in profit rates, except to secure necessary capital. Instead, there were explicit provisions requiring decisions on whether the return sought on investment could be lowered as an alternative to raising prices, and whether prices were based on excessive market power and should be reduced. There was no guidance on the interpretation of these provisions and nothing in the White Paper suggest that the prices policy was to be used to redistribute national income by a general reduction in the level of return on capital. [2]

2. Financial Enquiries

The financial data sought from firms were their costs, including unit costs of output, broken down into components such as labour, materials, advertising; profits and capital employed; often the prices, quantity of production and sales of particular goods; and certain cost and price indexes. The data covered a period of several years. In addition, forecasts of these items over the next year or two, and of the outcome of investment projects were also sought. Particular emphasis was placed on details of cost increases given as a reason for price rises. Accounting data was also useful in assessing efficiency and details were sought of areas in which savings were considered likely and some rough comparisons with cost trends in different firms were usually made. Data were normally sought from all the important firms; if the industry consisted of small firms, say motor garages, a sample was taken. Financial data about labour costs was also obtained in some incomes references. Not much data about productivity was collected in any references.

The NBPI did not normally examine a firm's books or records. Steps could be taken to test the validity and reasonableness of data supplied, and in cases of doubt checks were sometimes made for consistency with published accounts, market movements, with trends in other firms and other information such as published notices of raw material costs. In most references it was possible to visit and question the main firms. Detailed investigations of the basis of forecasts and investment projects, of the allocation of joint

---

1 To avoid confusion about this term, it should be understood that in this chapter it refers to a firm or industry's profit rate before any cost increase which led it to seek a price increase. It does not necessarily refer to a firm or industry's profit rate at the exact time it sought a price increase, when the rate may have temporarily fallen below some 'normal' level.

2 The December 1969 White Paper *Productivity Prices and Incomes Policy After 1969*, however, stated 'the Government does not believe that any general reduction in the level of return on capital invested in British industry ..... would be helpful in the context of the essential modernisation of the economy. But what is true in the case of the average level is not necessarily true of individual enterprises.' Para. 113.

costs, of calculations of depreciation, goodwill and the value of capital, and so on were made in this way. Multi-product firms were usually not asked for detailed information about non-reference products: on one or two occasions when asked they refused. It is later noted that the NBPI treated certain classes of cost increases as not justifying price increases, and that it similarly sometimes excluded certain items such as 'goodwill' in the valuation of capital employed. If the industry under reference accepted such adjustments to its case, they were not necessarily reported.

The Board therefore received post facto rationalisations of decisions to raise prices and make new investment. In the majority of cases this probably did not render its enquiries inadequate. To have discovered why and how firms actually arrived at decisions would have required the inspection of company minutes and internal documents, which are important, if imperfect, sources of such information, [1] and even such draconian investigatory procedures as the taking of testimony from executives. The NBPI appears to have been inhibited from taking these steps by the shortness of time available, and the desire to obtain voluntary co-operation.

Besides spotlighting publicly the reasons for price increases, publication of financial information, especially of a comparative nature, can be useful as a spur to improvement of firms, and the NBPI produced some valuable surveys. [2] The TUC also welcomed the publication of this information. Some of the best were about topics of which little was known previously: solicitors, architects, garages and different parts of the distribution sector. In *Beer Prices* (136), members of the Enquiry Team visited over 400 tenanted public houses in view of unsuccessful attempts in previous years by trade associations and others to collect data by post. The resulting product was the first ever useful financial survey of public houses.

3. Costs [3]

The most important element in the NBPI's price reference strategy was its requirement that enterprises attempt to avoid cost increases or offset them by reductions in other costs. It was believed that the revenue sought by price increases could often be obtained in this way instead, and therefore a contribution be made to the holding down of prices in the short and long run. It was also thought that this strategy would create pressure for greater efficiency. Only after that was it necessary to consider whether unavoidable,

---

1 The Monopolies Commission appears to collect more internal information of this kind.

2 A list of surveys is given in the appendix dealing with the NBPI's statistical work: these relate only to surveys which required statistical planning and processing, not to surveys involving only a few firms made in all price, and some incomes references.

3 J.F. Pickering 'The Prices and Incomes Board and Private Sector Prices: A Survey'. *The Economic Journal*, June 1971, pages 225-241 covers in more detail some of the topics dealt with in this section and some other parts of this chapter. A paper prepared inside the NBPI entitled 'Themes in Price References' by Mr. J.N. Stevens has been helpful in writing this and other sections of the chapter.

non-offsettable cost increases could be absorbed without a price rise.

This is indicated by the following passage about labour costs in the First General Report:

> 'The main convention we have found then in the field of prices is that of automatically translating increases in wages into increases in prices regardless of the trend in output per man and regardless therefore of the ability to absorb them. This automatic translation has followed the conclusion of wage settlements by automatic comparison with wage settlements elsewhere, often without regard to the more effective use of men. The principal purpose of our recommendations in the field of prices has been to restrain automatic price increases as a first stage, thus inducing in the second stage a search for increased efficiency and a tighter control over labour costs.' [1]

In principle, however, no element of cost under a firm or industry's control, whether in the field of labour or any other dimension of managerial efficiency, was excluded from the NBPI's scrutiny. For example, the structure of a firm or industry's prices in relation to its costs were studied to see if changes to secure more efficiency were possible. Industry-wide matters — the scope for mergers and other structural change, the effects of uncompetitive practices, and the need for reform of collective bargaining institutions — were also regarded as highly relevant.

A number of proposals for price increases were in fact fully or partly rejected on the grounds that there was scope for economies. These included *Costs, Prices and Profits in the Brewing Industry* (13), *Costs and Revenues of National Daily Newspapers* (43) and *Prices of Non-Alloy Bright Steel Bars* (118). More generally, however, the NBPI's long term proposals for greater efficiency were not of a kind that led to recommendations for an immediate abatement of price increases.

In some cases the NBPI refused to recommend price increases if industries were not in its view trying sufficiently hard to reduce costs. In this vein the Baking Industry which wanted price increases to pay for the extra overtime costs of a shorter standard working week were told that they had 'an obligation .... to demonstrate that the purpose of the settlement relating to hours ... was to secure the more efficient use of manpower.' [2] Later in 1969 because it was considered that the British Steel Corporation had made an insufficient attempt to save costs, an abatement of their price increase proposals was recommended. [3]

Various claims about cost increases were regarded as not being of a kind to justify higher prices. These included advertising costs judged to be excessively high in *Prices of Household and Toilet Soaps, Soap Powders and Soap Flakes, and Soapless Detergents* (4) and in *Tea Prices* (154);

---

1 Para. 80.

2 *Prices of Bread and Flour* (3), para. 64.

3 *Steel Prices* (111)

'cost-saving' cost increases such as the imposition of the training levy from which, the NBPI argued, firms could expect to benefit by having better trained workers e.g. in *Charges, Costs and Wages in the Road Haulage Industry* (48); the shortening of working hours which ought to have been accompanied by greater labour productivity (*Prices of Bread and Flour,* 3); and the increase in the cost of the Selective Employment Tax which it was asserted should have been offset by a reduction in the labour force (*Laundries and Dry Cleaning* 20). In later references, however, the NBPI did not always take the same attitude to S.E.T. and training cost increases.

The NBPI encountered a number of capital-intensive industries whose unit costs had risen following changes in capacity utilisation, especially after the recession induced by the Government's July 1966 economic measures. In practice this was treated as a cost issue although in reality, as the NBPI recognised, the question was whether firms should be allowed to make up recession-induced, possibly temporary losses in profits. In general the policy was to avert or mitigate price increases for this reason (except where this would have made it impossible to secure adequate funds for new investment), especially if prices had not been decreased when unit costs decreased. This was stated to be to avoid inflationary wage increases which might have resulted and would have meant that the NBPI was undermining the Government's deflationary policy and encouraging the co-existence of inflation with deflation. [1]

Abnormal temporary cost increases e.g. because of oil surcharges when the Suez Canal was closed, were generally rejected as a reason for price increases or else it was recommended that they be reflected in a temporary surcharge e.g. *Portland Cement Prices* (38). Tea companies partly justified their decision to raise prices with the argument that prices at which they bought tea from abroad were likely to continue rising. On economic analysis, however, a long run falling price trend was disclosed, and diagnosed as being due to a persistent tendency for world production to outstrip demand. The NBPI considered that these price increases had to be judged as temporary against this background, and did not constitute a justification for a permanent price rise. (*Tea Prices,* 154).

An important 'cost' which the NBPI regarded as not justifying a price increase was an anticipated cost increase although future cost increases which had already been contracted were acceptable. The doctrine was first laid down in *Bread* (3), firmly applied in a succession of references (e.g. *Electricity and Gas Tariffs* (7), *Coal Distribution* (21), and later *Bright Steel Bars* (118)) and eventually incorporated into White Papers. The NBPI was particularly firm about increases in costs which partly depended on the applicant's own actions.

An example of the application of the doctrine occured in the Coal Prices reference (153) in August 1970. The NBPI refused to recommend a large part of a price increase sought by the National Coal Board because its proposals rested on increases in costs which had not yet taken place and the

1 *Second General Report* (40) para. 30. See also J.F. Pickering, op. cit., pp. 229-230.

amount of which could not be prcisely determined. At that time the National Union of Mineworkers had decided to make a very substantial claim for a pay increase which would have led to cost increases of the order of £50 million. The NBPI did not think it right to anticipate in price increases the outcome of negotiations of the size impending, except insofar as it was reasonable to allow for pay to increase at a rate in keeping with the nation's economic growth. To make advance provision for increases in costs which were not yet certain would itself contribute to the inflationary process.

The consistently applied policy of not allowing firms to include an allowance in prices to take into account cost increases which would come about from a continuation of inflation was, in the context of moderately inflationary conditions, bound to lead to some reduction of profit rates, unless the firms had exaggerated the cost rises which they reported (e.g. by understating productivity gains already achieved or to come). This should not be overlooked in the account below of the NBPI's profits policy.

The NBPI operated during a period of continuously rising wages and costs, and it was inevitable that many cost increases had to be accepted as valid reasons for price increases, providing other offsetting cost reductions (or reductions in the return on new investment) could not be achieved. The White Paper itself explicitly permitted price increases that were the result of wage increases consistent with the criteria for incomes, if a firm had an unavoidably low rate of productivity increase and could not reduce its return on new investment. [1] The effect of devaluation was to increase prices of raw materials, food and other imports, and in a number of references these cost increases were accepted as valid reasons for price rises e.g. *Flour Prices* (53).

In many industries the ability of firms to absorb the increased costs caused by wage increases differed, and it was sometimes an issue whose costs should determine the price increase. It was not always clear that the NBPI had made a conscious decision when deciding to base prices on the costs of a selection of firms. However, the main doctrine was that whenever possible the price should be determined by the firms best able to absorb the cost increases rather than by those least able to do so. It was for this reason that the Road Haulage Association was criticised for giving advice to the effect that charges should be raised coupled with a statement of the maximum increase which was thought to have taken place in costs, since this might lead to charges being determined by the firms least able to absorb cost increases. [2] In the *Remuneration of Milk Distributors* (46) there was a suggestion that the Ministry's arrangements for determining prices

1 Perhaps one of the most important issues in any future long-term prices and incomes policy will be how to handle applications for price increases based on the fact that wages have increased at a rate in excess of the norm. The NBPI never confronted the problem head on. There were some references where above-norm wage increases had occured but they had the approval of the DEP.

2 *Road Haulage Rates* (1)

should be based on the cost of the more efficient firms. Where a choice was made it was usually implicit that the costs in the chosen firms were representative of the whole industry or alternatively those firms would have the capacity and incentive to make good a shortfall in supply occasioned by fixing prices on costs which were unrepresentative of parts of the industry. In some references (*Bright Steel Bars* (118) and Road Haulage Rates (1)) the NBPI refused to fix a common price based on a representative set of costs because this would lessen competition. The NBPI also refused to do this in the reference on *Distribution Costs of Fresh Fruit and Vegetables* (31) because it could not find a representative cost. In other references such as *Bricks* (47) and *Steel* (111) the Board used the costs of the dominant firm or firms to fix prices for the dominant firm only, recognising that such firms set the prices for the rest of the industry.

4. The Measurement of Profits

Before describing the NBPI's policies with respect to profits, it is necessary to discuss the problems which arose in defining and measuring capital and profits.

The 'profit rate' normally meant the rate of return on capital employed. In some cases, however, the main measures used were (net and gross) margins and profits in relation to turnover because of the inadequacy or lack of data about capital employed or because of its inappropriateness. Thus, where human resources were important as in the professions, the return on physical capital was of little significance:

> '... it would seem to us that the proper criterion for looking at the price of a service (apart, again, from the need to cover reasonable expense) is whether it produces a profit adequate to secure the investment of the necessary "resources", which in this case are trained manpower, and secures an efficient allocation of those resources.'[1]

It was also necessary to examine profit rates over a period of time in order to separate seasonal, cyclical and longer term trends and in order to form an impression of whether firms were attempting to increase profit rates above any 'usual' or 'going' level that they had observed in the past. Forecasted profit figures were also obtained.

The measurement of capital employed posed especially difficult problems. Capital employed was usually taken to be share capital, including preference shares (or proprietors' capital in other forms); reserves (including unappropriated profits); debentures stocks and other long-term loans and liabilities (including bank overdrafts). It was normally computed by ascertaining the average ascribed value of net assets (i.e. after deducting current liabilities) for the year or years in question. Any assets not productively employed in the business were excluded e.g. investment made in other concerns not associated with the company.

[1] *The Remuneration of Solicitors* (54), para. 7.

There are different ways of valuing assets. Many firms use the historical cost method of valuing assets at their original purchase price less depreciation to date. This method makes no allowance for the effects of inflation on the purchase price of an asset: a factory built 5 years ago would have a lower purchase price than an identical one built now by the same methods. Two alternative approaches, which aim to correct this undervaluation, are the periodic estimation of the cost of replacement or the current market price of the asset if it were sold. Unlike the historical cost approach, these approaches normally require arbitrary estimates of hypothetical situations, and in practice a variety of methods is used to make them. The difficulties may be illustrated by reference to the problem of obsolescence. Technological change may reduce the price of the latest plant (abstracting from inflation) needed to produce a product, and it may also render current products obsolete. Present or expected future developments of these kinds would affect the market price of a firm's current assets. How could this be taken into account? A variety of methods are used in practice and there is always room for widely varying assumptions about the current and expected future role of technology.

As the historical cost method often leads to a relatively low value being imputed to capital employed, and hence an apparently high rate of profit per unit of capital, the NBPI received many representations from companies for the substitution of current replacement values for the balance sheet values of fixed assets based on original purchase price. If the company or industry had done this, the replacement values were looked at. Otherwise an attempt at revaluation was not usually made. By way of exception there were one or two cases in which current values of single companies were ascertained on the basis of a professional revaluation. This was never or very seldom done when dealing with the accounts of a number of companies. In one such case a method of revaluation applied was the application of indices available from professional sources to the original cost of assets or group of assets by years of acquisition and deducting therefrom the accumulated depreciation on such theoretical values. However, these types of revaluation exercises were regarded as complex and time-consuming, especially when an industry comprised many firms, and were only rarely undertaken. It was also appreciated that the many possible methods that could be employed to arrive at revaluations would limit the usefulness of the exercise. In this respect the NBPI's investigations did not go as far as those of the Monopolies Commission which normally revalues capital at replacement cost if necessary. This partly reflected the lack of time which the NBPI had on references. It was thus a further disadvantage of 3 months references that it was often not possible to enquire as deeply as was desirable into the valuation of capital employed.

Capital employed net of depreciation often needs to be examined. The purpose of depreciation is to ensure recovery of invested funds over the economic life of the physical capital in which they have been embodied. The main limits on the economic life are wear-and-tear and obsolescence. Once again arbitrary estimates are necessary, and a variety of methods and assumptions may be used to calculate the annual allowance for depreciation.

When firms record their assets they sometimes include the item 'goodwill' and place a value on it. The NBPI generally accepted its inclusion in the computation of capital employed, providing it was included in the capital figures used for calculating the rate of return in other industries with which comparisons were made. [1] There were circumstances when it was excluded. In *Tea Prices* (154) goodwill was regarded as representing the purchase price for above-average profits in the course of one firm taking over another. There was therefore a circularity of reasoning in including goodwill in capital employed when assessing the rate of profit on capital employed. The question was whether profits on capital excluding goodwill was reasonable.

In the *Remuneration of Milk Distributors* (46) it was argued that insofar as one part of 'goodwill' represented payment by distributors for expansion of their business and for enlarging their share of the market it was the capital equivalent of promotion expenditure and was a legitimate part of capital employed so long as it did not anticipate the profits attributable to a rationalisation of the combined businesses. These profits, it was held, should be passed on to the consumer in any pricing formula set by the Ministry.

5. The Allocation of Capital Employed in Multi-Product Firms

The NBPI often received references requiring it to examine the justification for price increases of specific products or product groups of a firm or industry, rather than all of its profits and prices. (The Commission of Industry and Manpower would have had power to investigate the full range of a firm's activities). In these cases a serious problem that often arose concerned the allocation of capital employed in different sections of the business or in the production of different products when only some sections or products were under investigation. It may also be noted that a similar problem occurred in investigating a firm's price structure in relation to its cost structure.

From a score of references in which the problem arose, several examples may be given. In the 7 references concerned with the bakery industry, including *Flour Prices* (53), the problem kept recurring. Generally it was only bread prices which were under investigation, but flour milling shared some production facilities. Moreover, bread and cakes were distributed from the same delivery vans and trucks often, though cake prices were not under investigation. To complicate matters, the production of bread appeared to bring bakers a very low return on capital employed whilst the return from flour production was several times as great. The NBPI expressed the view that the traditional allocation formula used by all the five main bakers had the effect of allocating too great a share of costs to bread, though it was thought that profits on bread were only marginally affected (*Prices of Bread and Flour 3, Bread Prices and Pay in the Baking Industry* 144, 151).

With the reference *Man-Made Fibre and Cotton Yarn Prices* (127, Second

---

1 This discussion is a more accurate guide to the NBPI's practice than the Fifth General Report's discussion of goodwill.

Report) in investigating the price of acetate yarn produced by Courtaulds, the NBPI noted that it also manufactured staple fibre, chemicals and plastics in the course of the same process. Courtaulds attributed the greater part of an improvement in profits to chemicals and plastics, but because of the difficulty of attributing profits to jointly produced products this could not be established with certainty. In the event, in recommending a price reduction, the Board depended mainly upon evidence of a rate of increase of productivity above the national average and the ending of the oil surcharge.

In *Newspapers* (141), the NBPI referred to the problem of attempting to 'allocate the unallocable'[1] since although only morning and Sunday newspapers were investigated they were produced from the same plant as evening newspapers. It went beyond conventional accounting categories in collecting data concerning direct costs of newspapers i.e. those not shared with other activities, and sought to compare them with the revenue from sales and advertising. Whilst available data was insufficient for a full coverage even along their lines, it was sufficient to suggest the answer to the important question of whether any newspapers were making a loss. Four national newspapers did not cover their direct costs. Beyond that it was not possible to be sure of the position of the others — if direct costs were covered, and in addition a contribution was made to joint costs, it could not be assumed that there would be no net financial gain from the paper's issue, even though by conventional accounting methods it was shown as making a loss.

A few of the other references in which the NBPI encountered the joint cost problem were *Costs and Prices of the Chocolate and Sugar Confectionery Industry* (75) where the terms of reference precluded the NBPI from extending its detailed enquiries into those activities of manufacturers which extended to the point of sale to the consumer; in *Electric Motor Prices* (139) the Board investigated electric motors in the range 1-100 hp. It was precluded from investigating electric motors of less than 1 hp and more than 100 hp though they were produced in the same factories; in *Margarine and Compound Cooking Fats* (147) where the main weight of the enquiry was on Van den Burghs and Jurgens Ltd., a wholly owned subsidiary of Unilever Ltd.; *Manufacturers' Prices of Toilet Preparations* (113); and *Distributors' Costs and Margins on Furniture, Domestic Electrical Appliances and Footwear* (97). In all these cases the usefulness of the NBPI's report was in some way reduced by the limits of the terms of reference.

The significance of these problems of measuring capital employed is twofold from the point of view of an assessment of a firm or industry's current profit rates. First, profit per unit of capital employed may appear lower or higher depending upon the definition and method of measurement of capital employed. Second, it is difficult to make inter-firm or inter-industry comparisons. Even if similar definitions and methods are used in different firms being compared, there still remain many measurement decisions that

1 Para. 8.

are essentially arbitrary e.g. the allocation of jointly used capital, the estimates of replacement value and so on.

From the point of view of the NBPI's attempts to appraise the return on new investment, explained in section 8 below, very similar problems arose, though sometimes in a different guise. Instead of, for example, examining replacement costs of capital, it was necessary to examine capital costs of additional capacity.

6. The Assessment of Profit Rates

If a firm experienced an unavoidable, non-offsettable increase in costs, then the NBPI had to consider whether the increase could be absorbed without a rise in prices. This required a judgement about it's profitability, however measured and defined. In any event, *any* assessment of a firm or industry's prices necessarily requires a judgement, explicit or implicit, of its profitability. However, as has been observed, the White Paper offered little guidance on how to make this judgement.

Broadly speaking there were two types of overlapping questions which the NBPI had to deal with in assessing profit rates. First, was the level of return on capital reasonable? Was it, for example, so high that cost increases could be absorbed by a reduction in profit rather than a price increase? Second, would necessary new investment be cut back if a price increase was not granted?

The NBPI had a changing strategy in its assessment of profit rates. Until August 1967 profit rates were normally assessed by comparing the current level of return on capital of those firms or industries under reference with that for the whole economy. Occasionally when the main issue was whether a price increase was necessary to provide the capital for a new investment the proposal to raise prices was assessed with little refinement other than listening to the views of the industry and others in the light of information on its rate of return.

In August 1967 in *Portland Cement Prices* (38), however, the NBPI for the first time assessed the price increase in the cement industry by comparing the discounted cash flow with the cost of capital needed to finance new investment. (The industry fixed prices by trying to receive a 10 per cent return on its revalued capital employed.) At this point the NBPI might have decided to apply the d.c.f./cost of capital method to the assessment of most price increase proposals, but does not seem to have appreciated its potentialities for application in a greater number of cases.

One may speculate that events would possibly have taken a different turn at this stage had Professor Williams, an influential Board Member who played a big part in applying the method in the Cement reference, remained on the Board longer or had there been a senior economist adviser on the staff at the time to ensure continuity. Instead the new economists who become Board Members at the time were assigned to dealing with the important nationalised industry price references which had just been received. The Board was not required to have regard to the rate of return of a nationalised industry and could not apply the new investment approach in these references.

Whatever the reason, the NBPI continued without a consistent approach to the profit rate problem in any reference at all until around November 1969. In the *Price of Butyl Rubber* (66) and *Synthetic Organic Dyestuffs and Organic Pigments Prices* (100) the d.c.f./cost of capital method was used. Otherwise most private sector price references contained rather vague assessments of the rate of return on capital. Fairly often the rate was not revealed because of confidentiality requirements and either not formally compared or only cursorily examined, with such verdicts being reached as 'reasonable', 'low', 'not excessive'.

It is not possible to say in retrospect how many private sector price references could have been mainly handled by the d.c.f./cost of capital approach between 1965 and the end of 1969, but it is likely that some could have been.

It was not until late 1969, then, that the NBPI moved towards a more systematic strategy for handling those types of price references which turned primarily on the need for new investment. The method was applied in late 1969 in *Plasterboard Prices* (130) and in *Portland Cement Prices* (133). In *Beer Prices* (136), there were difficulties in assessing the cash flow from future investment, but a precise calculation of the cost of capital was employed.

In one or two later references the approach (or the best possible approximation to it) seems to have been used — *Prices of Primary Batteries (Ever Ready Company)* (148) and *Costs and Revenues of National Newspapers* (141). It was clearly explained in some other references why the approach could not be used e.g.: *Pay and Prices of the London Brick Company* (150).

It is thus clear that from the end of 1969 the NBPI sought to apply the d.c.f./cost of capital approach frequently, and if it had stayed in existence longer it is likely it would have sought to use it in most references in which it was possible to do so.

It is not clear that in *every* price reference in 1970-71 the NBPI sought very hard to apply the method. In some reports (electric motors, margarine, tea, ice-cream prices) there is no explanation of why the method was not used, although on the face of things the difficulties were not insurmountable. It is true that the Fifth General Report rationalised the decision not to use the method in *Tea Prices* (154) and *Ice Cream Prices* (160) by saying that no significant production investment was needed in the short term, but neither report explained this, and in *Ice Cream Prices* (160) there was an explicit statement that 'companies are experiencing difficulty in generating a sufficient cash flow to finance the normal capital investment requirements of the next few years.'[1] Otherwise there were hints that the problem of the allocation of joint costs in multi-product firms (*Margarine and Compound Cooking Fats* 147) and uncertainty about future investment (*Electric Motor Prices* 139) may have prevented application of the method, but no direct

1 Para. 36.

explanation.

Comparing the tenacity with which the NBPI sought data in some difficult references such as *Costs and Revenues of National Newspapers* (141) one tentatively concludes that two non-technical factors entered into decisions: (a) the different composition of Board Committees and staff working parties assigned to different references; (b) the degree of opposition of the firm or industry under reference to the use of d.c.f./cost of capital methods.

In view of its general lack of a consistent strategy in price references, and in view of the difficulties of using the comparison of profit rates method (see below) to assess whether current profit rates were unreasonably high, it is perhaps not surprising that there were few or no references in which the NBPI recommended or clearly implied that profit rates be cut.

Apart from the inherent difficulties of the comparisons method it may be mentioned that it seems that few companies with exceptionally high rates of return were referred. (A good deal of information about profit rates was not published because of confidentiality problems, so one can only surmise about some references). Moreover, the NBPI operated during a period in which profit rates were generally falling, and costs sharply rising.

Apart from some instances when it was recommended that profits be allowed to fall during the depressed phase of the business cycle, the main cases when profit reductions were recommended or openly implied were: *Beer* (13), where the NBPI took the view that a price increase should not be allowed so as to put greater pressure on breweries to contain costs; *Toilet Preparations Manufacturing* (113), where it concluded that in a system in which price was the main indication of quality, buyers of quality products were being exploited by price increases; and two cases — *Soaps and Detergents* (4) and *Tea* (154) — in which high advertising costs were involved. *Bread* (3) is also a case perhaps in which it was implied that profit rates could fall because of the industry's insufficient attempt to keep down costs. In *Mallory Batteries* (64), it was concluded that cost increases could be absorbed without increasing prices.

There were clearly special issues involved in the *Soaps and Detergents*, *Tea* and *Toilet Preparations Manufacturing* references. In *Beer* (13) and *Bread* (3), the issue was not really whether profit rates were too high but whether punitive action should be taken against inefficiency. Even in *Mallory Batteries*, the one clear case in which the NBPI found that a firm could absorb a cost increase without putting up prices, the main point about the reference was that the firm's 45 per cent increase in price was out of all proportion to the needs of the situation, and it was almost by way of an obiter dictum that the NBPI concluded that no price increase at all was necessary.

Accordingly, taking these reservations into account there were no references in which the NBPI judged a firm or industry's profit level to be 'too high' or 'unfair' (except perhaps in the special case of Mallory Batteries).

The subject of price reductions may be briefly discussed here. There were again very few companies referred which were, in terms of the White

Paper criteria, candidates for recommendations for price reduction because of rapid productivity increases. The NBPI only recommended them twice — for Courtaulds acetate yarn (127) and the recommended retail price of paint (80).

The NBPI's main role as regards profit rates was occasionally to block or discourage attempts by firms to raise profits rates unjustifiably. This most frequently occurred in respect of firms which automatically sought to pass on increases in part of their costs to their prices. The most prominent examples were the distributors' margins references. An important consequence of devaluation was that manufacturers costs — e.g. material costs — and therefore ex-factory prices increased. Where retailers were in the habit of including in their price a fixed percentage margin of profit for themselves, this margin expressed in terms of cash was thereby automatically increased, even though the retailer had not necessarily incurred the same percentage cost increase as the manufacturer. In a number of references the NBPI condemned this practice.

To sum up the discussion so far, the NBPI, although carefully looking at current profit rates, evolved no explicit criteria for judging whether they were too high or too low. It is of course difficult, if not impossible to suggest what operational rules it might have used, since contentious assumptions about income distribution, the economic function of profits and so on were involved. Nevertheless the absence of an objective method for assessing the level of profits was, in some respects, unfortunate because a central question in all price references had to go unanswered: in effect, the usual assumption was that the firm or industry's current 'normal' profit rates were acceptable, even though they displayed wide variation.

The absence of a well defined profit-rate policy also undermined to some extent the strategy of emphasising the cost element in prices. The cost rules seemed sensible enough in themselves but they would have been reinforced if they had been applied against the background of an assessment of a firm's profit position. For example the NBPI's doctrine that firms should not anticipate uncontracted future costs in their prices might have looked rather different when applied to firms whose profits were judged to be low, and those whose profits were judged high. This lack of an objective rule for assessing profits was unfortunate from the wider point of view because the NBPI had more definite, less arbitrary rules for determining the wage increases it was prepared to support than for price increases. The intrusion of bargaining or political factors in price references was also thereby made easier.

7. Comparisons of Profit Rates

The comparisons method was the main way of determining if a firm or industry's current profit rate was 'unfair' or 'too high' or 'excessive'. (The return on new investment costs method was mainly a way of assessing the different question of whether a price increase was necessary to permit investment to go ahead.)[1]

The NBPI's calculations of a firm or industry's average returns, whether based on historic or replacement costs, were usually compared with the average level for industry generally, in the series originally compiled by the Monopolies Commission for the period 1961-63[2] and subsequently kept up to date and published in certain of the Commission's later reports.[3]

There are well known difficulties in making comparisons. The measurement problems discussed earlier were often insuperable in making inter-firm and inter-industry comparisons, no matter which type or types of measure of capital employed were available. In addition above-average profit rates in a firm (and even in an industry) can be the reward for above-average efficiency. With the NBPI's emphasis on the importance of cost saving and efficiency, it was especially necessary to avoid penalising efficient enterprises. Moreover the circumstances of industries vary greatly, many facing far greater risk than others. There are difficult problems of principle involved in making adjustments for risk and anyway in the United Kingdom there are no data available which might enable systematic adjustments to be made. The NBPI's studies of managerial efficiency did not investigate the degree of risk which an industry faced, though had they continued they might have provided information which would have enabled a more precise assessment.

A final problem in making comparisons the basis of price recommendations is that, even if comparisons somehow show that firms are making unfair profits, this is only one factor which needs to be taken into account. Besides income distribution matters other consequences of allowing or quashing price increases need to be taken into account. 'One consequence of having one set of prices rather than another may be that it will affect the amount of capital expenditure undertaken by the client, by affecting the profitability of investment or by affecting the cost and availability of funds'.[4] If so it would seem necessary to consider whether it was in the national interest to undertake these projects and, if so, what level of prices would be necessary to make them profitable enough for the firm or industry to decide to undertake them.

It was against the background of these considerations and especially the last that the NBPI developed a new approach, for a British investigatory body, to the assessment of profit and the return on new investment.

1 See Ralph Turvey, 'Rates of Return, Pricing and the Public Interest', *Economic Journal*, September 1971. This article examines issues involved in the return on new investment approach in greater depth than here.

2 Monopolies Commission, Colour Film: a report on the supply and processing of colour film, April 1966, Appendix 7.

3 Monopolies Commission. A report on the supply of flat glass, February 1968; Appendix 7.

4 Ralph Turvey, op. cit.

8. The Return on New Investment

The White Paper required price increase proposals to be examined to see if they could be avoided 'by a reduction in the return on investment'. It also required the NBPI to decide in some cases if price increases were 'necessary to secure capital to meet future demand'.

At first the NBPI seemed to think that the comparison of a firm or industry's profit level with that of the rest of the economy, after allowance for its special circumstances such as risk, was a rule of thumb method for determining whether or not it would be able to secure capital to meet future demand without a price rise. The first report on the brewing industry is the main example of this philosophy:

> 'Our examination of the level of profits shows that in absolute terms the return on capital employed in brewing was higher than that in general manufacturing and distribution in 1962 and 1963, but lower in 1964. As far as the rate of return in relation to risk is concerned, we have formed the view that this is an industry of low risk. Its financial structure shows a high ratio of loan capital to equity capital. We conclude that increases in prices are not needed because of an inability to secure the capital required.'[1]

This seemed a simplistic way of interpreting the White Paper and by 1969 the return on new investment approach was applied in a number of references. The basic assumption was that a prices policy should not impair the ability of companies to meet demand for their products and hence should not hold up investment necessary for this purpose. It was therefore normally assumed to be in the national interest that any investment project directed to helping meet the demand for a particular product should go ahead. Prices are a determinant of the return on investment. They should not be set so low as to prevent a project from being worthwhile. The broad approach then was to compare the projected return from new investment projects assuming a continuation of the present price level, and the cost of finance of the projects. If the return was less than the cost, the present prices should be increased to cover this cost and, if necessary, risk. (In practice the feedback from higher prices to demand was difficult to assess and it was assumed it could largely be ignored).

To avoid confusion, it should be noted that this situation is *not* one in which a price increase is necessary to secure capital to finance a project, a case which is dealt with later. The present case is one in which a price increase is necessary to make an investment project profitable and it is assumed that finance would be available once it could be shown to be so.

In putting this approach into practice, the first step was to determine the return on new investment.

This required assessments of the industry or firm's demand projections and other forecasts. The NBPI normally relied on estimates provided by the

1 para. 52. *Costs, Prices and Profits in the Brewing Industry* (13).

industry or company concerned and by the sponsoring Government department, assessing their adequacy mainly in terms of whether correct techniques and reasonable assumptions underlay the forecasts.

The investment projects planned to meet the expected demand were then examined. Various methods are used in industry to appraise such projects. Some companies compute the period within which expected profits from a project must equal or exceed the capital outlay. According to this method, the shorter the period before recouping the capital outlay the more attractive the project. The NBPI, however, favoured the discounted cash flow (d.c.f.) method of appraisal.

There could be a wide range of possible cash flows for a particular project since there can be different estimates of the factors determining the cash flow, e.g. capital outlays, future demand for the product, actions of competitors, and operating costs over the life of the project. A factor of which particular account must be taken is technological obsolescence. To achieve any given rate of return a firm making an investment needs to adjust its prices upwards to allow for the possibility that because competitors who invest at a later date could produce more efficiently, it might have to reduce its price to compete with them, or else lose sales because the product itself became obsolete. [1] To look at this another way, if the technology available in the future is going to be better than current technology, then there is an extra cost of expanding capacity soon instead of later. Thus the higher the expectation of future technological progress, the lower will be the expected rate of return on new investment, given current product prices. [2]

It is of course exceptionally difficult to predict future events, and often the most that can be done is to use probability techniques to express how sensitive returns are to different assumptions e.g. about such key factors as capacity utilisation, length of life of the assets, etc. The NBPI could not normally hope to match the expertise and experience which industries or companies had in assessing the factors affecting the investment. For this reason it preferred to use d.c.f. calculations made by the industry or company concerned, if available, and to examine the underlying assumptions and techniques critically.

If only some of the companies in the industry had made d.c.f. calculations, it was necessary to assess the extent to which the results could be used to determine a price for all of them, that is, the extent to which the new investment under consideration was representative. For example, where all the companies concerned produced similar products and their investment projects were similar, the calculations could probably be regarded as representative of investment in the industry generally. In *Beer Prices* (136) it was considered that the different circumstances of individual brewers meant that no particular investment project could be considered typical of the industry. Where one company was the price leader in an industry, the results

1 In the second *Cement Prices* reference (133) an adjustment was made in the industry's favour to take account of the obsolescence factor.

2 See R. Turvey, 'Marginal Cost', *The Economic Journal*, June 1969, pp. 282-299.

of its calculations could sometimes be used to determine it's and the rest of the industry's price level. Finally, in the case of a monopoly firm which had not made its own d.c.f. calculations, the NBPI could carry out the calculation itself to determine if it was profitable. [1] In *Bricks* (150) there was not enough data available even to permit this. If the industry was one of many small firms, the fact that they did not make d.c.f. assessments meant that there was no point in the NBPI making them unless the firms could be persuaded they were useful. In these circumstances, however, the industry may well have been price competitive so that recommendations about its prices would have been both pointless and unenforceable.

On several occasions the NBPI encountered firms or industries which had already initiated projects and had no new projects in the offing. It assessed these projects in the same way as planned projects. It was necessary to look at these investment projects from the point of view of how they looked when originally formulated, not how they had actually turned out. [2]

There appears to be no reason in principle why this method could not have been applied in more price references. In particular there was no reason why it could not have been applied to industries faced with declining or static demand by calculating the cost of replacement investment or of keeping existing plants functioning rather than the cost of investment in new capacity, if this was necessary to meet demand. In at least two references, something like this was done. In *Man-Made Fibre and Cotton Yarn Prices* (*First Report*) 119, the NBPI agreed with price increase proposals because otherwise production would probably be stopped at one or two plants, although in this case there was no refined plant cost calculation. In the second *Newspapers* reference (141) prices were set which covered the identifiable costs of producing and distributing each newspaper under reference separately and jointly.

9. The Cost of Capital

Having determined the return on investment it was then necessary to determine the cost of capital (expressed as a d.c.f. rate) necessary to finance it. Two approaches were used by the Board.

In reports on I.C.I.'s *Dyestuffs* (100) and on *Cement* (38 and 133), for example, the assessment was made by calculating the cost of different sources of capital — equity share issues, retained earnings, loan capital — and determining the proportion of each source which would be used.

Calculating the cost of loan finance was relatively straightforward, and reflected the current rate of fixed interest loans after taking account of the fact that for Corporation Tax purposes, loan interest is deductible in computing profits.

---

1 This did not occur ab initio in any references, although in *Plasterboard Prices* (130) the NBPI helped formulate the analysis in more refined terms than the company normally used.

2 See Turvey, op. cit.

It was more difficult to calculate the cost of equity finance. One possible method would have been to add to the company's shares dividend yield the expected percentage growth in dividends, applying a formula which defines the cost of equity capital. The difficulty in this approach is to estimate what the market expects the annual percentage rate of increase in future dividends to be. However, the NBPI never used this method, no doubt because of its difficulty. Instead it proposed that the return on equity finance should be based on the average rate of return (net of all taxes and inflation) which a portfolio share investor has received over the last 30 to 40 years excluding wartime. Estimates prepared by Merrett and Sykes of returns shareholders received in the past found that equity shareholders could expect to receive about 10 per cent per annum in money terms (and in the region of 8.3 per cent in real terms allowing for inflation) on the basis of past experience. [1] The Merrett and Sykes analysis takes into account the fact that shareholders will either have to pay income tax on distributed earnings or capital gains tax on the increase in share values resulting from retained earnings. The NBPI used these results as estimates of the cost of capital. Whether the figures should have been recalculated on a pre-tax basis is an interesting issue. The post-tax calculations seemed to imply that taxation was being passed on in the form of higher (or lower) prices. It could, however, be argued that this was only realistic since investors have the choice of withholding their investment if they do not get the necessary return.

Two fairly obvious problems with this approach are that the return on equity share issues in future will not necessarily reflect past experience; and that average figures are not necessarily meaningful for a particular firm or industry.

There is more than one point of view on the cost of retained earnings. It is often argued that the value of retained earnings to the shareholders is its 'opportunity cost', the value which it would have if invested by the shareholder in the equity of other companies. This inputes to retained earnings a similar cost to that of raising new equity. The NBPI, however, took account of the fact that a shareholder does not have to pay income tax on retained profits, an advantage only partially offset by extra capital gains tax liability. It therefore assumed that the cost of retained earnings was somewhat less than that of new equity.

In the first *Cement Prices* reference (38) it was assumed that depreciation could be treated as a source of finance and it was treated as if it were retained earnings. Otherwise the NBPI ignored it in references, thereby implying that it was the same as the weighted average cost of finance from the other three sources.

It was then necessary to compute the proportion of each source of finance

---

1 A.J. Merrett and Allen Sykes, 'Return on Equities and Fixed Interest Securities: 1919-66', *District Bank Review*, June 1966, No. 158, p. 29. The subject of the cost of capital is generally dealt within A.J. Merrett and Allen Sykes, *The Finance and Analysis of Capital Projects* (Longmans, 1963).

which would be used. To some extent this was gauged against the background of an analysis by Merrett and Sykes of the capital structure of the 3,000 largest public quoted companies in the UK for the period 1954 to 1963 which showed, for example, that 22 per cent of finance of these companies was raised by fixed loan capital on average over the period.[1] However, the circumstances of the industry was the main factor taken into account. Usually the NBPI accepted the existing capital structure of an industry. But neither the Merrett and Sykes data, nor the actual practice of the industry were regarded as absolute guides to what an industry's capital structure should be. Thus in the first *Cement* report (38) the NBPI recommended that more efforts should be made to use loan finance than before and for this reason refused to sanction a price increase. This decision of course spotlights the difficulty, unresolved by the NBPI, of judging what the 'right' structure should be.

Moreover, as far as I can determine, the NBPI seems to have based the proportions on which the different sources of finance were used alternatively on short run and long run considerations. In following the industry's own capital structure it did not always necessarily base calculations on the average long term proportions of finance which the industry felt it could achieve, but sometimes varied these assumptions.

To all this was added an allowance for risk if it was believed that the circumstances of the industry warranted it. In *Cement* (38) for instance, an addition of 1 per cent was stated to have been made, and for *Fertilisers* (28) and *Dyestuffs* (100) 3 per cent. In making this calculation the NBPI seems to have been largely guided by the considerations which influenced the industry itself. In particular, it was believed that account should be taken of the possibility that an investment project might prove to be a failure, even in cases where the project was under way and seemed to be successful.[2]

The second main method was used in the *Plasterboard* (130) and *Beer Prices* (136) references. This was to obtain from merchant bankers an opinion of the cost of capital. They supplied this by projecting the current share price earnings yield as the rate of return required in real terms. This approach derived a cost of finance particular to the industry concerned, and reflected market factors in raising equity at the time. It was not always possible to use this method and it lacked justification in principle. Also, caution was necessary: share prices may be affected by market sentiment about future earnings without this being reflected in current yields. Finally, it may be noted that when used this method gave a lower cost of capital than the first method.

The cost of capital (net of Corporation Tax) calculated in staff papers submitted to the Board Meetings in the six references for which figures are most readily available, was on average 10.17 per cent, varying from 8 to 12 per cent, mainly because of different assessments of risk faced by the

1 Since 1964, the corporation tax has led to a higher use of loan finance by companies of course.

2 See R. Turvey, op. cit., for some reasons for this.

industry. This is, in effect, in real terms; it was stated in money terms because of an error explained later in this Chapter. The actual money cost of capital was about 3 per cent higher, on average 13.17 per cent. The named figure was quite low. In some cases it fell below the 10 per cent cut off rate used to test public sector investment. Therefore the NBPI was not especially generous in its assessment of the return, looked at from the capital cost angle, which it allowed from new projects.

Thus, having in one way or the other computed the cost of capital and allowed for risk, this was compared with the return on investment. If the return on investment was less than the cost of capital, after allowing for risk, an adjustment was made to prices to make the return from the project just exceed the cost.

10. Expected Inflation

When a firm makes computations of the above kind to determine whether or not to go ahead with an investment project, there is no need in principle to take account of the expected future general rate of inflation of the economy since the cash flow and the cost of capital should be equally affected. It is only when the movement of costs and prices specially relevant to the new investment is likely to differ from the general rate of inflation that adjustments are necessary. Otherwise analysis of cash flow and cost of capital should be conducted in real terms.

There is a further distinct issue which may be noted at this stage. The NBPI always held that general inflation should not be included in future cost figures used for present decision making since anticipating inflation helped to cause it. The cost of funds seems to reflect partly expectations of future inflation, and it would have appeared logical for the NBPI to have cleansed it of this element.

In practice the NBPI received discounted cash flow calculations in real terms from firms and amended any calculations assuming future general inflation. [1] The cost of the equity component of capital was normally assumed to consist of (a) the past average real rate of return enjoyed by shareholders as calculated by Merrett and Sykes plus (b) an allowance of 2-3 per cent for future expected inflation. The same assumption about future inflation was made in calculating the cost of retained earnings. The current cost of loan finance was not amended to take account of any inflationary element which it might contain either. In other words in a majority of cases in which d.c.f./ cost of capital calculations were made the NBPI mistakenly calculated the cost of capital in money terms whilst calculating the cash flow in real terms.

---

1 Labour costs forecasts and the underlying assumptions about the future course of wages were carefully examined. If the forecasts showed wages to be increasing rapidly, the NBPI substituted an expected rate of real wage increase of 3 per cent per annum. This figure recognised that the real reward to labour should increase each year at no more and no less than the expected rate of increase in national productivity, and excluded any element of increase based on the assumption that money wages would rise at more than 3 per cent because of general inflation.

This meant that prices were set to give returns on new investment which were 2-3 per cent higher than those stated in reports. The only defence of this practice which I have heard is that the Government's policy during these years raised the cost of capital significantly and that the NBPI's method of calculating the cost of capital largely on the basis of past experience understated its true cost. There may have been a practical justification for this because the cost of capital as calculated by the NBPI was low. This justification would be more convincing if the adjustment had been made explicitly for that purpose to those ingredients of capital cost (equity and retained earnings) to which it might have been applicable. In reality a simple mistake appears to have been made, and only rectified in 1970.

The problem of converting the cost of capital to real terms was not difficult given the NBPI's methods of calculating equity and retained earnings costs. It was simply necessary to take the Merrett and Sykes figures for the real return on equity investment in the past as the basis of the calculations. R. Turvey's article [2] notes the difficulties attaching to the inflation adjustment when the method of calculating the cost of shares depends on the current and expected percentage growth in dividends, but as the NBPI did not use this method, it avoided this problem.

There are difficulties in deducting from the cost of loan finance an allowance for future inflation. A crude method is to assume that the current rate of inflation is the expected future rate of inflation and to deduct this from the cost of loan capital. Another method, noted by Turvey and used in the U.S.A., is to attempt to calculate econometrically the size of expectations [3] using a surrogate variable for expectations in an econometric equation explaining interest rates. The best method for dealing with inflation on the cost flow side of the equation is given in Appendix J to *Coal Prices* (153); any official body using the same methods as the NBPI for evaluating price proposals should use this appendix as its starting point in considering what allowance should be made for future inflation, for productivity increases, and for a rising real reward to labour.

11. Price Increases to Secure Capital

The White Paper legitimised price increases if enterprises were unable to secure the capital required to meet home and overseas demand. As noted earlier this contemplates a quite different situation from one in which a price increase is necessary to increase the cash flow from a project sufficiently to exceed the given cost of finance. What the White Paper implied was apparently that in some situations where the market was unwilling to finance a new investment it was still permissible to increase prices now, thus generating funds to go ahead with the project. In effect the assumption was made that present consumers of a firm's products should finance its investment programme.

2 Op. cit.

3 ibid

The *Beer Prices* reference (136) is an example. New investment was, in the brewers' view, required to provide increased supplies of the new chilled and filtered beers, and to improve existing retail outlets and to provide new retail outlets to cater for new tastes and population movements. The overall growth of demand was slow, and the investment was claimed as necessary to meet a changed pattern of demand.

The NBPI obtained advice from merchant bankers which led it to conclude that it was doubtful whether finance for the investment could be obtained from the equity or loan market without some price increase. Other things being equal, some companies could have done so, at a rather high cost, but the NBPI concluded they were not equal. Prices had remained stationary since the introduction of the prices and incomes policy. The fact that the application for a price increase was couched in the name of the entire industry, on the basis in part of an estimated average increase in costs, had focussed attention on the situation of the entire industry. The position of any one company had become entangled with that of the whole industry, and the denial of a price increase would cast such doubts on the industry's profit potential that the NBPI doubted whether any company could successfully fight against the general current. The NBPI thus doubted the ability to raise capital without some price increase, and on this ingenious reasoning recommended an increase in the wholesale price at which beer was sold to retail outlets.

There seem to have been three other occasions in which the NBPI justified a decision to raise prices on the grounds of need for investment funds — Newsprint, Fertilisers and Newspapers. On none of these occasions was it explained why firms had to use self generated funds for financing investment rather than go to the market. It is, however, obvious that newspapers could not borrow on the capital market except at exorbitant rates, in view of their generally poor or negative profits.

In *Prices of Standard Newsprint* (26) it seems to have been thought that the low return on capital of the newsprint part of the paper and pulp industry would prevent the raising of funds from the market to finance investment which would offer an attractive rate of return. In *Prices of Compound Fertilisers* (28) the return on capital employed for the fertiliser part of the ICI and Fisons was, despite its high degree of risk, well below the average for all manufacturing industry. Already substantial calls on the market for additional capital had been made by both firms, and the NBPI accepted the contention that any further external capital could in Fison's case be raised only in the form of equity. Such capital would not be forthcoming unless the company could show an acceptable return to equity capital, higher than the present return. In view of the competing capital requirements of other parts of its business, ICI needed, at the end of the day, to adopt the same criteria as the market would apply to Fisons. To prohibit a price increase to these firms would be to prevent them from raising their return on capital and would thus be prejudicial to investment and therefore to its future efficiency.

In neither case was it made really clear why firms had to use self-generated funds for financing investment rather than go to the market i.e. it was not

222

really spelt out why the market would not finance investment projects with potentially good returns. It was merely asserted. The cost of capital calculations were not explicit (nor the d.c.f. calculations).

In the writer's view the NBPI could usefully have gone further in examining the question of why established firms said they were unable to raise money from the market for attractive investments. This would have given more substance to the NBPI's recommendations for increasing prices to provide funds for investment. One useful step which the NBPI might have taken would have been to have acquired high level staff with expertise in business finance.

12. The New Investment Approach — Some Comments

Insofar as it adopted the new investment approach, the NBPI's aim of using the price reference system to ensure that the momentum of investment in industry was sustained was more constructive and forward-looking than relying merely on difficult judgments about whether existing profit rates were high or low compared with elsewhere in the economy.

The approach also had the advantage that it was capable of generating systematic rules of application, despite the difficulties of principle that arose in estimating the cost of capital, and sometimes in adjusting cash flows. The NBPI did not, in fact, follow any pre-determined rules in assessing the cost of capital, but used somewhat different methods in different cases. The differences in the cost of equity and retained earnings computed by different methods were not, however, very great. The different attitudes towards the capital structure of an industry were important. At any rate by not adopting pre-determined rules the potential precision, in principle, of the method was not realised and a margin of imprecision was left in practice which meant that most of the relatively minor price adjustments considered were crucially affected by the particular assumptions used in assessing the cost of capital and in adjusting or not adjusting a firm's cash flow.

The NBPI had to accept d.c.f. calculations supplied to it largely as given, though in some cases the justification for new investments was carefully considered. Again, there was no systematic approach to the adjustments which were sometimes made to take account of risk factors and/or obsolescence possibilities which the industry had not satisfactorily taken into account. Had there been a longer period of experimentation no doubt some of these problems would have been solved.

In a future period of price control, there would be considerable difficulties with this approach. A firm or industry knowing that its d.c.f. calculations would be considered by the agency responsible for price policy would have an incentive to tailor them to ensure the largest possible increases of price. This in fact was probably a problem even from 1965-70. It has been remarked that the NBPI's financial investigations were often such that internal company data was not pressed for. Instead the d.c.f. forecasts which it examined were supplied by firms. This was a weakness in its investigations.

Of course the NBPI was only considering price levels at one point of time, whereas the investment projects extended over a period of time. As the price supervision was not of a continuing kind, a company could adjust its prices, anyway, at a later date in the project; and, if there were errors in forecasting future events, it could later adjust its prices. In looking at the price level at one point of time the NBPI perhaps aimed to recommend a relationship between price and cost which should prevail over the lifetime of the investment: the problem of obsolescence, however, greatly complicated this approach insofar as it was adopted.

13. Cost-Oriented Prices Policies

Price regulatory policies have traditionally mainly been concerned with profits despite the seemingly insuperable problems of determining what constitute 'fair' rates of return. It is doubtful that the NBPI would have achieved much by concentrating its attention mainly on profits in price references especially in a period when profits were falling and when also few high-profit firms were referred. It is appropriate to conclude this chapter then by enumerating some of the advantages of its emphasis on costs, in prices references.

Costs are of course a much larger component of prices than are profits. For that reason the prices set by a benevolent but inefficient monopoly, say, may be much greater than if it were a ruthlessly profit-maximising, but efficient, monopoly. Moreover, the national benefits of cost reductions achieved by greater efficiency are likely to be long-lasting; and, hopefully, to have some effect on keeping prices permanently lower than they otherwise would be. Officially-imposed or recommended profit reductions, on the other hand, can be ineffective or short-lived, especially when, as in 1966-70, the Government's powers are limited to delaying price increases for short periods of time.

Unlike practicable cost-reduction recommendations, profit-reduction recommendations do not accord with a firm's interests and for that reason also are less likely to be effective. It may be true that this difference was not very apparent to those firms which found their proposals to raise prices fully or partly rejected because of improvements in their efficiency. Those with some degree of market power believed that the main way in which they could benefit from greater efficiency was by raising profit-margins rather than cutting prices. Nevertheless, it was never against a firm's interests to cut costs, even if it had to cut prices and thus raise profits only a little. Another advantage (or disadvantage?) was the likely significant deterrent effect on price increases by firms threatened with possible exposure of managerial inefficiency. A by-product of the cost-emphasis, then, was that firms fearing reference must have examined more closely than usual the possible scope for cost-reduction and probably profit-reduction before putting up prices. From the NBPI's viewpoint, there was also a political advantage. The need for greater managerial efficiency was a subject around

224

which the various elements amongst the Board Membership could unite; it might have split if its only concern in prices references was with profits. If the revenue sought by price increases could instead be obtained by greater efficiency, this avoided asking difficult, controversial questions on whether the return on investment could be lowered.

Conclusion

It may be concluded therefore that it seemed eminently sensible for the NBPI as part of its price policy to have studied closely those elements of costs that were under managerial control, as well as profits. In an earlier chapter the practicability of such studies was established.

The policy, though, was one which looked to the long term. It is doubtful whether in the short run it did much to keep down costs. There may even have been occasions on which it led to a short run rise in costs and prices before longer term benefits were obtained. This is not a criticism, but merely intended to put the policy in perspective.

An important question that arises concerning the investigatory role of the NBPI is whether firms initially set their bids high in anticipation of investigation. If so, the Government's attempts to keep prices down may have been partially counterproductive; the NBPI may have been deceived into recommending prices that were higher than firms would have set if their decision had not been influenced by the possibility of investigation. On the other hand, fear of investigation and possible exposure of managerial efficiency may have deterred some firms from increasing prices, or only doing so by the minimum justifiable to the sponsoring government department. There were some cases where firms or federations indicated fairly clearly to the NBPI exactly how much they considered acceptable reductions of their bid for higher prices would be. However there is no conclusive evidence available about this subject.

The NBPI's approach was a first attempt to implement a policy for specific prices in Great Britain. This chapter has mainly aimed to set on record the methods adopted by the NBPI, although it has also drawn attention to a number of unresolved issues in its approach, such as the determination of the appropriate cost of capital, and the problem of controlling profits whilst stimulating innovation and efficiency. It is difficult to imagine how a future experiment in prices policy could fail to take account of the NBPI's experience, although many elements of the approach it adopted require much more examination.

It remains only to be said that the experience of the NBPI has demonstrated the need for a reconsideration of the criteria applied in investigating monopolies and restrictive practices by other official bodies, which are almost exclusively profit-oriented, and do not conduct studies of managerial efficiency at source.

13. Price Structure and Pricing Studies

This chapter briefly summarises some of the NBPI's numerous recommendations for changes in price structures to reflect cost structures more exactly.

No attempt is made to deal in detail with the NBPI's treatment of conflicts between policies designed to ensure more competition and those designed to achieve greater efficiency through the achievement of economies of scale, but there is a brief account of its treatment of the case of the London Brick Company. This typified the NBPI's general approach of encouraging expansion by large companies if this led to greater efficiency, providing they acted as competitive firms would have and did not abuse their market power.

Finally there is a brief account of a few of the NBPI's many useful, innovatory studies of pricing in nationalised industries, which again illustrate the NBPI's investigatory skills and capacity to deal with widely varying problems.

Before assessing a referent's general level of prices and profits the NBPI normally examined whether its price structure reflected its cost structure i.e., whether the prices of a referent's different products reflected their individual costs of production. If not, the NBPI was concerned because the allocation of resources tends to be most efficient when prices correspond to marginal costs.

The NBPI made many recommendations of changes in the price structure on the grounds that this would allow the consumer to choose sensibly the amount of a service that he was prepared to pay for or the producer to measure the most profitable use for his assets. Such recommendations were made, for example, with respect to delivery extras in *Bread* (3) and *Bricks* (47), quantity extras and discounts in *Plasterboard* (130), *Electric Motors* (139), *Passenger and Freight Charges to North Scotland* (67), *Architects' Fees* (71), *Solicitors' Charges* (54), and *Public House Rentals* (13), *Milk Prices* (46), and *Taxi Cost Charges* (87). *Bricks* (49) was a typical example: the prices of common bricks were being sold at less profit per brick than the more expensive facing bricks. As manufacturers found it more profitable to produce facing bricks, there tended to be shortages of common bricks at times of high demand. Again, rates charged for brick deliveries in small vehicles were the same as for larger vehicles, even though delivery costs per unit were greater. A change in the price structure to reflect this would have accorded with steps to replace small lorries with larger vehicles and thus

lower costs and would have been practicable. The NBPI accordingly recommended or accepted recommendations of the industry for rearrangements
of the price structure along these lines.

A further reason for investigating the price-cost structure was that
firms with substantial market power, or nationalised industries, were the
subject of many references. In competitive conditions, prices tend to equal
marginal costs and efficient resource allocation tends to occur. In non-competitive conditions, profit maximising firms tend not to set prices equal to
marginal costs and a less efficient allocation of resources tends to result
than if they do. Non-competitive conditions are a fact of life, and it may be
necessary for an industry's production to be concentrated in one or a few
enterprises to achieve economies of scale. A way of combining the exercise
of market power with efficient pricing and output practices is to require
oligopolies and monopolies to behave as if they were in a competitive situation and to make their price structure reflect their cost structure. In the
case of the London Brick Company, for example, the company enjoyed certain natural advantages over the other brick producers but was inhibited
from expanding its market and simultaneously obtaining economies of scale
from an expanded market by fear of a reference to the Monopolies Commission.
The NBPI suggested that it should not be deterred from doing this providing
it acted as a competitive firm would and adjusted its prices to reflect the
cost structure.

There were many cases where the NBPI sought to bring about behaviour
that would accord with competitive conditions. *Steel Prices* (111) was a
notable example. In dealing with the nationalised British Steel Corporation's proposals for general price increases, the NBPI had not been satisfied that the Corporation had taken adequate account in its forecasts of the
scope for cost reductions, and had recommended an abatement of 25 per cent,
that is, that the revenue raised by price increases should be reduced from
£50-55 million a year to £40 million a year. It went on to recommend that
the abatement should not be spread evenly over the proposed increases for
various products, because there was evidence that the Corporation had proposed greater price increases on some products where it had a predominant
share of the home market and smaller increases where it competed with the
private sector. The NBPI questioned whether this was in accordance with
the pledges given by the Government that competition between the public
and private sectors should be on a fair basis. It suggested that the Corporation's proposals be reviewed in the light of two criteria: first, where it had
a predominant share of the market and so might unduly have used its market
power; and, secondly, where the proposed selling prices exceeded 'required'
selling prices calculated to yield returns of specified amounts.

Nationalised industries are under an obligation normally to relate prices
to marginal costs as far as possible. [1] The NBPI undertook some novel
studies of marginal cost in for example *Gas* (102), *Coal* (153), and the *Post*

1 See A Review of the Economic and Financial Objectives of Nationalised
Industries. op. cit.

Office (58).

The NBPI, following in the line of similar studies in U.S.A., Belgium and Switzerland, can be credited with the first modern statistical study of the cost structure of the British Post Office. Although impressed by the thoroughness of the costing methods used, the NBPI did not consider that the results took sufficient account of long-run marginal costs to provide an appropriate basis for decisions on tariffs. Statistical techniques were used to identify sorting costs. The time scale of the reference did not permit the NBPI to do more than recommend the commissioning by the Post Office of studies of marginal costs in the total letter and telephone systems. (These recommendations were acted upon). A study was also made of telephone rental charges. The marginal costs of new and current subscribers were found to be markedly different. Since tariffs for new and existing subscribers had to be the same for practical reasons, the NBPI recommended that the connection cost should be used as the means by which the new subscriber paid the full marginal cost. This, and a tentative suggestion to increase the differential charges between hours of peak traffic and other times, were also adopted by the Post Office.

The NBPI summarised the background to its important study of coal pricing as follows:

'It is the present aim of the NCB to break even both on its colliery activities as a whole and on broad individual sectors of those activities such as production of general purpose coal. This means that the NCB is selling coal in each market at average cost. This has the appearance of being equitable but means that coal is being sold from high-cost pits at a loss. From the point of view of providing the nation's energy as efficiently as possible, it would be better to fix the price of coal at a level at which the highest-cost pit is at least breaking even. However the average-cost approach, enabling as it does the low-cost pits to subsidise the high-cost pits, helps to keep down the rate of contraction of the industry, and this is particularly important as high-cost coalfields are generally in places where miners would have most difficulty in finding new jobs and where therefore the social cost of pit closures is high. The limited protection which high-cost pits receive through the present system of pricing has been supplemented by *ad hoc* measures such as Ministerial directives to limit the conversion of power stations from coal to oil firing.

However, it is in principle quite possible to calculate a "resource cost" of employing manpower which takes into account the output foregone in other parts of the economy by retaining miners in the coal mining industry. In the circumstances of the coal industry the resource costs of many miners are lower than their equivalent accounting costs. If the price of coal is related to the resource costs of producing it in such a way that no coal is sold at less than such resource costs, this will mean that social considerations can be given their full weight in pricing decisions and that coal prices are fixed in such a way as to promote an efficient use of the country's resources. In such a system there would be no justification for *ad hoc* measures of the kind used in the past to protect the coal industry.'[1]

It therefore suggested that the Government should attempt to define more precisely the place the coal industry should occupy in the energy market taking into account not only social considerations but also the balance of payments and security of supply. It recognised that there were many problems in translating this principle into practice. The results of the studies undertaken to see how these might be resolved were published as a supplement to the main report.

Social costs of unemployed miners were calculated under a number of alternative hypotheses about the rate of manpower rundown in the coal mining industry as a whole. One hypothesis covered the extreme case of a miner's labour being a free input if on redundancy he were to remain wholly unemployed. What was novel, however, was the quantification of social opportunity costs which were greater than zero, but less than accounting costs, and the resulting exploration of the consequences of using these social costs instead of accounting costs for pricing decisions. The study was done in sufficient detail to compare prices, marginal accounting costs and five separate calculated marginal resource costs, in respect of 32 coal type region combinations.

The NBPI did not reach any really firm conclusion as to the level of resource costs relative to accounting costs. It concluded, however, that:

'Much pioneering work went into this part of the exercise and if it were now to be repeated much better estimates of resource costs could be made. Moreover ... iteration would be needed ... and because of lack of time and money we did not complete the iteration. We have outlined the work which has been done and we hope that it will be extended and developed by others.'[2]

The main conclusion from the study concerned not the general level of prices but the relationship between prices and marginal accounting costs, type of coal by type of coal. It was demonstrated that domestic consumers were subsidising consumers of coking coals (largely the British Steel Corporation) by over £20 million per annum. The NBPI's opinion was that in view of this considerable cross-subsidy its study should be repeated with more up-to-date information to establish whether there was continuing evidence of such cross-subsidy.

There was another novel aspect of the study. Since any change in the pricing policy of the NCB could be expected to alter the demand for coal, the Central Electricity Generating Board (CEGB) was asked to calculate how much coal they would take under specified assumptions as to coal prices and quantities. By iterating between the quantities and prices of coal notionally made available by the NCB and the quantities notionally demanded at each set of prices by the CEGB, the NBPI optimised simultaneously the cost of meeting the coal and oil requirements of the CEGB and the coal

1 *Coal Prices* (153), Supplement No.1. Introductory Note, paras. 3, 4.

2 paragraph 6, Supplement No.1, *Coal Prices* (153).

requirements of other consumers. This was the first occasion on which the operation of the two industries had been modelled in this way. From the results of these calculations it was possible to estimate the changes in the size of the industry and in its finances from 1974/5 which would result from alternative pricing policies. The cost savings to the nation from changing the NCB's pricing policy were also calculated. The conclusion, that there was no significant cost saving to the nation from moving from one coal pricing policy, and hence one combination of coal and fuel oil, to another was important:

'It means that the Government has a wide range of options, each different in its implications for the preservation of mining jobs and for the finances of the NCB, but each broadly equivalent in terms of net social cost. We have quantified the various options so far as we can, and we think it desirable that such calculations be made regularly in the future, partly because of their relevance to fuel policy and partly because of the benefit which we think joint planning would confer on the NCB and the CEGB — not to mention the South of Scotland Electricity Board, the British Steel Corporation, British Rail and others if they were brought into the exercise as well. To secure acceptance of the results it is desirable that the work be undertaken by experts acknowledged by the participating industries to be impartial.'[1]

More generally the fact that quantified results (together with sensitivity analyses showing the probabilities of alternative outcomes) were obtained demonstrated that it was possible to apply this kind of approach to a wide range of social policy questions involving many industries and to expect meaningful answers.

1   Ibid, Para. 9

Part IV Some Conclusions

14. Some Conclusions

In this chapter there is first a short survey of the quality and usefulness of
the investigatory work underlying NBPI reports; second, a brief recapitu-
lation of the main features of the operation and methods of inquiry of the
NBPI, and a discussion of their main lessons especially for other public
investigatory bodies in Britain and abroad; third, there is an outline of the
case for having retained the NBPI organisation, or something like it as a
permanent specialised investigatory body even after the discontinuation of
the prices and incomes policy. The NBPI's short term and long term roles
are then discussed. Finally there is a brief discussion of the overall impact
of the NBPI. This chapter is mainly a discussion of selected issues arising
from some parts of the book and is not a summary of its conclusions.

1. NBPI Investigations: An Appraisal

It is difficult, indeed dangerous, to generalise about the quality and usefulness of the investigations made by the NBPI in 170 reports on widely differing
subjects. Nevertheless it may be useful to present my impression of the
quality of the reports, giving most weight to their *apparent* quality and usefulness, rather than their actual effects, which are discussed briefly later
in this chapter. The main criteria for evaluation have been whether they uncovered important new information, or seemed likely to promote change and
greater efficiency, or contributed to the solution of important policy problems
in the prices and incomes field.

At the one extreme some reports were unimpressive, and some of the least
valuable included: a significant proportion of the price references completed
in less than three months, with little penetrating investigation of managerial
efficiency, and with no new contribution to policy. The succession of references on busmen's pay in 1968, where the main object was to block specific
wage increases, did nothing to solve general problems of the industry. In
addition, the reputation of the early reports does not rest on their supporting
investigations but on what they said, although they had a greater impact
than many of the later, more fully researched reports. But even in these
least impressive reports, the NBPI had nearly always something to say that

represented a serious attempt to discuss problems of the industry. There is practically no NBPI report which could be said to be of no interest to the industry studied, if only for the reason that one or two serious issues relating to efficiency were always isolated for substantial discussion, whether or not the discussion reached the right conclusion.

There were some later reports which seemed impressive because they provided a wealth of useful information and discussion for those within as well as outside the industry, but which were of limited value in stimulating efficiency, because of the inherent difficulty of producing in a short time useful recommendations about the particular industry. The report on the *Pay and Conditions of Workers in the Milk Industry* is an example. The NBPI carried out a large and thorough enquiry into nearly all aspects of this decentralised, complex, traditional industry. The report gave a full accurate picture of it, but contained few suggestions likely to have any major effect.

At the other extreme, there were some outstanding reports, such as many of the general study reports, on such topics as payments by results, job evaluation, top salaries, hours of work, overtime and shiftwork, general problems of low pay, and productivity agreements; the standing references on the Pay of the Armed Forces and the Remuneration of Solicitors (and a rather similar reference on the Costs and Fees of Architects); and studies of the efficiency and pricing policies of nationalised industries. These reports will perhaps prove to be those of the most enduring value.

In between there was also a host of valuable industrial relations studies of such previously largely or totally unexplored industries as clothing manufacturing, water supply, bricks, pottery, contract cleaners, industrial civil servants, nurses and midwives, and the exhibition contracting industry. And in the final phases of the NBPI's lifetime, some of the deeper, longer studies of managerial efficiency in the private sector were of considerable value. Between them and the least impressive reports, there were a fairly large number of reports with valuable substantial analyses of selected aspects of an industry, but which were weak in other respects. An example was the second report on *BeerPrices* (136). A survey, made for the first time, into the financial position of public houses will continue to serve as a work of reference on the subject for many years, unless it stimulates such bodies as the National Federation of Licensed Victuallers to hold these surveys regularly. But most of the remainder of the report on managerial efficiency and industrial relations was thin. My own view, on the basis of a reading of all reports, and an attempt to compare the best, worst, and intermediate reports, is that the bulk of the intermediate reports contained more than enough useful information, perceptive discussion, and constructive suggestions to justify the expenditure of resources of money and time by all concerned.

2. Some Lessons of the NBPI's Methods of Enquiry

More important now that the NBPI has gone, however, are the lessons of its methods of operation and enquiry, irrespective of the value or outcome of particular investigations. Some investigations had shortcomings not because

232

of inherent defects in the methods of enquiry but because of extraneous factors, such as shortage of time and staff, the complex nature of many industries, and the pioneering nature of enquiries. It is important to note therefore that certain methods of enquiry pioneered by the NBPI, faults not withstanding, have considerable potential for use by others.

The principal characteristic of the NBPI's enquiry methods was obtaining its own information, which then became the centrepiece of most reports. In this way a full and independent examination of the issues was possible; if the NBPI were to be influential, it had to be able to speak to the parties with knowledge and authority acquired from enquiry of a high standard; and it was sometimes possible to show the parties how they themselves should go about collecting information in future, and thereby improve their efficiency. The practice of doing investigations of its own had important advantages: speed, the progressive development of techniques of enquiry and investigatory expertise, a close integration of policy-making and fact-finding, and the effective use of an accumulation of experience of best — and worst — practices in a wide range of industries. In most references only secondary reliance was placed upon interested parties or other sources.

The NBPI did not usually rely upon the parties themselves because they often did not know the facts or could not provide evidence to support their own views. Another reason was the necessity at times of obtaining information to support making unacceptable recommendations. Nor did the NBPI rely much upon other sources of information — such as official statistics, expert evidence, commissioned research or management consultants — although it used them, whenever desirable. Official statistics of earnings, prices and productivity were usually inadequate for the Board's purposes. Experts were of value when their research had covered the exact issues in question, but references usually required up-to-date investigations in previously unstudied fields. Use of management consultants was necessary but the NBPI built up its own skills.

A closely related characteristic was that the NBPI usually sought to obtain all the information which could bear upon its decisions although it did not always succeed in doing so. But what was important was its refusal to be bounded by the limits imposed by following traditional lines of enquiry only, and to confine itself to accounting enquiries or interviews with top management. Whenever it was felt that the situation on the shop floor, for example, was important, an attempt was made to investigate it, even though no other public investigatory body in Britain (and possibly elsewhere) had ever made enquiries of this kind before. Broadly speaking it was the information needed which determined the nature of the enquiries, not the nature of the enquiry methods which determined the type of information sought. It is emphasised that this is a most important point.

Another distinctive element of the NBPI as an investigatory body was its speed of enquiry. As noted earlier, this had many advantages — relevance of findings, quick resolution of urgent disputes, minimum inconvenience to the parties. It also enabled the Board to cover a vast amount of ground in five years and to demonstrate how much investigation can be done in a short time by an inquiry body, given adequate resources and a desire to work quickly.

There were however certain disadvantages about its speed of enquiry. Three months was adequate for the 'narrow' prices and incomes references, providing the issues were identified clearly at the start, the data collected speedily and the analysis of information quickly made. But there was little safety margin for errors and if, as was sometimes inevitable, the real issues emerged only after the enquiries, it was then too late to make new ones. If the specialist staff or senior staff or Board Members were overwhelmed with a simultaneous inflow of data from several references, then three months proved to be too short a time in which to conduct references satisfactorily. In retrospect a less rigid deadline would probably have been desirable. During 1966—70, the Prices and Incomes Act might have specified three months as the normal time for a 'narrow' report, but might have given the NBPI the option occasionally to take one month more. The three month time limit also usually precluded 'depth' investigations which usually were of more lasting value: more is said of this later in this chapter.

Another nearly unique feature of the NBPI for an official body was its inter-disciplinary mix. No other British public investigatory body has had such a wide range of specialist staff at its disposal. In addition, there were the diverse backgrounds of Board Members, and the mix of Civil Service and non-Civil Service elements amongst the staff. These diverse groups were reasonably, though not perfectly, well integrated — as evidenced for example by the Board's unanimity and the satisfaction felt with staff working parties — and thus able to make effective contributions. This ensured that an unusually wide range of interests and viewpoints were brought together in the process of making the value judgements necessary for policy making.

These features put the NBPI in a stronger position than many other investigatory bodies such as Courts of Inquiry, which often have little independent or concrete information to guide them on the facts of the situation e.g. the level and structure of earnings in an industry under enquiry, the effects of alternative decisions on costs and prices, the underlying factors in an industrial relations situation which lie behind the immediate cause of a dispute. The Pearson enquiry on Docks in 1970 is a case in point, for the Court did not have the expertise to estimate the effects on costs of its recommendation to increase wages. The reports of the Wilberforce Court of Inquiry into Electricity Supply workers and the Scamp Court of Inquiry into Local Authority workers had a better factual basis on which to work — but only because they could use the NBPI's own reports on these subjects.

Although McCarthy and Clifford were of the opinion that Courts of Inquiry were not fact-finding bodies, providing the material on which the public decides, but simply useful devices for dispute settling, they doubt whether the elementary quasi-judicial techniques for fact-finding are always adequate and raise the question of whether it would not be better if courts dealing with more complex disputes could normally be expected to arm themselves with some sort of qualified assistance. [1]

Since then there has also been more discussion of the need for Courts of Inquiry to take more account of 'the national interest'. If they do need to, then they will need to undertake more research into the repercussions of their decisions. This was to some extent recognised by the appointment of a strong secretariat to service the Wilberforce Court of Inquiry into electricity pay: it would seem logical that this task should in future be allocated to the Office of Manpower Economics, which now conducts some of the functions of the NBPI.

This is not the place to draw a detailed comparison between the operation and methods of enquiry of the NBPI and those of the Monopolies Commission, but a number of contrasts immediately come to mind, and may be briefly mentioned, especially as the Commission is currently undergoing a reappraisal by the Government. A fuller comparison certainly would not be entirely in the NBPI's favour (for example, regarding the pains which the Commission takes to consult those upon whom it reports) and it might be observed that the Commission has stood the test of survival, whilst the NBPI has not. [2] The Commission has however some lessons to learn.

In certain respects the reports of the Monopolies Commission go deeper than those of the NBPI e.g. accounting enquiries, the historical background of the industry, analysis of market structure. But nearly always the Commission has confined its enquiries to a narrower field. Like the Restrictive Practices Court, it has not investigated managerial efficiency or industrial relations. Whether or not it should do so is, no doubt, open to debate, but it may be noted that Professor M. Peston has drawn attention to the following remark of the Monopolies Commission in the inquiry on Pilkington:

> 'It is not for us to speculate how long the traditional character of the management may continue, but there would, we think, have to be some quite unforeseen change in this respect before Pilkington would deliberately set out to exploit its position of strength at the expense of the public interest.'

As he indicates, the interesting thing here is the fact that a statement of this kind has never been made before about any organisation it has investigated, even though this is precisely the sort of thing which may be decisive in assessing a firm. Instead, he says, the Commission has relied upon simple textbook assumptions of profit maximisation in static conditions to judge the likely behaviour of firms, has commissioned very little work from outside, either from universities or management consultants, and 'although in principle all or nearly all the problems that have confronted it are cost-benefit problems, the Commission appears to have been happy merely to survey whatever evidence is easily available and then apply their judgement

---

1 W. E. J. McCarthy and B. A. Clifford, 'The Work of Industrial Courts of Inquiry', *British Journal of Industrial Relations*, March 1966. pp. 39—58.

2 Whether or not the ability to withstand this test is a measure of the successfulness of an investigatory or regulatory body is another matter which is not dealt with here.

to it... It is precisely the lack of this evidence that so limits the value of the work of the Monopolies Commission.'[1] It is also of interest to note in this case that the Commission went out of its way to praise the qualities of Pilkington's management although the firm's admitted weaknesses in labour management gave rise to one of the most serious strikes of 1970.

The Monopolies Commission also has not reported with the same urgency as the NBPI. The average time for its reports has been two and a half years (except in merger cases, where there was a six month time limit), and the time taken has ranged from one year to five years.[2] The report on the Supply of Metal Containers, for example, took three years. When published it appeared to be partly out of date in relation to the fast changing situation in that area of industry. At last one report in earlier days, which concluded that profits of one firm, Fisons, in the supply of chemical fertiliser were high in relation to the profits enjoyed by other industries, only appeared after the profits had trended downwards to a position close to the average for other industries,[3] later falling well below the average.

Yet another field of government to which some of the NBPI's methods of enquiry, particularly in the field of managerial efficiency, might be applied is in the auditing of efficiency of government. As E.L. Normanton, in the main book on the subject,[4] has shown, the principle of a high-level audit of administrative efficiency, greatly encouraged in Germany, France and the U.S.A., has not been encouraged in Great Britain. Instead Executive Class civil servants, who, according to Normanton, lack the skills and status within the Civil Service to attempt efficiency auditing, confine their activities largely to the detection of irregularities and extravagance. Should there be an attempt to apply a more comprehensive, higher level form of audit, a good starting point for the auditors would be to examine the methods used by the NBPI to conduct its studies of managerial efficiency.

A final point of general comparison with other investigatory bodies was made by the NBPI in its *Final General Report*:

'... among the Board members and staff were experts in such fields as economics, industrial relations, accounting, statistics and management operations, their effectiveness being the greater because they acted as a single instrument of investigation... In time also the Board accumulated a breadth of experience which was invaluable in many different types of enquiry.

'... we found the problems of incomes and prices inextricably bound

---

1 op. cit. Discussions of the limited sources of evidence in the Restrictive Practices Court are contained in R.B. Stephens and B.S. Yamey *The Restrictive Practices Court* (Weidenfield and Nicholson, London, 1965), passim.

2 Industrial Policy Group. *The Control of Monopoly*, Paper Number 8, (London 1971.) Page 14.

3 Ibid., page 21.

4 op. cit. passim.

together. In addition to industrial relations we found from the first that considerations of efficiency in the use of both labour and capital were equally bound up with the problems of incomes and prices. Now with the demise of the Board these subjects are being separated again. The Office of Manpower Economics is to look into problems relating to incomes, and an expanded Monopolies Commission is to look into problems related to prices where competition is muted or lacking. While we feel confident that each will do valuable work, the advantage which we have had of considering individual problems in the light of a consideration of productivity, prices and incomes as a whole will be denied them. . .'

It need only be added that in earlier chapters it has been noted that some of the NBPI's reports on industrial relations and labour management matters suffered from a rather one-sided orientation to industrial relations with insufficient attention being paid to the managerial dimension. This deficiency stemmed at least in part from the failure to employ staff who had occupied senior executive posts in industry. It is to be hoped that the lessons of this are not lost on the Office of Manpower Economics.

Whether the Board's policies and reports were acceptable, its methods of enquiry in general set an example to other official policy making and investigatory bodies in Britain. The Board demonstrated that a far wider range of questions − e.g. managerial efficiency, industrial relations, earnings − could be effectively and speedily investigated than had previously been believed possible and its experience suggests the need for a reappraisal of the methods and potentialities of other investigatory bodies in Britain, which have traditionally confined themselves to narrow fields of enquiry and have consequently often been unable to base their findings on crucial issues on anything more than supposition.

3. Retention of the NBPI Organisation as a Specialised Investigatory Body?

The best reports and the main features of the NBPI's methods of enquiry revealed its qualities and potentialities as an investigatory body. They also draw attention to some apparent gaps in the machinery of Government. It is useful to organise this section around a discussion of the case for retaining the NBPI organisation, or something like it, as a permanent investigatory body, even in the absence of a formal prices and incomes policy.

Because of its investigatory expertise the NBPI served to fill a gap in the machinery of government. Second, some reasons are given for concluding that the machinery of government is not well equipped to undertake all of its own research. Third, it is suggested that there is a permanent role for a specialised investigatory body servicing many of the research needs of Government departments, Courts of Inquiry, Royal Commissions and so on. It is noted that the Office of Manpower Economics is fulfilling some of those roles at present. Fourth, it is suggested that this idea is capable of extension into other fields of Government.

An analysis of NBPI reports shows that it could have played a useful role between 1965 and 1971, even had no prices and incomes policy existed.

First, in Chapter 4, it was noted that it served to fill a gap in the supervision of nationalised industries.

Second, it was noted that there was, albeit temporarily, a trend to the transfer to the NBPI of the functions of a plethora of bodies often using conflicting principles to determine pay in the public sector. There would have been a strong case for taking steps along these lines to ensure a closer measure of coordination of the determination of pay in the various parts of the public sector irrespective of the existence or otherwise of the prices and incomes policy. The establishment of the Office of Manpower Economics (OME) by a Conservative Government committed against a prices and incomes policy constitutes a (minimal) recognition of this point. In November 1970 it announced that it recognised the need for co-ordinated machinery for advising the Government on the remuneration of certain groups for whom no negotiating machinery was, for one reason or another, appropriate. It proposed to establish three review bodies with a small degree of interlocking membership. One would advise on the remuneration of the Boards of nationalised industries, the Judiciary, senior civil servants, senior officers of the Armed Forces and any other groups which might appropriately be considered with them. It was subsequently announced that this body would also report to the Government on the pay of members of Parliament. Another would advise on the pay of the Armed Forces generally. A third would advise on the remuneration of doctors and dentists in the National Health Service. The Review Bodies would have at their disposal and working to their directions a secretariat of 50 (later increased) provided by a new Office of Manpower Economics, manned mainly by former NBPI staff, and headed by a civil servant. The Office would not be part of the Government machine and its reports would be independent. Indeed there was some recognition of the usefulness of other aspects of the NBPI's work, for the Government also stated that it intended to use the new Office to service any ad hoc enquiries which were necessary from time to time to examine in depth particular pay structures and related problems. The Office would also carry out analytical and educational work on more general matters affecting pay and its relation to productivity, either at the request of Ministers or with the approval of Ministers. It has since received references about measured day work, equal pay, and wage drift (which seem likely to be a continuation of the NBPI's general study report series) and one about fire service pay. No doubt the OME will also make investigations into miscellaneous matters which may arise from time to time, such as arose in the reference, *London Weighting of the Civil Service* (42). In that reference, a major study was made of the additional pay allowance which should be made for civil servants who worked in London, in view of the high cost of living there. This study was also intended to be of help for similar decisions regarding private sector employees in London. It would also seem logical for the OME to service the needs of Courts of Inquiry.

Some examples of a third important class of references which could have been dealt with usefully, even had no prices and incomes policy existed, were the following: the three reports on *The Remuneration of Solicitors* – the remuneration of solicitors depends largely on their fees, which are set by committees under the Chairmanship of the Lord Chancellor. The NBPI's reports were designed principally to assist the Committees' decisions. The Lord Chancellor commented that before the publication of the reports the committee had not had one-tenth of the information about costs and incomes of solicitors with which to make the decision. The reference about London taxi-cab fares is a similar example, because their fares are controlled by the Home Office.

The reference *Architects Costs and Fees* originated largely from the needs of the inter-departmental Committee on Professional Fees. This body has to decide, in respect of architects fees amongst others, what the Government should pay architects who perform work for it. Since Government fees make up a large part of the total incomes of architects, the committee, in deciding whether to accept proposals for fee increases made by the Royal Institute of British Architects, was, in effect, determining whether the fees and total incomes of all architects should be increased or not. There are numerous other fields where the Government's role as a purchaser of private sector goods and services requires equally thorough investigations as those conducted in this case. The decision to use the secretariat of the OME to service a committee which will investigate the fees to be paid consulting engineers is again a recognition of the potential necessity of such an organisation.

Another example was the reference on *Increases in Local Authority Rents*(62). This was a highly political reference, but the NBPI was able to collect valuable information which allowed for the first time calculations to be made of the cost to a sample of local authorities of introducing the rent rebate scheme then being recommended by the Ministry of Housing and Local Government (and which demonstrated to authorities not in the sample how to go about costing the proposals). Another example was the reference *Costs and Revenues of Independent Television Contractors* (156). The Television Act of 1964 made provision for the payment by commercial television contractors to the Exchequer of a 'levy' in return for conferring upon them the sole right to operate a commercial television service within a given area. In 1970 the levy was reduced to produce annually some £23 million in revenue, instead of £29 million as previously, in the light of representations to the Government which appeared to show that the financial situation of the programme contractors was deteriorating. Within a month the NBPI was asked to report on their costs and revenues. Although the terms of reference specifically excluded the examination of any question as to the level of the levy, a comprehensive and detailed study of their financial position was clearly needed, and was made. The resulting information paved the way for the subsequent Government decision about the levy.

It thus emerges that in respect of this third class of examples an important subsidiary function of the NBPI was to serve as an adjunct to the whole governmental machine as a specialised investigatory body, fulfilling a role which, for one reason or another, could not be adequately performed by the existing machinery.

The above examples comprise only the tip of the iceberg of problems which might have come to the NBPI for investigation, had its main work not been the administration of a prices and incomes policy. The examples illustrate only a few of the large number of similar policy problems which the government must settle every day as a result of a proliferation of controls which have grown up over the years, as a result of its heavy involvement in one way or another — as purchaser, as protector of the consumer, as guardian of the balance of payments and of the environment. In every sphere of its activities any modern government must deal with a great and increasing number of policy problems requiring, for their satisfactory resolution, the quick collection and expert analysis of new information. Existing government departments and permanent official institutions are often inadequately equipped, and would find it uneconomical, to undertake the research and make the special enquiries necessary. Consequently important decisions are not infrequently taken with only a smattering of knowledge of the key factors.

It would take one too far afield to examine in depth why this is so, and why this situation is likely to continue always, or at least for the immediate future. Only one or two reasons need be noted.[1] Departments which are either considering extending their powers into new fields or simply wishing to examine problems for which they (and no other Departments) have no direct responsibility are unlikely to possess the resources necessary for collecting or evaluating advice. Second, Departments are often not properly organised to perform research or investigatory functions themselves: 'Where intelligence and operational duties are left to the same people, operational duties will tend greatly to distort the intelligence ones, if not to drive them out altogether. Where the intelligence function is specialised and given to a separate research unit, this risks either being ignored on the grounds that policy-makers have no time to spare from coping with immediate crises, or being deflected to deal with peripheral problems to keep it out of mischief. . . When specialised intelligence is needed, it is thus often necessary, and simpler, to set up a new body for the job.'[2]

There are other reasons why the existing permanent machinery may be an unsuitable instrument for the conduct of research: (a) one-off research projects do not require the appointment of permanent staff; (b) it may be uneconomical for a body to engage experts permanently when they are only needed from time to time; (c) there may be a shortage of research staff or they may be unprocurable; (d) the existing departmental structure can in practice often lead to inter-disciplinary imbalances in the research staff used for novel investigatory tasks.

In recognition of these shortcomings of the permanent executive, and

1 These points are taken from William Plowden 'An Anatomy of Commissions' *New Society*, July 15, 1971. p. 104–6.

2 Ibid., Page 106. Plowden cites example in support of his contentions.

especially in recognition of the growing need for the gathering and processing of new data, it has often been the case for Royal Commissions and other similar outside official bodies to be established. There were something like 25 Royal Commissions or bodies of a similar kind a year during the 1960's. [1]

It has also become increasingly common for these bodies, government departments themselves, planning bodies, Courts of Inquiry, interdepartmental committees and other official bodies to commission research. Even the Select Committees of the House of Commons have gone some way in this direction through the appointment of specialist advisers. However, 'The theoretical case (for outside bodies) in terms of the intelligence function is somewhat weakened in practice. Andrew Shonfield has noted... that commissions often fail to create any kind of research facility superior to whatever exists inside departments. Drawing on his experience on the Donovan and Duncan commissions he has identified what he describes as the "pragmatic illusion" which can dominate a commission's approach: "Just plunge into your subject; collect as many facts as you can; think about them hard as you go along; and at the end use your common sense, and above all your feel for the practicable, to select a few good proposals out of the large number of suggestions which will surely come your way." The alternative approach, he suggests, would be systematically to identify the main areas of difficulty and then, equally systematically, to explore these in some depth. It is striking how many commissions asked to advise on complex subjects have failed to collect the evidence needed to support their conclusions, or even to see the need for a supporting research programme. The major educational reports are outstanding exceptions; they may be contrasted with the magpie approach of Fulton, who accumulated a ragbag of miscellaneous and not wholly relevant information and then made various recommendations for which the essential research is only now being done by the Civil Service Department.'

Had the NBPI not been confined to investigating matters which bore a relationship to prices and incomes policy, and had it possessed enough staff there is no doubt that a considerable number of bodies could have used the services of its staff, instead of commissioning their own research. Some examples of this would be the Fulton Report on the Civil Service, the Maud Report on Local Government reform, the Donovan Report on trade unions and employers associations, all of which undertook large and expensive research programmes, the Duncan Committee on the diplomatic service, the report by Professor Phelps Brown on Labour-Only Subcontracting, numerous interdepartmental committees, such as that which reported in 1969 on the National Minimum Wage; the Parliamentary Committees on Nationalised Industries; Courts of Inquiry; and so on. It is not suggested that an NBPI-style body could necessarily have done all the research for these bodies on its own. But it could

---

[1] Ibid., p. 104. Plowden comments that their numbers have shown no signs of decreasing since.

have done a good deal of it, and commissioned and supervised the conduct of any research which the Royal Commission or official body considered necessary. It would have had a number of advantages in doing so — speed, interdisciplinary balance, and experience in the commissioning, conduct, and supervision of research.

It could not be contended that the NBPI was an organisation free of dogma and drawing its conclusions solely from the results of its disinterested enquiries. But towards the latter part of its life especially, it evolved much more in this direction. And at all times the overriding specialism of its large staff was not 'prices and incomes', but the business of impartial, balanced investigation. The staff made up an organisation for empirical inquiry the results of whose enquiries were presented to a body (the Board) whose role was to draw conclusions and make what were essentially political judgments. It was normally at the stage of the Board's consideration of the results of research that 'dogma' was, or should have been, injected.

There was then no fundamental reason why other bodies should not have been serviced by a similar organisation or organisations. Though the NBPI's staff were assembled to deal with, broadly, prices and incomes work, the techniques they applied and the procedures they followed were readily transferable to other kinds of investigations; and their multi-disciplinary approach would have helped avoid the risk of such bodies enquiring on too narrowly specialist a basis (though the need to develop a conceptual framework appropriate to the different areas of inquiry would have remained important in some instances.)

It is not contended that the organisation should have had anything like a monopoly over the conduct or the commissioning of research for all official bodies. There are obviously many areas where it is best for the official body possessing expertise in particular subjects itself to undertake, or commission directly and control, the outside research. But some questions requiring research, especially in the industrial, managerial, economic, industrial relations and social fields, could have been handled by the body. There would have been more than enough matters requiring investigation to ensure an even work flow; and the locating of this function in one body would have helped to ensure a more careful evaluation of the priority to be given to research in different areas of government than is now the case; and it would also have led to its more economical conduct, than by invariably engaging outsiders, at high prices, to do it.

Since the departure of the NBPI and the abandonment of the legislation on the Commission of Industry and Manpower (which body would have been the logical place in which to start an experiment along these lines) it has become difficult to see how the present set of independent regulatory or advisory bodies such as the Office of Manpower Economics or Monopolies Commission could be used for this experiment except on occasions when the subject needing investigation fits their speciality. In the long term, it may be that the Monopolies Commission and the Office of Manpower Economics will be integrated into a body not unlike the proposed Commission on Industry and Manpower with the conduct of an incomes policy being entrusted to an independent board whose main function would be to inspect and approve wage and price increases.

4. A digression and a tentative proposal

The idea of having a specialised independent investigatory body can be extended to at least one other broad area of government, that concerned with town and country planning and environment problems, and with certain types of problems to which it is useful to apply the techniques of cost-benefit analysis. It would take us far afield to consider in any depth the possibility of establishing a second permanent, probably independent, investigatory body, besides the one already discussed, but since the discussion of the case for the first body leads naturally onto this idea, it may be briefly aired, and then left to those professionally involved in the field to assess.

The Royal Commission on the Siting of the third London Airport is a natural starting point for this discussion. The origins of the Roskill Commission go back to at least 1964 when the report of an inter-departmental committee was published, recommending the siting of the third London airport at Stansted. This report was defective partly because a number of the subjects it dealt with were apparently not properly researched. [1] This report was almost immediately followed by a public inquiry, conducted by an inspector appointed by the Government, to hear objections to the recommendations.

> 'The result was that the inspector had to recommend that some basic research should be done, after the Government's case for Stansted had been presented. In effect, the Roskill Commission was invited to do what the Inter-Departmental Committee should arguably have done four years earlier with wider terms of reference.
> Perhaps the most lasting effect of the affair was that it revealed the limitations of the public local inquiry as an instrument for dealing with developments above a certain size and complexity.' [2]

The Roskill Commission proceeded by employing a team of experts to make a cost-benefit analysis of the alternative sites for the third London Airport, taking as given the assumption that there should be one. Some of the main questions dealt with included the evaluation of alternative sites, alternative planning strategies, the regional development of the South East, various abstruse technological problems, and a major political judgment; and in considering these matters it was necessary to take into account that the creation of an international airport could create a large new town, sterilise agricultural land, create an intolerable noise, and establish a large industrial complex. [3] The results of the calculations were submitted to legal

---

1 *Public Inquiries as an Instrument of Government* R.E. Wraith and G.B. Lamb (George Allen and Unwin, London, 1971) p. 206. The author is indebted to the authors for showing him a copy of the proofs of the book before publication.

2 Ibid. p. 208.

3 Ibid., p. 207—8, and p. 348.

style hearings. The cost of the exercise was over £1 million (which, incidentally, is more than the NBPI spent in any one year). The failure of the Commission's recommendations to win Government support is beside the point for the purposes of this study and could be largely attributed to the fact that the Government chose, rightly or wrongly, to make a political decision and select Foulness, the site to which there was least opposition and also to the difficulties encountered in quantifying to the satisfaction of all, the relevant costs and benefits.

More germane to this discussion is the fact that elaborate research of this kind was felt necessary. It will not always be the case in future inquiries that political factors will be so preponderant as to outweigh other considerations entirely; and future attempts to apply cost-benefit analysis may get to grips more satisfactorily with the problem of weighting non-measurable factors than did the Commission's research team. In my view, normally there would be a need in this situation for there to be conducted and published some kind of systematic expert analysis, using broadly the same principles as cost-benefit studies, of all the implications of all the alternatives as a prelude to the official decision, or inquiry, into such a matter. It would be for the Government or the inquiry body members to determine, in the last analysis, the weights to be given to key factors, including especially the political and less tangible ones.

The siting of the Third London Airport is in fact only one of several major planning subjects to which a form of cost-benefit analysis has been recently applied. There was for example a large-scale cost-benefit analysis of London's Victoria Underground project.

'One of the most formidable investigations of the century',[1] the inquiry into the Greater London Development Plan currently being conducted, perhaps illustrates the pattern of problems that will arise in the next few years in England, when something like 150 similar types of plans for the future development of cities and towns will be subjected to similar kinds of inquiry by ad hoc bodies. The Greater London Development Plan inquiry is not the same as Roskill inasmuch as no cost-benefit analysis has been applied, and there are a very great number of objections (more than 20,000 objections were received by December 1969) to be heard. But the existence of a permanent body capable of evaluating independently and systematically at least some of the factors involved, and some of the alternatives, would greatly assist the inquiries. In Britain, the scene for the next few years will be dominated by this wave of inquiries into development plans, which should then cease for another twenty years, but there is likely to be a continuing role for a body which can disinterestedly inquire into the complex implications of alternative courses of action, where environmental, economic and social considerations have to be investigated and weighed.

Again, as with our discussion of the possibility of having a permanent specialised investigatory body in the industrial relations, economics, management field, there is no suggestion that *all* or even most official research

1 Ibid., page 340.

into planning problems should be conducted by this body. Indeed in this case there might be a case for locating the body within existing government machinery, rather than making it independent. But there remains a case for establishing a body or a unit that would fill an apparent gap in the government machinery by investigating, in depth, problems of especial complexity that cannot be handled by the normal governmental procedures.

5. The Short Term Role of the NBPI

This study does not debate the question of the desirability nor practicability of different forms of prices and incomes policies, nor does it set forth proposals for how a future policy should be operated. The experience of the NBPI nevertheless suggests one or two important lessons which ought not to be neglected in any future policy conducted on lines similar to those of the period 1965-70.

How did the NBPI fare in its control role at the short term end of the prices and incomes policy? In Chapter 4 it was suggested that if the NBPI's task was conceived of as simply holding down seemingly unjustifiable prices or incomes increases, then, despite occasional generous exceptions, it was effective. Should an incomes policy experiment be conducted in future, the NBPI's experience has demonstrated the potential importance of a body set up to investigate and police individual cases of wage and price increase. The reference policy of the Government was the main cause of the breakdown in the short term task of controlling individual cases of wages and prices increases. Only some national wage agreements in excess of the norm, and hardly any local agreements, were referred to the NBPI. The Department of Employment and Productivity appeared to make no serious attempt to apply the NBPI's recommendations for the control of workers on PBR, and took a lenient attitude to productivity agreements. The flow of price references to the NBPI was also small, and poorly phased in relation to the different stages of the prices and incomes policy.

On his retirement the NBPI Chairman, Mr. Aubrey Jones, pointed to what he considered one of three sources of failure of the prices and incomes policy of 1965-70:

'... the department which initiated the policy and sponsored the Board was the Department of Economic Affairs. Whatever else may be said of the DEA it stood above other Departments all of which had their client groups, whether these were trade unions, or firms or industries. In the spring of 1968 the DEA disappeared and responsibility for the policy was transferred to the Ministry of Labour, rechristened the Department of Employment and Productivity. From that moment, the number of references made to the Board underwent a dramatic decline. In making that statement I am not implying any disrespect to Mrs. Barbara Castle (the Minister responsible), for whom I had and have the highest regard. If I look around me at Whitehall today, somewhat reshaped, there is not one Department which mirrors the objectivity of approach required if it is to send to the

Board significant and objectively phrased references'. [1]

The NBPI was the only body of its kind in market economies without power to initiate investigations. The Canadian Prices and Incomes Commission has used its power to conduct inquiries on the prices , and on the incomes side, though rather less in the case of the latter. In Australia and New Zealand independent bodies make national and individual wage decisions without being dependent upon Government reference. In the apparently successful (until the late 1950's) Netherlands incomes policy an independent body was responsible for inspection of all wage agreements and legal enforcement of the whole policy. In the United States during the Korean War an independent board administered national wage policy without being dependent upon Government references. There would be a strong case for automatically referring any wage increase in excess of the norm to an independent board should it play any part in a future policy. ·If its recommendations on short term proposals were not accepted by the Government, there would be the danger that the Board would be discredited and the policy seen to fail. But the force of public opinion would be mobilised against the offenders and make it easier for the Government to resist their pressures than if negotiations were conducted behind closed doors with the full facts and the main basis of decisions not being subject to public scrutiny. This would also reduce the possibility of two sets of standards — the board's, which generally would be closely in line with criteria laid down by the Government; and the inspection machinery's whose criteria would not be well known. Whilst it is difficult to imagine any Government being willing within the next few years to confer power of final decision on the board, this would be a logical long term direction in which to move.

The control of local agreements would be crucial to any future experiment in view of the increase in their importance. Action to block this potential breach could hardly be fully successful in preventing evasion, but the aim would be to reduce it substantially. The greater the reduction, the more acceptable the policy would be to others.

If the inspection machinery for local agreements were located in the board itself, this would imply a drastic change in its role. Automatic referral of above-norm wage increases to the board by an inspecting Government department would probably make better sense. A compulsory early warning system would be necessary. Automatic referral would undoubtedly lead to major changes in the role of an independent board. Unless the norm were generous, it would probably be regarded as an instrument of wage repression. Assuming that a substantial number of cases came to the board, it is difficult to imagine it carrying out efficiency studies on any scale. They might become the province of an expanded Monopolies Commission integrated with the Office of Manpower Economics. The disadvantage of the separation of functions is that it would give the policy a negative image. The board could however make limited attempts to encourage the development of genuine

[1] Aubrey Jones, 'The Price of Prosperity', *The Observer*, November 1, 1970, p. 15.

productivity bargaining.

The control of prices is an indispensable element in making an incomes policy acceptable. A well designed price policy could have another function. The problem of direct control of local wage agreements is so difficult that in many industries refusal to grant increases in prices because of above-norm wage settlements might be necessary as an additional control. The machinery from 1965-70 was spread through several departments, all with considerable knowledge of the industries they sponsored. It would be difficult to relocate this in an independent board, especially if the policy were short run. Again it would seem necessary to operate a compulsory early warning system for price increases. After the receipt of notification of price increases from these departments, together with their comments on them, the board would have the right to initiate its own investigations. It would also need powers to initiate investigations into firms which could reduce their prices. [1]

A disadvantage of linking the NBPI's efficiency role with its prices and incomes role was that often the NBPI had to, or wished to, report within too short a time for its reports to be useful. In addition it was not possible for the Government to select references in a way that was most systematic and helpful from the point of view of achieving the maximum effect on efficiency. Of necessity references largely depended on the contingencies of the prices and incomes policy.

If the NBPI were purely an efficiency stimulating body, with no role in prices and incomes policy, there is little doubt in the writer's mind that it would have been preferable to have conducted fewer, deeper studies, of six months duration, on average, using interdisciplinary teams of managers, industrial relations experts, civil servants, economists, statisticians, accountants and the Enquiry Team. They would largely have conducted their investigations independently of the top managers of the industry, but had much fuller consultations with them about proposed recommendations before issuing them than the NBPI. A smaller workload than the NBPI usually had would also have helped and the basis of selection of industries or firms for attention could have been made to depend on the likelihood that their efficiency or industrial relations could be improved.

This is not to say that more detailed studies would have solved all problems. Lack of time or expertise was not the reason for the failures of many recommendations. There were many insoluble problems, often intransigent parties, often the need for a different kind or a more permanent form of outside pressure to be applied than NBPI reports.

6. The Longer Term Role and Impact of the NBPI

Once again a full assessment of the NBPI's work, and its implications for the future of efficiency studies, is not undertaken. Instead a few issues have been selected for discussion. Did the NBPI's enthusiastic espousal of its long term role cause prices to rise more in the short term than if it had

[1] In a period with a high rate of inflation the number of such firms may be small.

taken a narrower view of its role?

To test this hypothesis raises a number of methodological problems, and, at the microeconomic level there is little available relevant evidence, and existing econometric studies generally refute the broader hypothesis that incomes policy was counterproductive.

It is possible, however, to record some relevant considerations. In some cases, the emphasis on efficiency probably kept costs and prices below the level they would otherwise have reached. The NBPI often applied pressure for long term change by opposing particular wage or price increases not designed to bring about such change. The condemnations of managerial efficiency seem to have deterred a substantial number of price increases, and possibly some incomes increases. Occasionally, immediate efficiency gains, lower costs and prices may have resulted from NBPI efficiency recommendations. More often the opposite was probably the case. Both the 1968 White Paper and the NBPI recognised that major wage or salary reorganisations could force up costs in the short term. The NBPI guidelines required that productivity agreements should have effective controls to ensure that projected increases in productivity were achieved and payment only made as productivity increased or as changes in working practice occurred. There are a number of reports in which the NBPI applied this and other guidelines strictly. Indeed some of these reports suggest that it felt obliged to do so even at the cost of delaying or preventing the conclusion of an agreement which would have led to significant productivity advances. The series of references on busmen's pay, for example, show that very low inducements were offered to busmen in return for the introduction of one-man busing. It may be, however, that the NBPI's wish to alter the wage structure was inflationary for reasons given in Chapter 8.

It was suggested in Chapter 7 that it was unlikely that the NBPI's earnings surveys were a significant inflationary influence. However, it is possible that the pointing up of pay differentials and exposure of inequitable and irrational pay structures may, by stimulating shop floor demands for pay increase and exacerbating leapfrogging tendencies, have been a more potent influence. The most important example was the *First Report on the Engineering Industry* (49) described in Chapter 7. Even here the NBPI clearly hoped that any such ill-effects would eventually be counterbalanced by the benefit of added pressure for a speedy reform of the pay structure: it is difficult to say if this calculation, in this instance, was correct or not. Perhaps a more serious adverse short term effect of many NBPI reports was their effect on wage expectations. The most striking example of all is the report on *The Pay and Conditions of Manual Workers in Local Authorities, the National Health Service, Gas and Water Supply* (29). The positive optimistic tone of the report and the ambitious plans for rapidly raising pay in the first of these industries in particular could only have sharply lifted the level of wage expectations. This would not have mattered if productivity had increased correspondingly, but the plans for improving it were unsuccessful, whilst events in 1970 suggested that the NBPI report may have been an important factor in the new militancy of local authority workers, whose demands in that year were an important element in the final collapse of the incomes policy. [1] The same kind of effect may have resulted from other NBPI reports which it could be argued were inclined to take a slightly exaggerated view of the potentiality for productivity gains, particularly when the context of a slowly growing economy is taken into account. To the extent that the NBPI had short term inflationary effects, this must, of course, be weighed up against any long term benefits of its reports.

The NBPI was also charged with superficiality in its reporting. How could a body which reported after several months of enquiry tell people who spent their lives in an industry how to do better? Clearly the details of the Board's reports could hardly be wholly satisfying to those employed in the industry. But superficiality is a relative concept: the question is whether the reports were adequate for the purpose in hand.

The NBPI's task was to identify broad problem areas and offer general solutions. Unlike many management consultants it was not assigned de-- fined specific problems and required to implement solutions. In dealing with problems at a general level, many matters of detail were not of consequence: what was essential, though, was to isolate the salient central facts. In many industries, this could be done quickly, in a few months, particularly by a body with experience of similar problems in many other industries, with a broader perspective than those involved in the industry, and a close acquaintance with best managerial practices throughout the economy. This is not, of course, to say that in practice the NBPI was invariably successful, or that 3 or 4 months was the right amount of time to spend investigating an industry. But its experience has shown the potentialities.

Given the generality of the NBPI's approach, one might suppose that few serious problems would be identified; and that even fewer general solutions would be proposed. There were in fact plenty of cases in which it was established virtually beyond question that because they lacked the information necessary to make correct decisions, management could not have been consistently optimising costs, or profits. In fact the picture which emerges from reports of the scope for the adoption of improvements in institutions, methods and practices in the fields of management and industrial relations is little short of astonishing. Few industries or firms were exempt from the NBPI's indictments which, even appropriately discounted at points, bear out the proposition that an important element in the relatively slow growth of the British economy is the failure of industry to modernise itself rapidly enough.

One can only offer an impression of what some of the NBPI's wider effects seemed to be. As was stated in Chapter 4, the NBPI seems to have played a major part in conveying several fundamental ideas to the population at large — that higher productivity permitted higher pay and that it

1 Because many local authority workers are relatively lowly paid and often do unpleasant arduous work, it could be argued that any inflationary effects of this report were excusable on income distribution grounds, providing the report did not raise expectations elsewhere in the economy, and providing the effects of pay increases granted to such workers did not spread through the rest of the economy.

was desirable to achieve a closer linking of pay and individual performance than in the past; that comparanility, at least in its crudest forms, was unacceptable as the sole basis for wage determination; that higher wages were likely to be inflationary unless justified by productivity considerations; and so on.

As was concluded in Chapter 9 the NBPI seemed to have had a good deal of success in injecting productivity considerations into bargaining about pay. Thereby it may have had a modest wider effect on raising national productivity — though one would feel more certain of this conclusion if the economic environment had been more favourable to change. The NBPI only had limited success in tempering the influence of comparability. It was probably more effective in reducing the influence of some other traditional factors such as cost of living considerations and manpower redistribution factors. The Board's general study reports in particular seem likely to have had a useful and probably enduring effect by influencing 'old habits, inherited attitudes and instititional arrangements', by introducing productivity into wage bargaining, and by securing rationalisation of wage and salary structures. The Board used individual and general study reports to publicise the importance for the whole economy of good labour management, the containment of costs under the control of management, the need for the adoption of best managerial practices, and speedy adaptation of industrial relations institutions and practices to the requirements of modernisation, and the important role of trade unions and workers in co-operating to secure improved efficiency.

Whilst it is difficult to say how successful it was in having any wider effect the Board probably helped substantially to accelerate the general improvement which seems to have occurred in management and industrial relations in the last six years in Great Britain, an improvement of which there is evidence in NBPI reports published in the later years of its lifetime. As was suggested in Chapter 3 it might have been more successful if the economic context of 1965-71 had been more favourable. The NBPI fairly certainly had some deterrent effects on price increases, which in turn may have stimulated a greater cost-consciousness on the part of management. The main effect, however, was probably to cut profit-rates somewhat at a time when they were generally declining, though it could hardly be contended that the NBPI or the prices and incomes policy was the main cause of the falling share of profits in the national income during these years.

Some other wider effects of the NBPI have been mentioned in the preceding parts of this chapter: lifting the level of wage expectations through the emphasis on productivity agreements, and, to some extent, through pointing up wage differentials — as has been said, these must be weighed up against any long term productivity gains which resulted from its work. This discussion is perhaps sufficient to indicate that any picture which ultimately emerges of the effects of the NBPI will be a mixed one.

But it would be quite unfair to measure the effects of the NBPI solely by examining the outcome of its recommendations in particular cases.

Very little is known about the outcome and effects of the NBPI's recommendations for change of a longer term nature; where it is known that the recommendations were implemented, it is not easy to know whether they would have occurred anyway, and, if so, whether they were accelerated or not by the NBPI; and finally, it is difficult to know if implementation of recommended changes in collective bargaining institutions, management methods and so on actually led in practice to cost savings or other benefits. In general it is too early to assess the effects of many of the NBPI's longer term recommendations; as time passes, however, they will become more and more difficult to isolate.

Reports in which the NBPI re-examined industries or firms reported on earlier furnish some information about the outcome of recommendations in earlier reports. There is a danger, however, that this selection is biased towards those who did not act upon NBPI recommendations. Moreover, this selection is biased to early reports. It would be a mistake to judge the effects of later NBPI reports by the outcome of early reports which were less detailed and often designed primarily to have a wider effect on the economy.

Nevertheless even a brief inspection shows that little effective action was taken on a significant number of early NBPI reports. Some examples include: road haulage workers; local authority, gas, water and the National Health Service workers; electrical contracting; solicitors; bricks; newspapers; engineering and buses. In a few of these, there had been some slight progress but the NBPI certainly regarded it as inadequate e.g. buses, and it was not clear that the progress was attributable to the NBPI's reports. Even worse, in some cases, recommendations had been acted upon with no apparent worthwhile effect − the bakery industry; and in one case, the industrial civil service, some adverse effects seemed to occur. These reports do show evidence of action on some recommendations. The recommendations in early reports on the brewing and cement industries for the adoption of operations research techniques were implemented, and the NBPI's first report on motor garages and services seems to have had some effects. However, the predominant impression from the evidence of second reports is that action on implementing early reports was generally slow.

It is fair to add, however, that most reports in which the NBPI took a second look at an industry (especially from after the middle of 1969) appeared to have been very carefully formulated after full consultation with the industry and to contain sensible, practicable and concrete suggestions for change which were likely to be of benefit to the industry. Some examples are the report on *Pay and Prices of the London Brick Company* (150) (LBC has in fact continued work on the construction of a model which the NBPI formulated in some detail in the report); it is evident that the national newspapers should have taken measures suggested by the NBPI in the second report to control newsprint utilisation and, in fact, a number of the main recommendations were almost immediately implemented. The second report on the *Industrial Civil Service* (146) contained very careful proposals for reforms, which will certainly serve as the starting point, probably the basis, of the future reorganisation of the collective bargaining structure of the

Industrial Civil Service; the NBPI's second report on Pay of Ancillary Workers in the National Health Service contains some specific proposals for greater efficiency which will undoubtedly be acted upon.

Turning to what little is known about the effects of recommendations which were not dealt with in return references, the NBPI had some definite successes. It was noted in Chapter 4 that the main recommendations of the report on Bank Charges are in the process of being put into effect, though the Board's report was only one factor in the change. The work on the reorganisation of the pay of the armed forces was an important achievement. The NBPI's pricing recommendations especially in the nationalised industries were strikingly successful. The Post Office accepted most of the Board's recommendations concerning marginal cost pricing and the recommendations on the structure of telephone charges were eventually adopted. British Rail introduced a more flexible pricing policy after the NBPI's recommendations in Report 72. A good number of the specific recommendations on pricing policy in the gas and coal industries were successful.

It is very clear that the detailed recommendations of a number of reports published in 1970 and 1971 will be implemented. Following the report on ITV Contractors in 1970, several programme contractors discussed the practical application of the manpower and studio scheduling model developed in that report. As was noted, similar followup discussions were held with national newspapers after the NBPI's second report. It was too close to the end of the NBPI's life for this followup procedure to be developed.

On the other hand, it is known that very little action was taken on other reports, of which the report on local authorities is a well-known example. One reason for the apparent slowness in making changes was that many NBPI recommendations were for change of a long term character and quick results could not be expected. The most that could be hoped for was some acceleration of the rate of change. NBPI reports themselves did not always seem to recognise that much of the change it sought would take years rather than months; in addition, it should be taken into account that the NBPI probably exaggerated somewhat the potential for change as a deliberate tactic to accelerate change; in such cases, it is a mistake to measure the success of its report by comparing results with recommendations.

In general, in a number of cases where no significant action was taken to implement NBPI reports, it is difficult to know whether the failure of the NBPI's recommendations amounts to an indictment of the NBPI or the incompetence or intransigence of management or trade unions or both.

It would be going too far to draw many conclusions about the usefulness of the NBPI from this sketchy information though it is not unreasonable to note that considered simply as an efficiency stimulating body the NBPI's costs were not very great; it probably had few perverse effects. On the other hand, where it was successful, the benefits seemed to be very large. There is one other very important consideration to take into account in examining the effects of NBPI reports on those reported on. The effects of a report cannot be assessed simply by determining if specific recommendations were or were not adopted. There were reports in which the adoption of work study, productivity bargaining, or job evaluation for example, was proposed. Even if these specific remedies were not adopted, industries may have been spurred into taking other steps to overcome problems pointed up by the NBPI. The mere fact that an investigation is undertaken into a firm or industry's efficiency or its institutions may sometimes lead to significant changes, even if not along the lines recommended by the investigator. In addition, measures suggested for improvement in one part of a business may spread to another part. Thus recommendations for the use of performance indicators in the production area may prove to be applicable in other parts such as marketing.

In conclusion, this discussion of the effects of the NBPI has been deliberately inconclusive, because it has been outside the main purpose of the study to examine the impact of the Board. The chief object has been to provide an historical account of its role, operation and methods of enquiry. It is hoped that a picture has emerged of a body from whose work and methods of operation there is much to learn.

Appendix A. Members of the National Board for Prices and Incomes

The Rt. Hon. Aubrey Jones, B.Sc.(Econ).	26.4.65 – 31.10.70	Chairman	Formerly Chairman of Stavely Industries Ltd. and previously Minister of Fuel and Power and Minister of Supply
The Lord Peddie, M.B.E., J.P.	26.4.65 – 31.3.71	26.4.65 – 31.8.68 Full time Member 1.9.68 – 31.10.70 Joint Dep. Chairman 1.11.70 – 31.3.71 Chairman	Formerly Director of the Co-operative Wholesale Society Ltd and the Co-operative Insurance Society Ltd.
The Rt. Hon. H.A. Marquand, M.A., D.Sc.	3.5.65 – 2.5.68	Joint Deputy Chairman	Formerly Minister of Pensions (1948–51) and Minister of Health (1951)
D.A.C. Dewdney, B.Sc., C.B.E.	8.6.65 – 31.12.69	8.6.65 – 30.6.66 Joint Dep. Chairman 1.7.66 – 31.12.69 Part time Member	Managing Director of Esso Petroleum Ltd. and subsequently Chairman, Anglesey Aluminium Co. Ltd.
R. Turvey, B.Sc. (Econ).	1.9.67 – 31.3.71	1.9.67 – 31.8.68 Full time Member 1.9.68 – 31.10.70 Joint Dep. Chairman 1.11.70 – 31.3.71 Deputy Chairman	Formerly Chief Economist with the Electricity Council
Dr. J.E. Mitchell, M.A., Ph.D.	26.4.65 – 25.10.68	Part time	Reader in Economics, University of Nottingham
R.G. Middleton D.S.C., LL.B.	26.4.65 – 11.10.68	Part time	Senior Partner in Coward Chance & Co., Solicitors
J.F. Knight, B.A., F.C.A.	26.4.65 – 25.4.67	Part time	Financial Director of Unilever Ltd.
P.E. Trench, C.B.E., T.D., J.P., B.Sc.	26.4.65 – 10.5.68	Part time	Director of the National Federation of Building Trade Employers
R. Willis.	26.4.65 – 31.7.67	Part time	Formerly Joint General Secretary of the National Graphical Association

Prof. H.A. Clegg, M.A.	1.3.66 – 31.8.67	Full time	Formerly Fellow of Nuffield College, Oxford
Prof. B.R. Williams, M.A.	12.12.66 – 31.8.67	Part time	Stanley Jevons Professor of Political Economy, University of Manchester
Prof. W.B. Reddaway, M.A. F.B.A.	1.9.67 – 31.3.71	Part time	Director of the Department of Applied Economics, and subsequently Professor of Political Economy, University of Cambridge.
R.C. Mathias, O.B.E.	1.9.67 – 15.4.68 (deceased)	Full time	Formerly South Wales Regional Secretary of Transport and General Workers Union
E. Brough, M.A.	1.10.67 – 31.3.70	Part time	Head of Marketing Division, Unilever Ltd.
Prof. H.A. Turner, B.Sc., M.A., Ph.D.	1.10.67 – 31.3.71	Part time	Montague Burton Professor of Industrial Relations, University of Cambridge.
Prof. J. Woodward, M.A., D.P.S.A.	1.2.68 – 31.8.70	Part time	Reader and subsequently Professor of Industrial Sociology at the Imperial College of Science and Technology, London
W.L. Heywood, C.B.E.	1.3.68 – 30.6.70	Full time	Formerly Lay Member of the Restrictive Practices Court and previously General Secretary of the National Union of Dyers, Bleachers and Textile Workers, member of the General Council of the Trades Union Congress
M.B. Forman, T.D.	1.4.68 – 31.3.70	Part time	Personnel Director, Steel Tube Division, Tube Investments Ltd. Director of Steel Tube Division Services Ltd.
The Lord Wright of Ashton-under-Lyne, C.B.E.	1.7.68 – 31.3.71	Part time	Formerly General Secretary of the Amalgamated Weavers' Association and Chairman of the Trades Union Congress.
J.E. Mortimer.	5.8.68 – 31.1.71 / 1.2.71 – 31.3.71	Full time / Part time	Formerly a National Official of the Draughtsmen's and Allied Technicians Association and subsequently Board Member for Industrial Relations, London Transport Executive.

G.F. Young, C.B.E., J.P., M.I.Mech.E.	19.9.68 – 31.3.71	Part time	Chairman of Tempered Group Ltd., and formerly Pro-Chancellor and Chairman of the Council of the University of Sheffield
Admiral Sir Desmond Dreyer G.C.B., C.B.E., D.S.C., J.P.	28.10.68 – 31.3.71	Part time	Formerly Chief Adviser (Personnel & Logistics) Ministry of Defence; formerly Chief of Naval Personnel & Second Sea Lord.
Dr. H.G. Reid, B.Sc., Ph.D.	1.4.69 – 31.3.70	Part time	Formerly General Manager (Commercial Services), Imperial Chemical Industries Ltd.

The appointments shown are those held either before or at the time of membership of the Board.

Secretaries to the Board

A.A. Jarratt, C.B.   1.6.65 – 31.3.68

K.H. Clucas, C.B.   1.4.68 – 31.3.71

Appendix B. Productivity, Prices and Incomes Policy: White Papers and Legislation

	Date	*Cmnd No.*
Joint Statement of Intent on Productivity Prices and Incomes	December, 1964	
Machinery of Prices and Incomes Policy	February, 1965	2577
Prices and Incomes Policy	April, 1965	2639
Prices and Incomes Policy: An 'Early Warning' System	November, 1965	2808
Prices and Incomes Standstill	July, 1966	3073
Prices and Incomes Act 1966	August, 1966	
Prices and Incomes Standstill: Period of Severe Restraint	November, 1966	3150
Prices and Incomes Policy after 30th July 1967	March, 1967	3235
Prices and Incomes Act, 1967	July, 1967	
Productivity, Prices and Incomes Policy in 1968 and 1969	April, 1968	3590
Prices and Incomes Act, 1968	July, 1968	
Productivity, Prices and Incomes Policy after 1969	December, 1969	4237

Appendix C. NBPI Published Reports

Report No.	Reference	Gazetted (i.e. formally referred)	Published	Cmnd. No.
1.	Road Haulage Rates (Interim)	6.5.65	28.6.65	2695
2.	Wages, Costs and Prices in the Printing Industry	18.5.65	17.8.65	2750
3.	Prices of Bread and Flour	6.5.65	1.9.65	2760
4.	Prices of Household and Toilet Soaps, Soap Powders and Soap Flakes, and Soapless Detergents	6.5.65	11.10.65	2791
5.	Remuneration of Administrative and Clerical Staff in the Electricity Supply Industry	16.6.65	25.10.65	2801
6.	Salaries of Midland Bank Staff	17.6.65	24.11.65	2839
7.	Electricity and Gas Tariffs—London Electricity Board and Scottish, South Western and Wales Gas Board	18.6.65 +20.10.65	22.12.65	2862
8.	Pay and Conditions of Service of British Railways Staff (Conciliation, Salaried and Workshop Grades)	15.10.65	14.1.65	2873
9.	Wages in the Bakery Industry (First Report)	3.12.65	19.1.66	2878
10.	Armed Forces Pay	25.11.65	28.1.66	2881
11.	Pay of the Higher Civil Service	25.11.65	28.1.66	2882
12.	Coal Prices	20.12.65	24.2.66	2919
13.	Costs, Prices and Profits in the Brewing Industry	26.1.66	19.4.66	2965
14.	Road Haulage Charges (Final Report)	6.5.65	21.4.66	2968
15.	Scottish Teachers' Salaries	24.1.66	24.5.66	3005
16.	Pay and Conditions of Busmen	4.3.66	26.5.66	3012
17.	Wages in the Bakery Industry (Final Report)	3.12.65	9.6.66	3019
18.	Pay of Industrial Civil Servants	21.10.65	21.6.66	3034
19.	General Report, April 1965 to July 1966	—	23.8.66	3087
20.	Laundry and Dry Cleaning Charges	4.1.66	7.9.66	3093

Report No.	Reference	Gazetted (i.e. formally referred)	Published	Cmnd. No.
21.	Coal Distribution Costs	7.3.66	7.9.66	3094
22.	Rate of Interest on Building Society Mortgages	24.5.66	14.11.66	3136
23.	Productivity and Pay during the Period of Severe Restraint	24.8.66	15.12.66	3167
24.	Wages and Condition in the Electrical Contracting Industry	1.7.66	22.12.66	3172
25.	Pay of workers in Agriculture in England and Wales	16.12.66	2.2.67	3199
26.	Prices of Standard Newsprint	8.12.66	23.2.67	3210
27.	Pay of Workers in the Retail Drapery, Outfitting and Footwear Trades	16.12.66	9.3.67	3224
	Pay of Workers in the Retail Drapery, and Footwear Trades: Statistical Supplement	—	18.4.67	3224—1
28.	Prices of Compound Fertilisers	8.12.66	13.3.67	3228
29.	The Pay and Conditions of Manual Workers in Local Authorities, the National Health Service, Gas and Water Supply	6.8.66	16.3.67	3230
	The Pay and Conditions of Manual Workers in Local Authorities, the National Health Service, Gas and Water Supply Statistical Supplement	—	4.5.67	3230—1
30.	Pay and Conditions of Limbfitters employed by J.E. Hanger and Co.	9.1.67	6.4.67	3245
31.	Distribution Costs of Fresh Fruit and Vegetables	3.10.66	26.4.67	3265
32.	Fire Service Pay	19.12.66	16.5.67	3287
33.	The Remuneration Of Milk Distributors (Interim Report)	13.1.67	23.5.67	3294
34.	Bank Charges	22.6.66	24.5.67	3292
35.	Pay and Conditions of Merchant Navy Officers	26.4.67	2.6.67	3302
36.	Productivity Agreements	24.8.66	13.6.67	3311
37.	Costs and Charges in the Motor Repairing and Servicing Industry	24.8.66	8.8.67	3368
38.	Portland Cement Prices	24.2.67	10.8.67	3381
39.	Costs and Prices of Aluminium Semi-Manufactures	24.8.66	11.8.67	3378
40.	Second General Report July 1966 to August 1967	—	31.8.67	3394
41.	Salaries of Staff employed by the General Accident Fire and Life Assurance Corporation Ltd.	9.6.67	7.9.67	3398
42.	Pay of Electricity Supply Workers	11.8.67	19.9.67	3405

Report No.		Gazetted (i.e. formally referred)	Published	Cmnd. No.
43.	Costs and Revenue of National Daily Newspapers	27.7.67	19.10.67	3435
44.	London Weighting in the Non-Industrial Civil Service	21.3.67	2.11.67	3436
45.	Pay of Chief and Senior Officers (1) in Local Government Service and (2) in the Greater London Council	(1) 6.12.66 (2)29.11.66	23.11.67	3473
46.	The Remuneration of Milk Distributors (Final Report)	17.1.67	28.11.67	3477
47.	Prices of Fletton and Non-Fletton Bricks	26.5.67	30.11.67	3480
48.	Charges, Costs and Wages in the Road Haulage Industry	18.8.67	6.12.67	3482
	Statistical Supplement:	—	8.3.68	3482–1
49.	Pay and Conditions of Service of Workers in the Engineering Industry (First Report on the Engineering Industry)	16.5.67	19.12.67	3495
	Statistical Supplement: Pay and Conditions of Staff Workers in the Engineering Industry	—	6.3.68	3495–1
50.	Productivity Agreements in the Bus Industry	25.7.67	21.12.67	3498
51.	Pay and Productivity of Industrial Employees of the United Kingdom Atomic Energy Authority	17.10.67	2.1.68	3499
52.	Costs and Charges in the Radio and Television Rental and Relay Industry	26.1.67	25.1.68	3520
53.	Flour Prices	12.1.68	1.2.68	3522
54.	Remuneration of Solicitors	10.2.67	8.2.68	3529
55.	Distributors' Margins in Relation to Manufacturers' Recommended Prices	28.12.67	22.2.68	3546
56.	Proposals by the London Transport Board for fare increases in the London Area	5.10.67	7.3.68	3561
57.	Gas Prices (First Report)	5.10.67	18.3.68	3567
58.	Post Office Charges	5.10.67	18.3.68	3574
59.	Bulk Supply Tariff of the Central Electricity Generating Board	5.10.67	18.3.68	3575
60.	Pay of Nurses and Midwives in the National Health Service	30.6.67	28.3.68	3585
61.	Prices of Secondary Batteries	13.2.68	10.4.68	3597
62.	Increases in Rents of Local Authority Housing	12.12.67	25.4.68	3604
	Increases in Rents of Local Authority Housing (Statistical Supplement)	—	1.10.68	3604–1
63.	Pay of Municipal Busmen	27.1.68	26.4.68	3605
64.	Increase in Prices in Mecury Hearing Aid Batteries manufactured by Mallory Batteries Ltd.	13.2.68	13.5.68	3625

Report No.	Reference	Gazetted (i.e. formally referred)	Published	Cmnd. No.
65.	Payment by Results Systems	23.3.67	14.5.68	3627
	Payments by Results Systems (Supplement)	–	10.12.68	3627–1
66.	Price of Butyl Rubber	16.2.68	13.5.68	3626
67.	Passenger Fares and Freight Charges of the North of Scotland, Orkney and Shetland Shipping Company Ltd.	30.1.68	16.5.68	3631
68.	Agreement made between certain Engineering Firms' and Draughtsmens' and Allied Technicians' Association	20.2.68	16.5.68	3632
69.	Pay and Conditions of Busmen Employed by the Corporation of Belfast, Glasgow and Liverpool	1.3.68	23.5.68	3646
70.	Standing Reference on the Pay of the Armed Forces	2.11.67	30.5.68	3651
71.	Architects' Costs and Fees	11.4.67	29.5.68	3653
72.	Proposed Increases by British Railways Board in certain Country-wide Fares and Charges	5.10.67	30.5.68	3656
73.	The Prices of Hoover Domestic Appliances	13.2.68	8.6.68	3671
74.	Agreement relating to Terms and Conditions of Employment of Staff employed by the Prudential and Pearl Assurance Companies	22.3.68	21.6.68	3674
75.	Costs and Prices of the Chocolate and Sugar Confectionery Industry	4.1.68	3.7.68	3694
76.	Increase in Rental Charges for the Equipment hired from I.B.M. U.K. Ltd.	11.4.68	10.7.68	3699
77.	Third General Report August 1967 to July 1968	–	25.7.68	3751
78.	Award Relating to Terms and Conditions of Employment in the Road Passenger Transport Department of Rochdale County Borough Council	30.5.68	26.7.68	3723
79.	National Guidelines Covering Productivity Payments in the Electricity Supply Industry	3.5.68	30.7.68	3726
80.	Distributors' Margins on Paint, Childrens' Clothing, Household Textiles and Propri-etary Medicines	14.5.68	13.8.68	3737
81.	Pay Awards made by the City and County of Bristol to staff employed in its dock undertaking	30.5.68	23.8.68	3752
82.	Report on an Agreement relating to the Pay of Sawyers and Woodcutting Machinists in the Sawmilling Industry	21.6.68	20.9.68	3768
83.	Job Evaluation	23.3.67	26.9.68	3772
	Job Evaluation (Supplement)	–	10.12.68	3772–1

Report No.	Reference	Gazetted (i.e. formally referred)	Published	Cmnd. No.
84.	Report on a Settlement relating to the Pay of certain workers employed in the Thermal Insulation Contracting industry	16.8.68	8.10.68	3784
85.	Pay and Conditions of Busmen employed by the Corporation of Dundee	13.8.68	15.10.68	3791
86.	Pay of Staff Workers in the Gas Industry	25.7.68	24.10.68	3795
87.	Proposed Increase in London Taxicab Fares	28.6.68	25.10.68	3796
88.	Pay of Pilots employed by the British Overseas Airways Corporation	31.5.68	29.10.68	3789
89.	Office Staff Employment Agencies Charges and Salaries	22.3.68	14.11.68	3828
90.	Pay of Vehicle Maintenance Workers in British Road Services	27.8.68	4.12.68	3848
91.	Pay and Conditions in the Civil Engineering Industry	31.5.68	28.11.68	3836
92.	Pay and Conditions in the Building Industry	31.5.68	28.11.68	3837
93.	Pay and Conditions in the Construction Industry other than Building and Civil Engineering	31.5.68	28.11.68	3838
	Statistical Supplement: Reports Nos. 91, 92 and 93 (Supplement). Pay and Conditions in the Building Industry, the Civil Engineering Industry, and the Construction Industry other than Building and Civil Engineering	—	1.4.69	3982
94.	Productivity Agreements in the Road Haulage Industry	13.8.68	5.12.68	3847
95.	Pay and Conditions of Busmen employed by the Corporation of Wigan	10.9.68	6.12.68	3845
96.	Pay of Busmen employed by the Corporation of Great Yarmouth	10.9.68	6.12.68	3844
97.	Distributors' Costs and Margins on Furniture, Domestic Electrical Appliances and Footwear	17.8.67	17.12.68	3858
98.	Standing Reference on the Pay of University Teachers in Great Britain (First Report)	2.11.67	18.12.68	3866
99.	Pay of Maintenance Workers Employed by Bus Companies	13.9.68	2.1.69	3868
100.	Synthetic Organic Dyestuffs and Organic Pigments Prices	19.9.68	28.1.69	3895
101.	Pay of Workers in Agriculture in England and Wales	3.1.69	30.1.69	3911
102.	Gas Prices (Second Report)	5.10.67	13.2.69	3924
103.	Pay and Productivity in the Car Delivery Industry	8.10.68	18.2.69	3929

Report No.	Reference	Gazetted (i.e. formally referred)	Published	Cmnd. No.
104.	Pay and Conditions of Service of Engineering Workers (Second Report on the Engineering Industry)	16.5.67	20.2.69	3931
105.	Pay of General Workers and Craftsmen in Imperial Chemical Industries Ltd.	28.11.68	25.2.69	3941
106.	Pay in the London Clearing Banks	29.11.68	28.2.69	3943
107.	Top Salaries in the Private Sector and Nationalised Industries	2.7.68	25.3.69	3970
108.	Pay and Conditions in the Electrical Contracting Industry in Scotland	24.12.68	20.3.69	3966
109.	Pay of Salaried Staff in Imperial Chemical Industries Ltd.	31.12.68	28.3.69	3981
110.	Pay and Conditions in the Clothing Manufacturing Industries	1.10.68	17.4.69	4002
	Pay and Conditions in the Clothing Manufacturing Industries (Supplement)	—	17.7.69	4002–1
111.	Steel Prices	24.12.68	21.5.69	4033
112.	Proposals by the London Transport Board for Fares Increases	20.2.69	15.5.69	4036
113.	Manufacturers' Prices of Toilet Preparations	24.12.68	3.6.69	4066
114.	Pay and duties of Light-Keepers	28.2.69	4.6.69	4067
115.	Journalists' Pay	11.3.69	10.6.69	4077
116.	Standing Reference on the Pay of the Armed Forces (Second Report)	2.11.67	16.6.69	4079
117.	Pay and Conditions of Workers in the Exhibition Contracting Industry	18.3.69	18.6.69	4088
118.	Prices of Non-Alloy Bright Steel Bars	7.3.69	19.6.69	4093
119.	Man-made Fibre and Cotton Yarn Prices (First Report)	20.2.69	19.6.69	4092
120.	Pay and Conditions in the Electrical Contracting Industry	13.12.68	27.6.69	4097
121.	Post Office Charges: Inland Parcel Post and Remittance Services	16.5.69	15.7.69	4115
122.	Fourth General Report July 1968 to July 1969	—	29.7.69	4130
123.	Productivity Agreements	26.11.68	5.8.69	4136
124.	Coal Prices	22.5.69	21.8.69	4149
125.	Salaries of certain staff employed by B.I.C.C. Ltd.	27.6.69	24.9.69	4168
126.	Remuneration of workers in Smithfield Market	24.4.69	9.10.69	4171
127.	Man-made Fibre and Cotton Yarn Prices (Second Report)	20.2.69	17.10.69	4180

Report No.	Reference	Gazetted (i.e. formally referred)	Published	Cmnd. No.
128.	Pay of Ground Staff at Aerodromes	11.4.69	28.10.69	4182
129.	Pay of Pilots employed by B.O.A.C.	5.6.69	4.11.69	4197
130.	Plasterboard Prices	5.8.69	5.11.69	4184
131.	Pay of certain employees in the Film Processing Industry	8.8.69	6.11.69	4185
132.	Salary Structures	25.7.68	18.11.69	4187
133.	Portland Cement Prices	15.8.69	12.11.69	4215
134.	Standing Reference on the Remuneration of Solicitors (First Report)	13.3.69	19.11.69	4217
135.	Pay Structure within H.M. Stationery Office	5.8.69	21.11.69	4219
136.	Beer Prices	24.4.69	28.11.69	4227
137.	Proposals by the British Railways Board for fare increases in the London Commuter Area	22.8.69	22.12.69	4250
138.	Coal Prices (First Report)	18.11.69	2.1.70	4255
139.	Electric Motor Prices	7.10.69	6.1.70	4258
140.	Pay and Conditions of Workers in the Milk Industry	22.7.69	22.1.70	4267
141.	Costs and Revenue of National Newspapers	19.9.69	5.2.70	4277
142.	Standing Reference of the Pay of the Armed Forces (Third Report)	2.11.67	25.2.70	4291
143.	Hours and Overtime in the London Clearing Banks	28.11.69	27.2.70	4301
144.	Bread Prices and Pay in the Baking Industry (First Report)	6.1.70	7.4.70	4329
145.	Standing Reference on the Pay of University Teachers in Great Britain (Second Report)	2.11.67	9.4.70	4334
146.	Pay and Conditions of Industrial Civil Servants	7.10.69	29.4.70	4351
147.	Margarine and Compound Cooking Fats	3.2.70	14.5.70	4368
148.	Prices of Primary Batteries proposed by the Ever Ready Company (Great Britain) Ltd.	24.2.70	19.5.70	4370
149.	Pay and other terms and conditions of employment of workers in the Pottery Industry	24.10.69	21.7.70	4411
150.	Pay and other terms and conditions of employment in the Fletton Brick Industry and the prices charged by the London Brick Company	27.1.70	23.7.70	4422
151.	Bread Prices and pay in the Baking Industry	6.1.70	28.7.70	4428
152.	Pay and Productivity in the Water Supply Industry	27.1.70	4.8.70	4434

Report No.	Reference	Gazetted (i.e. formally referred)	Published	Cmnd. No.
153.	Coal Prices (Second Report)	18.11.69	13.8.70	4455
	Coal Prices (Second Report) (Supplement)	—	27.4.71	4455–1
	Coal Prices (Second Report) (Supplement)	—	27.4.71	4455–2
154.	Tea Prices	14.5.70	14.8.70	4456
155.	Costs and efficiency in the Gas Industry	20.1.70	19.8.70	4458
156.	Costs and Revenues of Independent Television Companies	31.3.70	29.10.70	4524
157.	Standing Reference on the Pay of the Armed Forces (Fourth Report) – The Pay of Senior Officers	2.11.67	8.12.70	4513
158.	Standing Reference on the Pay of the Armed Forces (Fifth Report) – Separation Allowance	2.11.67	12.11.70	4529
159.	London Transport Fares	28.5.70	26.11.70	4540
160.	Costs, prices and profitability in the Ice-Cream manufacturing industry	16.6.70	3.12.70	4548
161.	Hours of Work, Overtime and Shiftworking	29.4.69	30.12.70	4554
	Hours of Work, Overtime and Shiftworking (Supplement)	—	30.12.70	4554–1
162.	Costs, charges and Productivity of the National Freight Corporation	9.6.70	13.1.71	4569
163.	Costs and charges in the Motor Repair and Servicing Industry	11.6.70	16.2.71	4590
164.	Standing Reference on the Remuneration of Solicitors (Second Report)	13.3.69	1.4.71	4624
165.	Prices, Profits and Costs in Food Distribution	29.5.70	20.4.71	4645
166.	Pay and Conditions of Service of Ancillary Workers in National Health Service Hospitals	22.5.70	28.4.71	4644
167.	Pay and Conditions of Service of Workers in the Laundry and Dry Cleaning Industry	22.5.70	28.4.71	4647
168.	Pay and Conditions in the Contract Cleaning Trade	22.5.70	28.4.71	4637
169.	General Problems of Low Pay	—	28.4.71	4648
170.	Fifth and Final General Report July 1969 to March 1971	—	29.4.71	4649
	Fifth and Final General Report (Supplement)	—	29.4.71	4649–1

Appendix D. Industries Reported on More than Once (Including Standing References)

Incomes

1. Agriculture (25, 101)

*2. Armed Forces (10, 70, 116, 142, 157, 158)

3. Bakery (9, 17, 144, 151)

4. Banks (6, 106, 143)

5. BOAC Pilots (88, 129)

6. Buses (16, 50, 63, 69, 78, 85, 95, 96, 99)

7. Electricity Supply (5, 42, 79)

8. Electrical Contracting (24, 108, 120)

9. Engineering Industry (49, 68, 104)

10. Gas (29, 86, 102, 155)

11. Industrial Civil Service (18, 146)

12. Insurance Prudential)
    Pearl)(41, 74)
    General Accident)

13. NHS Ancillary Workers (29, 166)

*14. Remuneration of Solicitors (54, 134, 164)

15. Road Haulage (48, 90, 94)

*16. University Teachers (98, 145)

17. Water Supply (29, 152)

* Denotes standing reference

Prices

1. Bakery — Bread, Flour (3, 53, 144, 151)

2. Brewing (13, 136)

3. British Rail (56, 72, 137)

4. Bricks (47, 150)

5. Portland Cement (38, 133)

6. Coal (12, 21, 124, 138, 153)

7. Gas Prices (7, 57, 102, 155)

8. London Transport (56, 112, 159)

9. Motor Repair and Servicing (37, 163)

10. Newspapers (43, 141)

11. Post Office Charges (58, 121)

12. Road Haulage (1, 14, 48)

Note: Some industries were investigated twice, once as an incomes reference, once as a prices reference. For example, Report 20 dealt with Laundry and Dry Cleaning Charges, whilst Report 167 dealt with Pay and Conditions of Service of Workers in the Laundry and Dry Cleaning Industry. Examples of this kind have been excluded from this Appendix.

Appendix E. NBPI Recommendations on Incomes

(a) Incomes increases were *fully approved* in 10 references

1. Electricity Clerical and Adminstrative Staff, Report No. 5;

2. Armed Forces, No. 10;

3. Higher Civil Service, No. 11;

4. Agricultural Workers, No. 25;

5. Prudential and Pearl Assurance Companies Staff, No. 74;

6. Bristol Docks Staff, No. 81;

7. Sawmilling, No. 82;

8. Thermal Insulation, No. 84;

9. Gas Staff, No. 86;

10. Agricultural Workers, No. 101.

(b) Incomes increases were *partly approved* in 24 references

1. Printing, No. 2;

2. Baking (interim report), No. 9;

3. Busmen, No. 16;

4. Baking (final report), No. 17;

5. Electrical Contracting, No. 24;

6. Retail Drapery, No. 27;

7. Local Authorities, N.H.S., Gas, Water Manuals, No. 29;

8. Firemen, No. 32;

9. Merchant Navy Officers, No. 35;

10. General Accident Staff, No. 41;

11. Electricity Supply, No. 42;

12. Chief Officers in Local Government, No. 45;

13. Road Haulage, No. 48;

14. Engineering, No. 49;

15. Atomic Energy Authority, No. 51;

16. Nurses and Midwives, No. 60;

17. Busmen in Liverpool, Glasgow and Belfast, No. 69;

18. British Road Service Maintenance, No. 90;

19. University Teachers, No. 98;

20. Bus Maintenance Workers, No. 99;

21. I.C.I. Manuals, No. 105;

22. Journalists, No. 115;

23. BICC Staff;

24. University Teachers, No. 145.

(c) Incomes Increases were *rejected* in 17 cases

1. Midland Bank Salaries, No. 6;

2. British Rail, No. 8;

3. Limb Fitters, No. 30;

4. Municipal Busmen, No. 63;

5. Draughtsmen, No. 68;

6. Busmen in Dundee, No. 85;

7. Civil Engineering, No. 91;

8. Building, No. 92;

9. Busmen in Wigan, No. 95;

10. Banks, No. 106;

11. Electrical Contracting in Scotland, No. 108;

12. I.C.I. Staff, No. 109;

13. Light-Keepers, No. 114;

14. Exhibition Industry, No. 117;

15. BOAC Pilots, No. 129;

16. Film Processing, No. 131;

17. Bank Overtime, No. 143.

Note: No distinction has been made been proposals/claims/offers/agreements for incomes increases. In general it is difficult to make satisfactory classification along the above lines. Thus, some partial acceptances were generous; others were not. In many reports the N.B.P.I., although rejecting incomes increases, pointed to ways in which earnings could be increased, sometimes at once, providing appropriate action was taken. The N.B.P.I. itself never attempted to construct a table of the above kind.

Appendix F. NBPI Recommendations on Prices

(a) *Price rises were fully accepted in 23 references*

1. Coal Prices, Report No. 12; 2. Laundry and Dry Cleaning, No. 20; 3. Building Society Interest Rates, No. 22; 4. Prices of Standard Newsprint, No. 26; 5. London Transport Fares, No. 56; 6. Gas Prices (First Report), No. 57; 7. Butyl Rubber, No. 66; 8. Fares and Charges of the North of Scotland Orkney & Shetland Shipping Company Ltd, No. 67; 9. British Rail Countryside Fares, No. 72 (the type of increase sought was rejected); 10. Chocolate and Sugar Confectionery, No. 75; 11. Synthetic Organic Dyestuffs and Organic Pigments Prices, No. 100; 12. London Transport Fares, No. 112; 13. Post Office Charges, No. 121; 14. Coal Prices, No. 124; 15. Plasterboard Prices, No. 130; 16. British Rail Fares in London Commuter Area, No. 137 with modifications; 17. Coal Prices (First Report), No. 138; 18. Bread Prices, No. 144; 19. Margarine and Compound Cooking Fats, No. 147; 20. Ever Ready Batteries, No. 148; 21. Gas Prices, No. 155; 22. London Transport Fares, No. 159; 23. Ice Cream Prices, No. 160.

(b) *Price rises were partly accepted in 20 references*

1. Soap and Detergent Prices, No. 4, standstill on prices and reductions in some cases; 2. Electricity and Gas Tariffs, No. 7, South West Gas Board 8% instead of 13%, other proposals agreed; 3. Compound Fertilisers, No. 28, 2s. instead of 5s. per ton; 4. Brick Prices, No. 47, increase limited to 4½% for London Brick Company; 5. Flour Prices, No. 53, increases limited to 8s. 3d. a sack for Bakers flour and 12s. 1d. for Springs flour; 6. Post Office Charges, No. 58, increases deferred for 6 – 12 months; 7. CEGB Tariff, No. 59, 3.75 per cent instead of 4.1 per cent; 8. Secondary Batteries, No. 61, 4 per cent instead of 3.75 to 7.5 per cent; 9. Local Authority Housing Rents, No. 62, increases limited to 7s. 6d. per dwelling in a 12 month period; 10. Hoover Domestic Appliances, No. 73, 3 per cent instead of 7.6 per cent for floor care appliances; 11. IBM Rental Charges, No. 76, 5 to 7 per cent instead of 10 per cent; 12. London Taxicab Fares, No. 87, 11½ per cent instead of 20 per cent; 13. Steel Prices, No. 111, increases to produce £40 millions instead of £50 – 55 millions; 14. Non-Alloy Bright Steel Bars, No. 118, 10 per cent instead of 20 per cent; 15. Man-made Fibres (First Report), No. 119, 5 per cent instead of 9 per cent originally proposed; 16. Portland Cement Prices, No. 133, 13s. 6d. per ton instead of 23s. 4d.; 17. Beer Prices, No. 136, 2d. per pint instead of 4.5d.; 18. Electric Motor Prices, No. 139, 4 per cent instead of 6.5 to 7.5 per cent; 19. Costs and Revenue of National Newspapers, No. 141, Daily Telegraph

1d. instead of 2d., other proposals accepted; 20. Coal Prices (Second Report), No. 153, 15 to 16 per cent on coking coal instead of 12.8 per cent on general purpose coal and 12.3 per cent on coking coal.

(c) *Price rises were rejected in 7 references*

1. Road Haulage Rates (Interim), No. 1, 5 per cent sought; 2. Prices of Bread and Flour, No. 3, various increases sought; 3. Costs, Profits and Prices in the Brewing Industry, No. 13, ½d. per pint sought; 4. Costs and Revenues of Newspapers, No. 43, 'Daily Mirror' sought 1d. increase; 5. Remuneration of Solicitors, No. 54, increase in county court charges approved but reduction in income from conveyancing recommended (Report No. 134 said much the same thing); 6. Mercury Hearing Aid Batteries, No. 64, 45 per cent sought; 7. Tea Prices, No. 154, increases of 2d. a 1 lb. could have been delayed or avoided.

Notes:

1) Classifications are necessarily somewhat arbitrary. 2) Price restructuring recommendations having little or no effect on the total amount of revenue obtained have been ignored. 3) References in which no specific price increase was examined are omitted (e.g. distributors margin 5 (Report 55), aluminium (39))

Appendix G. Industrial Relations Case Study Brief

The Clothing Manufacturing Industry Reference
Brief for Case Study Workers

The Clothing Industry has 20,000 establishments and 10 wages councils, therefore any programme of case studies that we are able to carry out can cover only a small fraction of the establishments concerned. If we are to be in any position to understand the operation of payment systems, negotiating procedures, the circumstances of low pay, the effects of cheap labour on production techniques and the special characteristics of women in employment, we shall require to undertake a number of case studies in depth. This paper is concerned with these depth studies.

1. *Background Information.* Obtain information relating to; type of company (part of group or individual company) private company, public company, partnership, whether it is expanding or contracting, its product range and production technology; Is the firm, or establishment, associated with any other company? Customers and how they are secured. Number of operatives, male and female and how distributed by grade and trade. Geographical position, the part of the trade in which it operates, and its position relative to other firms in the trade.

From this information it should be possible to decide how typical the establishment is within the trade and the degree of managerial and other sophistication that can be expected. Sufficient information should be collected to place the company within its industrial setting.

2. *Managerial Structure, and policy.* Managerial structure. What information on costs is available? Investment policy and investment programme over the last five years. Labour costs as a proportion of total costs.

3. *Productivity.* Productivity agreements? Any technical process which has increased productivity. If earnings are at or barely above wages council minima assess the reasons (could be poor quality labour, economic conditions, managerial efficiency, low productivity etc.). Assessment of the extent to which labour is being properly utilised.

4. *Industrial Relations.* Is the firm a member of a trade association if so what benefits arise from membership? Is it covered by any national voluntary agreements? Are there any local agreements? If so are they formal or informal When was the last general wage increase? What is the effect of wages council awards? Is the union recognised, how many members? Are there shop floor

representatives? If so how are they appointed and what kind of grievances do they handle? Do foremen and supervisors have industrial relations responsibilities? If so of what kind? How effective is shop floor organisation? Is there any problem in organising women workers? Have any shop stewards, or other union representatives attended any conferences of shop stewards courses run by the union, or organised by an educational authority? Naturally, workers and managements' views on these questions should be reported.

What attitudes are there towards Wages Councils, the possibility of their abolition, and if so on what could take their place. Does the existence of Wages Councils and National Voluntary Agreements mean that employers pay more or less than they otherwise would or do they make no difference?

5. *Manpower Questions*. How does management determine the general level of payments? Effect of local labour market. How is labour recruited? Is there a general labour shortage? Absenteeism. Training and skills — the extent to which skills have changed over the last five years. Labour turnover. Operatives interviewed should be asked about their working histories.

6. *The Production Cycle*. A pronounced production cycle is supposed to be a common feature of the industry and it is necessary to make some judgment on the extent to which management/labour relations are affected. It will be necessary to examine the extent to which production changes are outside management control. (The effect of fashion is clearly important, and the extent to which stocks can be held).

The firms' product market. Do they export and are there any special problems associated with production for export? The extent of demand fluctuation. Are fluctuations in production increased by the policy of retailers or cloth manufacturers? To what extent can demand fluctuation be anticipated so that production can be stabilised? Are fluctuations in demand met by using the level of employment or earnings of operatives? If so how does this operate? (Changing levels of work for home workers or sub-contractors, shorter hours for operatives, reduced piece-work earnings, short time, redundancy, extensive overtime working).

Production and earnings changes over five years would be of considerable interest — although the value of any statistics and the amount of time that should be spent collecting them is a decision which case study workers will have to make in the light of the time available and the significance of a production cycle to the firm. Workers and management views of all these questions should be sought.

7. *Earnings and Payments Systems*. Earnings and hours of a sample of operatives including home workers, except those who are self employed, one week each month over the past 12 months. Distinguish between bonus and other payments where relevant and possible. If there are ten or less operatives in the firm include every operative. 10 – 100 choose 10 on a random basis. For larger numbers use a 10% sample up to a maximum of 25. Where possible take one or two occupational groups (e.g. women machinists) and workers who have been working at the same job, at the same grade, for twelve months.

Describe fringe benefits – aid for travel, sickness, superannuation schemes, canteen benefits etc. Describe payments systems in detail. Is piece-work or production bonus paid for work issued (dead horse) or work completed? Are there 'good' 'bad' jobs? Who issues work and on what basis and is work study used? Is there a 'Recognised' level of bonus over and above which rates are cut or an investigation takes place? Whether a particular payments system operates efficiently or has 'broken down' should be considered in the light of the criteria contained in Report No. 65 'Payment by Results Systems' (availabl on request). How is work timed? Are times negotiated? What happens if there is a disagreement?

It will be necessary to decide whether there is any evidence which suggests that groups of women workers take up a 'less militant' attitude to payments questions than do men. It will be interesting to discover whether age or status (e.g. young single girls, young marrieds, married or unmarried with children, widows, and older workers) or any other common factors, would appear to explain attitudes. Together with detailed questioning and the accounts of various payments systems it may be possible to form an impression of the extent to which present payments systems are able to work to the satisfaction of management because women workers take a non-militant attitude in the bargaining process.

8. *Low Pay and Equal Pay.* Case study workers may be able to discover the extent to which women workers earning somewhere near or below the average for women workers make significant contributions to a household's income. Some parts of the industry regard this reference as relating to the equal pay issue. It would be interesting to have some views both from the management and a selection of employees on the question of equal pay. And upon the comparability of mens' and womens' employment.

This brief may be regarded as providing general guidelines. Within the terms of the reference case study workers may use their discretion about which aspects should be investigated in greater depth.

It will considerably help in the analysis of Case Studies if reports follow the plan of this brief.

Clothing Case Studies: Some possibilities for more precise information

2. Information on costs: especially standard and actual direct labour costs of the regular garment.

Labour costs and material costs (with trim) as % of total costs.

2. Investment programme (including leasing) over the last five years.
   – total invested
   – what machines and for what % of workers?
     Automatic sewing machine
     thread cutter on machine
     folder on machine
     automatic cutter; pattern grader
     powered pressing equipment
     specially designed workplaces with/without moving parts
     other

6. Exports
- exports as % of sales
- how far is export production concentrated in the home slack period?
- how are customers secured? own outlets, own or other sales force, franchised or unfranchised agents?

6. Any shiftwork

1. Industry organisation or employers' association:
Membership
What does your organisation or association do for you —

promotion, advertising
buying cloth
buying machinery
selling: contracting
market research
market information: prices, import
/export, new regulations; production and sales figures; forecasts
technical information

conduct labour negotiations
provide labour statistics, wage data
inform on conditions of work,
availability of labour,
health and safety
inform on training
standardise contracts
consultancy; interfirm comparisions
any other services

Appendix H. Industrial Relations Case Studies Analysis

Name of Reference (Number of Report)	Type of Case Study Worker	Number of Studies	Average days per study	Statistics data collected	Main subjects covered*												Labour Utilisation			Trade union organisation
					Employment, numbers, age structure etc.	Labour turnover, absence etc.	Hours of work, overtime etc.	Wage/salary system	Wage/salary structure	Low Pay	Labour Market Conditions	Productivity agreements considerations	Recent settlements	Conditions of employment	Workplace bargaining & I.R.	Local effects of national bargaining	Work measurement	Management control of costs	Restrictive practices	
Contract Cleaning Workers (168)	Mainly outside specialists	28	4	Yes	2	2	1	2	2	2	2	1	—	2	2	1	1	2	—	2
Laundry & Dry Cleaning Workers (167)	Mainly outside specialists	23	5	Yes	2	2	2	2	2	2	2	—	—	1	2	1	1	2	—	2
N.H.S. Ancillary Staff (166)	Mainly outside specialists	21	10	Yes	2	2	2	2	2	2	1	1	—	1	2	1	2	2	—	1
Hours of work, Overtime, and Shiftwork (161)	Outside specialists	50	20	Yes	1	2	2	1	2	2	2	2	1	1	2	2	1	2	1	1

* 1 = basic information collected
2 = studied in detail

Main subjects covered*

Name of Reference (Number of Report)	Type of Case Study Worker	Number of Studies	Average days per study	Statistics data collected	Employment, numbers, age structure etc.	Labour turnover, absence etc.	Hours of work, overtime etc.	Wage/salary system	Wage/salary structure	Low Pay	Labour Market Conditions	Productivity agreements considerations	Recent settlements	Conditions of employment	Workplace bargaining & I.R.	Local effects of national bargaining	Labour Utilisation — Work measurement	Labour Utilisation — Management control of costs	Labour Utilisation — Restrictive practices	Trade union organisation
Coal Prices (153)	Outside specialists	20	17	Yes	2	2	2	2	1	1	1			1	2	2	1	1		2
Gas Prices (155)	Outside specialists	25	6	Yes	1	1	2	2	2			2	2	1	1	2	1	1		1
Industrial Civil Servants (146)	IR Advisers and Enquiry Team	5	10	Yes	1	1	1	2	2	1	1	1	1	1	1	1	1	1		1
Milk Workers (140)	Mainly Enquiry Team	28	4	Yes		2	1	2	2			1		1	2					1
Salary Structures (132)	Outside specialists	23	15	Yes	1	1		2	2		2			2						
Pay of Airport Ground Staff (128)	Mainly Enquiry Team	18	5	Yes	1	1	1	1	2			1	1	1		1	1	1	1	1

* 1 = basic information collected
  2 = studied in detail

277

Name of Reference (Number of Report)	Type of Case Study Worker	Number of Studies	Average days per study	Statistics data collected	Employment, numbers, age structure etc.	Labour turnover, absence etc.	Hours of work, overtime etc.	Wage/salary system	Wage/salary structure	Low Pay	Labour Market Conditions	Productivity agreements considerations	Recent settlements	Conditions of employment	Workplace bargaining & I.R.	Local effects of national bargaining	Labour Utilisation: Work measurement	Labour Utilisation: Management control of costs	Labour Utilisation: Restrictive practices	Trade union organisation
Smithfield Market (126)	Enquiry Team	17	3	No	1	1	1	2	2		1	1		2	2		1	1	2	1
BICC (125)	Enquiry Team	7	3	No	1	1	1	2	2			1			2		1	1	2	
Productivity Agreements (123)	Mainly Outside specialists	40	7	Yes	1	1	2	2	2		1	2	1	1	2	1	1	1	2	
Exhibition Workers (117)	Enquiry Team	19	3	Yes	1	2	1	1	2			1		1	2	1	1	1	1	
Electrical Contracting (108 & 120)	Mainly Enquiry Team	30	4	Yes	1	1	1	2	2		1	2	2	1	1	2	1	1	1	1
Journalists' Pay (115)	Mainly Enquiry Team	17	2	No	1	1	1	2	2		1	1	2	1	2	2	1	1	1	

Main subjects covered*

* 1 = basic information collected
2 = studies in detail

278

Main subjects covered*

Name of Reference (Number of Report)	Type of Case Study Worker	Number of Studies	Average days per study	Statistics data collected	Employment, numbers, age structure etc.	Labour turnover, absence etc.	Hours of work, overtime etc.	Wage/salary system	Wage/salary structure	Low Pay	Labour Market Conditions	Productivity agreements considerations	Recent settlements	Conditions of employment	Workplace bargaining & I.R.	Local effects of national bargaining	Labour Utilisation: Work measurement	Labour Utilisation: Management control of costs	Labour Utilisation: Restrictive practices	Trade union organisation
Lightkeepers Pay and Duties (114)	Enquiry Team	10	2	No	1	1	1	1	2					2	1	1				1
Pay and Conditions in Clothing Manufacturing (110)	IR Branch and outside specialists	20 lge. 50 sml.	10 / 3	Yes	1	1	1	2	2	2	1	1	2	2	2	2				1
ICI Staff Salaries (109)	Enquiry Team	7	4	No	1	2		1	1			1					1			
ICI General Workers (105)	Enquiry Team	7	5	No	1	2	1	1	1		1	2	2		2	1				1
Engineering Workers (49 and 104)	IR Branch, outside specialists and Enquiry Team	47	3					2	2			1	1	1	1	1				1

* 1 = basic information collected
  2 = studies in detail

Name of Reference (Number of Report)	Type of Case Study Worker	Number of Studies	Average days per study	Statistics data collected	Employment, numbers, age structure etc.	Labour turnover, absence etc.	Hours of work, overtime etc.	Wage/salary system	Wage/salary structure	Low Pay	Labour Market Conditions	Productivity agreements considerations	Recent settlements	Conditions of employment	Workplace bargaining & I.R.	Local effects of national bargaining	Labour Utilisation — Work measurement	Labour Utilisation — Management control of costs	Labour Utilisation — Restrictive practices	Trade union organisation
					Main subjects covered*															
Car Delivery Industry	Enquiry Team	7	8	Yes	1	1	1	2	2			2		1	2	2	1			1
Bus Maintenance Workers (99)	Enquiry Team	9	5	Yes	1	1	1	2				2							1	
Busmens' Pay References (50, 63, 69, 78, 85, 95, 96)	Outside specialists and Enquiry Team	28	15	Yes	1	1				2	1	2					1	2	1	
Construction Industries (91, 92 & 93)	Mainly outside specialists	38	7	Yes	1	2		2	2			1	1	1	2	1		1	1	1
BRS Vehicle Maintenance Workers (90)	Enquiry Team	9	3	No	1	1	1		1			1		1	2		1	1	1	1

*1 = basic information collected
2 = studied in detail

Main subjects covered*

Name of Reference (Number of Report)	Type of Case Study Worker	Number of Studies	Average days per study	Statistics data collected	Employment, numbers, age structure etc.	Labour turnover, absence etc.	Hours of work, overtime etc.	Wage/salary system	Wage/salary structure	Low Pay	Labour Market Conditions	Productivity agreements considerations	Recent settlements	Conditions of employment	Workplace bargaining & I.R.	Labour Utilisation — Local effects of national bargaining	Labour Utilisation — Work measurement	Labour Utilisation — Management control of costs	Labour Utilisation — Restrictive practices	Trade union organisation
Thermal Insulation Workers (84)	Enquiry Team	7	3	Yes	1	1		2	2			1			2	1				1
Job Evaluation (83)	Enquiry Team	100 sml.	2	No	1			1	1			1			1	1				1
	Outside specialists	12 lge.	12	Yes	2	1		2	2			2			1					
Sawmilling Workers (82)	Enquiry Team	12	2	Yes	1	1	2	2			1	1		1						
Payment by Results (65)	Outside specialists and IR Branch	40	15	Yes	1	1	1	2	2		1	2			2	2	2			2
Nurses and Midwives (60)	Mainly outside specialists assisted by the Enquiry Team	11	20	Yes	2	2	2				1			2						
Productivity Agreements (36)	IR Branch & outside specialists	15	20	Yes	1	1	2	2	2			2		1	2			2	2	

* 1 = basic information collected
  2 = studied in detail

281

Notes:

1. The analysis has been based on the case study briefs. Hence, the emphasis may have been put on the wrong subjects in some cases.

2. In most cases the statistics collected by case study workers were of a fairly elementary nature, e.g. details of earnings to illustrate particular points.

3. Often it has been necessary to guess the number of days per study. The accuracy is greatest for the most recent references, so they have been put first.

4. The table relates to the main case studies made by the NBPI. There may be some exclusions.

5. Studies conducted by the Enquiry Team when made principally under the direction of the Management Operations Branch are included in Appendix I.

Appendix I. Enquiry Team Studies Analysis

Report No.	Title	No. of man days spent on visits	E.T. or Supp. Assistance	No. of Places visited	Av. no. of man days study	Were stats data collected?	Work Study O & M J.E.	Prod. Plan/& Control	Invest. Plan. Corporate Plan	Purchasing	Labour Utilisation	Plant Utilisation	Cost Reduction Fields	Productivity	Maintenance	Management Structure	Marketing	Distribution	Pricing Policy	Or Effectiveness	OR and other Man. Techniques	Pay and Conditions	Studies for I.R. Branch	Studies for Financial Adviser	Comment
26	Standard Newsprint	9	4	7	1	×		×		×															Obtain background information for SWP
27	Retail Drapery Workers	–	2	3	?	×																			Feasibility Study of Statistical Quest.
29	LAS/NHS/Gas/Water Manual Workers	14	3	13	1	×																			Feasibility Study
30	Limb Fitters	20	5	14	1½	×																			All Reference Work
31	Distribution Costs of Fresh Fruit and vegetables	22	4	10	2¾	×	×				×			×											Use of Clerical Labour
32	Fire Services	12	1	8	1½	×					×														Pilot Survey
35	Merchant Navy Officers	6	5	9	¾	×					×			×											Ascertain effects of Productivity Agreements
36	Productivity Agreements	19	4	23	¾			×			×			×											Technological Study
38	Portland Cement Prices	34	3	17	2	×								×											Assisting Consultant in Analysis of Survey (Desk Study)
39	Costs and Prices of Aluminium Semi-Manufacturers	–	1																						Study of Salary Structures
41	Salaries of Staff Employed by the Accident and Life Assurance	2	1	1	¾												×								Obtaining information from PRU for SWP
44	London Weighting	2	1	1		×																			Investigating Milk Packaging Methods
46	Renumeration of Milk Distributors (Final)	6	2	7	1																				Obtain information about rise in rates and current practice in demurrage
48	Road Haulage – Charges, Costs and Wages	2	2	10	¼	×													×						
50	Productivity Agreements in the Bus Industry	9	5	6	1½	×	×				×			×											
52	Radio and Television Rental Relay Industry Charges	–	2												×				×						Ascertain rental charges + Paper on International Comparison No Visits
54	Solicitors Renumeration	140	6	88	1¾	×					×								×						Survey of activities in County Courts and Offices
55	Distributors Margins in Relation to Manufacturers Recommended Prices	179	37	160	1	×												×	×						Questionnaire retrieval. 30 Customs and Excise Officers used.

Enquiry Team Studies Analysis

Main Fields or Subjects of Enquiry

Report No.	Title	No. of man days spent on visits	E.T. or Supp. Assistance	No. of Places visited	Av. no. of man days study	Were stats data collected?	Work Study O & M J.E.	Prod. Plan/& Control	Invest. Plan, Corporate Plan	Purchasing	Labour Utilisation	Plant Utilisation	Cost Reduction Fields	Productivity	Maintenance	Management Structure	Marketing	Distribution	Pricing Policy	Or Effectiveness	OR and other Man. Techniques	Pay and Conditions	Studies for I.R. Branch	Studies for Financial Adviser	Comment
56	Proposals by London Transport and British Rail for Fare Increase in the London Area	7	2	3	2						x			x					x		x	x			
59	The Bulk Supply of the Central Electricity Board	2	2	2	1		x				x			x						x	x				International Comparisons Plus Desk Study on Technology
60	Nurses and Midwives Pay	67	6	37	2	x	x				x			x							x				+ International Comparisons
61	Prices of Secondary Batteries	–	2	–	–																				Telephone Enquiries re: Prices of Batteries
63	Pay of Municipal Busmen	184	13	12	15	x	x				x			x											+ Low Pay Staff Shortages
65	Payment by Results	95	9	24	4	x	x				x			x						x					WAGON Utilisation
68	Agreements on Draughtsmen Pay	–	4	–	–									x											Desk Study of Productivity Agreements
69	Pay of Busmen in Belfast, Glasgow, Liverpool	73	10	3	24	x	x				x			x							x				+ Low Pay Staff Shortages
71	Architects Fees and Costs	114	4	125	1	x	x				x			x					x	x					+ International Comparison
72	British Rail Countrywide Fares and Charges														x										
74	Pay Conditions – Prudential and Pearl Assurance Cos.	7	1	5	1½	x	x				x			x											
75	Chocolate and Sugar Confectionery	32	6	13	2½							x													
78	Rochdale Buses	19	4	1	19	x	x				x			x								x			E.T. not involved to great extent
80	Distribution Margins on Paint, Children's Clothing, Household Textiles, Proprietory Materials	184	18	?	?									x					x			x			+ Low pay Staff Shortages
81	Bristol Docks, Clerical Workers' Pay	9	2	2	4½	x	x				x			x								x			Retrieval of Questionnaires from numerous retailers
82	Pay of Sawyers and Woodcutting Machinists in the Sawmilling Industry	31	4	12	2½	x	x				x	x									x	x			Recruitment
83	Job Evaluation	153	8	104	1½	x	x x				x	x										x			
84	Pay of Thermal Insulation Workers	21	4	7	3	x	x				x			x								x			+ Manpower Shortages
85	Pay of Dundee Busmen	16	4	1	16	x	x				x			x							x	x			+ Low Pay Staff Shortages
86	Pay of Staff Workers in the Gas Industry	20	6	7	3	x					x			x								x			
87	London Taxicabs Fares	68	6	286	4	x	x							x								x			

Enquiry Team Studies Analysis

Main Fields or Subjects of Enquiry

Report No.	Title	No. of man days spent on visits	E.T. of Supp. Assistance	No. of Places visited	Av. no. of man days study	Were stats data collected?	Work Study O & M J.E.	Prod.Plan/& Control	Invest. Plan. Corporate Plan	Purchasing	Labour Utilisation	Plant Utilisation	Cost Reduction Fields	Productivity	Maintenance	Management Structure	Marketing	Distribution	Pricing Policy	Or Effectiveness	OR and other Man Techniques	Pay and Conditions	Studies for I.R. Branch	Studies for Financial Adviser	Comment
89	Office Staff Employment Agencies – Charges, salaries	54	4	27	2	×	× ×				×			×					×			×			
90	Vehicle Maintenance Workers BRP	28	5	9	3	×	×				×			×											
91	Pay and Conditions in the Civil Engineering Industry	55	5	7	8	×	×				×			×								×			
92	Pay and Conditions in the Building Industry	17	3	3	5	×	×				×			×								×			
93	Pay and Conditions in the Construction Industry	—	—	—	—																				Included in Building
94	Road Haulage Industry	51	6	7	7	×	×				×			×	×				×			×			Pay Structure Industrial Relations
95	Pay of Wigan Busmen	28	6	1	23	×	×				×			×								×			+ Low Pay Staff Shortages
96	Pay of Gt. Yarmouth Busmen	—	6	?	?																				E.T. Not Involved
97	FEF Dist. Margins	75		?	?			×				×			×						×				Retrieval of Questionnaires from from numerous retailers
99	Pay of Bus Companies Maintenance Workers	46	7	9	5	×	×				×			×	×							×			E.T. not seriously invo.ved
100	Dyestuff and Organic Pigments	—																							
102	Gas Prices (Second Report)	23	2	8	3	×	× ×				×			×					×				×		Examination of Consumer Service with
103	Car Delivery (Pay and Productivity)	56	8	7	8	×					×			×								×			
104	Engineering Workers	29	5	15	2	×					×			×								×			Labour Turnover Recruitment
105	ICI (Workers and Craftsmen) Pay	34	6	6	6	×		×			×	×		×								×			Desk Studies – Analysis of Productivity
106	Bank Staff Salaries	—		—	113	×					×			×								×			E.T. not involved
107	Top Salaries	—																							
108	Electrical Contracting Industry	8	3	4	2	×	×				×			×		×						×			
109	ICI Salaried Staff Scotland	32	9	7	4½	×	×				×			×								×			Recruitment and Turnover Pay Systems
110	Pay and Conditions in the Clothing Industry Industries	117	14	70	1½	×	×	×			×	×		×		×	×	×	×			×			
112	Proposals by London Transport Board for Fares Increases	65	10	6	10	×	×				×			×								×	×		Restrictive Practices Union Attitudes
113	Manufacturers Prices of Toilet Preparations	9	4	6	1½	×																			
114	Pay and Duties of Light-Keepers	20	5	8	2¾	×					×			×								×			Recruitment
115	Pay of Journalists	32	8	17	2	×					×			×					×			×			+ Social Survey

Enquiry Team Studies Analysis

Main Fields or Subjects of Enquiry

Report No.	Title	No. of man days spent on visits	E.T. or Supp. Assistance	No. of Places visited	Av. no. of man days study	Were stats data collected?	Work Study O&M J.E.	Prod. Plan/& Control	Invest. Plan, Corporate Plan	Purchasing	Labour Utilisation	Plant Utilisation	Cost Reduction Fields	Productivity	Maintenance	Management Structure	Marketing	Distribution	Pricing Policy	Or Effectiveness	OR and other Man Techniques	Pay and Conditions	Studies for I.R. Branch	Studies for Financial Adviser	Comment
116	Pay of Armed Forces (Second Report)	575	14	?	?	x	x				x			x								x		x	Extraction of Financial Data (Desk Study)
117	Pay of Exhibition Workers	32	7	20	1½	x																x			
118	Prices of Non-Alloy Bright Steel Base	–	9	–	–																				
119	Man-Made Fibre and Cotton Yarn Prices (Final Report)	–																							E.T. not deeply involved
120	Pay and Conditions in the Electrical Contracting Industry	75	8	24	3	x	x				x			x								x			Trade Union Attitudes Effects of Agreements
123	Productivity Agreements Evaluations	144	11	42	3½	x	x				x			x											+ Work Measurement
124	Coal Prices	48	7	12	4	x	x				x	x	x	x											
125	BICC Staff	20	5	7	3	x					x			x											
126	Smithfield Market Workers	61	7	17	3¾	x					x			x											
127	Man-Made Fibres and Cotton Yarn Prices (Second Report)	–						x	x																E.T. not involved
128	Pay of Ground Staff at Aerodromes	84	7	16	5	x	x				x	x		x								x			
130	Plasterboard Prices	25	4	7	3½	x					x	x	x	x		x	x		x						
131	Pay of Film Processing Workers	8	3	4	2		x				x			x											
132	Salary Structure	–																							E.T. not involved
133	Portland Cement Prices	49	8	7	7	x	x	x	x		x	x	x	x		x	x		x						
134	Solicitors Renumeration	152	4	150	1	x	x				x		x	x		x			x						
135	HMSO Presses & Binderies	6	2	8	½	x	x	x	x		x	x	x	x	x		x	x	x		x				Worked with Consultants
136	Brewing Industry Costs & Prices	274	19	400+	14	x					x			x							x				Study of London Bridge Station
137	British Rail Fares – London Area	14	2	1	½	x				x	x	x		x											See Report No. 153
138	Coal Prices – First Report	16	2	23	1½	x													x						
139	Electric Motors Prices	118	11	28	4¼	x																			
140	Milk Industry & Pay	128	10	8	16	x					x	x		x		x	x								
141	National Newspaper Costs					x				x	x	x						x							Worked with Consultants See Report No. 116
142	Armed Forces Pay – Third Report	45	7	11	4½	x					x		x	x					x			x			Worked with Consultants
143	London Cleaning Banks						x																		Worked with Consultants See Report No. 151
144	Bread Prices & Bakery Wages	9	2	15	½	x					x			x											
145	Pay of University Teachers										x											x			Recruitment of Graduates
146	Pay and Conditions of Industrial Civil Servants	95	11	44	2	x	x				x	x		x	x	x						x			
147	Margarine, Cooking Fats	8	1	4	2		x	x			x	x	x	x	x	x	x	x							Worked with Consultants Case Studies

Enquiry Team Studies Analysis

Main Fields or Subjects of Enquiry

Report No.	Title	No. of man days spent on visits	E.T. or Supp. Assistance	No. of Places visited	Av. no. of man days study	Were stats data collected?	Work Study O & M J.E.	Prod. Plan & Control	Invest. Plan, Corporate Plan	Purchasing	Labour Utilisation	Plant Utilisation	Cost Reduction Fields	Productivity	Maintenance	Management Structure	Marketing	Distribution	Pricing Policy	Or Effectiveness	OR and other Man Techniques	Pay and Conditions	Studies for I.R. Branch	Studies for Financial Adviser	Comment
148	Prices of Primary Batteries	9	4	123	?	x	x x				x	x		x			x	x				x			Case Studies of 3 Manufacturing plants
149	Pay of Pottery Workers	141	12	23	7	x					x			x										x	+ Survey of 120 Retailers
150	Brick Industry Prices	9	3	8	1	x	x					x													+ Labour Turnover, Training. Handling & Storage of Bricks
151	Bread Prices & Pay in the Bakery Industry (2nd)	32	6	24	¼	x	x x	x		x	x	x	x	x											
152	Water Industry Pay	77	8	24	3	x	x x	x		x	x	x	x	x	x	x	x	x	x	x	x				+ Industrial Relations
153	Coal Prices (Second Report)	151	7	16	9	x	x x	x	x	x	x	x		x		x	x	x	x		x				
154	Tea Prices	40	6	131	¾	x	x							x			x								Survey of Wholesalers & Retailers
155	Gas Industry – Costs & Efficiency	108	9	25	4						x	x		x		x	x	x							+ Staff Negotiations
156	ITV Costs & Revenue																								E. T. not used
157	Armed Forces Pay																								E. T. not used
158	Armed Forces Pay																								E. T. not used
159	Ice Cream Prices	64	7	15	4	x		x			x	x	x	x		x	x	x	x						Includes Survey of Retailers
161	Hours of Work, Overtime & Shiftwork	32	4	71	½	x	x				x			x								x	x		
162	National Freight Corporation Charges	80	6	55	1½	x	x				x			x			x	x	x			x	x		+ Recruitment & Industrial Relations
163	Motor Repairs & Servicing Costs & Charges	48	4	25	2	x					x		x				x	x							
164	Solicitors Renumeration	120	2	133	1	x					x														
165	Food Distribution	190	5	122	1.3	x					x														
166	National Health Service	100	5	30	3.3	x					x														Office Efficiency etc.
167	Laundries and Dry Cleaning	48	4	23	2	x					x											x	x		
168	Contract Cleaning	53	4	22	2.4	x					x											x	x		
169	Low Pay General	35	5	38	1						x											x	x		Interviews in the home

Appendix J. Some Management Studies (after 1968)

*Report
No.*

88/129   *BOAC Pilots* Cost benefit analysis of pilot scheduling agreements — mathematical model of rate structure — industrial relations study in Europe and USA — personnel organization

103   *Car Delivery* 50% increase in return loads — optimisation of balance between vehicles and drivers

111   *Steel Prices* Revision of price structure — cost reduction programme — development of marginal cost pricing

112/159   *London Transport Fares* Improved service reliability — increased use of one-man buses — use of performance indices

118   *Bright Steel Bars* Improvements in stock and production control — statistical quality control — new shift working system

121   *Parcel Post* Planning future system — capital budgeting — advice on better use of internal resources of scientific manpower

130   *Plasterboard* Efficiency studies of production, R & D, production planning, plant location, new project appraisal, demand forecasting, product variety, potential labour problems

133   *Cement* Efficiency study of production and distribution — recommended use of work study — benefits of decentralization

136   *Beer* Unit costing — rationalization of distribution — national study of retail outlets, cost reduction programmes

138/153   *Coal* Organisation structure — outline of planning procedures — forecasting output — area by area analysis of output — marketing strategy — in house models for individual collieries — investment project appraisal, role of supervision in productivity, corporate planning, motivation of management — training

         Coal Supplement Joint optimization of coal and electricity — cost benefit analysis — industry run-down

140   *Milk* Improvement of bulk distribution — study of potential savings due to zoning — retail rounds and outlets

141   *National Newspapers* Manning — waste control — management control — marketing methods — distribution efficiency, paging profitability, detail follow-up with each paper, action programme for industry

143   *London Clearing Banks* Control of overtime working — improved methods of measuring and controlling non-routine work

146   *Industrial Civil Service* Workers in docks, shipbuilding, aircraft, munitions, research and development — job evaluation — manpower planning — management audit — management information systems — management training

147   *Margarine and Cooking Fats* Cost structure — optimal blending — role of advertising — integrated planning and control, sales organisation, warehousing and distribution — waste — control of short interval manufacture and distribution operations

149   *Pottery Industry* Plant layout — variety reduction — management information — efficiency audit

150   *Bricks* Production efficiency — cost of stockholding — transport and distribution cost studies — revision of price structure — total systems approach

155   *Gas* Improvements in methods of marketing, purchasing world wide, conversion — utilization of labour and staff — depot rationalization — stock control — tariff for bulk supplies, first line supervision contribution to efficiency, cost of rework, cost of debtors, the use of High street sites, the role of management services, corporate planning, dispersion of resources, £100m saving

156   *Independent Television Companies* Programme scheduling — use of studio resources — savings in manpower — merger studies — marketing effectiveness

160   *Ice Cream* Examination of 'exclusive' contracts and retail outlets — study of unit costs — effect of weather on sales — relationship between costs, prices and marketing, costs of product variety — trends in USA

162   *National Freight Corporation* Depot rationalisation — vehicle scheduling — vehicle replacement — organisation structure — management control — corporate planning — recasting of 'realisable market' potential

163   *Motor Vehicle Repair and Servicing* Study of set up required for efficient repair and maintenance work — proposal for national scheme for 'approved' garages — quality control — accident repair — problem of supervision in small units

165   *Food Distribution Industry* Structure of the industry — study of manufacturers' marketing and distribution methods — scope for improvement — consumer attitude survey — competition in the market place — use of purchasing power

166   *National Health Service — Ancillary Service* Management and organization — new approach to productivity — manpower budgeting — financial control — performance indices — management training

167   *Laundries and Dry Cleaning* Analysis of future of the industry — survey of labour type and living conditions — problems of increasing productivity — industry rundown

168   *Contract Cleaning* Analysis of structure of service operations of the kind — problems of management control in scattered units — motivational study of workforce

Appendix K. Statistical Questionnaire Surveys

Table 1: Summary of questionnaire surveys† 1967–1971.

		All surveys			Earnings surveys only						
		Questionnaires				Questionnaires				Workers	
Year	No. of Surveys	Issued	Usable returns	Response rate	No. of Surveys	Issued	Usable returns	Response rate	No. in sample	Total no. covered	Average sampling fraction
				%				%	000	000	%
1967	32	27,821	16,531	59.4	12	5,480	3,473	63.4	139.9	2,647.2	5.3
1968	61	48,244	28,812	59.7	14	12,532	8,530	68.1	47.4	1,367.8	3.5
1969	30	18,718	13,431	71.8	16	5,487	4,170	76.0	29.9	734.2	4.1
1970	15	8,204	5,614	68.4	9	2,306	1,513	65.6	36.6	650.5	5.6
1971	13	12,000	5,306	44.2	4	1,392	925	66.5	35.0	377.0	9.3
Total	151	114,987	69,694	60.6*	55	27,197	18,611	68.4	288.8	5,776.7	5.0

* Based on the ratio of total usable returns to questionnaires issued. The unweighted average of the response rates for each survey was 72 per cent. Either figures understates the true response since substantial numbers of questionnaires issued were out of scope.

† This summary relates only to surveys initiated and/or processed by the NBPI Statistics Branch. Thus, some financial surveys which did not require statistical processing are not included.

Report	Subject of Report	Date of pubc'n	If published as Supplement(S) or Appendix(ces)(A)	Subject of survey	Number of surveys	Questionnaires Issued	Usable response	Response rate %	Earnings Surveys Workers in sample 000	Surveys Total number covered 000
1	2	3	4	5	6	7	8	9	10	11
27	Pay in retail drapery outfitting & footwear	3/67	A	Pay and hours	1	1,488	1,382	93.1	10.4	336.5
		4/67	S*	Conditions	1	1,488	1,382	93.1		
29	Pay in local authorities, NHS, Gas & Water Supply	3/67	A	Pay and hours	5	685	658	96.1	54.0	1,117.0
		5/67	S*	Finance	5	685	658	96.1		
31	Distribution costs of fresh fruit	4/67	A	Wholesalers' & retailers' costs & margins	3	1,688	860	50.9		
32	Fire service pay	5/67	A	Pay and hours	1	142	140	98.6	4.5	27.8
34	Bank charges	5/67	A	Costs and charges	1	17	17	100.0		
35	Pay of Merchant Navy Officers	6/67		Comparison of salary scales	1	34	34	100.0		
37	Costs and charges in motor repair and servicing	8/67	A	Charges	1	2,300	1,050	45.7		
				Costs and margins	1	347	138	39.8		
44	London weighting in the non-industrial civil service	11/67	A	Travel and housing expenses	1	7,400	5,300	71.6		
47	Prices of bricks	11/67		Costs and margins	1	72	36	50.0		
48	Charges, costs and wages in the road haulage industry	11/67	A	Pay and hours	1	907	344	37.9	4.0	212.1
		11/67	S*	Costs and margins	1	38	38	100.0		

Report	Subject of Report	Date of pubc'n	If published as Supplement(S) or Appendix(ces) (A)	Subject of Survey	Number of surveys	Questionnaires			Earnings Surveys	Surveys
						Issued	Usable response	Response rate	Workers in sample	Total number covered
1	2	3	4	5	6	7	8	9 %	10 000	11 000
49	Pay and conditions of engineering workers	12/67 3/68	A S*	Pay and hours: Staff Conditions: Staff Conditions: Manual workers	1 1 3	2,105 2,105 6,167	815 815 2,730	38.7 38.7 44.3	9.0	815.6
50	Productivity agreements in the bus industry	12/67	A	Pay and hours, staff shortage	3	153	134	87.6	58.0	138.2
52	Costs and charges radio and TV rental and relay	1/68	A	Charges Costs and margins	1 1	316 25	81 20	25.6 80.0		
54	Remuneration of solicitors	2/68	A	Income Practices and Staff	1 1	718 695	449 440	62.5 63.3	0.7	0.7
60	Pay of nurses and mid-wives in the NHS	3/68	A	Management analysis	1	587	535	91.1		
62	Increases in rents of local authority housing	4/68 10/68	A S*	Rents Tenants' income Local authority finance	1 1 2	20 10,116 413	20 6,155 387	100.0 60.8 93.7		
63	Pay of minicipal busmen	4/68	A	Pay and hours Manning Costs and margins	1 2 1	28 190 95	28 184 92	100.0 96.8 96.8	3.0	71.0
71	Architects' costs and fees	5/68	A	Income Practices Design costs	1 1 2	4,065 793 5,200	3,104 467 1,286	76.4 58.9 24.7	4.1	20.0

Report	Subject of Report	Date of pubc'n	If published as Supplement(S) or Appendix(ces) (A)	Subject of Survey	Number of surveys	Questionnaires Issued	Usable response	Response rate	Earnings Workers in sample	Surveys Total number covered
1	2	3	4	5	6	7	8	9 %	10 000	11 000
75	Costs and prices in the chocolate and sugar confectionery industry	7/68	A	Costs and margins	1	39	25	64.1		
78	Terms and conditions Rochdale County Boro' Council – Road passenger transport department	7/68	A	Pay and hours Manning Costs and margins	1 1 1	1 1 1	1 1 1	100.0 100.0 100.0	0.2	0.5
80	Distributors margins on paint, children's clothing, household textiles & proprietary medicines	8/68	A	Costs and margins	2	326	175	53.7		
82	Report on agreement relating to pay of sawyers & woodworking machinists in the sawmilling industry		See report no. 93	Pay and hours	1	506	321	63.4	1.8	1.8
83	Job evaluation	9/68 12/68	S*	Analysis of schemes	1	7,700	5,000	64.9		
84	Report on pay settlement for certain workers employed in the thermal insulation contracting industry	10/68	See Report No. 93	Pay and hours	1	109	72	66.1	0.7	7.6
85	Pay and conditions of busmen – Dundee corporation	10/68	A	Pay and hours Manning Costs and margins	1 2 1	1 2 1	1 2 1	100.0 100.0 100.0	0.2	1.0

						Questionnairesm			Earnings Surveys	
Report	Subject of Report	Date of pubc'n	If published as Supplement(S) or Appendix(ces) (A)	Subject of Survey	Number of surveys	Issued	Usable response	Response rate	Workers in sample	Total number covered
1	2	3	4	5	6	7	8	9 %	10 000	11 000
87	London taxicab fares	10/68	A	Owner drivers	1	400	286	71.5		
				Fleet owners	1	90	78	86.7		
89	Office employment agencies charges and salaries	11/68	A	Agency charges	1	232	68	29.3		
				Pay of temporary staff	1	232	68	29.3	0.8	4.2
90	Pay of vehicle maintenance workers in BRS	12/68	A	Pay and hours	1	257	257	100.0		
				Manning	2	134	134	100.0	2.6	2.6
91	Pay and conditions in the civil engineering industry	11/68	A	Pay and hours	3	6,558	4,174	63.6		
				Conditions	3	6,558	4,174	63.6	31.1	1241.8
92	Building industry	11/68								
93	Other construction industries including sawmilling & thermal insulating	11/68								
–93	Statistical supplement	4/69	S*							
95	Pay and conditions of busmen – Wigan corporation	12/68	A	Pay and hours	1	1	1	100.0		
				Manning	1	1	1	100.0		
				Costs and margins	1	1	1	100.0	0.2	0.6
96	Pay of Busmen – Great Yarmouth corporation	12/68		Pay and hours	1	1	1	100.0		
				Costs and margins	1	1	1	100.0		
97	Distribution costs and margins on furniture, domestic electrical appliances and footwear	12/68	A	Retailers' and wholesalers' costs and margins	11	1,718	612	35.6		

294

Report	Subject of Report	Date of pubc'n	If published as Supplement(S) or Appendix(ces) (A)	Subject of Survey	Number of surveys	Issued	Usable response	Response rate	Workers in sample	Total number covered
1	2	3	4	5	6	7	8	9 %	10 000	11 000
99	Pay of maintenance workers employed by bus companies	12/68	A	Pay and hours / Manning	1 / 1	56 / 56	54 / 54	96.4 / 96.4	2.0	16.0
103	Pay and productivity in the car delivery industry	2/69	A	Pay and hours	1	100	78	78.0	0.5	3.0
106	Pay in the London clearing banks	3/69	A	Pay and hours	1	11	11	100.0	3.8	153.0
107	Top salaries	3/69	A	Pay and hours	1	113	99	87.6	2.0	5.2
108	Pay and conditions in the electrical contracting industry – Scotland	3/69	A (Reprocess from construction survey – Rpts 91–93)	Pay and hours	1	(See column 4)			0.2	7.9
109	Pay of salaried staff in ICI Ltd	3/69	A	Pay (from ICI staff records)	1	2,000	1,936	96.8	2.0	40.0
110	Pay and conditions in the clothing manufacturing industries	4/69	A	Pay and hours / Conditions	1 / 1	2,234 / 2,234	1,401 / 1,401	62.7 / 62.7	9.4	440.8
111	Steel prices	5/69	A	Prices	1	36	36	100.0		
113	Manufacturers' prices of, toilet preparations	6/69	A	Costs and margins	1	35	35	100.0		
114	Pay and duties of light keepers	6/69	A	Pay	1	Trinity House and Northern Lighthouse Board sample			0.2	0.4
115	Journalists' pay	6/69	A	Pay	1	20	20	100.0	3.3	3.3
116	Armed forces pay (2nd	6/69	A	Attitude surveys	2	7,600	6,148	80.9	3.3	

Report	Subjects of Report	Date of pubc'n	If published as Supplement(S) or Appendix(ces) (A)	Subject of Survey	Number of surveys	Questionnaires			Earnings	Surveys
						Issued	Usable response	Response rate	Workers in sample	Total number covered
1	2	3	4	5	6	7	8	9 %	10 000	11 000
117	Pay and conditions in the exhibition contracting industry	6/69	A	Pay and hours / Conditions	1 / 1	199 / 199	124 / 124	62.3 / 62.3	0.8	4.8
118	Price of non-alloy bright steel bars	6/69	A	Costs and margins	1	37	27	73.0		
120	Pay and conditions in the electrical contracting industry	6/69	(Reprocessed from const'n survey Rpts 91/93)	Pay and hours / Conditions	1 / 1	See column 4			1.8	58.5
125	Pay of staff in British Insulated Callenders' Cables Ltd	8/69	A	Pay	1	(Sample drawn from BICC Ltd)			0.5	4.3
126	Smithfield market	10/69	A	Pay and conditions / Costs and margins	1 / 1	76 / 76	57 / 76	75.0 / 100.0	0.7	1.1
128	Pay of ground staff at aerodromes	10/69	A	Pay	1	35	35	100.0	1.2	3.8
131	Pay of certain employees in the film processing industry	11/69	A	Pay and hours / Manpower	1 / 1	12 / 12	12 / 12	100.0 / 100.0	1.2	5.8
132	Salary structures	11/69	A	Salary structures	2	1,806	561	31.1		
134	Renumeration of solicitors (1st Report)	11/69	A	Income / Costs	1 / 1	687 / 687	397 / 378	57.8 / 55.0	N/A	N/A
135	Pay structure in HMSO presses and binderies	11/69	A	Pay	1	(From data supplied by HMSO)			2.3	2.3

Report	Subject of Report	Date of pubc'n	If published as Supplement(S) or Appendix(ces) (A)	Subject of Survey	Number of Surveys	Questionnaires Issued	Questionnaires Usable response	Questionnaires Response rate	Earnings Surveys Workers in sample	Earnings Surveys Total number covered
1	2	3	4	5	6	7	8	9 %	10 000	11 000
163	Costs and charges in the motor repairing & servicing industry	2/71	A	Charges and efficiency Costs and margins	1	2,272 331	696 33	30.6 10.0		
164	Remuneration of solicitors	4/71	A	Income	1	293	97	33.1	N/K	N/K
165	Food distribution	4/71	A	Prices, costs and margins	3	2,923	1,039	26.1		
166	Pay and conditions of NHS workers	4/71	A	Pay and hours Conditions	1 1	529 529	470 470	88.8 88.8	6.6	220.0
168	Pay and conditions of cleaning workers	4/71	A	Pay and hours Conditions	1 1	261 261	168 168	64.4 64.4	3.0	91.5
167	Pay and conditions laundry & dry cleaning workers	4/71	A	Pay and hours Conditions	1 1	331 293	190 190	61.5 61.5	25.4	64.9
168	Low pay and general report	4/71	A	Social survey	1	3,983	1,785	61.5